I0759617

MILITARY TRANSPORT

51
51

MILITARY TRANSPORT

THE DEFINITIVE VISUAL HISTORY

Contents

TO 1830: WHEELS, SAILS, AND GUNS

Armies have always needed to be mobile. For thousands of years, the most basic form of transport was marching on foot, and from around 4000 BCE until the industrial era, military transport was dominated by horses on land, and on water by ships powered with oars and sails.

1830–1918: THE MECHANIZATION OF WAR

The steam engine revolutionized transport, and military forces were quick to adapt it to ships, trains, and later, road vehicles. Improvements in the internal combustion engine further accelerated the development of military transport, and World War I ushered in a new generation of vehicles such as tanks and fighter planes.

1918–1945: THE BATTLEFIELD REDEFINED

After World War I, armies explored technological advances in the air and on land. As the world plunged once more into conflict in World War II, a period of dramatically swift progress took place in military technology.

1945–1989: THE COLD WAR

In the postwar world, transport platforms for nuclear arms became paramount, including long-range bomber aircraft and nuclear submarines. Many already powerful weapons systems increased their threat and lethality.

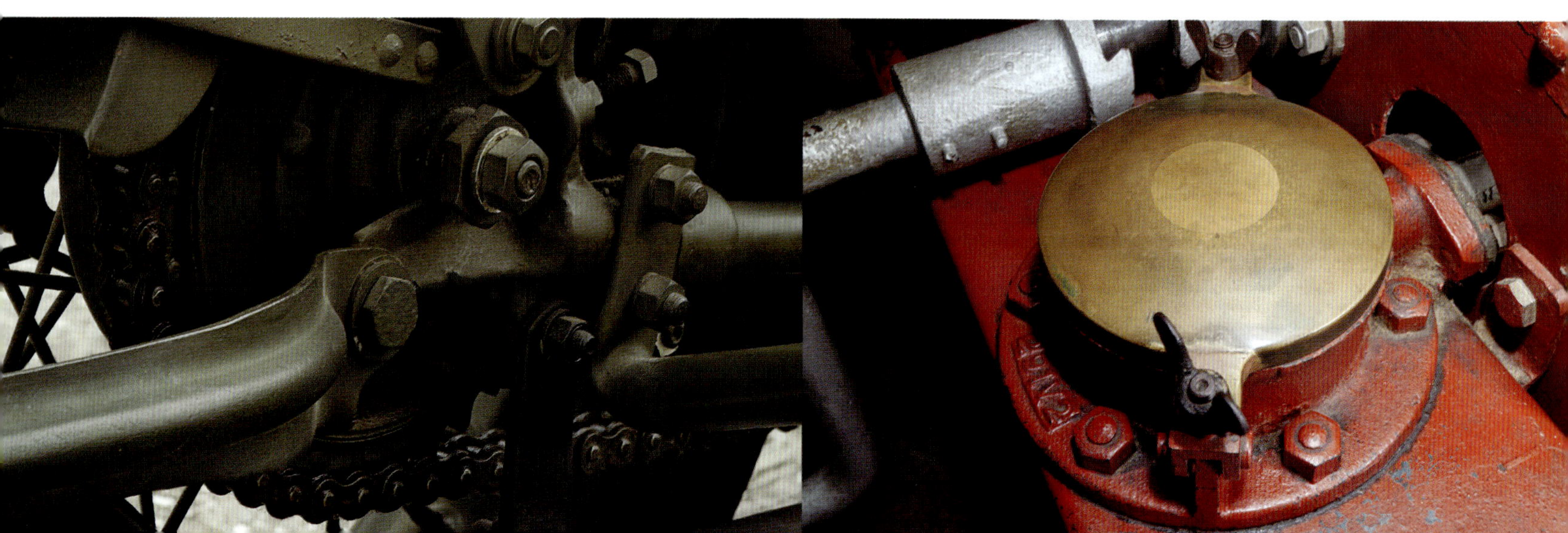

1989–PRESENT: THE HIGH-TECH AGE

The modern era has seen the deployment of massive aircraft carriers and nuclear submarines. The invasion of Ukraine brought a return of trench warfare and tank combat, as well as the use of drones. Future battlefields seem likely to be dominated by digital technology and increasing numbers of unmanned vehicles.

REFERENCE

Introduction

War has been a part of human history since records began. Throughout this time, military forces have had three basic requirements, which remain as pressing today as they were in ancient times: weapons, protection, and mobility. The third necessity is particularly notable—for military forces, a means of getting to the fight, or taking the fight to the enemy, is the key to victory.

The Military Transport Book illustrates and explains the technology that has made this possible. Covering land, sea, and air, it features military vehicles and mobile weapons platforms from antiquity to the present day, from the first chariots and the earliest warships to the latest nuclear submarines, jet fighters, and drones. The book explains these machines' roles and uses, and looks at key inventions and technological milestones.

War on the move

The need for transport in war is universal. In static (or attritional) warfare, armies meet and remain in relatively fixed positions, and try to wear each other down with repeated attacks and counterattacks. Mobile warfare, by contrast, employs speed to achieve strategic advantage. However, both types of warfare require vehicles to move troops and munitions—and on the battlefield, the more mobile an army is, the more easily it can outmaneuver or surround its opponent. Mobility makes it easier for an army to retreat to fight another day, rather than remaining to be defeated by an enemy's overwhelming force. Mobile warfare can also particularly benefit smaller armies that cannot match an enemy soldier-for-soldier or weapon-for-weapon. It enables the swift concentration of force on vulnerable areas, or on key targets such as headquarters, transport hubs, and supply centers.

Across land and sea

On land, for much of history, the distance a soldier could march in a day, and still be able to fight, was the limit of military mobility. The domestication of the horse in around 4,000 BCE revolutionized land warfare. A horse—which could carry not only its rider, but also his supplies—had far greater range, speed, and endurance than a foot soldier. These animals enabled mounted warriors to ride forward and scout for the enemy, charge into battle to fight as archers, swordsmen, and lancers, or dismount in a location that gave a tactical advantage. Horses could also pull chariots—the first vehicles used in an offensive role—and supply wagons.

The industrial revolution that took hold during the 19th century further transformed land warfare. The arrival of steam power and the internal combustion engine introduced railroads and motor vehicles that sped up troop mobilization, while in World War I (1914–18), the first tanks brought mobile firepower to the battlefield.

> **"**Since the **dawn of history**, the **mobility of combat forces** has always been a **decisive element** in warfare.**"**
>
> COL. ROBERT E. MCMAHON, US ARMY, "AIRMOBILE OPERATIONS," 1959

At sea and on waterways, boats provided a way of transporting soldiers swiftly to engage with the enemy, often over great distances, while avoiding land obstacles. They were also an efficient way to carry supplies. Boats soon opened up seas and rivers as a theater of war, with the first recorded naval battle, the Battle of the Delta, taking place around 1175 BCE in Ancient Egypt.

Over the next millennia, fleets of vessels were able to bring whole armies ashore or evacuate them to safety, notably during the era of the Western Roman Empire (*c.* 27 BCE–476 CE). The "age of sail" (mid-1600s to mid-1800s) saw European sail-powered, ocean-going warships take center stage. These were vital for protecting trade routes, while naval blockades of ports could starve an enemy into submission or prevent escape or rescue by water. In the early 1900s, the invention of the submarine took naval warfare beneath the waves, and these stealthy vessels rapidly became a mainstay of navies.

Taking to the skies

The sky, too, eventually became a battlefield. In the late 18th century, the French army first deployed balloons carrying observers to monitor enemy forces, and in 1804 Napoleon Bonaparte considered using balloons to invade Britain (he was advised against the idea due to the variable winds in the English Channel). Balloons also delivered military messages, and in 1849 Austrian forces attempted to use balloons to drop explosives onto Venice. Just over one decade after the first powered, heavier-than-air flight by the Wright brothers' *Flyer* in 1903, purpose-built aircraft were taking to the skies during World War I in reconnaissance, bomber, and fighter roles; this era also saw the first takeoff from an aircraft carrier.

During World War II (1939–45), both Axis and Allied powers realized that air power could bring destruction to cities and industrial centers far from the front line, which necessitated the creation of fleets of airplanes for defense. It also resulted in the movement and dispersal of factories out of bomber range, or even underground. Planes were also used to supply ground forces, and to drop or land ground troops by parachute or glider. From the 1940s, helicopters took on supply and transport roles, being well-suited to landing in difficult terrain; when equipped with weapons, they could defend themselves and carry out attacks on ground targets. From the jet age in the 1950s onward, the need to fly faster to outpace enemy defences, to extend the range and altitude of flight, and to carry greater loads, has produced rapid technological developments in military aircraft. In the early 21st century, a new generation of remotely piloted drone aircraft is reshaping strategy and tactics.

Spotlighting these examples and many more, *The Military Transport Book* showcases in detail the numerous types of vehicles that humanity has invented to aid mobility in warfare. Often ingenious and groundbreaking, and in many cases lethal, these machines have shaped the world we live in today, and their successors will continue to do so in the centuries ahead.

To 1830

WHEELS, SAILS, AND GUNS

The Rise of Battlefield Mobility

By the end of the 4th millennium BCE, the foundations of military mobility for the next few thousand years were already in place—the foot, the horse, the wheel, the oar, and the sail. Based on these elements, a slow process of innovation paved the way for modern warfare.

For much of human history, the primary means of transport for land armies were the soldiers' own legs. Although simple, this could be very effective: a well-trained and fit army could traverse long distances and difficult terrain. In 218 BCE, for example, the Carthaginian commander Hannibal famously led his army across Spain, through Gaul, and into Italy to fight the Romans. During the ordeal of this five-month trek, the soldiers maintained an average daily distance of 13 miles (21 km), a figure made even more impressive because they crossed the Alps in the process. There are numerous other historical examples of epic military marches, some even in the 20th century. However, there are clear limits to foot mobility. The fastest walking pace is about 5 mph (8 km/h), but it can drop considerably depending on the nature of the landscape, the amount of load carried, and the physical well-being of the soldiers.

Horses in warfare

Horses were critical to improving military mobility (other animals used in similar capacities included mules, camels, and, occasionally, elephants). From the domestication of the horse in the 4th millennium BCE, horses provided armies with three main benefits. Firstly, they functioned as mounts for cavalry, which by the 1st millennium BCE was being used for fast maneuvers and shock battlefield attacks, as well as offering mobile reconnaissance, screening, and other tactical functions. Secondly, horses could pull wheeled combat platforms such as chariots, war wagons, siege engines, and gun carriages, enabling armies to deploy heavy fighting equipment. Thirdly, they greatly improved the logistical side of war. A powerful draft horse, for example, could pull a wheeled load of supplies weighing as much as 9,000 lb (4,500 kg).

However, employing horses in large numbers could require the transportation of immense volumes of forage, itself a logistical challenge—particularly if the campaign passed through land with poor grazing. During the fall and winter months, a horse needed approximately 22 lb (10 kg) of grass, oats, or hay each day. Campaigns such as Napoleon's invasion of Russia in 1812, which used around 250,000 horses, give a sense of the potential scale of the amount of supplies that might be needed.

TALKING POINT

Wheels

Predated by crude log rollers, the first vehicular wheels are dated to around 3500 BCE. Wheels not only transformed human social and commercial history, but also revolutionized military logistics and tactics. Spoked wheels emerged around 2000 BCE. Lighter and with better shock-absorbing properties than their solid predecessors, they made possible the development of fast, horse-drawn battle chariots. Chariot engineers in the ancient Near East and Middle East perfected the maneuverability of battle chariots by adjusting the placement of the axle relative to the centerline of the box (the chariot "carriage"). After this, solid wheels were reserved for drawing unusually heavy loads.

Egyptian pharaoh Ramesses II takes aim with bow and arrow from the back of his war chariot during the Battle of Kadesh, in 1274 BCE, between Egyptian and Hittite armies.

Galley warfare
The Battle of Lepanto in 1571 between the Holy League and the Ottoman Turks mainly involved galleys and galleasses—ships that were still driven in battle by oars rather than by sails.

Timeline
It did not take long for humans to utilize horses, wheels, oars, and sails as tools of warfare. In the first millennia of recorded history, chariots provided nimble mobile platforms for archers, warships evolved from oar-powered galleys into multi-gundeck galleons, and soldiers even made their first forays into the air.

Air
Land
Water

c.3000 BCE Egypt and Crete develop rowed galleys intended purely for warfare

c.2500 BCE Mesopotamian armies deploy four-wheeled war wagons, drawn by donkeys or onagers

c.1600 BCE Two-wheeled horse-drawn chariots appear in the Middle East, Africa, and Asia

c.700 BCE The Phoenicians introduce the bireme, with two banks of oars on each side

c.600 BCE War elephants are fielded by Indian Imperial armies as "living tanks"

c.480 BCE The Greek trireme (three banks of oars) transforms Mediterranean warfare

c.250 BCE The Chinese use *Muyuan* military kites for signaling, communications, and weather observations

c.119 BCE Armored wagons are utilized as mobile fortifications at the Battle of Mobei, China

Battle of Waterloo, 1815
At Waterloo, Napoleon's French forces were defeated by a coalition of European armies. As in ancient times, the battle was fought on foot and on horseback. Horses also drew field artillery.

On water, from ancient times until the 19th century, naval mobility relied on two devices: oars and sails. Oars propelled galleys, longships, and many small riverine craft. Speed was dictated by the numbers of oars in the water, but more rowers necessarily meant a heavier vessel. A Greek trireme of the 5th century BCE, for example, could achieve a maximum speed of about 9 knots (17 km/h) for short fighting distances, driven by 170 oars. Oar propulsion was ultimately restricted by the finite power of human muscle.

Harnessing the wind

Sails, by contrast, drew on the vast but often unpredictable power of the wind. Ships were fitted with masted sails by around 3500 BCE, but for centuries these sails were basic designs with limited efficiency, suitable mainly for short coastal journeys. Improvements in sail and ship design eventually gave rise to sail warships, which became instruments of global strategic power. These developments included the introduction of lateen sails (triangular sails that enabled ships to tack forward into even light winds); increases in the numbers and efficiency of both masts and sails, supported by extensive rigging; improvements in hull shape and construction, especially the shift from clinker-built (overlapping planks) to caravel-built (smoothly joined planks) hull profiles; and the introduction of centrally aligned rudders at the stern, fitted to a sternpost. These advances, and many others, allowed ships to increase dramatically in size—by the 15th century, a fully rigged galleon might weigh around 518 tons (470 tonnes)—and cross entire oceans laden with guns, cargo, and crew. They also gave warships better maneuvering capabilities in battle, albeit at slow pace—10 knots (18.5 km/h) would have been considered a good speed for a 17th-century ship-of-the-line.

The great "age of sail," which ran from the 16th to the 19th century, revolutionized naval mobility in terms of range, carrying capacity, and gunnery. Toward the end of the 19th century, the first steam boats entered civilian service. Spotting the potential, in 1814 the US Navy launched the *Demologos*, a floating battery that was the first military steamship. The future promised mobility for navies that was not dependent on the wind.

> "An aptitude for **war** is an aptitude for **movement.**"
>
> NAPOLEON BONAPARTE, IN *MAXIMS FOR WAR*, 1831

c.350 CE The first Viking longships are built in Scandinavia

1400 Civilian masted sailing vessels, such as cogs and carracks, are converted to warships

1420 In central Europe, the Hussites use heavy war wagons at the Battle of Sudomer

1450 Limbers are developed in Europe to help tow wheeled artillery pieces

1485 Leonardo da Vinci designs a prototype wheeled, armored fighting vehicle

1520 Three- or four-masted galleons emerge as the defining vessels of the age of sail warships

1765 French artillery officer Gribeauval standardizes artillery caissons to transport ammunition

1792 French surgeon Dominique-Jean Larrey designs military horse-drawn "flying ambulances"

1794 The French Aerostatic Corps flies manned observation balloons at the Battle of Fleurus

1814 *Demologos*, a steam-powered floating battery, is launched in the US

Chariots and War Wagons

Horse-drawn chariots were first used as weapons of war in the 2nd millennium BCE, notably in southern Europe, the Near East, Central Asia, and the Indian subcontinent. The ancient equivalent of modern armored fighting vehicles (AFVs), chariots carried archers, spear-throwers, or other soldiers in a small, low, open carriage called a box. They provided mobile fighting platforms that, directed by a skilled commander, could break up enemy troop formations, leaving them unable to resist a follow-up infantry assault. Chariots were less effective over rough ground, and they tended to fight at the speed of a brisk canter, since at a gallop they became difficult to control.

▽ **Egyptian war carriage**

Date 13th century BCE

Origin Egypt

Over time, Egyptian chariots moved the axle to the rear of the box to give a tight turning cycle and better performance at speed. They had two-man or three-man crews and operated in large chariot formations composed of a "host" of 250 chariots divided into five squadrons.

◁ **Hittite chariot**

Date 10th–8th century BCE

Origin Türkiye

The Hittites were pioneers of chariot warfare. As seen here, they manned their chariots with three warriors: a charioteer, an archer, and a third man who would dismount and fight on foot in close action. Here, the occupants carry shields to protect themselves against incoming arrows.

◁ **Etruscan bronze chariot**

Date 6th century BCE

Origin Italy

Found in Umbria, Italy, in 1902, the so-called Monteleone chariot dates from *c.*530 BCE. This Etruscan funerary chariot, 4 ft 4 in (1.3 m tall), is exquisitely decorated with hammered bronze plates showing scenes in relief from ancient Greek mythology.

Relief depicts combat between Achilles and Memnon

Yoke for attaching two horses

Draft pole emerges from a boar's mouth

Nine-spoked wooden wheel with iron tire

Four horses abreast harnessed to a pair of draft poles

◁ **Greek chariot**

Date 6th century BCE

Origin Greece

Greek chariots were generally of unsophisticated design, with simple, four-spoked wheels and the axle running under the center of the box. This axle position improved stability, but it also reduced maneuverability compared to chariots that had their axle at the rear of the box.

△ **Indian chariot**

Date 3rd century BCE

Origin India

Depictions of ancient Indian chariots show vehicles with either spoked or solid wheels. The chariot box, known as a *kosha*, was made of either wicker or a leather-coated wooden framework. This scene from the Great Stupa at Sanchi shows King Ashoka on his chariot.

Umbrellalike canopy had a ceremonial function

△ **Chinese chariot**

Date 3rd century BCE

Origin China

Chariots were used in Chinese warfare from about 1200 BCE. They were pulled by either two or four horses, and the wheels could have up to 30 spokes. This chariot model dates from the Qin Dynasty (221–206 BCE).

◁ **Persian chariot**

Date 4th–5th century CE

Origin Persia

Less than 3 in (8 cm) tall, this finely detailed gold model of a square-fronted Persian chariot carries a driver and a robed figure, possibly a satrap (a governor of the Persian Empire). The chariot is drawn by four horses under a single four-bay yoke, rather than the more typical two-horse arrangement.

Wheel studs were attachment points for a tire and bronze sheath

▽ **War wagon**

Date 2600 BCE–16th century

Origin Mesopotamia

The Standard of Ur—a Sumerian wooden box from the 3rd millennium BCE inlaid with shell, red limestone, and lapis lazuli—bears depictions of war wagons with four solid wheels. War wagons were used in battle by various cultures in Asia and Europe until around the 1500s.

▽ **Roman chariot**

Date Unknown

Origin Rome

Roman chariots were designed for speed; chariot teams often competed against one another in public races. Iron tires might be applied to the wheels to enhance their grip. Chariots also featured in triumphal processions, but the Roman Army did not use them for warfare.

Ram's head motif atop draft pole

Leonardo da Vinci's "Tank"

"I can make armored cars, safe and unassailable, which will enter the closed ranks of the enemy… behind these our infantry will be able to follow quite unharmed." So boasted Italian artist and inventor Leonardo da Vinci in 1482, in a letter to Ludovico Sforza, Duke of Milan, in an attempt to win the patronage of the powerful nobleman.

Around 1485, Da Vinci made sketches for military inventions, including a "war car." Regarded as one of the precursors of the tank, Da Vinci's vehicle comprised a protective wooden shell reinforced by metal plates, with holes around the perimeter through which light cannons could fire in all directions. Two manually turned cranks would have driven four wheels to propel the vehicle. With angled surfaces to deflect incoming projectiles, the design looks surprisingly modern.

Da Vinci's sketch was primarily a concept to win favor with the duke. It contains a flaw, possibly intentionally, to protect his work: the cranks would have turned the wheels in opposite directions, making the vehicle impossible to drive. The technology to make the "tank" a reality did not exist at the time, but modern recreations (with the flaw corrected) have shown it could only have traveled over very flat surfaces, rendering it unsuitable for the rugged terrain of contemporary battlefields.

Leonardo da Vinci's sketches of his "war car" (lower left and right) show the crank mechanism and the vehicle's exterior, below his idea for a chariot armed with rotating scythes.

The Sea as a Battlefield

For over two millennia, naval warfare was dominated by galleys, which were propelled into combat by oars and often supported by merchant sailing ships that delivered logistics and could land troops ashore. The rise of the great fleets of sail warships, which began in the 1500s, transformed the strategic potential of navies from largely coastal forces into blue-water fleets able to traverse the oceans.

Ancient galley battle
This depiction of the Battle of Actium in 31 BCE provides a window into the reality of galley warfare, which often involved infantry combat taking place on floating platforms. At Actium, the Roman triumvir Octavian defeated the fleets of Mark Antony and Cleopatra.

From the start of recorded military history until the Renaissance, naval forces had a limited operational range. The primary instrument of war across this entire period was the galley—a vessel propelled by banks of oars with the assistance of two or three masts rigged with triangular lateen sails.

Muscle-powered navies

Galley-design variations were largely limited to the number of oars, the size of the vessel, and displacement. For example, an Athenian trireme of the 5th century BCE had 170 oarsmen manning three banks of oars, with the ship itself measuring about 120 ft (37 m) long and displacing about 49 tons (45 tonnes). A typical Roman quinquereme of the 1st century BCE was significantly upscaled—it had five banks of oars powered by 300 rowers, was around 148 ft (45 m) in length, and had a displacement of around 110 tons (100 tonnes) with its full complement. However, the overall design principle changed very little. In fact, the galleys fighting in the Battle of Salamis in 480 BCE and the Battle of Lepanto, over 2,000 years later in 1571 CE, shared the same core design. Used at Lepanto, the Venetian innovation of the "galleass" was essentially a double-sized galley. Naval combat at this time was basic: enemy ships were typically sunk by ramming or captured after a successful boarding action.

The predominance of shallow-draft, oar-and-sail-powered galleys meant that prior to the 1500s, battles at sea were typically fought relatively close to coastlines (especially across the Mediterranean and its adjacent seas) or within reach of home or friendly ports. Of course, some vessels did travel long distances, notably the sail-powered Viking longships, which had made transatlantic journeys by the 10th century.

Raising the sails

From around the 1500s, multiple revolutions in the design of warships transformed naval tactics and maritime strategy. In Europe, the rise of the three-masted galleon, with raised "castles" fore and aft and broadside cannons arranged across multiple decks, ushered in the age of fighting sail. Properly provisioned and with favorable winds, these formidable vessels eventually gave nations hemispheric range. As well as range, protection also saw advances in this era. In Korea, Admiral Yi Sun-sin (1545–98) developed the *kŏbuksŏn* ("turtle ship"), essentially a cannon-armed wooden galley, but fully enclosed by iron plates. Turtle ships were, in effect, the first armored warships.

The great fleets

The English, Spanish, Portuguese, Dutch, French, and others built vast fleets of sail warships to establish, maintain, and protect their empires and oceanic shipping lanes. Naval warfare was now fought ever further from home and the shore, although the needs of provisioning meant that coastlines were usually kept

Viking longship
The longships of the Vikings were ideal raiding vessels. Powered by oars and a single square sail, longships had a slender design and a shallow-draft hull that made them fast, maneuverable, and easy to beach.

The age of sail ships
Unleashing broadsides as they fight in the "line of battle," French and British warships engage at the Battle of the Chesapeake on September 5, 1781, during the American Revolutionary War. Victory went to the French.

within comfortable range. By the 18th century, the British Royal Navy had built the world's largest and most formidable fleet, eclipsing those of Spain and the Netherlands. France challenged for the naval crown in the Napoleonic age, but Britain retained the edge through its command professionalism and its superior seamanship and gunnery.

The frequent and lengthy wars between 1500 and 1830 saw naval tactics honed and tested, especially through the debate between those who advocated rigid lines of attack and those who favored a less structured "melee" approach to engaging enemy vessels. By 1830, the world's first steamships had also made an appearance, inaugurating the next revolution in naval warfare.

"… **no Captain** can do very wrong if he **places his ship** alongside that of the **enemy.**"

BRITISH ADMIRAL HORATIO NELSON, MEMORANDUM TO SHIP COMMANDERS BEFORE THE BATTLE OF TRAFALGAR, OCTOBER 1805

TALKING POINT

Greek fire

An incendiary composition, "Greek fire" was developed by the Byzantine Greeks during the 7th century CE as an anti-ship weapon. Its exact formula is unknown, but it probably included naphtha or gasoline mixed with sulfur or pitch. The result was a viscous substance that glued itself to wooden ships and burned ferociously; according to the accounts of ancient writers, it even flamed on the water's surface. Either ejected under air pressure from metal tubes or hurled in pottery grenades, Greek fire was highly effective. It played a key role in repelling the first Arab siege of Constantinople in 674–78 CE and in several major battles thereafter, and it was still being used as late as the 13th century.

This Byzantine manuscript depicts Greek fire being launched under pressure from a metal tube mounted at the prow of an attacking ship, engulfing an enemy vessel in flames.

Olympias Greek Trireme

Light, speedy, maneuverable galleys called triremes helped the ancient Greeks extend their influence and power throughout the Mediterranean. While no trireme has survived from antiquity, a full-scale reconstruction based on historical evidence, the *Olympias*, was built at Piraeus, Athens, between 1985 and 1987.

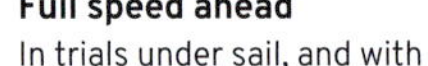

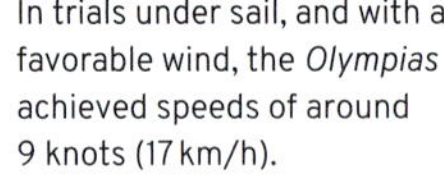

Full speed ahead
In trials under sail, and with a favorable wind, the *Olympias* achieved speeds of around 9 knots (17 km/h).

APPROXIMATELY 120 FT (37 M) LONG and 18 ft (5.5 m) wide, the shallow-draft *Olympias* proved to be agile and fast in sea trials, turning about in twice its own length and reaching almost 9 knots (10 mph; 17 km/h) under oar. Steered by a helmsman operating a pair of tillers, a trireme like *Olympias* would have cruised under sail but relied on oarsmen for propulsion in battle. The 170 rowers sat in three staggered tiers, each with its own type of oarsmen: 54 thalamites at the bottom, 54 zygites in the middle, and 62 thranites on top. Thranites were paid the most, since the steep angle at which their oars entered the water made for harder work. Around 30 other men, including marine hoplites and archers, completed the crew. There was room for only a few basic supplies and insufficient space for everyone to sleep on board.

In battle, a well-trained, disciplined trireme crew could use the ship's bronze prow ram to hole an enemy vessel, or ride over its oars and then reverse to render it helpless. If its own hull was pierced, a trireme would not sink because it was made of buoyant wood such as pine, poplar, or fir.

SPECIFICATIONS	
Model	*Olympias*
Origin	Greece
Date	Built 1985–87; replica of a c.5th century BCE trireme
Displacement	51.8 tons (47 tonnes)
Length	121 ft 1 in (36.9 m)
Propulsion	Two sails; 170 oarsmen
Armament	Bronze prow ram, 10 spears, 4 archers
Maximum speed	Approx. 9 knots (17 km/h)

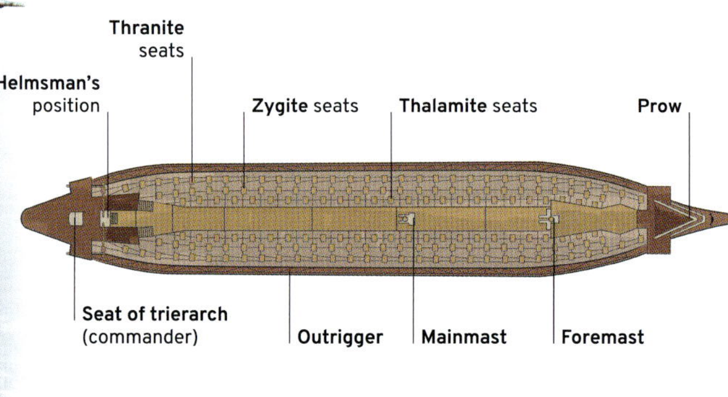

EXTERIOR

Sailors dropped and weighed anchor from platforms called *epotides* (ears) near the prow. Oars on the lowest tier had leather sheaths to keep water of the hull. Outriggers on the top tier allowed the thranites to row in a position outboard of the tiers below. The two steering oars (rudders) could also be used as a brake.

1. Bronze prow ram **2.** Ear and anchor **3.** Tiers of oars (showing leather sheaths) **4.** Outrigger **5.** Steering oar

INTERIOR

Each rower sat level with the shoulders of the oarsman on the tier below. The helmsman at the stern overlooked the slot between the decks, where the mast was stowed. *Olympias* tested various rowing techniques, including securing one foot to the stretcher.

6. Thranites' benches **7.** Stretcher (to push against when rowing) **8.** Oarsmen's seats **9.** View from the stern **10.** Tiller

Early Warships

Purpose-built warships took to the waves in the Mediterranean during the 1st millennium BCE, in the form of fighting galleys. In combat, these vessels were powered by banks of oars, the number of oars increasing over time depending on the period and the culture. Galley warfare prevailed until the medieval era, when sail power gradually took over. In Europe, simple cargo sailing ships known as cogs were converted for warfare, with high "castles" added fore and aft as fighting platforms for archers and other missile troops. From such ships evolved the large cannon-armed carracks, galleons, and other vessels of the age of sail.

▷ Greek trireme

Date 7th–4th century BCE **Origin** Greece
Displacement 55 tons (*c.*50 tonnes)
Length 121 ft (37 m)
Propulsion 7–9 knots (13–17 km/h)

The defining warship of the Mediterranean and adjacent seas in ancient times was the trireme, a type of galley. Most of a trireme's crew of 200 were oarsmen. Triremes played a major role in the wars of the 5th century BCE.

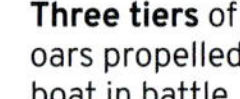

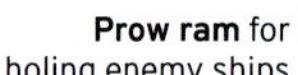

◁ Viking longship

Date 3rd century BCE–9th century CE **Origin** Scandinavia
Displacement 22 tons (*c.*20 tonnes)
Length Up to 75 ft (23 m)
Propulsion 10–12 knots (19–22 km/h)

A design so successful that it lasted for more than 1,000 years, the Viking longship had excellent sailing abilities in rough, open seas. Its shallow draft also allowed it to sail up rivers and onto beaches, making it an ideal raiding vessel.

△ Roman troop ship

Date 27 BCE–476 CE **Origin** Rome
Displacement 165 tons (*c.*150 tonnes)
Length 98 ft (30 m)
Propulsion 5–6 knots (9–11 km/h)

The Roman Army ferried its soldiers across the sea in merchant ships, or *navis oneraria*, that it repurposed for military transport. Large examples of these vessels could carry up to 300 troops, although with limited space for cargo and equipment.

◁ Venetian galley

Date 15th–16th century CE **Origin** Italy
Displacement 132 tons (*c.*120 tonnes)
Length 138 ft (42 m)
Propulsion 6–7 knots (11–13 km/h)

This large Venetian galley has lateen-sail masts in addition to its banks of oars, indicative of the fact that when such ships were not at war they were often used for long-distance trading voyages.

▽ Algerian xebec

Date 16th century CE **Origin** Algeria
Displacement 165 tons (*c.*150 tonnes)
Length 98 ft (30 m)
Propulsion 12–14 knots (22–26 km/h)

The *xebec* (or *chebec*) was a trade ship that operated in the Mediterranean Sea. The Barbary corsairs of the North African coast converted xebecs into warships by adding up to 40 guns, although 15–30 guns was a more typical armament.

▷ **Korean turtle ship**

Date 15th–16th century CE **Origin** Korea
Displacement 220 tons (c.200 tonnes)
Length 112 ft (34 m)
Propulsion 5–6 knots (9–11 km/h)

The *kobukson*, or "turtle ship," was one of the first armored warships. It featured an upper deck covered with spiked iron plates, making it resistant to missiles and boarding attacks.

Banner had command or identification purposes

Dragon's head sometimes concealed cannons

Sails were reinforced by wooden batons

Armor plate covered the entire upper deck

Stern in the shape of a turtle's tail

△ **Portuguese caravel**

Date 16th century CE **Origin** Portugal
Displacement 88 tons (c.80 tonnes)
Length 75 ft (23 m)
Propulsion 8–10 knots (15–19 km/h)

The caravel was a relatively small sailing ship used by the Portuguese and Spanish during the age of exploration. As with most sailing ships of the time, the caravel could, and often did, incorporate armament.

◁ **Maori waka taua**

Date 19th century CE **Origin** New Zealand
Displacement 6.6 tons (c.6 tonnes)
Length 82 ft (25 m)
Propulsion 10–12 knots (19–22 km/h)

The *waka taua* was a Maori oar/sail-powered war canoe, with similar performance characteristics to a Viking longship. In war, it tended to be used for the movement of warriors along the New Zealand coastline to achieve tactical advantage.

Ornate prow with figurehead

Hull carved from a single tree trunk

Tall, carved sternpost, crucial for balance and steering

HMS Victory

Built from the wood of around 6,000 trees, mostly oak, this first-rate British ship of the line was launched in 1765. The *Victory* was the flagship of Admiral Horatio Nelson at the Battle of Trafalgar, in 1805, when the Royal Navy defeated the combined Spanish and French fleets. It is the world's oldest ship still officially in naval service.

LAUNCHED IN 1765 but held in reserve for its first 13 years, the *Victory* first saw action in 1778, when the British fleet engaged the French at the Battle of Ushant. It later became the Royal Navy's flagship in the Mediterranean, and spearheaded the action that destroyed the Spanish fleet at the Battle of Cape Saint Vincent in 1797. It played a key role in the Battle of Trafalgar, and remained in active service until 1812.

The *Victory*'s 104 smoothbore, muzzle-loading cannons gave it phenomenal firepower. For stability, the *Victory*'s heaviest guns, the 32-pounders, were positioned on the lower gun deck. The middle gun deck held the 24-pounders, while the 12-pounders were located on the upper gun deck. To keep its cannons fed with ammunition, the ship carried about 134 tons (122 tonnes) of cast-iron shot, the largest weighing 32 lb (14.5 kg).

SPECIFICATIONS	
Name	HMS *Victory*
Commissioned	1778
Displacement	3,920 tons (3,556 tonnes)
Length	227 ft 6 in (9.34 m)
Depth of hold	21 ft 6 in (6.55 m)
Propulsion	Sail
Armament	At Trafalgar: 104 guns, including 32-, 24-, and 12-pounders
Maximum speed	Up to 11 knots (20 km/h)

Warship at rest
The *Victory* has gone through five major repairs since its launch in 1765; it had been almost entirely rebuilt by the time of Trafalgar in 1805. Now restored to its pre-Trafalgar condition, HMS *Victory* sits in dry dock at Portsmouth, England.

EXTERIOR

Men climbed along the yards (horizontal spars) of the three masts to set or furl the sails. The masts are supported by ropes known as standing rigging; running rigging refers to the ropes that raise, lower, and manipulate sails. In total, the *Victory*'s 26 miles (42 km) of rigging used 768 blocks, or pulleys, the biggest of which are called jeer blocks. Ropes were also used to open and close the gun ports along the hull. Two powerful, short-barreled carronade guns were mounted on the forecastle. The *Victory* had seven anchors; the largest and heaviest required 144 men to raise it. The double wheel was located aft on the quarterdeck, under the poop.

1. Stern **2.** Wheel and binnacle holding a lantern and two compasses **3.** Gun ports **4.** Mainmast and rigging **5.** Carronade **6.** Figurehead

INTERIOR

The *Victory* carried 820 men, including 146 marines, most of whom lived among the cannons on the gun decks. The men slept in hammocks slung from the beams; meals were taken at mess tables suspended between the guns. The magazines were on the orlop deck and in the hold, which both lay below the waterline, safe from enemy fire. The hold also held stores and ballast. In the stern were cabins for the admiral, captain, and other officers.

7. 32-pounder guns **8.** Nelson's sleeping cabin **9.** Sick berth **10.** Captain's day cabin

End of an Era

The Battle of Navarino on October 20, 1827, during the Greek War of Independence (1821–29), was the last great action of the age of sail. The Treaty of London in July had committed Britain, Russia, and France to work together for Greek independence from Ottoman rule. Under the British vice-admiral Sir Edward Codrington, a combined fleet from the three nations entered the bay at Navarino (modern Pylos in southern Greece), where a larger Ottoman fleet was anchored. Codrington tried to open negotiations, but firing broke out. The ensuing battle was utterly one-sided: the allies' achieved a decisive victory through superior firepower, skill, and tactics, losing no ships but destroying much of the opposing fleet. A pivotal moment in the war, the battle ended Ottoman naval dominance in the region and helped pave the way for an independent Greek state.

With cannons blazing and ships burning, this engraving conveys the drama of the battle. Navarino caught the public imagination: many prints and souvenirs were made, and Codrington became a national hero.

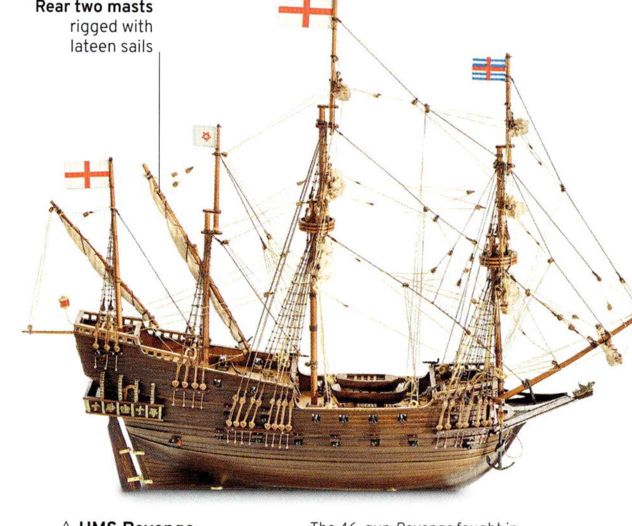

△ **Adler von Lübeck**

Date 1567 **Origin** Lübeck
Displacement 3,360 tons (3,050 tonnes)
Length 256 ft (78 m)
Propulsion Sail (4 masts)

Built as a warship to protect trade between ports of the Hanseatic League during the Northern Seven Years War (1563–70), *Alder von Lübeck* was one of the largest seagoing vessels of its day. Converted into a merchant vessel when peace was declared, the ship carried cargo until 1588.

△ **HMS Revenge**

Date 1577 **Origin** England
Displacement 492 tons (447 tonnes)
Length 140 ft (43 m)
Propulsion Sail (4 masts)

The 46-gun *Revenge* fought in numerous actions, including the defeat of the Spanish Armada in 1588 under the command of Sir Francis Drake. The ship was captured by the Spanish after a long fight off the Azores in 1591, but then sank after running into cliffs.

◁ **Spanish galleon**

Date 1698 **Origin** Iberian Peninsula
Displacement 550–1,100 tons (500–1,000 tonnes)
Length 130–200 ft (40–60 m)
Propulsion Sail (3 or 4 masts)

Developed in Spain and Portugal in the 16th and 17th centuries, galleons were armed cargo ships with a raised rear quarterdeck. Their armament depended on the period of their use and the threats they might encounter. Galleons transported wealth from colonies in the Americas to the Iberian Peninsula, braving encounters with enemy navies, privateers, and pirates, as well as the Atlantic weather.

Galleried stern, the most comfortable part of the ship, contained the senior officers' quarters

The Great Age of Sail

The development of large, well-armed, sail-powered warships gave navies the ability to protect trade routes around the world and extend their power. Ships designed to line up and engage the enemy in broadsides during battle were known as ships of the line. The British Royal Navy classed the largest of these ships, which carried over 100 guns of varying calibers, as first-rate ships; second-rate and third-rate ships carried correspondingly fewer guns. Frigates were fourth-rate ships not considered suitable for the line of battle; they were less well armed than ships of the line, but significantly faster.

△ **Santisima Trinidad**

Date 1769 **Origin** Cuba
Displacement 5,545 tons (5,030 tonnes)
Length 200 ft (61 m)
Propulsion Sail (3 masts)

Designed by an Irishman, Michael Mullan, working for the Spanish in Havana, Cuba, the *Santisima Trinidad* carried 136 guns, more than any other ship of its day. After fighting in numerous engagements against the British Royal Navy, sometimes as the Spanish flagship, *Santisima Trinidad* was captured at Trafalgar in 1805, and eventually scuttled off Cadiz. A full-sized replica is shown here.

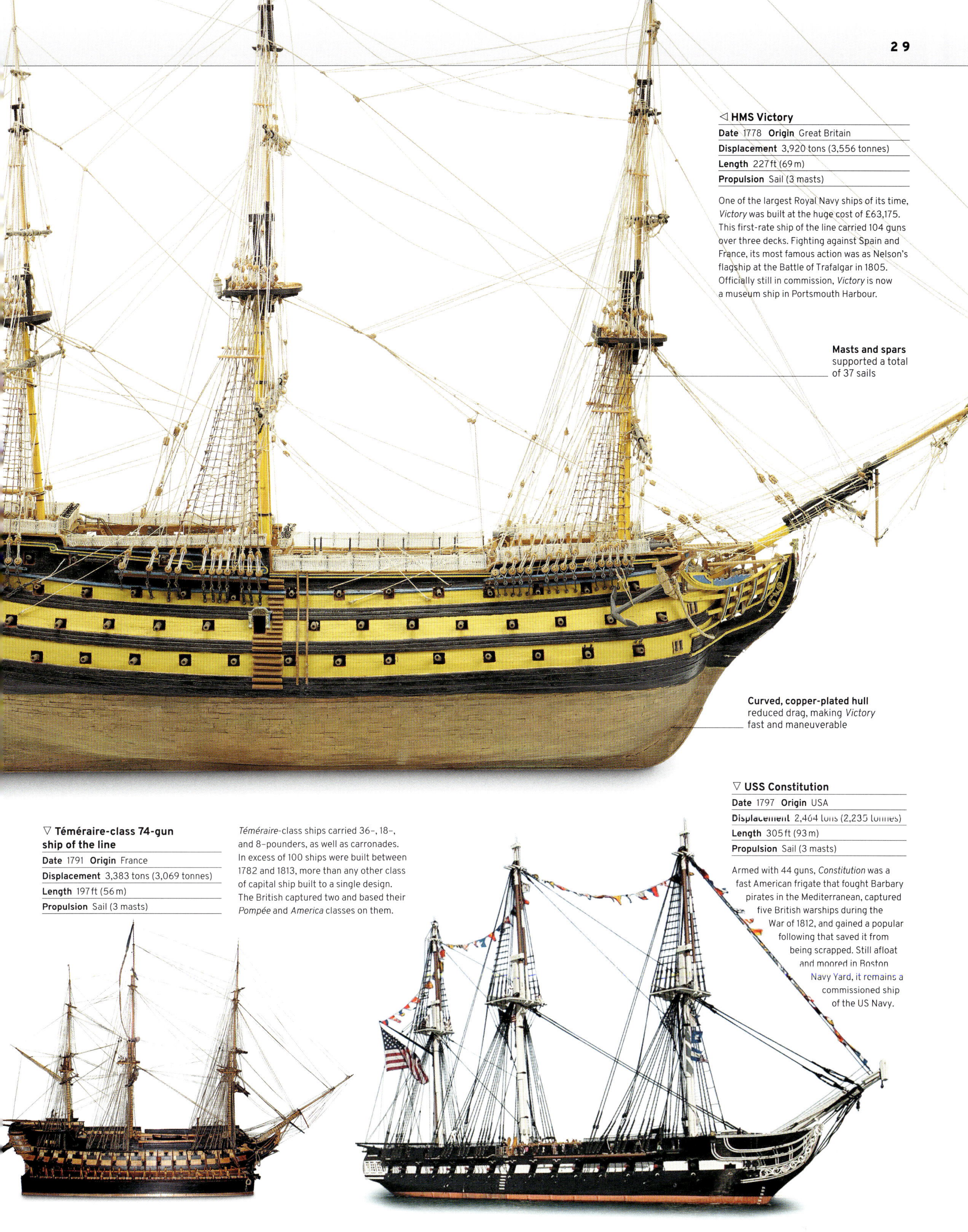

◁ **HMS Victory**

Date 1778 **Origin** Great Britain

Displacement 3,920 tons (3,556 tonnes)

Length 227 ft (69 m)

Propulsion Sail (3 masts)

One of the largest Royal Navy ships of its time, *Victory* was built at the huge cost of £63,175. This first-rate ship of the line carried 104 guns over three decks. Fighting against Spain and France, its most famous action was as Nelson's flagship at the Battle of Trafalgar in 1805. Officially still in commission, *Victory* is now a museum ship in Portsmouth Harbour.

Masts and spars supported a total of 37 sails

Curved, copper-plated hull reduced drag, making *Victory* fast and maneuverable

▽ **Téméraire-class 74-gun ship of the line**

Date 1791 **Origin** France

Displacement 3,383 tons (3,069 tonnes)

Length 197 ft (56 m)

Propulsion Sail (3 masts)

Téméraire-class ships carried 36-, 18-, and 8-pounders, as well as carronades. In excess of 100 ships were built between 1782 and 1813, more than any other class of capital ship built to a single design. The British captured two and based their *Pompée* and *America* classes on them.

▽ **USS Constitution**

Date 1797 **Origin** USA

Displacement 2,464 tons (2,235 tonnes)

Length 305 ft (93 m)

Propulsion Sail (3 masts)

Armed with 44 guns, *Constitution* was a fast American frigate that fought Barbary pirates in the Mediterranean, captured five British warships during the War of 1812, and gained a popular following that saved it from being scrapped. Still afloat and moored in Boston Navy Yard, it remains a commissioned ship of the US Navy.

1830–1918

THE MECHANIZATION OF WAR

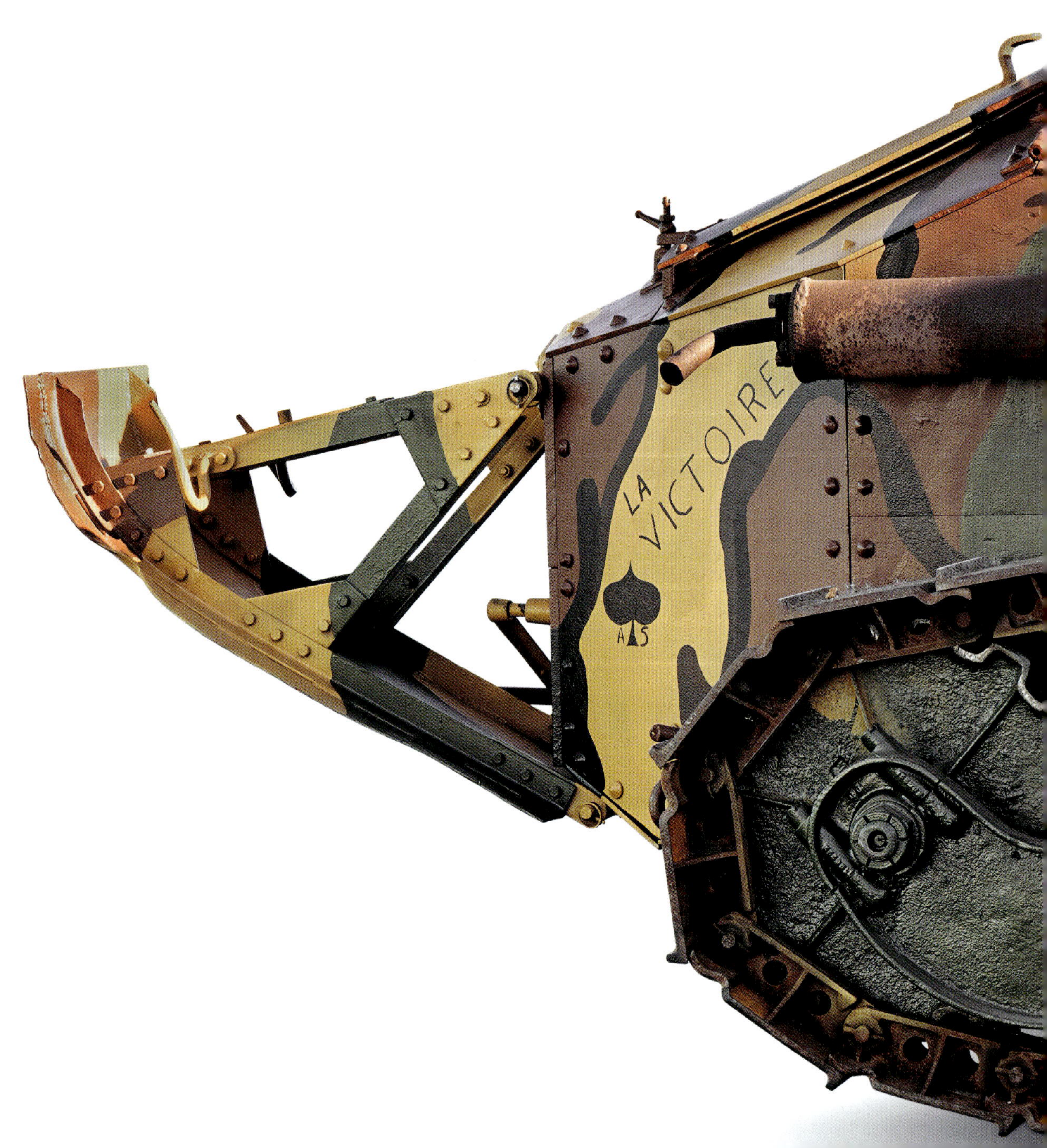

66724
1

Engines of War

The age of mechanically driven military vehicles emerged between 1830 and 1918. The invention of engines fueled by coal, oil, gasoline, and diesel heralded new types of transport, from huge dreadnought battleships to military aircraft.

The transformative force in military transportation during the 19th century was steam power. Steam engines were initially developed in the 18th century for industrial and agricultural applications. As power outputs and efficiency increased, the new engines gave rise to steam-powered trains and ships, which in turn quickly found military applications.

The first steam locomotives were designed by Englishman John Blenkinsop in 1812–13 to haul coal in mines, and by 1822 Britain had its first passenger railroad line, the Stockton and Darlington Railway. Rail networks subsequently spread across Britain and its empire, Europe, the US, and, eventually, the rest of the world. In trains and railroads there was great potential for scaling up military mobilization and deployment. Railroads could concentrate the mass movement of men and materiél in timetabled, reliable journeys, less constrained by terrain and free from the challenges of overland horse logistics.

TALKING POINT

Rail and War

The first major use of rail in warfare occurred in the late 1840s. During the European revolutions of 1848, trains were used to move soldiers rapidly to contested cities, and Prussia deployed thousands of troops by rail during its war against Denmark of 1848–51. While the Prussians refined military rail transportation to a high degree of efficiency during the Franco-Prussian War of 1870–71, the American Civil War of 1861–65 stakes its claim to being history's first large-scale "railroad war." In the fall of 1863 alone, around 20,000 men were transferred 1,200 miles (1,930 km) by rail to the front lines. The war also featured the first railroad guns and armored rail cars that could function as mobile fortifications.

The "Dictator" was a heavy mortar used by Union forces in 1864, during the American Civil War. It fired from a rail flatcar, although the recoil of its first firing destroyed the platform.

Navies under steam

The steam revolution soon found its way onto ships. Sails remained in use throughout the 19th century, and continuing improvements in sail layouts and hull design raised the speed of sail vessels. However, by 1840, steamships were making unassisted crossings of the Atlantic. Civilian steamships, like civilian railroads, were soon repurposed as troop transports. The first transatlantic steamer, Isambard Kingdom Brunel's *Great Western*, made its maiden voyage in April 1838, but by 1856 it was being used to ferry British soldiers to the Crimean War. Furthermore, from 1859, "ironclad" warships began to emerge, steam-powered and clad in steel or iron armor. In 1860, the inaugural steam-powered, fully iron-hulled warship, HMS *Warrior*, took to the waves. This began the rise of the steel-and-steam warship, which by the "dreadnought" age of the early 20th century included powerful battleships with transoceanic range, heavy turreted guns, and crews of more than 1,000.

Land vehicles

On land, steam power was not just adopted by locomotives. In Britain, the first steam traction engine purpose-built to pull artillery was developed in 1870. Such vehicles became relatively common in the late 19th century and during World War I, not least because field artillery pieces were growing considerably heavier. These vehicles had serious limitations, being slow and cumbersome, and their smoking chimneys could act as markers for enemy artillery. There was, however, an alternative power source available in this era.

Battle of Tsushima, 1905
Tsushima, fought in the waters between Korea and Japan during the Russo-Japanese War, was a crushing defeat for the Russian fleet against a confident Japanese Navy.

Timeline
As the 19th century progressed, literal horsepower increasingly gave way to the mechanical "horsepower" that engines could generate by steam and internal combustion. As a result, by the beginning of World War I, armies had entered a new industrial age. It was an era of iron, motorization, armor, and the early stages of combat aviation.

Air

Land

Water

1846 The Prussian Army pioneers the use of trains for military transportation

1859 The French launch the first ironclad warship, the *Gloire*

1860 The British launch HMS *Warrior*, the first iron-hulled, armored warship

1861 A rail baggage wagon is converted to an armored carriage during the American Civil War

1864 In the American Civil War, a Confederate submarine CSS *Hunley* becomes the first submarine to sink another ship in combat

1870s Fast torpedo boats enter service in European navies

World War I railroad gun
US Navy gunners pose for the camera, distributed along a 14 in (357 mm) railroad gun on a Mark 1 Army mount. Able to engage targets beyond the range of traditional artillery, the gun was used to support US troops on the Meuse-Argonne battlefield in northern France.

By World War I, modern armies had embraced the possibilities of the internal combustion engine (ICE), which had been invented in Germany in the 1870s. The ICE gave birth to the civilian car, motorbike, and truck, and it gradually became clear that all three modes of transport could be adapted for military use. The first steps into the mechanization and motorization of armed forces began around 1910, principally using trucks as supply vehicles. During World War I, many thousands of trucks, including types designed specifically for military use, performed logistical and support roles on all fronts.

The conflict also saw the rise of ICE-powered armored fighting vehicles (AFVs), including armored cars and the first tanks. The performance and reliability of military vehicles at this time were poor. British Mk IV tanks of World War I, for example, had a top speed of just 4 mph (6.4 km/h), were deafening and suffocating to operate, and broke down constantly. They did, however, demonstrate the shock value of mobile, armored firepower, particularly when used en masse.

Airborne warfare

The early 20th century saw a completely new addition to vehicular warfare: the airplane. Powered, pilot-controlled airplane flight was born in 1903, and just a decade later planes had developed sufficiently to be useful for military purposes. At first these purposes were mainly reconnaissance and observation, but aircraft types soon diversified, producing bombers, fighters, and ground-attack aircraft. As with early tanks, performance was limited. A typical biplane fighter had a top speed of around 110 mph (177 km/h) and a range of around 300 miles (482 km). Although dangerous to fly, let alone to fight in, the impact of these warplanes was profound: they opened up a new kind of warfare, and the use of military technology in the skies would become one of the defining features of warfare in the 20th century and beyond.

“We need **bold and free flight,** we need **mobility!”**

SOVIET REVOLUTIONARY AND MILITARY COMMANDER MIKHAIL FRUNZE, 1921

1880s The destroyer emerges as a new type of warship

1884 Driven by an electric motor, *La France* makes the world's first fully controlled airship flight near Paris

1902 Design of the first armored car, the French Charron, Girardot et Voigt

1903 The American Wright brothers' *Flyer* makes the first flight of a manned, powered, controllable, heavier-than-air aircraft

1904 The French vessel *Aigrette* becomes history's first diesel-electric powered submarine

1906 French and Austrian armies develop gasoline-powered artillery tractors

1909 In the US, the Wright Military Flyer, the world's first military aircraft, enters service

1914 Introduction of the first bomber aircraft

1915 The armies of World War I use increasing numbers of military trucks

1916 The first use of tanks in combat—British Mark Is at the Battle of Flers-Courcelette

Military Trains and Railroad Guns

The use of railroads for military purposes began in the 1840s and became well-established during the second half of the 19th century. At first, civilian freight and passenger trains were repurposed to transport military materiel and personnel. However, such trains became high-profile targets for sabotage, ambush, and artillery strikes, particularly trains that ran through contested regions or came close to the front lines. As a result, many military trains were fitted with armor and defensive weaponry. During World War I, some combatants produced enormous railroad guns. These outsized artillery pieces were too heavy and logistically complex to move by any other means than rail.

△ Railroad battery

Date 1861 **Origin** USA	
Wheel arrangement	Four axles
Armament	1 x 24-pounder cannon; infantry muskets
Crew	Up to 60 infantrymen
Armor	Heavy boilerplate

This boxy, boilerplate mobile battery was developed in the first year of the American Civil War (1861–65) to protect engineers repairing railroad bridges that had been damaged or destroyed by Confederate forces. It had a 24-pounder cannon as its main armament; the infantry inside could fire their muskets through hinged firing ports.

◁ B&O L Class No.57 Memnon

Date 1848 **Origin** USA	
Wheel arrangement	0-8-0
Boiler pressure	75 psi (5 kg/sq cm)
Driving wheel diameter	44 in (1,118 mm)
Top speed	approx. 30 mph (48 km/h)

With eight driving wheels for extra traction and power, *Memnon* was originally used by the Baltimore & Ohio Railroad to haul freight. During the American Civil War, it transported supplies and troops for the Union Army.

Tall stack created strong draft for better combustion and helped capture sparks

Cowcatcher (also called a pilot) deflected objects on track

Eight driving wheels, with no leading or trailing wheels

▷ American Standard locomotive

Date 1862 **Origin** USA	
Wheel arrangement	4-4-0
Boiler pressure	Up to 140 psi (9.8 kg/sq cm)
Driving wheel diameter	Up to 66 in (1,676 mm)
Top speed	60 mph (c.97 km/h)

The American Standard was an iconic steam locomotive type put to work during the American Civil War in troop transport and logistical roles. This particular train, the *W. H. Whiton*, pulled President Abraham Lincoln's railcar, which was later converted to his funerary car.

Headlights were powered by oil or kerosene

◁ **Armored train (British)**

Date 1900 **Origin** South Africa

Wheel arrangement 4–8 axles total

Armament 1 x 12-pounder QF gun; multiple machine guns; infantry rifles and carbines

Crew 40–60

Armor Boilerplate and steel cladding on gun trucks and engine cab

The British forces in the Boer War (1899–1902) made extensive use of armored trains. The trains were essentially railway wagons fitted with steel plating for protection, and firing ports and gun positions for defense. They proved to be vulnerable to well-planned Boer ambushes.

Tender carried on two four-wheel bogies

△ **British Imperial Military Railways armored CSAR Class E 4-10-2T**

Date 1902 **Origin** UK

Wheel arrangement 4-10-2T

Boiler pressure 175 psi (12.3 kg/sq cm)

Driving wheel diameter 45 in (1,143 mm)

Top speed 28–31 mph (c.45–50 km/h)

During the Boer War, the British Imperial Military Railways (IMR) commissioned the construction of 35 armored variants of the "Reid Tenwheeler" locomotive designed by George W. Reid. The engines, which became the Class E 4-10-2T, had good traction and were ideal for pulling heavy loads up the steep inclines common in South Africa.

△ **280 cm SK L/40 "Bruno"**

Date 1916 **Origin** Germany

Wheel arrangement 2 x 5-axle bogies (10 axles total)

Armament 1 x 280 mm naval gun

Crew c.25–30 artillery personnel, plus support and security troops

Armor Minimal

The "Bruno" was a 280 mm railway gun that operated on the Western Front during World War I, where it bombarded targets up to a maximum range of 11 miles (18 km). The gun was actually a type used on German Navy warships, adapted to rail in 1916.

Barrel measured 54 ft (17 m) in length

△ **M1895 railroad gun**

Date 1917 **Origin** USA

Wheel arrangement 2 x 8-axle bogies (16 axles total)

Armament 1 x 16 in M1895 coastal defense gun

Crew c.40–50

Armor None

This mighty American railroad gun was constructed in 1902 as a mobile coastal defense weapon, being deployed around Panama in 1917. It married an M1895 16 in (406 mm) gun to two eight-axle bogies. The total weight of the entire assembly was a hefty 284,000 lb (129,000 kg).

▽ **Ordnance BL 12 in gun Mk IX**

Date 1916 **Origin** UK

Wheel arrangement 11 axles total

Armament 1 x 12 in Mk IX W naval gun

Crew c.30–55

Armor None

The British deployed four of these heavy railroad guns to the Western Front between 1915 and 1918. The guns were surplus Royal Navy 12 in Mk IX W naval models set on railroad mountings; shown here is a Mk II mounting made by the Elswick Ordnance Company of Newcastle-upon-Tyne.

Battleships and Cruisers

Britain's Royal Navy was seen by many rival nations as the bedrock of the country's success in expanding the British Empire during the 19th century. Nations wanting to acquire colonies overseas felt compelled to boost their naval strength with increasingly powerful warships. Of all fighting ships, cruisers and battleships carried the biggest guns and had the best armor protection; consequently, they became part of a technological arms race—and a symbol of the global power struggles of the late 19th and early 20th centuries.

88 mm gun for defense against torpedo boats

24 cm gun (was main armament)

△ **HMS Trafalgar**

Date 1890 **Origin** UK

Displacement 14,100 tons (12,792 tonnes)

Length 345 ft (105 m)

Top speed 16.7 knots (31 km/h)

This was the last of a series of British low-freeboard battleships. With a short distance from waterline to main deck, the hull sat low in the water, so the ship presented a smaller target. Such ships were best suited for calmer waters, like the Mediterranean.

▽ **USS Atlanta**

Date 1886 **Origin** USA

Displacement 3,570 tons (3,240 tonnes)

Length 283 ft (86.3 m)

Top speed 16.3 knots (30 km/h)

Atlanta was a cruiser with 2 in (5 cm) of armor protection, one of the first four steel ships built for the US Navy as part of its "New Navy" drive in the 1880s. *Atlanta*'s armament included two 8 in and six 6 in guns, and a range of smaller weapons.

Rigging supported the masts and was used to raise and lower the sails

Sails (here furled) increased *Atlanta*'s cruising range

◁ **Siegfried-class ship**

Date 1890 **Origin** Germany

Displacement 3,860 tons (3,500 tonnes)

Length 259 ft (79 m)

Top speed 26 km/h (14 knots)

The six *Siegfried*-class ships, built 1888–94, were designed to patrol and protect the German coast and the entry to the Kiel Canal. Armament was three 24 cm main guns (able to fire two rounds per minute), eight 88 mm guns, and torpedo tubes.

△ **Navarin**

Date 1896 **Origin** Russia

Displacement 11,430 tons (10,370 tonnes)

Length 351 ft (107 m)

Top speed 28 km/h (15 knots)

Ordered in 1890 by the Imperial Russian Navy, changes in design and delays in construction meant this battleship did not enter service until 1896. *Navarin* saw action in the Russo-Japanese War, being sunk in 1905 at the Battle of Tsushima by mines laid in its path by Japanese destroyers. Only three of her crew of over 600 survived.

▷ **USS Indiana**

Date 1895 **Origin** USA

Displacement 11,522 tons (10,453 tonnes)

Length 350 ft (107 m)

Top speed 15 knots (28 km/h)

The US Navy's first battleship, *Indiana* was built for coastal protection work (with its low freeboard, it would have struggled in heavy open seas). In the Spanish-American War, *Indiana* took part in the 1898 Battle of Santiago de Cuba, a decisive US victory.

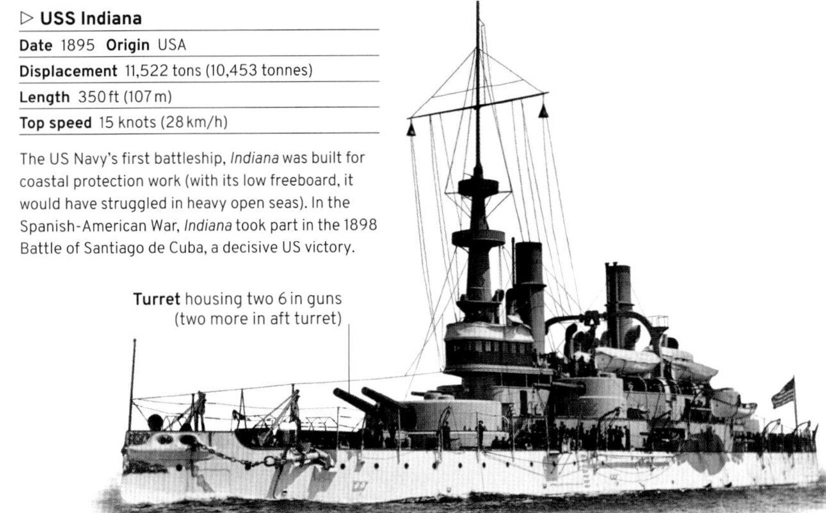

Turret housing two 6 in guns (two more in aft turret)

▷ **Fuji**

Date 1897 **Origin** Japan

Displacement 13,700 tons (12,430 tonnes)

Length 412 ft (125 m)

Top speed 18 knots (33 km/h)

Fuji was one of two British-built battleships ordered by Japan in response to the Chinese acquiring two new battleships from Germany. *Fuji* was involved in the battles of the Yellow Sea (1904) and Tsushima (1905) during the Russo-Japanese War. Later used for coastal patrols, it ended its life as a training ship.

◁ **HMS Leviathan**

Date 1903 **Origin** UK

Displacement 15,850 tons (14,380 tonnes)

Length 533 ft (162 m)

Top speed 23 knots (43 km/h)

One of four *Drake*-class armored cruisers, with two 9 in and sixteen 6 in guns, *Leviathan* served in East Asia and the Mediterranean before being put in reserve. Recommissioned in 1914, *Leviathan* chased commerce raiders and escorted convoys across the Atlantic during World War I.

▷ **SMS Dresden**

Date 1908 **Origin** Germany

Displacement 4,705 tons (4,268 tonnes)

Length 388 ft (118 m)

Top speed 44 km/h (24 knots)

Built as part of the Imperial German Navy's efforts to rival the Royal Navy, the light cruiser *Dresden* saw action in World War I as a commerce raider in the South Atlantic. It fought at the battles of Coronel and the Falkland Islands (1914), but was cornered and scuttled off the Chilean coast in 1915.

Mikasa

Renowned as the Japanese flagship at the 1905 Battle of Tsushima, which saw the fleet of the Imperial Russian Navy virtually annihilated, the *Mikasa* is the only surviving example of a pre-dreadnought battleship. The *Mikasa* was one of the first ships to be fitted with "Krupp cemented" steel armor. This armor proved highly effective at Tsushima, when some 30 hits from Russian guns failed to put the *Mikasa* out of action.

BASED ON THE ROYAL NAVY'S Majestic class, the *Mikasa* was built by Vickers at Barrow-in-Furness—the last of four similar battleships made in British yards for the Imperial Japanese Navy. Powered by 25 coal-burning boilers, the *Mikasa* entered service in 1902.

The ship's main armament consisted of four 12 in guns mounted in twin centerline turrets fore and aft; these guns could be fired at a rate of three rounds every two minutes. The *Mikasa*'s array of secondary armaments included fourteen 6 in quick-firing guns, lighter guns to defend against destroyers and torpedo boats, and four torpedo tubes submerged below the waterline.

In addition to forming the main deck, Krupp cemented armor was fitted in belts around the waterline up to 9 in (23 cm) thick, and in 14 in- (356 mm-) thick barbettes around the 12 in gun installations. Other features that proved influential at Tsushima included up-to-date wireless communication and superior range finders, which gave the Japanese fleet long-range firepower superiority. Ironically, having survived the Russian guns at Tsushima, the ship sank in harbor four months later, following an accidental explosion in a magazine. Raised in 1906 and repaired, the *Mikasa* never fought again. Decommissioned in 1923, it is now a museum ship at Yokosuka.

EXTERIOR

The *Mikasa* supplemented its main armament with a variety of smaller-caliber weapons, ranging from 6 in guns for use against cruisers and destroyers, to 12-, 3-, and 1-pounders, in addition to machine guns. From the command post on top of the bridge, which gave uninterrupted views to the front and sides, orders were passed to the pilothouse via a speaking tube beside the compass. The gilded characters on the railings of the walkway to the admiral's cabin spell out *Mi-ka-sa*.

1. Rear view of bridge **2.** Bridge searchlight **3.** Fore anchor **4.** Bridge **5.** Stern walkway **6.** Porthole **7.** Mainmast **8.** Aft skylight **9.** Hotchkiss 3-pounder gun **10.** Funnels **11.** Command post with speaking tube **12.** 6 in guns **13.** Range finder **14.** Port to 3 in battery **15.** 6 in gun breech

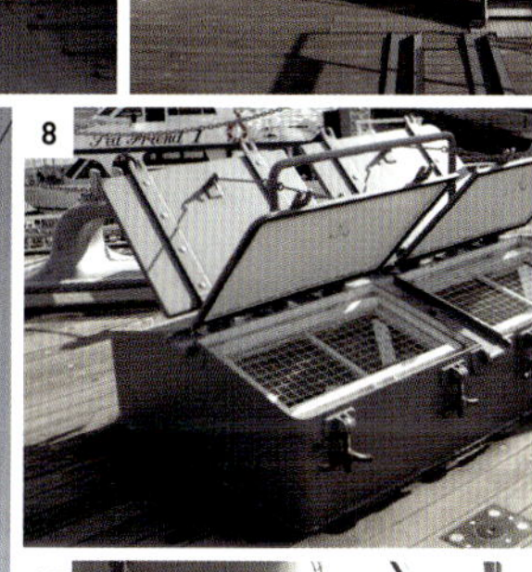

12 in gun turret
The *Mikasa's* two turrets originally housed 12 in guns, 40 calibers long, that could fire an 850 lb (385 kg) projectile 8½ miles (13.5 km). In the 1906 rebuild, the turrets were fitted with 45-caliber pieces.

SPECIFICATIONS	
Name	*Mikasa*
Commissioned	1902
Type	Pre-dreadnought battleship
Displacement	16,954 tons (15,380 tonnes)
Length	432 ft (131.7 m)
Propulsion	2 triple-expansion steam engines
Armament	2 × twin (12 in) guns
Armour	Krupp cemented armor
Maximum speed	18 knots (33 km/h)

INTERIOR

The ship was controlled, or "conned," from the pilothouse, whose wheel, compass, and engine-room telegraphs (used to indicate the speed required) were duplicated in an armored conning tower one deck below. Living conditions for the crew were almost unchanged from the days of sail, with the men sleeping in hammocks and eating at foldaway tables. Officers dined in the wardroom, which also hosted meetings; the admiral, who had his own bathroom, took formal meals in his saloon.

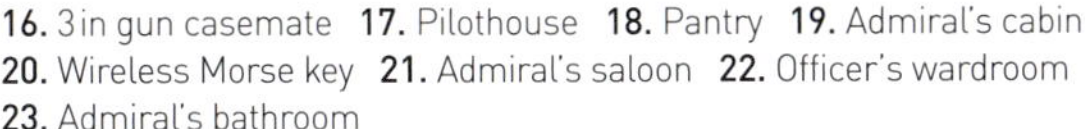

16. 3in gun casemate **17.** Pilothouse **18.** Pantry **19.** Admiral's cabin **20.** Wireless Morse key **21.** Admiral's saloon **22.** Officer's wardroom **23.** Admiral's bathroom

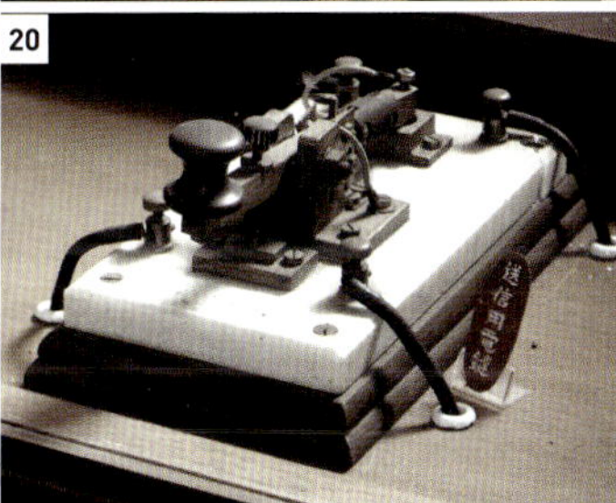

Torpedo Boats, Destroyers, and Submarines

A new chapter in naval warfare began in 1866, when the English engineer Robert Whitehead, working at Fiume (modern-day Rijeka in Croatia), perfected the self-propelled torpedo. Soon, boats were being designed specifically to deploy the revolutionary weapon; this, in turn, prompted the production of torpedo-boat "destroyers" to combat the new threat. Able to defend other ships and also take on the offensive role of torpedo boats if needed, destroyers became an indispensable element of the fleet. The torpedo gave the emerging generation of submarines a powerful weapon to use against surface vessels while remaining underwater.

▽ HMS Lightning

Date 1876 **Origin** UK
Displacement 37 tons (33.5 tonnes)
Length 87½ ft (26.7 m)
Top speed 18.5 knots (34 km/h)

Built at the urging of constructor John Thornycroft, *Lightning* was the British Royal Navy's first torpedo boat. This experimental craft incorporated a variety of innovative features, including a divided rudder ahead of the single propeller.

Torpedo launch tube

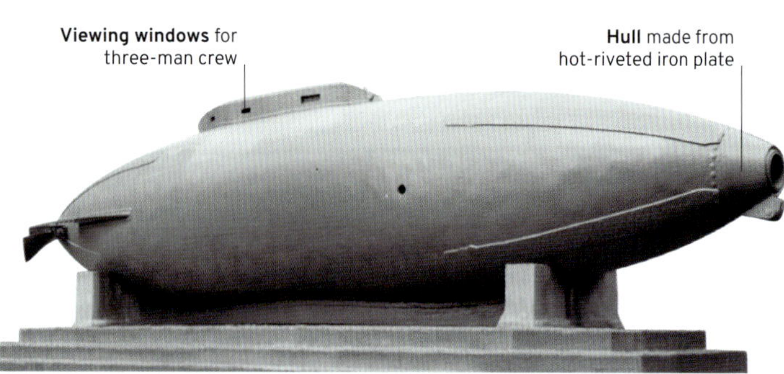

△ Fenian Ram

Date 1881 **Origin** USA
Displacement 19 tons (17.2 tonnes)
Length 31 ft (9.4 m)
Top speed 9 knots (17 km/h)

Designed by Irish émigré John Philip Holland and funded by the Irish Republican Brotherhood in the US for use against British ships in Ireland, *Fenian Ram* was armed with a 9 in pneumatic gun for firing explosive projectiles from its bow. It never saw action. Holland later designed the USS *Holland*, the US Navy's first commissioned submarine.

△ SMS S90

Date 1899 **Origin** Germany
Displacement 437 tons 396 tonnes
Length 207 ft (63 m)
Top speed 26.5 knots (49 km/h)

Armed with a trio of 5 cm guns and three torpedo tubes, *S90* was the lead vessel of a class of large torpedo boats built from 1898 to 1907. In 1914, during the siege of the German port of Tsingtao (Qindao) in China, *S90* sank the Japanese cruiser *Takachiho*, before being scuttled to avoid capture.

△ HMS Havock

Date 1893 **Origin** UK
Displacement 308 tons (279 tonnes)
Length 185 ft (56 m)
Top speed 27 knots (50 km/h)

Havock and its sister ship, *Hornet*, were the first operational Royal Navy destroyers. *Havock* carried a 12-pounder gun, three 6-pounders, and three torpedo tubes—a fixed bow tube and a pair of deck tubes on a rotating mount.

▷ Sokol

Date 1895 **Origin** Russia
Displacement 265 tons (240 tonnes)
Length 190 ft (57.9 m)
Top speed 29 knots (54 km/h)

Constructed by British shipbuilder Yarrow, *Sokol*—Russia's first destroyer—was claimed to be the fastest warship of its day. Renamed *Pruitki* in 1902, it served with the Imperial Russian Navy in World War I, then, after the October Revolution, with the Bolshevik Red Fleet, fighting White Army forces during the Russian Civil War (1917–22).

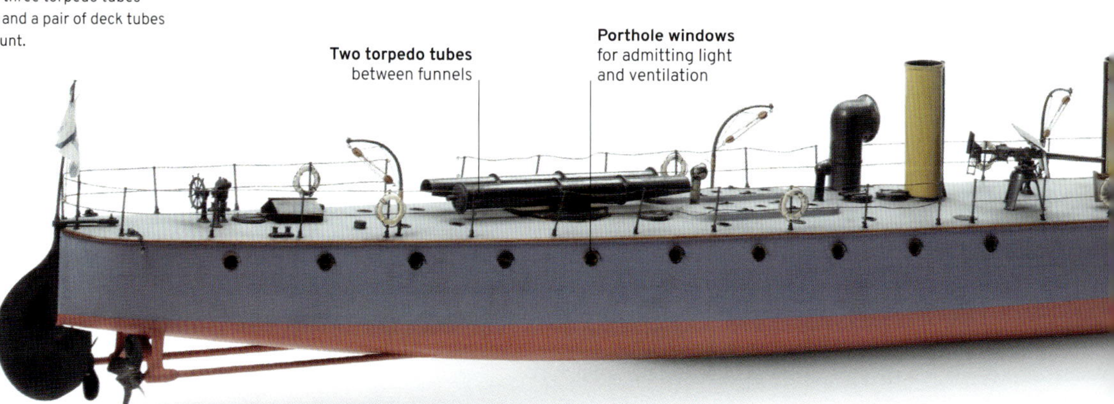

▷ **Kagerō**

Date 1899 **Origin** Japan
Displacement 403 tons (366 tonnes)
Length 210 ft (64 m)
Top speed 30 knots (56 km/h)

Kagerō was one of six *Murakano*-class destroyers built for Japan in the late 1890s by Thornycroft in the UK, based on Thornycroft's design for HMS *Angler*. *Kagerō* featured in the Battle of Tsushima and other engagements of the Russo-Japanese War of 1904–05, and saw action in World War I.

Divided rudder for improved maneuverability

"Four-stack" (four funnel) arrangement

△ **USS Hull (DD-7)**

Date 1903 **Origin** USA
Displacement 457 tons (415 tonnes)
Length 249 ft (75.8 m)
Top speed 29 knots (54 km/h)

Hull and other *Bainbridge* class vessels were the inaugural US destroyers. *Hull* was equipped with two torpedo tubes, a pair of 3 in guns, and five 6-pounders. Put into reserve in 1912, the ship was recommissioned in 1917. It took part in patrols, escorts, and training exercises during World War I.

△ **USS Tarantula (B-3)**

Date 1907 **Origin** USA
Displacement 162 tons (147 tonnes)
Length 82½ ft (25.1 m)
Top speed 9 knots (17 km/h)

Tarantula was one of three B-class US Navy vessels, the last submarines directly designed by John Holland. With a 10-man crew, it carried four torpedoes and could dive to around 150 ft (46 m). It sailed with the US Atlantic and Asiatic Fleets, ending its operational life in the Philippines.

Steamboat Battles in the American Civil War

The American Civil War (1861–65) generated a range of new weapons. On the water, the first engagements of "ironclads" took place, with iron-hulled ships at sea and armored monitor vessels sporting turrets operating nearer to shore. Both types were powered by effective steam engines, meaning that fighting was no longer dictated by the wind's direction. Early ironclads were converted wooden sailing ships, but innovative designs soon appeared, spawning new maritime battle tactics. Since armor plate was effective at protecting a vessel against cannon fire, ships were fitted with rams to hole and sink their adversaries. Submarines were used with varying degrees of success, along with torpedoes and mines. The blockading of ports by Union forces prevented the Confederate South from trading or importing weaponry—a major factor in its defeat.

The Battle of Mobile Bay by J. O. Davidson depicts the victorious assault by Union ships on a smaller Confederate fleet and three defensive forts around Mobile Bay in the Gulf of Mexico in 1864.

J.O. DAVIDSON

World War I: Mobile Warfare on Land

World War I was a conflict forged in the industrial age. The vast material requirements of the war depended heavily upon railway logistics, plus an ever-growing fleet of motor vehicles. On the front line, the war saw the introduction of history's first armored fighting vehicles, which provided mobile firepower. However, horses and mules were also widely used for logistics.

Motorcycle unit
Britain's Motor Machine-Gun Service (MMGS) used motorbikes (here a 532 cc Scott) and sidecars armed with Vickers guns to provide mobile antiaircraft defense and suppress ground fire.

British historian A. J. P. Taylor described World War I as being "imposed on the statesmen of Europe by railway timetables." Trains made possible the swift, mass transportation of soldiers and materials. Taylor argued that, prewar, nations believed the ability to mobilize by rail faster than their adversaries would act as a deterrent, but in reality planning for such rapid mobilization made war inevitable.

Home front to front line

When the conflict began in 1914, continental Europe—including western Russia—was connected by over 186,400 miles (300,000 km) of railroad. Rail tracks allowed newly mobilized armies to be sent rapidly to major rail hubs close to emerging battlefields. Above all, railroads offered logistical scale. An infantry division of 12,000 men required around 1,100 tons (1,000 tonnes) of supplies each day just to meet its noncombat demands, equivalent to two 50-wagon supply trains.

For this reason, railroads were integral to the strategic and operational planning of the war. Germany's opening offensive, the so-called "Schlieffen Plan," was developed closely around rail timetables and transportation volumes, underpinning the belief that the German Army would be able to secure a quick victory in the west before moving its forces east to face the Russians. In France, the mobilization of 3.7 million men in August 1914 was converted into a practical offensive–defensive response by 39,150 miles (63,000 km) of rail (including local lines).

In matters of logistics, rail power enabled armies to build up vast supply dumps located several miles from the fighting front. To take those stores forward to the troops, the French and Germans in particular, and later the British, laid thousands of miles of 24-in (60-cm) gauge railroad track, across which small, lightweight engines pulling supply trains rolled endlessly.

Beyond the rails

World War I demonstrated rail's limitations, as well as its usefulness. The chaos and destruction wrought by fighting could disrupt rail traffic, especially near the artillery-ravaged front lines, and ultimately trains had to stop short of the combat zone, with the final miles of supply movement often being undertaken by horse and mules (see panel below).

However, the war also saw the first substantial military use of mechanical horsepower, especially by the British and, later, the Americans. Cars, buses, and trucks were requisitioned and sent to the front line, while steam-, gasoline-, and diesel-driven tracked tractors were used to haul heavy artillery pieces. By 1915–16, large fleets of purpose-built military trucks were in use, such as the British 3-ton AEC Type Y and the US 3- and 5-ton "Liberty" trucks. Although these vehicles were limited in reliability, speed, and off-road performance, they nevertheless demonstrated the viability of military motorization.

Armored warfare

Another World War I innovation was mobile, mechanized armor. The first crude iterations of armored cars were little more than actual road cars with some sheet metal protection and a machine gun. Particularly on the Western Front, however, heavier armored vehicles were developed as a means to break the trench deadlock. While there were many precursors, Britain led the way with the first tank, the prototype "Little Willie," in 1915. More significantly, in September 1916 Britain launched the lozenge-shaped Mark I tank into action at the Somme, followed in June 1917 by the more capable Mark IV at the Battle of Messines. The Germans and French developed their own tanks, and in April 1918 the first tank vs. tank duel was fought between a Mark IV and a German A7V—the former prevailed. The age of armour had begun.

Artillery tractor
During the British retreat on the Western Front in spring 1918, an artillery gun and assorted personnel are pulled by what appears to be a US-built Holt tracked artillery tractor.

> "Employment of **tanks in mass** is our greatest **enemy.**"
>
> GENERAL ERICH LUDENDORFF, FIRST QUARTERMASTER GENERAL OF THE GERMAN GENERAL STAFF

Modes of transport
Here, at the Second Battle of Bapaume, August–September 1918, the full spectrum of World War I mobility can be seen: horse-drawn logistics, military trucks, and British Mark IV tanks alongside Canadian infantry.

TALKING POINT

Horses in World War I

Across the many fronts of World War I, millions of horses and mules were drafted into war service (as well as camels in the Middle East). In the UK alone, the British Army's Remount Department sent more than 368,000 domestic and agricultural horses to the Western Front between 1914 and 1917. Although there were still some horse-mounted cavalry units in service during the war, particularly on the Eastern Front, horses were mainly employed in logistical work, moving heavy loads over rough terrain that proved impassable to military vehicles. Their roles included carrying ammunition between forward rail hubs and frontline troops, drawing field ambulances, and pulling heavy artillery pieces. Often, the requisitioned horses were terribly unsuited for the hard labor at the front lines—it is estimated that around eight million horses died, most of them on the Western Front.

Horses, like their handlers, needed protection from sudden gas attacks. British equine gas masks consisted of a dual-layer flannelette bag, impregnated with a "Komplexene" chemical treatment and expanded out from the horse's nose and mouth by a canvas frame.

△ **Nash Quad**

Date 1913 **Origin** USA

Engine 4-cylinder gasoline, 52 hp (39 kW)

Payload 1.5 tons (1.4 tonnes)

A versatile and durable utility truck, the Nash Quad was developed specifically for military use by the Thomas B. Jeffery Company, itself acquired by the Nash Motors Company in 1916. More than 11,500 vehicles were produced by 1919.

▷ **Fiat 15 Ter**

Date 1912 **Origin** Italy

Engine 4-cylinder gasoline, 40 hp (30 kW)

Payload 1.65 tons (1.5 tonnes)

The Fiat 15 Ter, Italy's first military truck, served initially in the Italo-Turkish War. The Italian, British, French, and Russian armies all used the light truck in large numbers throughout World War I.

△ **Latil TAR**

Date 1913 **Origin** France

Engine 4-cylinder gasoline, 30 hp (22.5 kW)

Payload 4.4 tons (4 tonnes)

During World War I, the 4x4 Latil TAR took the place of horses to pull heavy artillery, including 14.3-ton (13-tonne) 155 mm field guns. By 1922, more than 3,000 trucks had been built and many were still in service at the start of World War II.

Utility and Troop Trucks

World War I heralded the arrival of industrialized, highly mechanized conflict. Horses struggled to haul the larger artillery pieces or carry the sheer weight of soldiers, equipment, and supplies that modern warfare demanded. As war broke out in 1914, huge numbers of trucks were needed, but development time was limited, so civilian vehicles, such as London buses and Paris taxis, were drafted in, hastily painted green or brown, and sent to the front to supply and transport troops, including the wounded. Even purpose-built trucks were often ill-suited to the shell-blasted terrain, struggling to steer through the mud and terrifyingly vulnerable to attack. The lessons from such extreme conditions were quickly learned, leading to a new generation of robust battlefield trucks—and drivers who could carry their skills into transport roles at home.

△ **Ford Model T Ambulance**

Date 1916 **Origin** USA

Engine 4-cylinder gasoline, 20 hp (15 kW)

Payload Up to six casualties

The readily available Ford Model T chassis offered a practical battlefield ambulance platform in World War I. The back cabin could transport three litters or four seated casualties, with two more wounded carried in the front cabin.

▷ **Berliet CBA**

Date 1916 **Origin** France

Engine 4-cylinder gasoline, 22 hp (16.5 kW)

Payload 3.9 tons (3.5 tonnes)

With more than 25,000 in service, the CBA was the most used French truck of World War I. It played a particularly important role in supplying French forces at the Battle of Verdun in 1916.

Paraffin-powered headlamp

△ **Pierce Arrow R8**

Date 1916 **Origin** USA

Engine 4-cylinder gasoline, 38 hp (28 kW)

Payload 4 tons (3.6 tonnes)

More than 14,000 R8 trucks, with their cross-braced chassis design, were delivered to British and French forces during the war. The R8 proved to be a durable and easy-to-repair military workhorse.

Electricity-powered headlamp

△ **Thornycroft J Type**

Date 1916 **Origin** UK

Engine 4-cylinder gasoline, 40 hp (30 kW)

Payload 3.3 tons (3 tonnes)

Thornycroft supplied more than 5,000 J Type trucks for Britain's war effort on the Western Front, as well as service in Egypt and India. The J Type operated as both a cargo carrier and mobile antiaircraft gun platform.

△ **Berliet CBA Surgical Truck**

Date 1917 **Origin** France

Engine 4-cylinder gasoline, 22 hp (16.5 kW)

Payload 5.5 tons (5 tonnes)

By 1917, hundreds of cars and trucks had been converted into ambulances and stretcher carriers on the Western Front. Some, such as this Berliet, were used for surgery.

Pierce-Arrow R Type

Between 1901 and 1938, Pierce-Arrow of Buffalo, New York, was one of the leading US manufacturers of luxury automobiles, its models used by presidents and movie stars alike. After the outbreak of World War I, the company switched its focus from expensive cars for the rich and famous to trucks for military use. The high quality of the Pierce-Arrow R Type truck made it a popular choice for the Allied war effort.

PIERCE-ARROW described its R type as the "American Rolls-Royce of trucks." During World War I, over 14,000 Pierce-Arrow trucks were produced for the French and British armed forces. Most were general cargo types, but some were fully equipped workshop trucks, and a few were even armored and equipped with guns.

The R8 truck pictured here was one of many delivered to the French government in 1916. Transporting the trucks from the US to France was a perilous affair: the vehicles were hoisted onto barges at the docks in New York and towed across the ocean to Le Havre, but many did not survive the rough Atlantic voyage.

CLOSED REAR VIEW

OPEN REAR VIEW

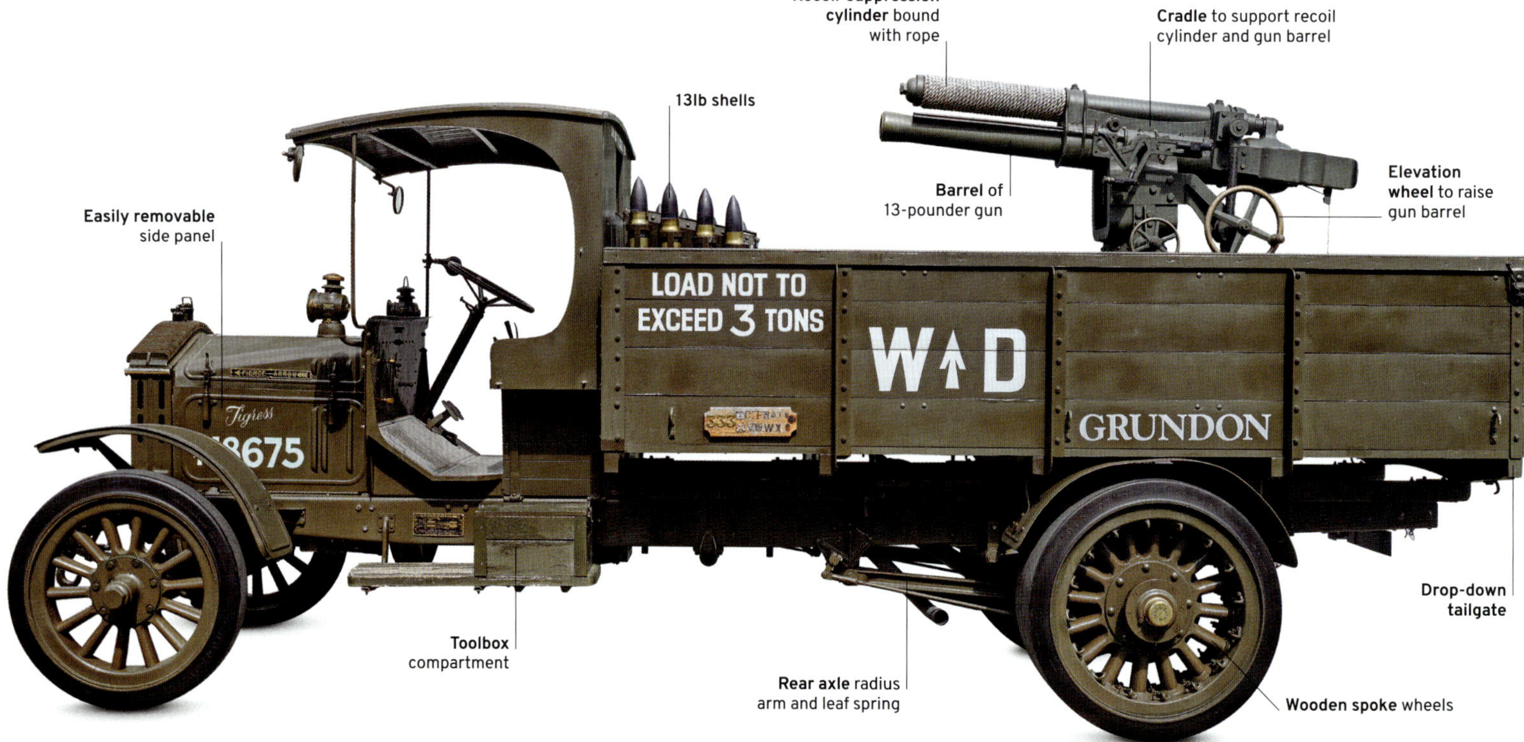

SPECIFICATIONS	
Model	Pierce-Arrow R Type
Origin	USA
Assembly	Buffalo, New York
Production run	1911–19, approx. 16,500
Weight	4.95 tons (4.5 tonnes)
Payload	3.3 tons (3 tonnes)
Engine	4-cylinder gasoline, 3880 cc, 30 hp (22 kW)
Transmission	3-speed manual
Maximum speed	18 mph (29 km/h)

Restored survivor
After wartime service, this cargo truck remained in military use until the late 1920s, when it was sold for civilian purposes in the south of France. In 1991, it was brought to the UK in 1991 and restored. Sporting British Army paintwork, this R type now has a 13-pounder antiaircraft gun mounted on the truck bed.

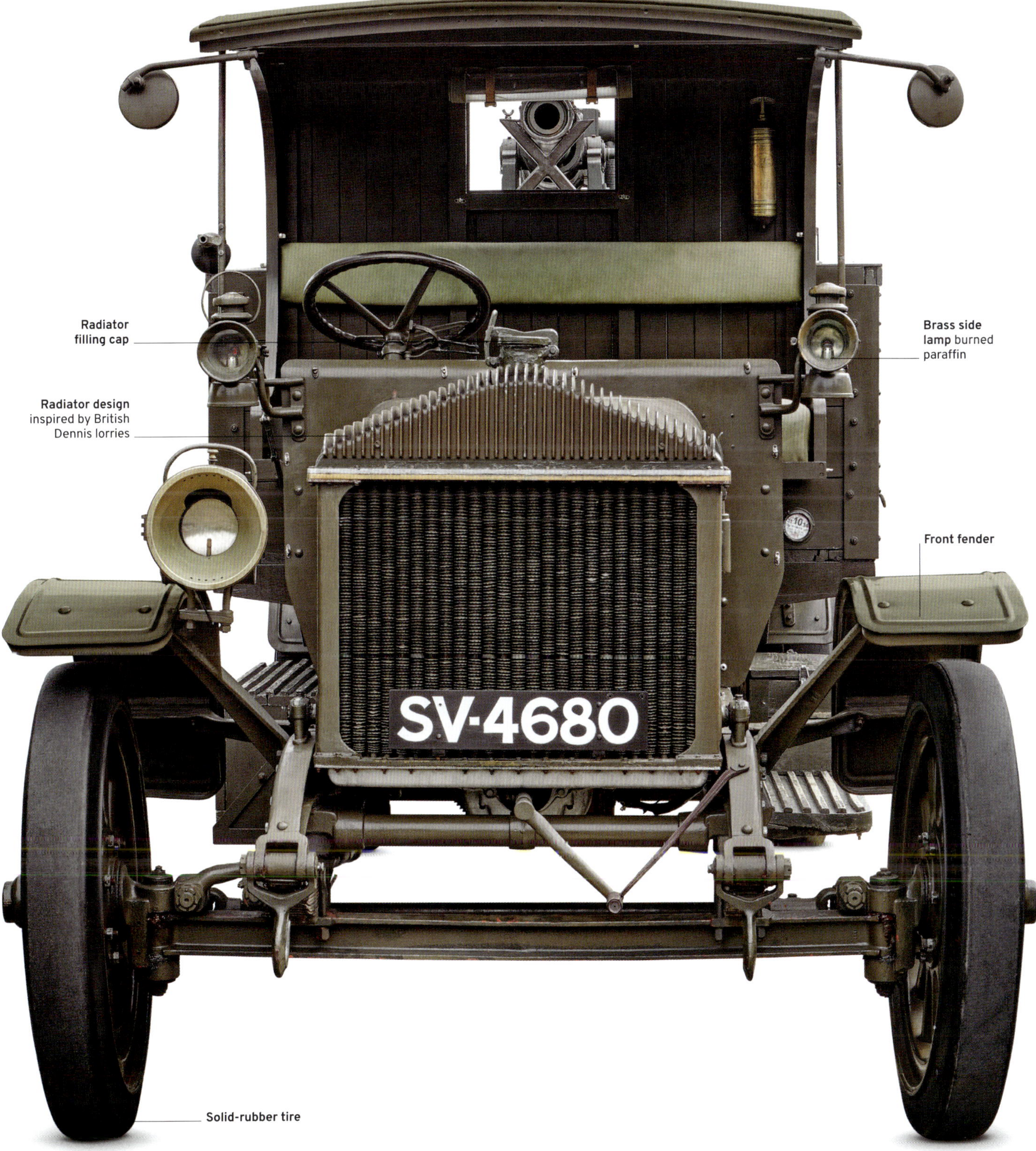

Radiator filling cap

Radiator design inspired by British Dennis lorries

Brass side lamp burned paraffin

Front fender

Solid-rubber tire

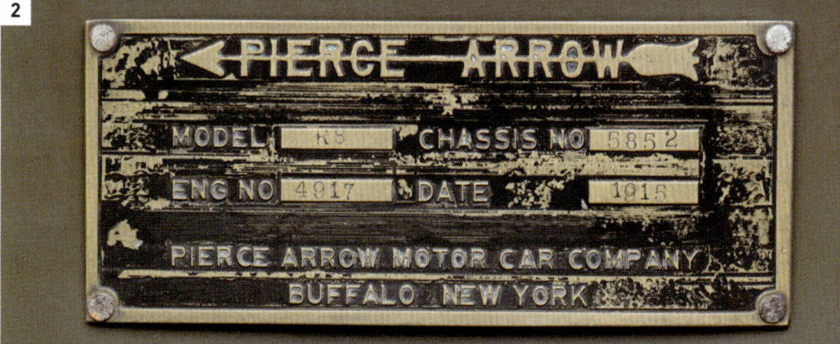

EXTERIOR

With no windscreen or doors, the driver and passenger were at the mercy of the elements. While glass was forbidden, due to the risk of shell bursts causing shattering, some trucks were fitted with a canvas apron that at least gave the crew some protection from wind and rain—as well as a small measure of warmth. Except for the hood and wings, the truck's bodywork is mostly wood, painted a drab army-camouflage green.

1. Maker's badge **2.** Chassis plate with identification numbers **3.** Hood catch **4.** Main headlamp, fitted for wartime use **5.** War Department vehicle number and adopted name **6.** Footplates to gain access **7.** Fuel feed from tank selector lever **8.** Heavy-duty wooden spoked wheel with detachable rim **9.** Rear spring hanger bracket

ENGINE

The R type's four-cylinder engine consists of two blocks bolted on to a shared alloy crankcase, with each block housing a pair of cylinders. A handle protruding from the front of the vehicle is turned to start the engine. External metal engine parts in trucks of this period were often made of brass—the water pump (seen bottom center in image 11) being one such example. Having a pump at all made the engine relatively sophisticated compared to many truck-engines of the time.

10. Engine bay, showing the magneto—an early form of ignition system **11.** Engine bay; the hood hinges upward to provide access to the engine

10

11

14

15

17

18

INTERIOR

The simple, doorless cab design has little that could get in the way and impede access, allowing for rapid entry and exit—a great asset in wartime. The foot pedals are typical of the era, with a clutch pedal on the left, a center throttle pedal, and a brake pedal on the right. Only one light (if any) was used for night driving during the war: that would be the light closest to the driver, so that it could be extinguished quickly.

12. Ignition switch and engine starter button
13. Dashboard and driving controls layout
14. Cab-mounted fire extinguisher **15.** Handbrake lever and gear lever selector **16.** Steering wheel and advance/retard ignition control levers
17. Sight glass for fuel tank **18.** Foot pedals: clutch left, accelerator center, brake right

World War I Locomotives

Formed in 1915, the Railway Operating Division (ROD) of the British Royal Engineers was set up to operate railroads in the European and Middle East theaters during World War I. The British network of narrow-gauge trench railroads was operated by the War Department Light Railways. The French had already standardized portable, 1 ft 11⅝ in (600 mm) gauge, military Decauville equipment to supply ammunition and stores to their forces on the Western Front; German trench railroads used a similar system, the Heeresfeldbahn. After the US entered the war in 1917, many American-built locomotives were shipped across the Atlantic for wartime service in France.

▷ **GWR Class 2301 "Dean Goods"**

Date 1883 **Origin** UK
Wheel arrangement 0-6-0
Cylinders 2 (inside)
Boiler pressure 180 psi (12.65 kg/sq cm)
Driving wheel diameter 62 in (1,575 mm)
Top speed 45 mph (72 km/h)

Between 1883 and 1899, the Great Western Railway's Swindon Works produced 260 William Dean-designed standard-gauge Class 2301 freight locomotives. The ROD shipped 62 to northern France in 1917 to haul supply trains, with 16 later transferred to Salonika, Greece. Some engines also served in France during World War II.

◁ **O&K Feldbahn**

Date 1903 **Origin** Germany
Wheel arrangement 0-8-0T
Cylinders 2
Boiler pressure 180 psi (12.65 kg/sq cm)
Driving wheel diameter Approx. 22¾ in (580 mm)
Top speed 15 mph (24 km/h)

Several German companies made these 1 ft 11⅝ in (600 mm) gauge "Brigadelok" locomotives, with around 2,500 produced in total. The engines were widely used on the military light railroads constructed by the Germans to supply their forward army positions. Shown here is No. 7999, a 1915 Orenstein & Koppel engine with Klein-Lindner articulation of the front and rear axles.

▷ **GCR Class 8K**

Date 1911 **Origin** UK
Wheel arrangement 2-8-0
Cylinders 2
Boiler pressure 180 psi (12.65 kg/sq cm)
Driving wheel diameter 56 in (1,422 mm)
Top speed 60 mph (97 km/h)

The Great Central Railway's Class 8K freight engine entered service in Britain in 1911 and served as the ROD's standard 2-8-0 locomotive during World War I. Many of the 521 Class 8Ks built for ROD were used to haul troop and freight trains in wartime France, and during World War II a number were sent on active service to the Middle East.

◁ **Henschel meter-gauge**

Date 1914 **Origin** Germany
Wheel arrangement 0-6-0T
Cylinders 2
Boiler pressure 200 psi (14 kg/sq cm)
Driving wheel diameter $31\frac{1}{2}$ in (800 mm)
Top speed 19 mph (30 km/h)

In 1914, the Henschel company supplied a pair of 3 ft $3\frac{3}{8}$ in (1 m) gauge locomotives to Germany's Army Technical Research Institute. The two engines were later transferred to the Harz Mountains in central Germany, where they ran on the Nordhausen–Wernigerode Railway, put to work hauling trains of standard-gauge freight wagons.

△ **Baldwin Class 10-12-D**

Date 1916 **Origin** USA
Wheel arrangement 4-6-0PT
Cylinders 2
Boiler pressure 178 psi (12.5 kg/sq cm)
Driving wheel diameter $23\frac{1}{2}$ in (597 mm)
Top speed 19 mph (30 km/h)

These 1 ft $11\frac{5}{8}$ in (600 m) gauge pannier tank locomotives, based on a French design, were built by the Baldwin Locomotive Works in the US. They were supplied to Britain's War Office for frontline use on railways in northern France and the Middle East. The engine above joined the Glyn Valley Tramway, Wales, after the war.

▷ **Pershing Nord**

Date 1917 **Origin** UK
Wheel arrangement 2-8-0
Cylinders 2
Boiler pressure 190 psi (13.4 kg/sq cm)
Driving wheel diameter 56 in (1,422 mm)
Top speed 56 mph (90 km/h)

The Glasgow-based North British Locomotive Company supplied 113 Consolidation Pershings to France for wartime use by the Compagnie des Chemins de fer du Nord. The railway (often referred to simply as Nord) operated these large engines at up to 56 mph (90 km/h); other French railways preferred to run them at lower speeds.

◁ **Baldwin "Spider"**

Date 1917 **Origin** USA
Wheel arrangement 4-6-0
Cylinders 2
Boiler pressure 190 psi (13.4 kg/sq cm)
Driving wheel diameter $61\frac{3}{4}$ in (1,570 mm)
Top speed 65 mph (105 km/h)

Between 1917 and 1918, America's Baldwin Locomotive Works built 70 of these mixed-traffic, bar-frame locomotives for Western Front service. Nicknamed "Spiders" by British soldiers, they later became Class 40 engines on the Belgian State Railways.

World War I Tanks

On September 15, 1916, during the Battle of the Somme, the tank—a British Mark I—made its battlefield debut. The heavy Mark I and its successors, with tracks around their entire rhomboid-shaped bodies and armed with 6-pounder guns and machine guns, were designed to cross trenches and support infantry. The French developed their own tanks, and in 1918, as fighting became more open, sent large numbers of light FT-17s into battle to support cavalry. The British did the same, in smaller numbers, with the Whippet medium tank. Germany built only one tank, the A7, as did Italy, the Fiat 2000.

△ **"Little Willie"**

Date 1915 **Origin** UK
Weight 18 tons (16.3 tonnes)
Engine Daimler 6-cylinder gasoline, 105 hp (78 kW)
Main armament None

"Little Willie" was a prototype armored, tracked fighting vehicle, built to prove the viability of the concept to British military chiefs.

△ **Mark I**

Date 1916 **Origin** UK
Weight 31.3 tons (28.4 tonnes)
Engine Daimler 6-cylinder gasoline, 105 hp (78 kW)
Main armament 2 x 6-pounder guns

Of the 150 Mark I tanks built, half were Male (as shown here) and half Female, the latter replacing each of the Male's 6-pounder guns with two .303 Vickers machine guns. The crew of eight—four to drive and steer, four to fire the weapons—were protected by armor ½ in (12 mm) thick.

△ **Schneider CA-1**

Date 1917 **Origin** France
Weight 14.9 tons (13.5 tonnes)
Engine Schneider 4-cylinder gasoline, 60 hp (45 kW)
Main armament 75 mm Schneider Blockhaus gun

Based on the American Holt tractor, the six-crew CA-1 was the first French tank to go into battle—on April 14, 1917. It struggled to cross trenches, and its field of fire was limited by a gun offset to the right, but the tank fared better in the more open advances of 1918, by which time 400 CA-1s had been built.

Dome-shaped rotating turret

Front armor

△ **Fiat 2000**

Date 1917 **Origin** Italy
Weight 44 tons (40 tonnes)
Engine Fiat 6-cylinder gasoline, 240 hp (179 kW)
Main armament 65 mm Turin Arsenal M.1910/M.1913 mountain howitzer

The FIAT 2000 was conceived as a "mobile fortress." It was a true heavyweight, weighing in at 44 tons (40 tonnes), heavily armored, and bristling with guns from its hull and top cupola. However, it was ponderously slow, and the tank never entered series production, with only two examples being produced.

102

2324

High angle for crossing trenches

◁ **Mark IV**

Date 1917 **Origin** UK
Weight 31.3 tons (28.4 tonnes)
Engine Daimler 6-cylinder gasoline, 105 hp (78 kW)
Main armament 2 x 6-pounder guns

More than 1,200 Mark IVs were built, seeing action from June 1917 until the end of the war. The Mark IV was better protected than Britain's earlier tanks, and its mobility was enhanced by shortening the guns and shrinking the sponsons. Larger, armored gasoline tanks, now vacuum- rather than gravity-fed, increased the Mark IV's operational range.

37 mm main gun

Vertical spring suspension

Rear drive sprocket

△ **Renault FT-17**

Date 1918 **Origin** France	
Weight 7.2 tons (6.5 tonnes)	
Engine Renault 4-cylinder gasoline, 35 hp (26 kW)	
Main armament 37 mm SA18 Puteaux gun	

The FT-17, which played a major role in the French victories of 1918, departed radically from earlier tanks. It was smaller, lighter, and followed what is now the standard layout of a fully rotating turret, the driver positioned at the front, and the engine and gearbox at the rear. More than 3,000 FT-17s were built, with many still in use in 1940.

Allied insignia

△ **Mark VIII "International"**

Date 1918 **Origin** UK, USA	
Weight 41.4 tons (37.6 tonnes)	
Engine Ricardo or Liberty V12 gasoline, 300 hp (224 kW)	
Main armament 2 x 6-pounder guns	

Designed jointly by Britain and the US, the Mark VIII "International" was longer and more powerful than previous tanks, with thicker $\frac{2}{3}$ in (16 mm) armor. It improved conditions by separating the crew from the engine. After the war, 100 Mark VIIIs were built in the US, serving until 1930.

57 mm Maxim-Nordenfelt gun

△ **A7V Sturmpanzerwagen**

Date 1918 **Origin** Germany	
Weight 35.3 tons (32 tonnes)	
Engine 2 x Daimler 4-cylinder gasoline, 100 hp (74.5 kW) each	
Main armament 57 mm Maxim-Nordenfelt gun	

Based on the running gear of the American Holt tractor, the A7V—a kind of mobile fortress—had a crew of at least 18 and was armed with six machine guns and a 57 mm gun. The image above shows a replica.

◁ **M1918 3 Ton Tank**

Date 1918 **Origin** USA	
Weight 3.1 tons (2.8 tonnes)	
Engine 2 x Ford Model T 4-cylinder gasoline, 45 hp (33.5 kW) each	
Main armament .30-caliber machine gun	

A light tank with a crew of two sitting side by side, the M1918 was designed for mass production by the Ford Motor Company using Ford car parts. Of a planned 15,000 tanks, just 15 examples were built and only two arrived in France, with the US Tank Corps preferring the Renault F-17 for its superior combat capability.

▷ **Medium Mark A Whippet**

Date 1918 **Origin** UK	
Weight 15.7 tons (14.2 tonnes)	
Engine 2 x Tylor JB4 four-cylinder gasoline, 45 hp (33.5 kW) each	
Main armament 4 x .303 Hotchkiss machine guns	

Named the "Whippet" for its top speed of $8\frac{1}{3}$ mph (13.4 km/h), which was more than twice that of Britain's heaviest tanks, the Medium Mark A played a significant role in the open warfare of late 1918. Each track had its own engine, and steering was controlled by adjusting the two throttles.

Mark IV

The British Mark IV made its impact at the Battle of Cambrai in November 1917, the first effective massed tank attack. More than 450 tanks—moved at night by rail to the quiet front line at Cambrai—launched an assault that cut deep into the German Hindenburg line. This attack demonstrated the potential destructive power of heavy tanks. More Mark IVs were made than any other British tank during World War I.

THE MARK IV featured improvements on the earlier, similar-looking Mark I, including thicker 0.5 in (12 mm) frontal armor to protect against armor-piercing bullets and an armored rear fuel tank. The gun sponsons, one on either side, could be pushed inside the tank for transport by train; those on the Mark I had to be removed.

Mark IVs came in "male" and "female" variants: males carried two 6-pounder guns and four machine guns; females had six machine guns. Females were thought more useful, as their machine guns could pin down the enemy while troops advanced; males had to stop so the 6-pounder gunners could aim. "Hermaphrodites," with one male and one female sponson, were introduced after April 1918.

SPECIFICATIONS	
Name	Tank, Mark IV
Date	1917
Origin	UK
Production	1,222
Engine	Daimler/Knight straight six, 105 hp (78 kW)
Weight	31.4 tons (28.4 tonnes)
Armament (male)	2 x 6-pounder guns; 4 x .303 Lewis machine guns
Armament (female)	6 x .303 Lewis machine guns
Crew	8
Armor thickness	0.5 in (12 mm)

Loader
Gunner
Commander
Gearsman
Gearsman
Loader
Gunner
Driver

Training vehicle
Having served in World War I, this Mark IV male tank was transferred to a Royal Navy facility at Whale Island, Portsmouth, UK. Tank gunners were trained at Whale Island by naval personnel who were skilled at firing weapons from moving platforms.

2324

Serial number
A unique four-digit number—often at the rear behind the sponsons—stayed with the tank, regardless of moves between units.

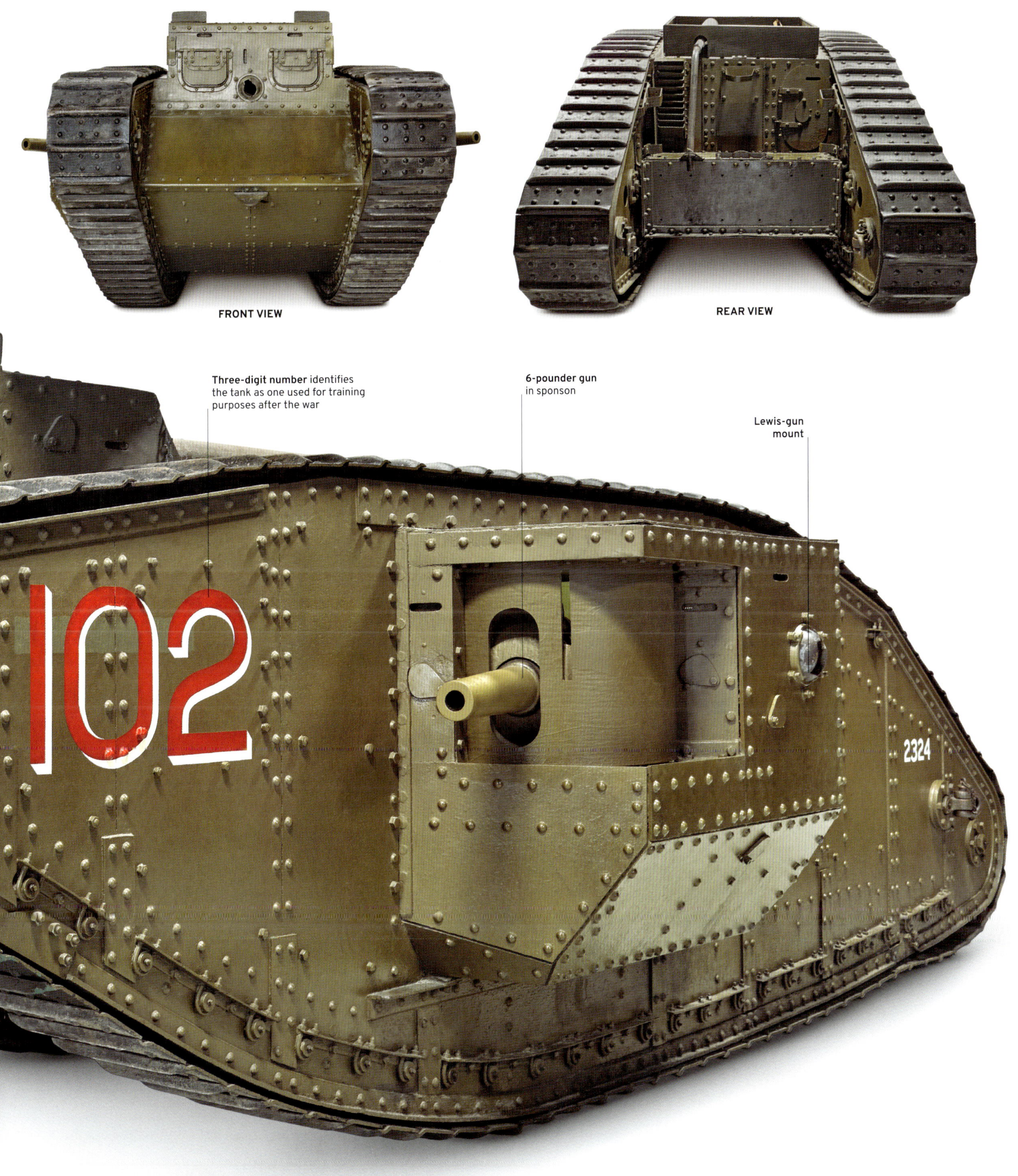

FRONT VIEW

REAR VIEW

Three-digit number identifies the tank as one used for training purposes after the war

6-pounder gun in sponson

Lewis-gun mount

EXTERIOR

The Mark IV's construction—a metal framework with armor plates hot-riveted or bolted on—is characteristic of early tanks. However, this riveted build allowed bullet "splash" to enter through small gaps. To protect their faces from hot metal splinters, tank crews were issued with leather-covered steel masks.

1. Training number **2.** Driver's vision port (closed) **3.** Ventilation louvers **4.** Male sponson with 6-pounder gun **5.** Rear escape hatch **6.** Towing eye **7.** Track tensioner **8.** Location of final drive **9.** Sponson ball machine-gun mount (without gun) **10.** Track plates

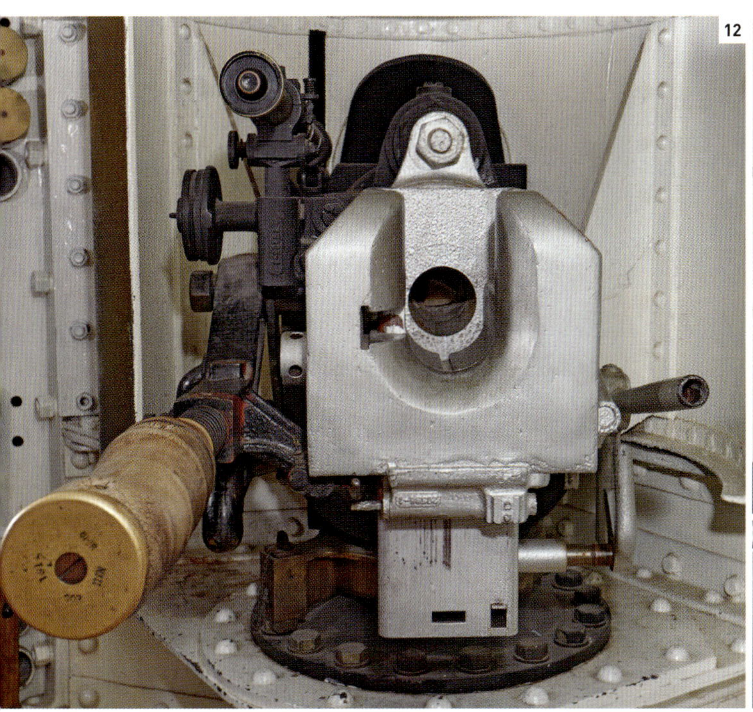

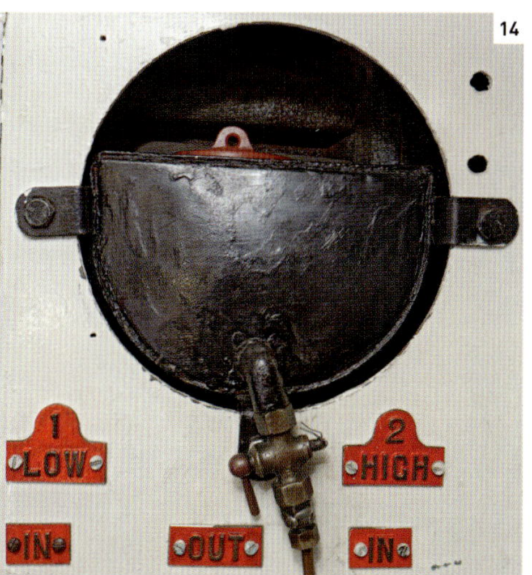

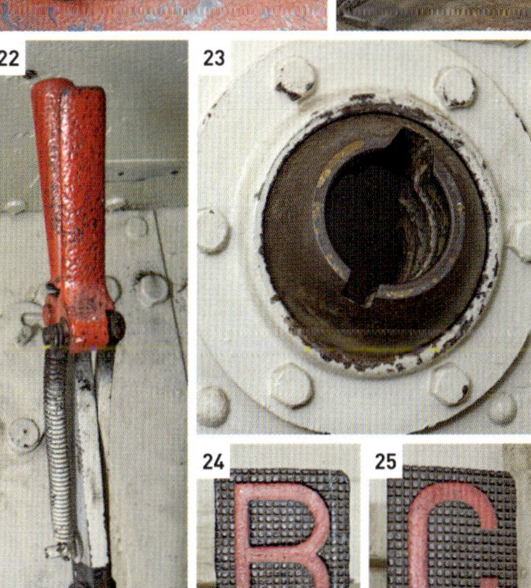

INTERIOR

With the Daimler 105 hp engine positioned in the center of the interior compartment, conditions for the crew were cramped, hot, noisy, and fume-filled. It was also a rough ride, since the Mark IV lacked suspension. There were no seats for gunners or loaders, so they often rode on top or walked beside the tank when not in action.

11. 6-pounder ammunition stowage **12.** Starboard-side 6-pounder gun breech **13.** Machine-gun ammunition stowage **14.** Oil tank to lubricate secondary gears **15.** Differential lock lever **16.** Secondary gear levers **17.** Engine **18.** Oil filler cover **19.** Differential housing **20.** Front commander and driver's positions **21.** Vision port lever **22.** Steering lever **23.** Front machine-gun ball mount (without gun) **24.** Brake pedal **25.** Clutch pedal

Tank Battles in World War I

The need to cross "no-man's-land"—the barbed-wire-strewn and machine-gun-swept ground between entrenched armies—led to the invention of the tank during World War I. Both Britain and France developed the idea of an armor-plated vehicle with caterpillar tracks to help it cross rough terrain. With armament fitted to suppress enemy machine guns, the tank would crush the wire to allow infantry to advance. Britain deployed 49 tanks toward the end of the Battle of the Somme in September 1916. They were not a great success, but Douglas Haig, the British Commander-in-Chief, saw their potential and ordered 1,000.

Tanks were a work in progress during World War I, with each new model incorporating improvements learned from battlefield experience. They undoubtedly had an impact on German forces, and were used to best effect when combined in an "all arms battle"—that is, with artillery, air power, and infantry working in cohesion, such as at Cambrai in 1917 and Amiens in 1918. Britain was determined to exploit the new armored vehicle's potential, designing armored personnel carrier, self-propelled artillery, and engineer variants, as well as faster light tanks, although not all made it into service before the war's end. In contrast, the Germans made only 20 tanks of their own design, and used captured British and French tanks on the battlefield.

British Mark V tanks carry roof-mounted "cribs" to help cross trenches as they advance ready for the Battle of St. Quentin Canal in September 1918.

World War I Armored Cars

Belgium pioneered the combat deployment of armored cars in World War I, using them to engage German forces around Antwerp in August 1914 and operate behind enemy lines. The earliest vehicles of this type were civilian cars with improvised armor and weaponry—such as the Belgian Minerva and, later, the British Rolls-Royce—but specialist versions soon appeared. Trench warfare and stalemate on the Western Front limited the effectiveness of armored cars, but where combat was more mobile, their value as fighting machines increased.

△ Peugeot modèle AC
Date 1914 **Origin** France
Weight 5.5 tons (5 tonnes)
Engine Peugeot 4-cylinder gasoline, 40 hp (30 kW)
Main armament 37 mm Puteaux SA 18 cannon or 8 mm Hotchkiss machine gun

Cannon-carrying Peugeots were given the designation AC (*autocannon*); AM (*automitrailleuse*) denoted those armed with machine guns. Not suited to trench warfare, Peugeots were few in number by 1918; some vehicles later served with the Polish and Serbian armies.

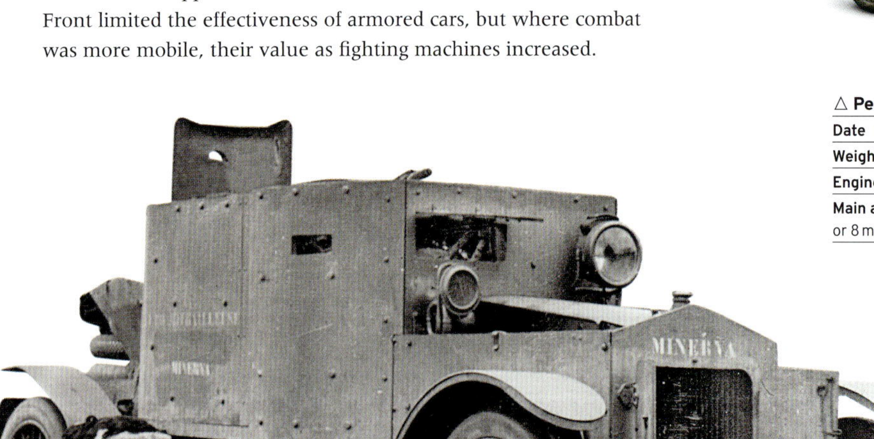

△ Minerva Armored Car
Date 1914 **Origin** Belgium
Weight 4.5 tons (4.1 tonnes)
Engine Minerva 4-cylinder gasoline, 40 hp (30 kW)
Main armament 8 mm Hotchkiss machine gun

In 1914, the Belgian car manufacturer Minerva converted around 30 of its civilian vehicles into armored cars. The earliest model, with a top speed of 25 mph (40 km/h), had no doors or roof. More armor, including a roof and machine-gun protection, was added later. Minervas were the first armored cars to see combat in World War I.

▽ Lanchester Armored Car
Date 1915 **Origin** UK
Weight 5.4 tons (4.9 tonnes)
Engine Lanchester 6-cylinder gasoline, 60 hp (45 kW)
Main armament .303 Vickers machine gun

Around 36 Lanchesters were built, initially for the Royal Naval Air Service (RNAS) to serve in Belgium, harassing German forces and carrying out reconnaissance missions. A detachment of Lanchesters was deployed to the Caucasus in 1916, reaching as far as Persia and Turkey. Some Lanchesters took part in the Russian Civil War from 1918.

△ Mgebrov-Renault
Date 1915 **Origin** Russia
Weight 3.7 tons (3.4 tonnes)
Engine Renault 4-cylinder gasoline, 30 hp (22.5 kW)
Main armament 2 x 7.62 mm Maxim M1910 machine guns

A Russian army captain, Vladimir Mgebrov, designed the Mgebrov-Renault's distinctive sloped armor to deflect enemy fire or minimize damage without adding excessive weight. The original hand-cranked triple-turret arrangement proved too heavy for the Renault chassis, and it was replaced in 1916 by two smaller turrets.

△ Lancia Ansaldo 1Z

Date 1916 **Origin** Italy
Weight 4.2 tons (3.8 tonnes)
Engine Lancia V-6 gasoline, 40 hp (30 kW)
Main armament 3 x 6.5 mm FIAT-Revelli M1914 machine guns

Only 10 double-turreted 1Z armored cars—based on a Lancia frame—were built by the Ansaldo engineering firm. In 1917, the company developed the 1ZM ("M" for *modificato*), producing 110 armored cars similar to the 1Z, but with a single, more stable turret housing two machine guns. The 1ZM remained in use in Italy's African colonies until World War II.

△ Ehrhardt E-V/4

Date 1917 **Origin** Germany
Weight 8 tons (7.3 tonnes)
Engine Daimler 6-cylinder gasoline, 80 hp (60 kW)
Main armament 3 x 7.92 mm MG08 or MG15 machine guns

Developed in 1915, Germany's E-V/4 was purpose-built for military action, rather than converted from a civilian vehicle like most World War I armored cars. A lighter version with enhanced armor served on the more mobile Eastern Front from 1917, and was used in 1919 by German police and paramilitary to subdue urban rioting.

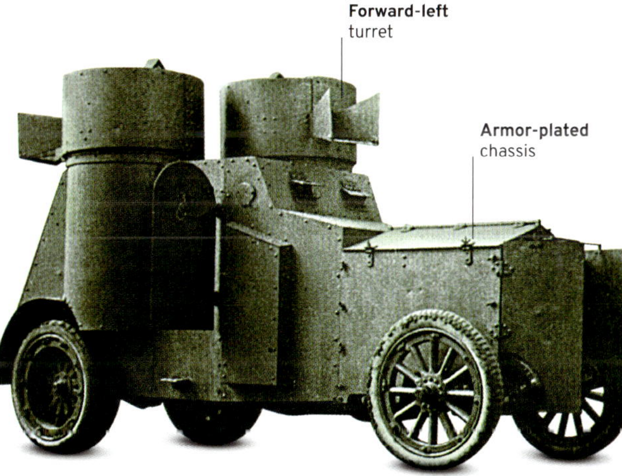

△ Izhorski Fiat

Date 1917 **Origin** Russia
Weight 5.3 tons (4.8 tonnes)
Engine FIAT 6-cylinder gasoline, 72 hp (54 kW)
Main armament 2 x 7.62 mm Maxim M1910 machine guns

The Russian Izhorski company used a Fiat chassis to create this five-man armored car, which featured two turrets, each armed with a machine gun. Around 70 of these vehicles were built, many serving with the Bolsheviks from 1918 in the Russian Civil War.

◁ White Model AEF Armored Car

Date 1918 **Origin** USA
Weight 6.6 tons (6 tonnes)
Engine White 4-cylinder gasoline, 45 hp (33.5 kW)
Main armament M1895 Colt-Browning machine gun

The White Motor Company of Cleveland, Ohio, had been providing chassis for French and American armored cars since 1915. The White AEF was a variant produced from 1918 for the American Expeditionary Force.

War Takes to the Air

The first flight of a piloted heavier-than-air vehicle took place in December 1903, and little more than a decade later the first combat aircraft were in military service. Strategists were quick to see the potential of this new form of transport. By the end of World War I, air power had become the most important emerging arm of modern warfare.

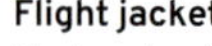

Flight jacket
Most early military aircraft had open cockpits, so a fur-lined leather flight jacket was an essential item of clothing for airmen. Also vital was a silk scarf to prevent the neck from rubbing raw against the jacket collar.

When World War I began in 1914, the aircraft had already been tested as a tool of destruction. On November 1, 1911, Italian aviator Giulio Gavotti had hand-dropped four bulky grenades over the side of his Etrich Taube monoplane, targeting Ottoman troops around the Ain Zara oasis in Libya during the Italo-Turkish War (1911–12)—the first known example of aerial bombing. However, early military aircraft were primarily used for reconnaissance and observation.

The first fighters

The majority of World War I military aircraft were biplanes. The biplane layout—two wings, one over the other, linked by struts—provided structural rigidity to aircraft made largely of wood and canvas, gave greater lift for short takeoffs with typically underpowered engines, and delivered superb maneuverability. The trade-offs were low speed, poor range, and slow climb rates, but these limitations did not hamper the early reconnaissance and observation planes, which operated above battle lines that, especially on the Western Front, were often static and close together. As they overflew the combat zone, aircraft such as Britain's B.E.2 and Germany's Aviatik B.I carried out tasks including deep reconnaissance, battle-damage assessment, artillery spotting, and intelligence gathering.

Rival reconnaissance pilots soon began trading shots using handheld pistols, rifles, and, eventually, flexibly mounted machine guns. More martially significant was the rise of "interceptors"—aircraft purpose-built to catch and shoot down observation planes. By 1916, interceptors had become "fighters" that engaged one another with fixed machine guns in twisting dogfights as they attempted to gain air supremacy.

Fighters became the most important and numerous combat aircraft type of World War I. An important technical innovation came in 1915, with the invention of the synchronizer, or interrupter gear, which enabled machine guns to fire safely through the arc of the propeller without hitting the spinning blades. The synchronizer put the fighter pilot in a line-of-sight relationship with his weapons; crudely put, his bullets went where his aircraft was pointed. This German invention, which was soon copied in detail or principle by the other combatants, turned aerial duels between fighters into a lethal battle of firepower and pilot skill.

Strategic bombing

World War I also saw the birth of what is now known as "strategic bombing"—the use of bomber aircraft to attack significant industrial or military targets at long ranges. The tactic was pioneered by Germany, primarily because air power was one of the few ways in which it could strike at the distant British homeland.

The first aerial bombardments were delivered by large, slow Zeppelin airships. In 1915 and 1916, Zeppelins made regular raids, particularly over England's north and Midlands. From 1917, however, twin-engined Gotha bomber airplanes also began hitting targets in southern England. The Zeppelin and Gotha raids caused comparatively light damage, but it was enough to shock the British public. In total, German bombing raids killed 1,414 people and injured another 3,416. It was in developing a coherent response to these air raids that Britain formed history's first independent air force—the Royal Air Force (RAF).

Antiaircraft defenses
Four gas-mask-clad German infantrymen operate a heavy antiaircraft machine gun in World War I. By the war's end, ground fire from automatic weapons had become a significant threat to air operations.

Fighters and pilots
Pilots of No. 1 Squadron, RAF, pose alongside their British S.E.5a biplanes at Clairmarais aerodrome, near Ypres, July 1918. Life expectancy for young combat aviators was appallingly low, often measured in weeks.

Military planners continued to find new battlefield roles for aircraft. Between December 1915 and April 1916, the Royal Flying Corps (RFC), the RAF's predecessor, made airdrops of food and materials to besieged British troops at Kut-el-Amara (in what is now Iraq). Although these clumsy efforts could not save the garrison, they did show that resupplying ground forces by air was possible. Similarly, in 1917–18, the Germans began using aircraft for ground-attack missions, making tactical aerial strikes against enemy targets on the battlefield in support of infantry maneuvers.

Military leaders were just beginning to exploit the potential of aircraft, but it was already clear that warfare had gained a completely new dimension.

> "**Fight on** and **fly on** to the last drop of **blood**... the last drop of **fuel**... the last beat of the **heart**."
>
> MANFRED VON RICHTHOFEN, WORLD WAR I GERMAN AIR ACE

TALKING POINT

Manfred von Richthofen

World War I gave rise to the fighter "ace": a pilot who had shot down five or more aircraft in aerial combat. Manfred Freiherr (Baron) von Richthofen was the greatest ace, officially credited with downing 80 enemy aircraft. Born in 1892 in Kleinburg, Lower Silesia, von Richthofen served in the cavalry and infantry before joining the Imperial Air Service from September 1916. Having shown astonishing skill and courage as a fighter pilot, he was given the command of Jagdgeschwader 1 (Fighter Wing 1), known as "Richthofen's Flying Circus" because of its plane's bright colors. The Allies nicknamed von Richthofen the "Red Baron," for his red-painted Fokker triplane. Fate caught up with von Richthofen on April 21, 1918, when he was shot down and killed over Morlancourt Ridge, northern France.

Manfred von Richthofen, the "Red Baron," stands in front of his famous Fokker Dr.I (Dr = Dreidecker, "triplane") on the Western Front.

Reconnaissance Aircraft

When World War I began, the primary roles of military aircraft were observation and reconnaissance, not combat. On the Western Front, with no open flanks for land-based reconnaissance troops to penetrate, aircraft provided an invaluable means to monitor enemy activities, increasingly using aerial photography to map trench systems. These two-seater aircraft could maintain surveillance for two to four hours, flying up to 56 miles (90 km) behind the front line at altitudes above 19,700 ft (6,000 m). Although messages continued to be hand-dropped throughout the war, from 1915 some aircraft were fitted with wireless radios for airborne artillery observations.

▷ Royal Aircraft Factory B.E.2

Date 1912 **Origin** UK
Engine 90 hp (67 kW) RAF 1a air-cooled V8 (B.E.2c onward)
Length 27 ft (8.3 m)
Top speed 72 mph (116 km/h)

Although primarily a reconnaissance aircraft, the B.E.2 was also one of the first aircraft in the Royal Flying Corps (RFC) to be fitted with a machine gun. It was a stable platform for observation and aerial photography, but poor maneuverability made the aircraft an easy target for enemy fighters.

△ Nieuport 12

Date 1915 **Origin** France
Engine 110 hp (82 kW) Clerget 9Z 9-cylinder rotary
Length 23 ft (7 m)
Top speed 91 mph (146 km/h)

The Nieuport 12 was a sesquiplane—meaning that its lower wing was smaller than the upper wing. This layout reduced drag and so improved performance, and also gave the pilot and observer better downward visibility, which was especially useful for a reconnaissance aircraft.

Fabric-covered wings

◁ Lebed XII

Date 1916 **Origin** Russia
Engine 150 hp (112 kW) Salmson water-cooled radial
Length 26 ft (8 m)
Top speed 84 mph (135 km/h)

The Lebed XII was one of few aircraft produced indigenously by Russia in World War I. Although it drew inspiration from captured German aircraft, the two-seater XII was notoriously unreliable and underpowered, and losses in both combat and training were high.

△ DFW C.V

Date 1916 **Origin** Germany
Engine 200 hp (149 kW) Benz Bz IV 6-cylinder in-line water-cooled
Length 26 ft (7.9 m)
Top speed 96 mph (155 km/h)

Reliable, structurally sound, easy to control, and a nimble performer, the DFW C.V was also heavily armed for a reconnaissance aircraft. The pilot had a fixed, forward-firing LMG 08 machine gun, while the observer had a flexible-mount LMG 14 machine gun for rear and side defense.

△ LFG Roland C.II

Date 1916 **Origin** Germany
Engine 160 hp (119 kW) Mercedes D.III 6-cylinder in-line water-cooled
Length 25 ft (7.7 m)
Top speed 103 mph (165 km/h)

Despite its popular name of *Walfisch* ("Whale"), the LFG Roland C.II actually had a low-drag design, partly achieved by limiting the number of wing struts. This gave the aircraft a relatively high top speed, which enabled it to outrun many enemy interceptors.

▷ **Royal Aircraft Factory R.E.8**

Date 1917 **Origin** UK

Engine 150 hp (112 kW) RAF 4a 12-cylinder in-line air-cooled

Length 28 ft (8.5 m)

Top speed 102 mph (164 km/h)

Nicknamed the "Harry Tate" after a popular music-hall comedian, the R.E.8 was an artillery-spotting, reconnaissance, and light bomber aircraft. Early variants were plagued by a series of fatal spins, but this fault was rectified by fitting a ventral fin to the base of the tail.

Wired-braced linen-covered fuselage

Curved tailplane to aid flying stability

▽ **Salmson 2**

Date 1917 **Origin** France

Engine 230 hp (172 kW) Salmson 9Za 9-cylinder water-cooled radial

Length 28 ft (8.5 m)

Top speed 117 mph (188 km/h)

In the final two years of World War I, around 3,200 Salmson 2s were built—the majority for the French Air Force and about 700 for the American Expeditionary Force. The aircraft was also used in daylight bombing and ground attacks.

△ **Armstrong Whitworth F.K.8**

Date 1917 **Origin** UK

Engine 160 hp (119 kW) Beardmore 6-cylinder in-line water-cooled

Length 31½ ft (9.6 m)

Top speed 95 mph (153 km/h)

The F.K.8 (nicknamed the "Big Ack") was a stable aircraft to fly, which made it ideally suited for a reconnaissance role in World War I. It was also used for ground-attack and bombing missions, and could carry up to 260 lb (118 kg) of bombs.

◁ **LVG C.VI**

Date 1918 **Origin** Germany

Engine 200 hp (150 kW) Benz Bz.IV 6-cylinder in-line water-cooled

Length 24½ ft (7.45 m)

Top speed 106 mph (170 km/h)

A distinctive feature of the LVG C.VI was the top-mounted exhaust pipe, which projected above the engine like a chimney. The aircraft was also fitted with wireless Morse code transmission equipment, useful for transferring real-time coordinates and information.

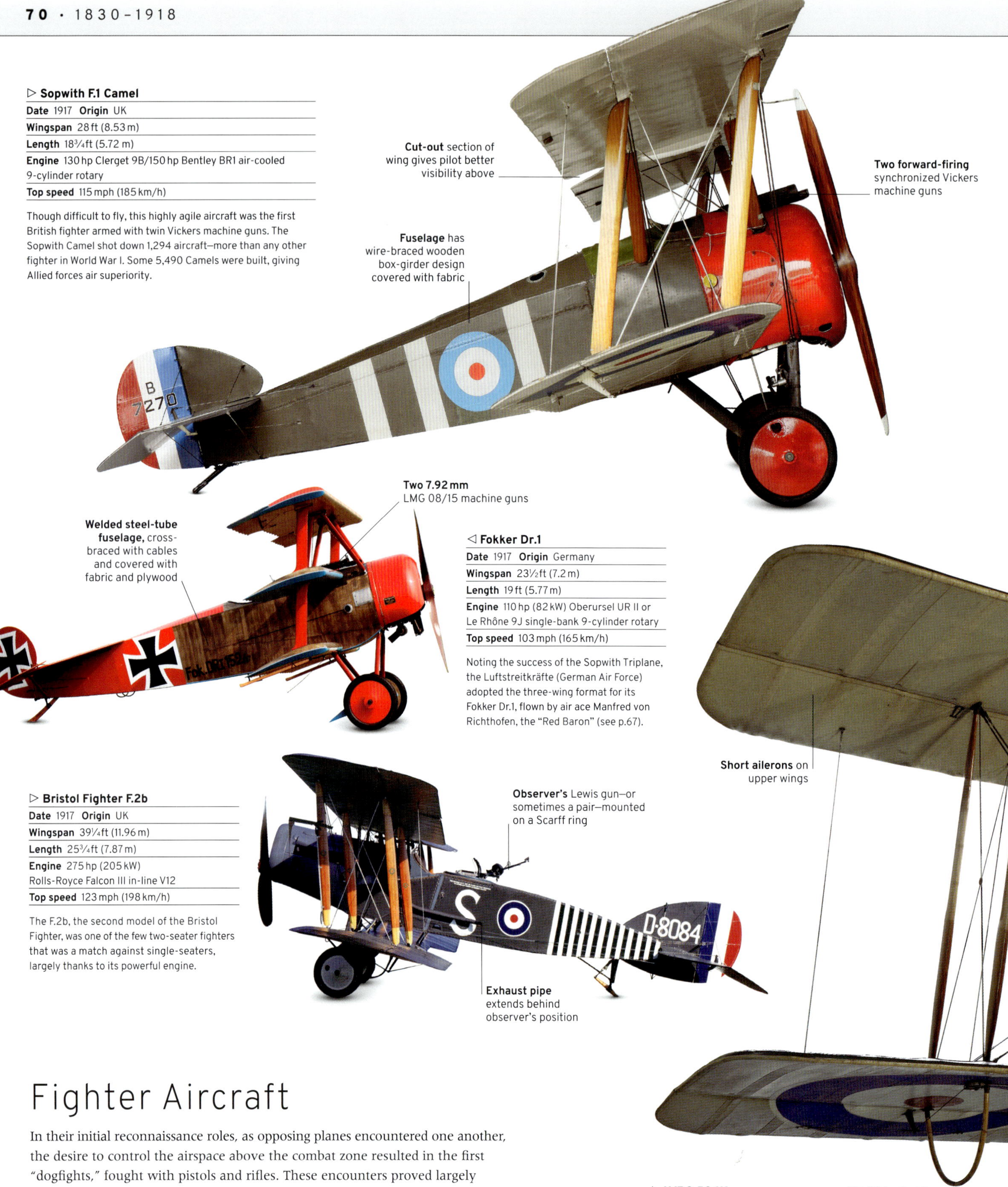

▷ **Sopwith F.1 Camel**

Date 1917 **Origin** UK
Wingspan 28 ft (8.53 m)
Length 18¾ ft (5.72 m)
Engine 130 hp Clerget 9B/150 hp Bentley BR1 air-cooled 9-cylinder rotary
Top speed 115 mph (185 km/h)

Though difficult to fly, this highly agile aircraft was the first British fighter armed with twin Vickers machine guns. The Sopwith Camel shot down 1,294 aircraft—more than any other fighter in World War I. Some 5,490 Camels were built, giving Allied forces air superiority.

◁ **Fokker Dr.1**

Date 1917 **Origin** Germany
Wingspan 23½ ft (7.2 m)
Length 19 ft (5.77 m)
Engine 110 hp (82 kW) Oberursel UR II or Le Rhône 9J single-bank 9-cylinder rotary
Top speed 103 mph (165 km/h)

Noting the success of the Sopwith Triplane, the Luftstreitkräfte (German Air Force) adopted the three-wing format for its Fokker Dr.1, flown by air ace Manfred von Richthofen, the "Red Baron" (see p.67).

▷ **Bristol Fighter F.2b**

Date 1917 **Origin** UK
Wingspan 39¼ ft (11.96 m)
Length 25¾ ft (7.87 m)
Engine 275 hp (205 kW) Rolls-Royce Falcon III in-line V12
Top speed 123 mph (198 km/h)

The F.2b, the second model of the Bristol Fighter, was one of the few two-seater fighters that was a match against single-seaters, largely thanks to its powerful engine.

Fighter Aircraft

In their initial reconnaissance roles, as opposing planes encountered one another, the desire to control the airspace above the combat zone resulted in the first "dogfights," fought with pistols and rifles. These encounters proved largely inconclusive until aircraft began to be fitted with machine guns. Enabling such weapons to follow the pilot's natural sight line and fire through the propeller's arc—without destroying the propeller blades—led to the evolution of dedicated fighter aircraft. Early efforts involved fitting the blades with steel strips to deflect bullets; these were soon superseded by "interrupter" mechanisms, which shut off the gun as the blade passed through the line of fire.

△ **AVRO 504K**

Date 1917 **Origin** UK
Wingspan 36 ft (10.97 m)
Length 29½ ft (8.97 m)
Engine 110 hp (82 kW) Le Rhône 9Ja single-bank 9-cylinder rotary
Top speed 90 mph (145 km/h)

The 504 enjoyed a production run of nearly 20 years, during which time over 10,000 were built. Initially a reconnaissance and combat plane, the 504's greatest success was as a trainer in its K variant.

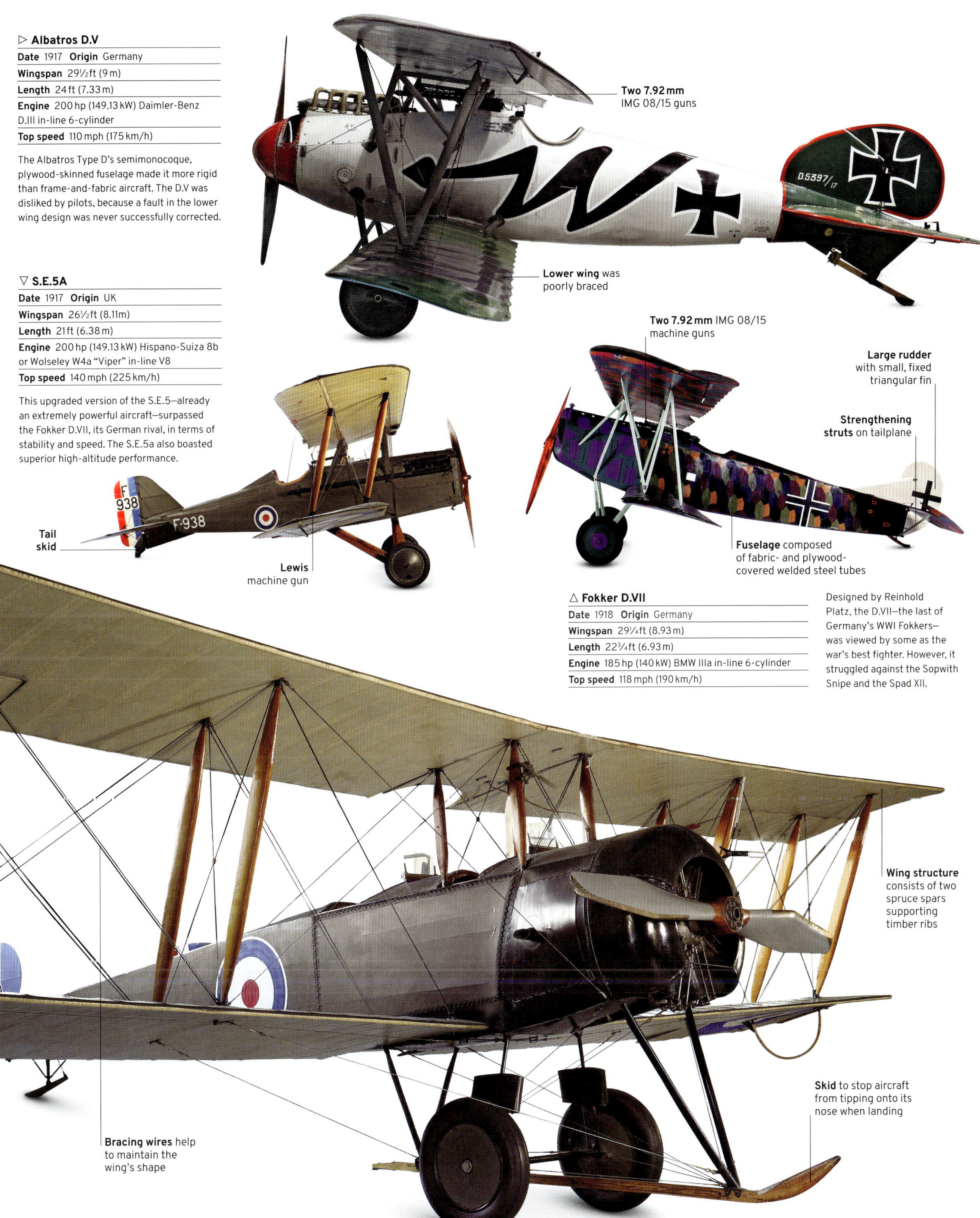

▷ Albatros D.V

Date 1917 **Origin** Germany
Wingspan 29½ft (9 m)
Length 24 ft (7.33 m)
Engine 200 hp (149.13 kW) Daimler-Benz D.III in-line 6-cylinder
Top speed 110 mph (175 km/h)

The Albatros Type D's semimonocoque, plywood-skinned fuselage made it more rigid than frame-and-fabric aircraft. The D.V was disliked by pilots, because a fault in the lower wing design was never successfully corrected.

▽ S.E.5A

Date 1917 **Origin** UK
Wingspan 26½ft (8.11m)
Length 21 ft (6.38 m)
Engine 200 hp (149.13 kW) Hispano-Suiza 8b or Wolseley W4a "Viper" in-line V8
Top speed 140 mph (225 km/h)

This upgraded version of the S.E.5—already an extremely powerful aircraft—surpassed the Fokker D.VII, its German rival, in terms of stability and speed. The S.E.5a also boasted superior high-altitude performance.

△ Fokker D.VII

Date 1918 **Origin** Germany
Wingspan 29¼ft (8.93 m)
Length 22¾ft (6.93 m)
Engine 185 hp (140 kW) BMW IIIa in-line 6-cylinder
Top speed 118 mph (190 km/h)

Designed by Reinhold Platz, the D.VII—the last of Germany's WWI Fokkers—was viewed by some as the war's best fighter. However, it struggled against the Sopwith Snipe and the Spad XII.

RAF S.E.5a

Developed from the S.E.5, the square-nosed Royal Aircraft Factory (RAF) S.E.5a was an exceptionally robust single-seat fighter. In the hands of such World War I Victoria-Cross aces as Albert Ball, Billy Bishop, "Mick" Mannock, and James McCudden, the S.E.5 and S.E.5a proved formidable aerial weapons, valued by pilots for their strength and steadiness, superior speed, excellent all-round field of vision from the cockpit, and good levels of performance—even at high altitude.

THE S.E.5 ("S.E." stood for "Scout Experimental"), which first flew in November 1916, was designed under Henry Folland at the Royal Aircraft Factory in Farnborough, Hampshire. Early Royal Flying Corps fighters, such as the DH2 and FE8, were "pushers"—biplanes with their engines and propellers mounted behind the pilot. The S.E.5's "tractor" configuration, with front-mounted engine and propeller, allowed for a more streamlined design. The upgraded S.E.5a entered service in June 1917 with a powerful 200 hp engine in place of the S.E.5's 150 hp unit, making it one of the fastest aircraft of the war.

The S.E.5a is often seen as the World War I equivalent of the later Hawker Hurricane, of Battle of Britain fame, since both were very stable gun platforms. Likewise, the lighter, more maneuverable Sopwith Camel is equated with World War II's Supermarine Spitfire. Together, the S.E.5a and Camel dominated the skies over the Western Front from mid-1917 until the war's end.

SPECIFICATIONS	
Model	Royal Aircraft Factory S.E.5a, 1916 (in service from 1917)
Origin	UK
Production	5,205 (including the S.E.5)
Construction	Wooden frames, fabric covering
Maximum weight	1,980 lb (898 kg)
Engine	200 hp (149 kW) Hispano-Suiza/Wolseley Viper water-cooled V8
Wingspan	26 ft 7 in (8.1 m)
Length	20 ft 11 in (6.38 m)
Range	300 miles (483 km)

Fin is wire-braced to tailplane

Rear decking made of fabric over wooden stringers

Perfect blend
The S.E.5a combined a powerful engine with a simple, slab-sided fuselage and single-bay, strut-and-wire-braced biplane wings. The result was a fast, easily maintained, reliable fighting machine that blended strength with practicality.

Side panel of fabric fuselage can be opened for maintenance and inspection

Tail is wood and steel-tube frame, fabric-covered

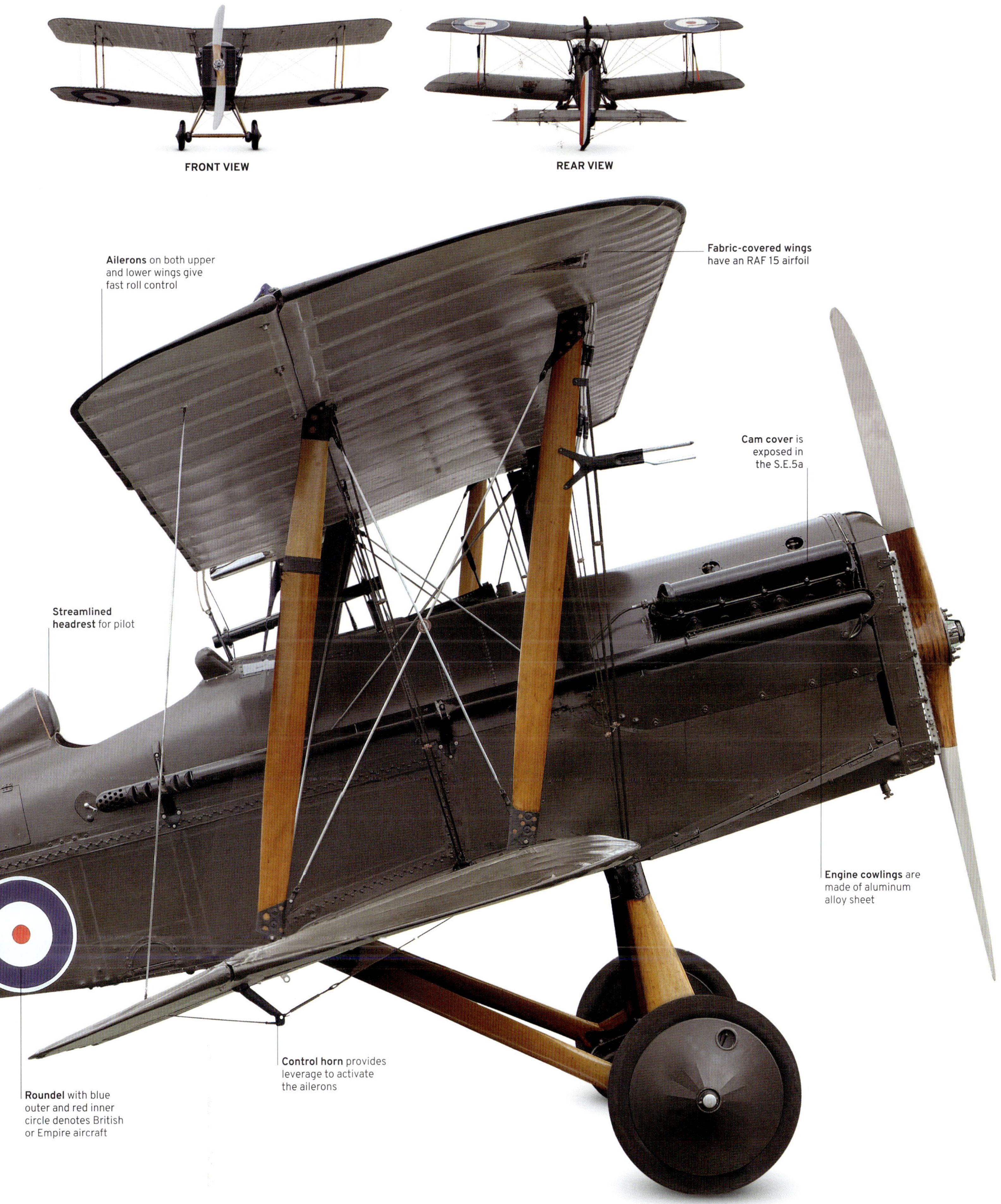
FRONT VIEW
REAR VIEW
Ailerons on both upper and lower wings give fast roll control
Fabric-covered wings have an RAF 15 airfoil
Cam cover is exposed in the S.E.5a
Streamlined headrest for pilot
Engine cowlings are made of aluminum alloy sheet
Control horn provides leverage to activate the ailerons
Roundel with blue outer and red inner circle denotes British or Empire aircraft

EXTERIOR

With an urgent need for aircraft that could be got to the front line quickly and kept combat-ready, the design of the S.E.5a emphasized simplicity, durability, ease of manufacture, and practical serviceability. Problems with the thin structures of the wings and tail on the S.E.5 were ironed out, and a weakness in the aircraft's steel-tube undercarriage struts was solved by replacing them with wooden struts, which were more resilient.

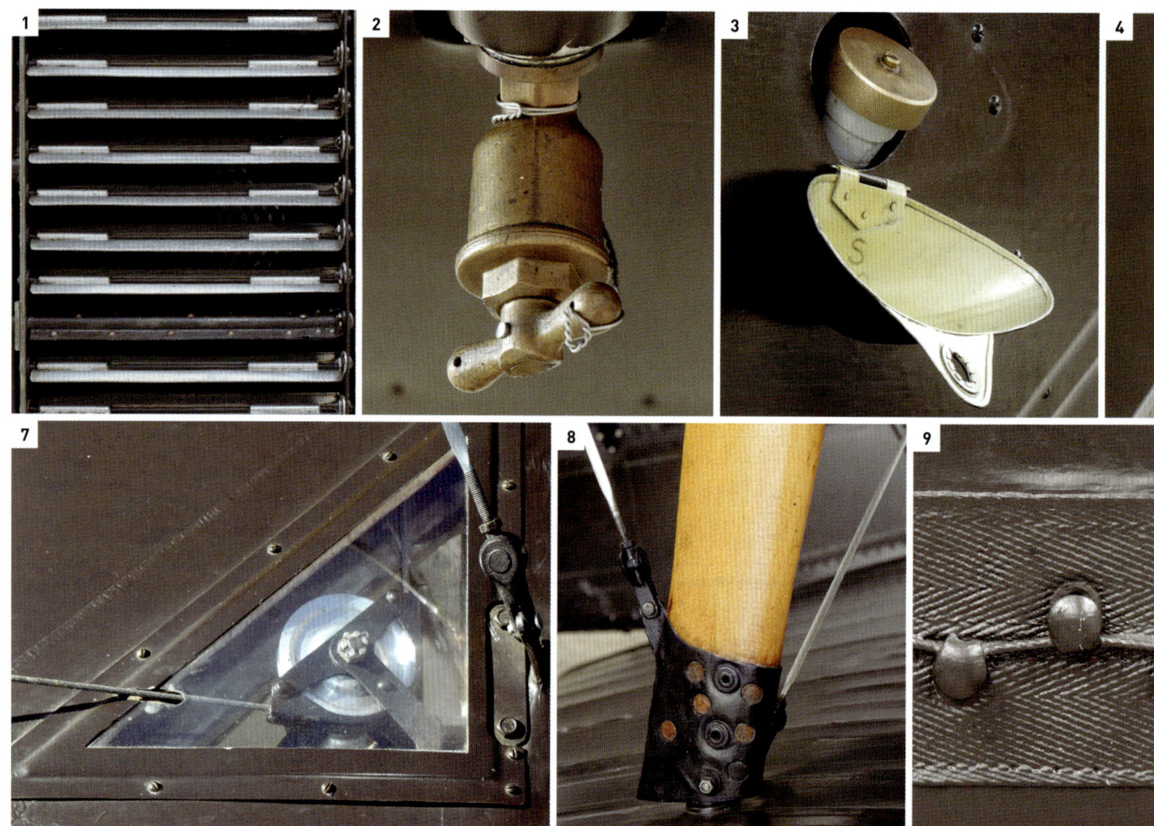

1. Radiator shutters **2.** Radiator drain **3.** Oil filler **4.** Bullet spacer on bracing wires **5.** Leather "boots" on bracing-wire ends **6.** Perforated exhaust **7.** Control pulley inspection panel **8.** Wing strut end **9.** Fabric panel join **10.** Control horn **11.** Bungee suspension **12.** Gun sight **13.** Control-wire grommet **14.** Lewis machine gun

COCKPIT

All varnished wood, copper tubes, and brass fittings, the S.E.5a's no-frills "office," which looks spartan by today's standards, was typical of the period. Instruments and controls are seemingly positioned wherever they would fit, with few concessions to pilot comfort or ease of use. The cockpit gave the pilot in-flight access to the aircraft's two machine guns—the movable, rail-mounted Lewis over the wing and the fixed internal Vickers—in order to clear jams and, in the case of the Lewis, change the drum-shaped ammunition magazine.

15. Cockpit general view **16.** Fuel pump control **17.** Fuel cock **18.** Compass **19.** Airspeed indicator **20.** Control column "spade" with gun firing buttons **21.** Rudder bar **22.** Radiator shutter lever

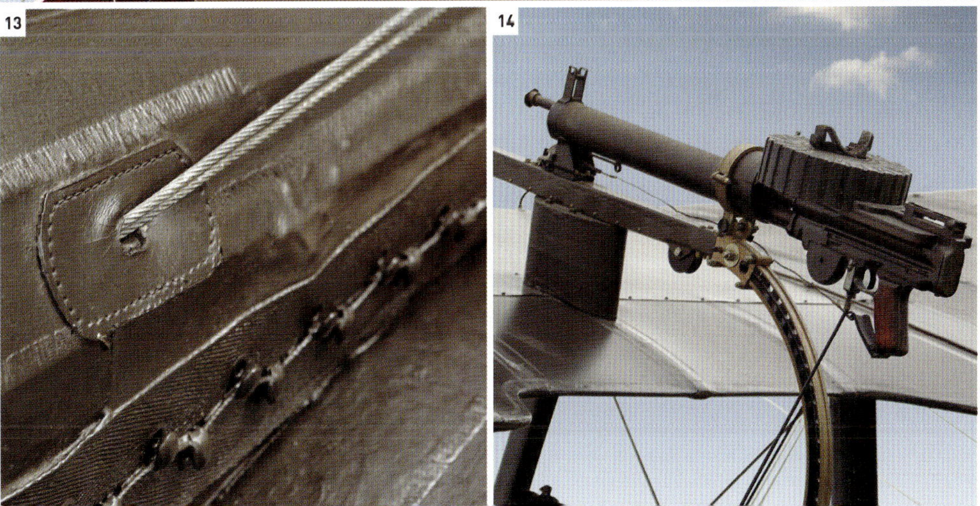

Airship Bombing Raids

Balloons had been deployed to overlook enemy forces on the battlefield during the Napoleonic Wars at the start of the 19th century. Their first use to drop munitions came in 1849, when the Austrians launched paper balloons to send explosive charges over the besieged city of Venice. Many militaries established balloon sections, mainly to assist artillery by spotting targets and observing the fall of shot, but it was World War I that saw the real debut of the airship as a weapon. The designs of Germany's Count Ferdinand von Zeppelin were used to bomb London, creating a great deal of alarm but little actual damage for the effort involved. The Royal Navy saw the need for airships to use as blimps, known as Sea Scouts, that could remain in the air for up to 24 hours and keep watch for German submarines around the coast of Britain. As the war progressed, it gradually became clear to military commanders that airplanes were better suited to the tasks performed by airships, which were vulnerable to adverse weather conditions and presented a large, slow target to their enemies.

The British Army airship Beta II at Aldershot in World War I. A rebuilt version of the Beta I airship, Beta II, was an experimental craft tested for a potential role observing troop movements and photographing ground positions. Beta II ended its service life as a training airship for the Royal Naval Air Service in 1916.

Bomber Aircraft

In November 1911, an Italian pilot dropped grenades on ground targets during Italy's campaign to wrest Libya from Ottoman Empire control. This was the first use of an aircraft as a bomber. World War I showed that there was a need to design machines specifically for this role, but progress in producing dedicated bomber aircraft was slow. By the war's end, only the bombing of built-up areas had proven at all effective. The large aircraft needed to carry bomb payloads over long distances were easy prey for fighters, so they quickly became restricted to nighttime operations.

△ **RAF F.E.2b**

Date 1915 **Origin** UK
Wingspan 47¾ft (14.5m)
Length 32¼ft (9.8m)
Engine 160hp (119kW) Beardmore 6-cylinder
Top speed 91mph (147km/h)

Although an unusual configuration, the "pusher" propeller of the F.E.2 series of biplanes allowed the gunner an uninterrupted field of fire. Intended as a fighter, the F.E.2b later found success as a night bomber. Nearly 2,000 of the aircraft were produced.

Observer had one or two Lewis guns

Tail skid

△ **RAF R.E.8**

Date 1916 **Origin** UK
Wingspan 42½ft (13m)
Length 27¾ft (8.5m)
Engine 140hp (104kW) RAF 4a in-line V12
Top speed 103mph (165km/h)

The R.E.8 was better armed and carried a heavier payload than the B.E.2, its predecessor. Although slow, cumbersome, and difficult to fly, it performed well in the hands of skilled pilots and remained in service until the war's end. More than 4,000 R.E.8s were built.

▽ **AEG G.IV**

Date 1916 **Origin** Germany
Wingspan 60⅓ft (18.4m)
Length 31¾ft (9.7m)
Engine 2 x 260hp (194kW) Daimler-Benz D.IVa in-line 6-cylinder
Top speed 103mph (165km/h)

The G.IV's advanced equipment included an all-metal welded-tube frame, radios, and heated suits for the crew. Lacking range, it was used mainly as a tactical bomber to attack battlefield targets, although on the Italian front it also bombed cities, including Padua, Venice, and Verona.

Underwing racks could carry around 397lb (180kg) of bombs

△ **Voisin 8**

Date 1916 **Origin** France
Wingspan 59¾ft (18.2m)
Length 34ft (10.4m)
Engine 220hp (164kW) Peugeot 8Aa in-line V8
Top speed 82mph (132km/h)

The first purpose-built night bomber of the French air service (*Aéronautique Militaire*), the Voisin 8 was hampered by the limited capabilities of its Peugeot engine. Changing the engine to a 300hp (220.6kW) Renault V12 improved performance, but the Voisin 8 was never more than mediocre.

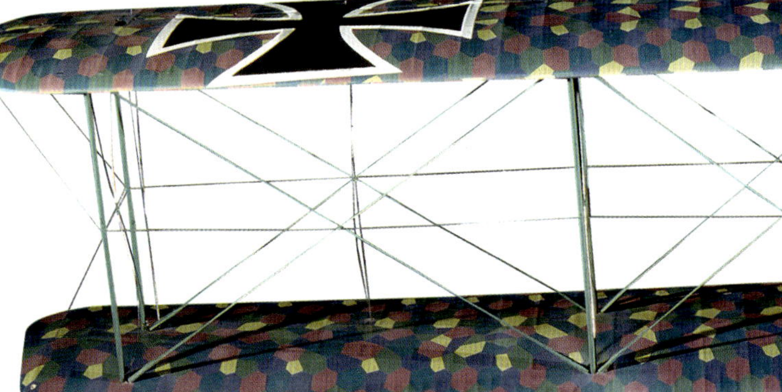

△ **Zeppelin-Staaken R.IV**

Date 1916 **Origin** Germany
Wingspan 138½ft (42.2m)
Length 72½ft (22.1m)
Engine 4 x 220hp (164kW) Benz Bz.IV in wing nacelles; 2 x 160hp (119kW) Mercedes D.III in nose
Top speed 84mph (135km/h)

The giant R-series Zeppelins were the most remarkable aircraft built for the *Luftstreitkräfte* (the German Air Force). Equipped with four, five, or six engines, they could accurately deliver up to 4,410lb (2,000kg) of bombs to targets in Britain.

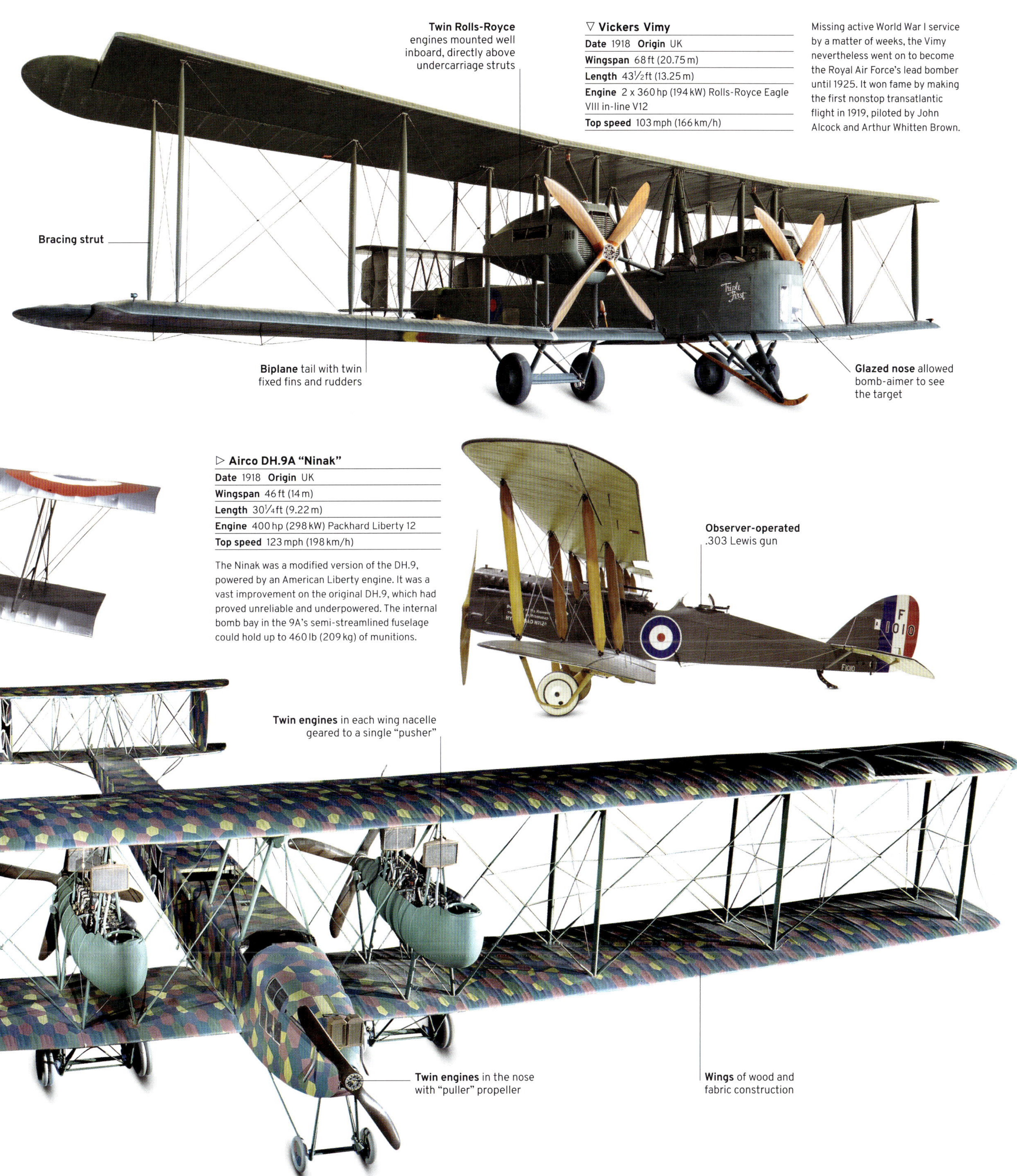

▽ Vickers Vimy

Date 1918 **Origin** UK
Wingspan 68 ft (20.75 m)
Length 43½ ft (13.25 m)
Engine 2 x 360 hp (194 kW) Rolls-Royce Eagle VIII in-line V12
Top speed 103 mph (166 km/h)

Missing active World War I service by a matter of weeks, the Vimy nevertheless went on to become the Royal Air Force's lead bomber until 1925. It won fame by making the first nonstop transatlantic flight in 1919, piloted by John Alcock and Arthur Whitten Brown.

▷ Airco DH.9A "Ninak"

Date 1918 **Origin** UK
Wingspan 46 ft (14 m)
Length 30¼ ft (9.22 m)
Engine 400 hp (298 kW) Packhard Liberty 12
Top speed 123 mph (198 km/h)

The Ninak was a modified version of the DH.9, powered by an American Liberty engine. It was a vast improvement on the original DH.9, which had proved unreliable and underpowered. The internal bomb bay in the 9A's semi-streamlined fuselage could hold up to 460 lb (209 kg) of munitions.

Sea Battles in World War I

The navies of World War I were initially dominated by enormous battleships. However, the reality of the conflict gradually undermined the rationale of these great vessels. As the war progressed, submarines, torpedo boats, and sea mines emerged to challenge the battleships' supremacy, both tactically and strategically.

Recruitment poster
This stirring US Navy poster is a bold attempt to attract new recruits. The US Navy began combat operations from April 6, 1917, with its principal roles being convoy escort duties and anti-submarine warfare.

U-boat engine room
German engineers monitor the operation of a U-boat power plant. The typical submerged speed of a U-boat was about 9 knots (17 km/h), and about 17 knots (31 km/h) on the surface, where the U-boats spent most of their time.

When World War I began, the power of a navy was mainly determined by the numbers of battleships it had in service. Fitted with turreted heavy guns, plated in armor, and with oceanic reach, these powerful ships projected influence and security around the globe. In battle, they could engage enemies with massive shells at ranges beyond the horizon, relying on complicated (and often fallible) fire-control technologies. The British Royal Navy—at the time, the most powerful navy in the world—entered hostilities with 52 battleships against the 34 capital vessels of the German Kaiserliche Marine.

Big-gun battles

The first year of the war produced a few major clashes between opposing battleships and cruisers at disparate points on the globe. On August 28, 1914, the Germans lost three light cruisers and a torpedo boat during the Battle of Heligoland Bight near Germany's northern coast. The tide turned on November 1 at the Battle of Coronel off Chile, when the formidable German battle cruisers *Scharnhorst* and *Gneisenau* sank two British armored cruisers. However, both German warships were later destroyed, along with a pair of light cruisers accompanying them, in the retaliatory Battle of the Falkland Islands on December 8. The Germans also lost an armored cruiser, *Blücher*, on January 24, 1915, during a huge North Sea gun battle at Dogger Bank.

The zenith of battleship warfare was the Battle of Jutland, fought on May 31–June 1, 1916. This large-scale action brought the full might of the German High Seas Fleet and the British Grand Fleet into contact off the coast of Denmark; the objective was potential control of the North Sea. In a chaotic, rather random engagement, the British came off worst materially, with three of their battle cruisers, three armored cruisers, and eight destroyers being sunk. Although the Germans lost two battleships, four light cruisers, and five destroyers, the bulk of their fleet made it safely home to port. The Kaiser's government declared a victory, but in reality no strategic advantage had been gained.

Changing threats

While surface actions such as this were awe-inspiring events, with huge shells arcing from billowing heavy guns across miles of ocean, the battleships had already begun their slide toward obsolescence. New threats meant that for much of the war, many battleships spent their time at anchor in protected ports.

Among the emerging threats were sea mines: contact-detonated canisters of explosives that were deployed in their tens of thousands off enemy coasts and along contested sea lanes. These passive weapons sank many warships and merchant vessels. At the Battle of the Dardanelles on March 18, 1915, for example, three Allied warships were lost to mines during an Allied attempt to force passage up the Dardanelles Strait.

Light and fast torpedo boats also posed a serious challenge to heavier vessels; at Jutland, the British

HMS *Ramillies*
One of five British *Revenge*-class battleships, HMS *Ramillies* was launched in September 1916. It survived the war, and one of its 15-in main guns now stands on permanent display outside the Imperial War Museum in London.

"Our **losses were heavy**, and we miss many most **gallant comrades**"

ADMIRAL SIR JOHN JELLICOE, IN A MESSAGE TO THE BRITISH FLEET AFTER THE BATTLE OF JUTLAND IN 1916

commander, Admiral Sir John Jellicoe, felt sufficiently intimidated by torpedo-boat attacks to break off pursuit of the German fleet.

Submarine war

As successful as the new sea mines were, arguably the most important development of World War I naval warfare was the submarine, which Germany used to great strategic effect, unleashing its growing fleet of U-boats against Allied vessels. On September 22, 1914, a single U-boat, *U-9*, sank three British armored cruisers in less than an hour in the southern North Sea. The submarines of the Central Powers also began preying on merchant ships, sinking approximately 5,000 such vessels and killing 15,000 sailors by the end of the war.

Losses to submarines eventually compelled the Allies to adopt a system of escorted convoys to elevate the statistical likelihood of merchant ships reaching transatlantic shores without being intercepted and sunk. With the rise of the submarine, the battleship was no longer the most influential vessel on the high seas.

TALKING POINT

The Blockade of Europe

The British naval blockade of Germany and its allies is considered one of the most controversial aspects of World War I. The blockade was established in August 1914 and ran until June 1919, not finishing until seven months after the signing of the Armistice. Britain used mine-laying ships to deploy vast numbers of sea mines off enemy coastlines, while its warships attempted to cut off access to the English Channel and the North Sea. By early 1915, all merchant vessels bound for Germany could be stopped and their cargoes seized. The impact of the blockade by the end of the war was profound. Estimates of deaths from malnutrition and associated diseases range from about 400,000 to more than 700,000. The blockade was not impenetrable, but it made a significant contribution to Germany's final defeat.

German submarine captains Paul Konig, left, (*Deutschland*) and Wolfgang Schwartzkopf, right, (*Bremen*) became famous for blockade-running exploits.

Dreadnoughts and Battleships

The launch of HMS *Dreadnought* in 1906 began an international arms race to build new generations of fast and thickly armored "all-big-gun" warships. By 1914, these had evolved into "super-dreadnought" monsters such as the British *Queen Elizabeth* class, with a steam-turbine-driven top speed of 24 knots (44 km/h), armor plate 13 in (330 mm) thick, and guns with a maximum range of around 16 miles (26 km). Battle cruisers also emerged as a new type of battleship—heavily armed but more lightly armored for greater speed.

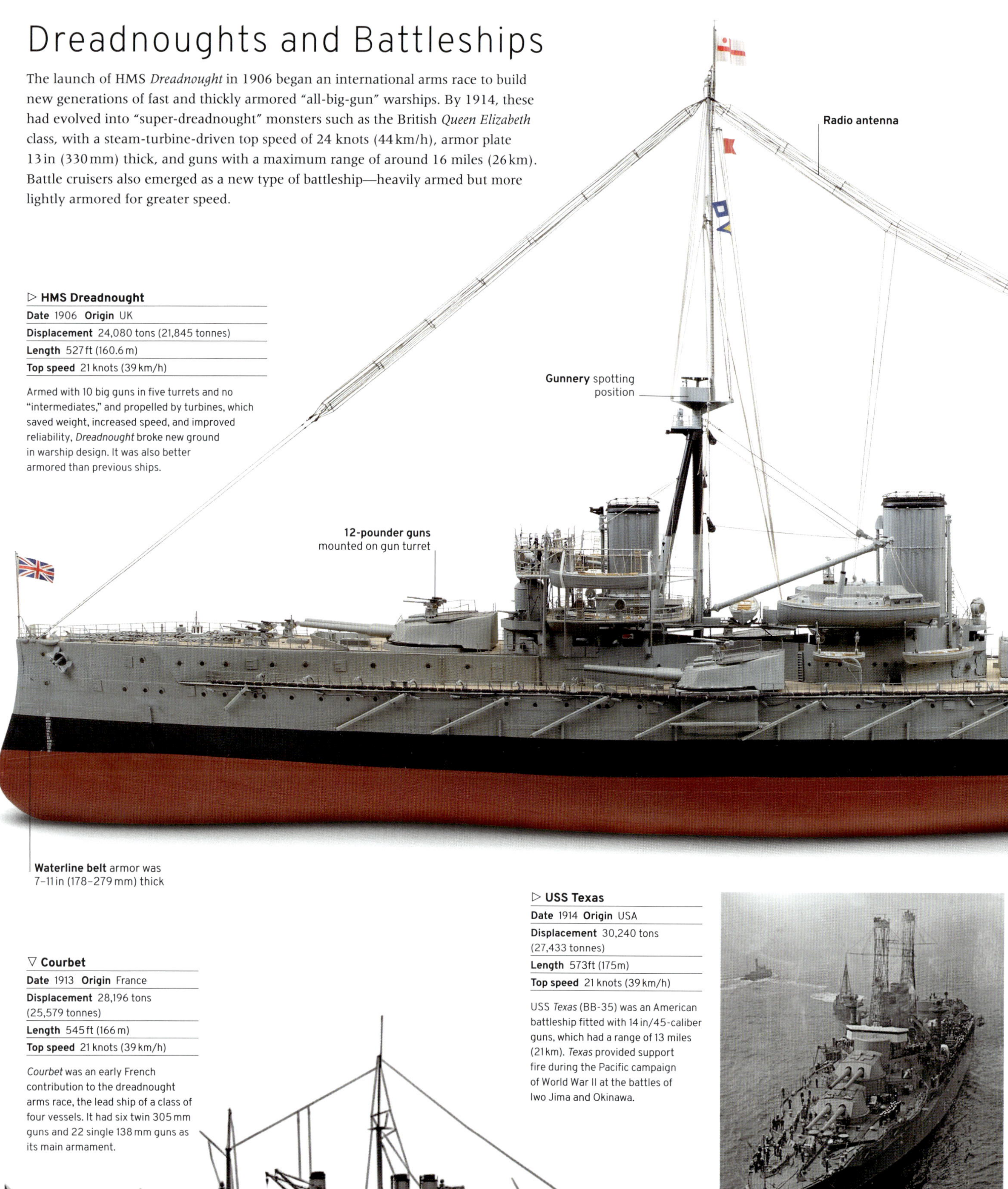

▷ HMS Dreadnought

Date 1906 **Origin** UK
Displacement 24,080 tons (21,845 tonnes)
Length 527 ft (160.6 m)
Top speed 21 knots (39 km/h)

Armed with 10 big guns in five turrets and no "intermediates," and propelled by turbines, which saved weight, increased speed, and improved reliability, *Dreadnought* broke new ground in warship design. It was also better armored than previous ships.

▽ Courbet

Date 1913 **Origin** France
Displacement 28,196 tons (25,579 tonnes)
Length 545 ft (166 m)
Top speed 21 knots (39 km/h)

Courbet was an early French contribution to the dreadnought arms race, the lead ship of a class of four vessels. It had six twin 305 mm guns and 22 single 138 mm guns as its main armament.

▷ USS Texas

Date 1914 **Origin** USA
Displacement 30,240 tons (27,433 tonnes)
Length 573 ft (175 m)
Top speed 21 knots (39 km/h)

USS *Texas* (BB-35) was an American battleship fitted with 14 in/45-caliber guns, which had a range of 13 miles (21 km). *Texas* provided support fire during the Pacific campaign of World War II at the battles of Iwo Jima and Okinawa.

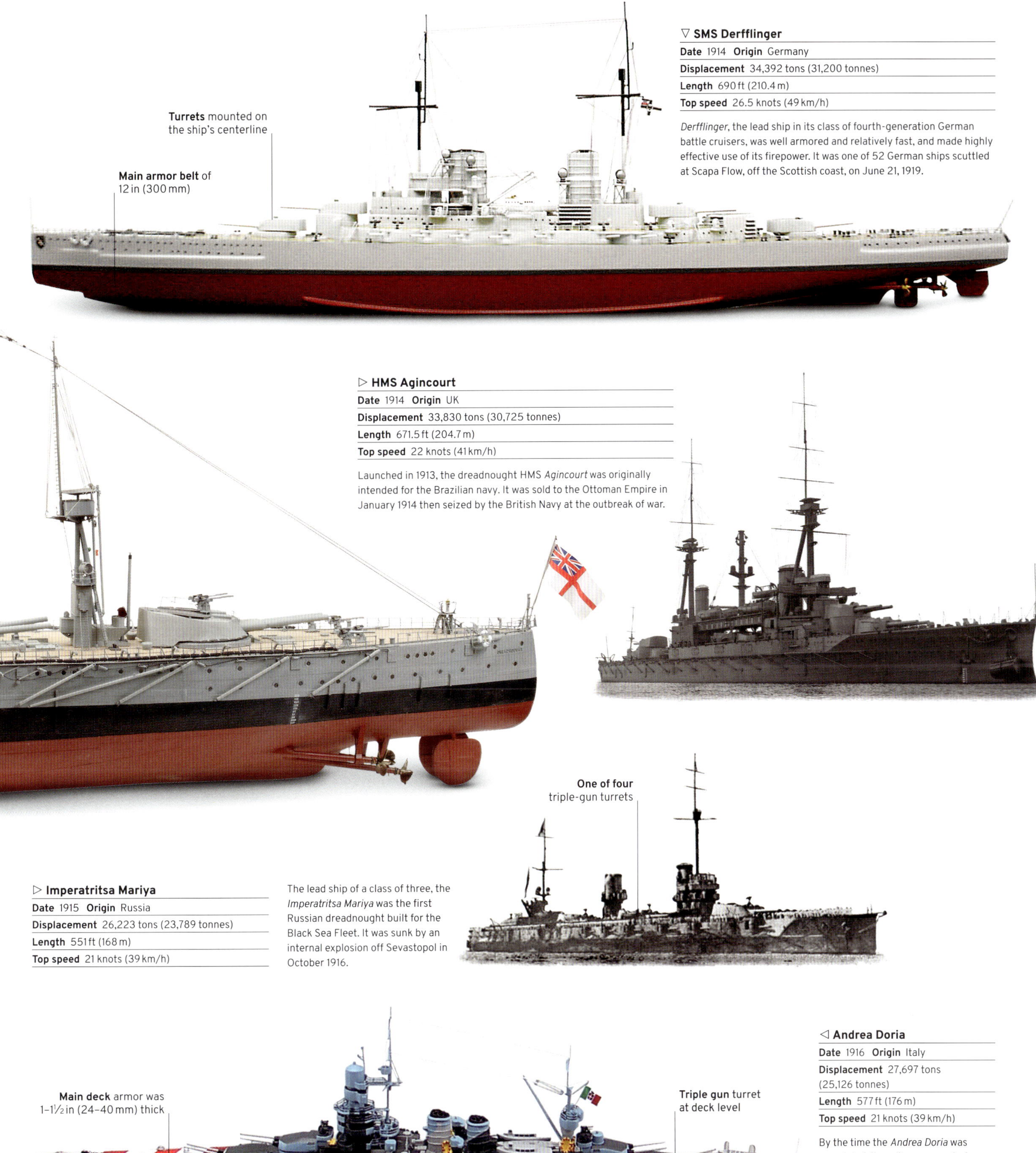

▽ SMS Derfflinger

Date 1914 **Origin** Germany
Displacement 34,392 tons (31,200 tonnes)
Length 690 ft (210.4 m)
Top speed 26.5 knots (49 km/h)

Derfflinger, the lead ship in its class of fourth-generation German battle cruisers, was well armored and relatively fast, and made highly effective use of its firepower. It was one of 52 German ships scuttled at Scapa Flow, off the Scottish coast, on June 21, 1919.

▷ HMS Agincourt

Date 1914 **Origin** UK
Displacement 33,830 tons (30,725 tonnes)
Length 671.5 ft (204.7 m)
Top speed 22 knots (41 km/h)

Launched in 1913, the dreadnought HMS *Agincourt* was originally intended for the Brazilian navy. It was sold to the Ottoman Empire in January 1914 then seized by the British Navy at the outbreak of war.

▷ Imperatritsa Mariya

Date 1915 **Origin** Russia
Displacement 26,223 tons (23,789 tonnes)
Length 551 ft (168 m)
Top speed 21 knots (39 km/h)

The lead ship of a class of three, the *Imperatritsa Mariya* was the first Russian dreadnought built for the Black Sea Fleet. It was sunk by an internal explosion off Sevastopol in October 1916.

◁ Andrea Doria

Date 1916 **Origin** Italy
Displacement 27,697 tons (25,126 tonnes)
Length 577 ft (176 m)
Top speed 21 knots (39 km/h)

By the time the *Andrea Doria* was completed, its main armament of 305 mm guns had been outclassed by heavier armaments on other international battleships. The ship was rebuilt in 1937–40 and served in the Italian navy until 1956.

USS Texas

With a main armament of ten 14in guns, the USS *Texas* entered service in 1914 as the world's most powerful warship. This *New York*-class battleship, which cost around $6 million to build, was the product of the naval arms race that preceded World War I.

DESPITE THE HEAVY FIREPOWER of this "superdreadnought," the *Texas* was behind the times as it used coal-fired reciprocating engines rather than oil-fired steam turbines. Oil-fired boilers were installed in 1927 as part of a major overhaul, with the ship's armor and fire-control systems also being upgraded. Antiaircraft guns and fire-control and air-defense radars were added at a later date.

By the outbreak of World War II, the *Texas* was no longer fast enough to keep up with more modern capital ships in combat. Before the US entered the war, the *Texas* escorted merchant convoys across the Atlantic. Subsequently, it was used for shore bombardment, since its 14in guns could fire 1,500lb (680kg) shells at targets more than 12 miles (20km) away, at a rate of one round every 45 seconds. In this role, the *Texas* provided fire support for landings in North Africa, Normandy, Iwo Jima, and Okinawa.

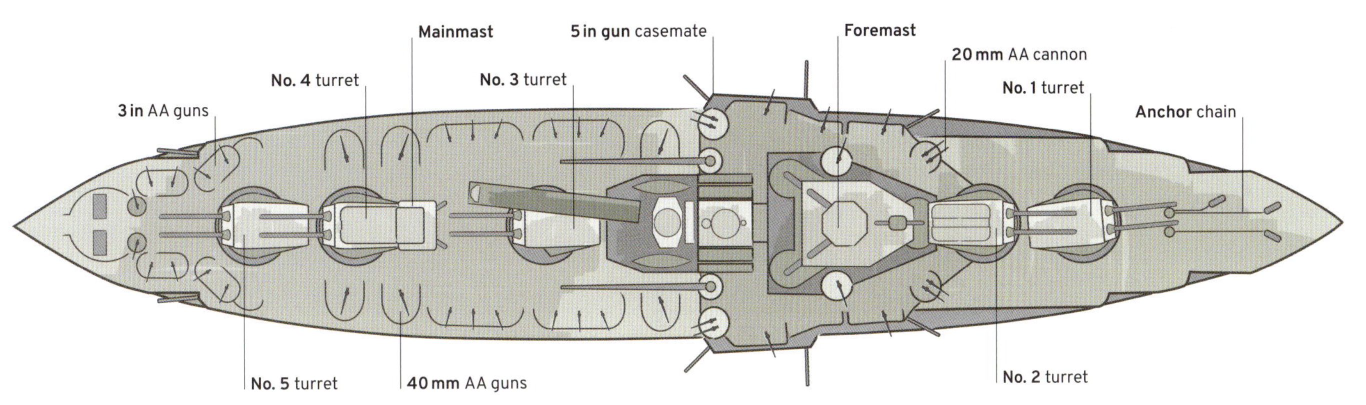

SPECIFICATIONS	
Name	USS *Texas*
Commissioned	1914
Class and type	*New York*-class battleship
Displacement	30,240 tons (27,433 tonnes)
Length	573 ft (175 m)
Propulsion	2 × triple-expansion steam engines
Armament	10 × 14 in/45-caliber guns
Armor	14 in (356 mm) max.
Maximum speed	21 knots (39 km/h)

Illustrious career
Having served with the Grand Fleet in World War I, the *Texas* earned five battle stars during World War II, before being decommissioned in 1946. The last surviving dreadnought-era battleship, it is now a museum ship at San Jacinto, Texas.

EXTERIOR

Observers in the battery control, situated at the top of the foremast, relayed readings of range, speed, and bearing that were used to instruct the gunners. Below the battery control sat other areas that needed a high, clear line of sight, such as the bridge and lookout platforms. The *Texas* carried two paravanes, which were towed behind the ship to snag or cut the lines of submerged mines.

1. Rear view of foremast **2.** Anchor capstans **3.** Battery control **4.** Ship's bell **5.** Antiaircraft guns **6.** Bofors 40mm antiaircraft gun **7.** Forward gun turrets **8.** 20mm antiaircraft cannon **9.** Paravane **10.** Line cutter of paravane **11.** Breech of 14in gun

1

2

6

7

12

13

14

19

20

21

22

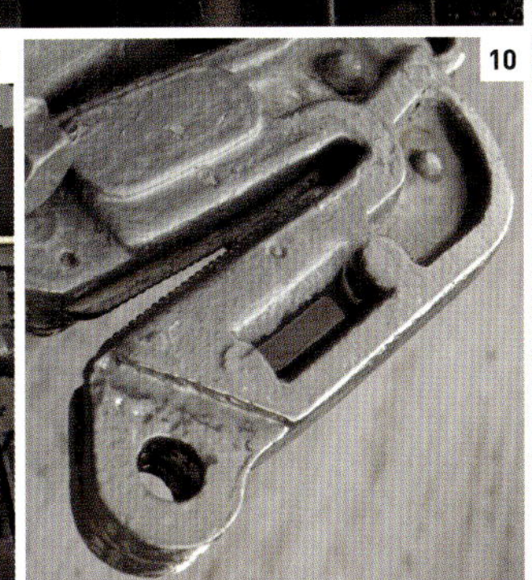

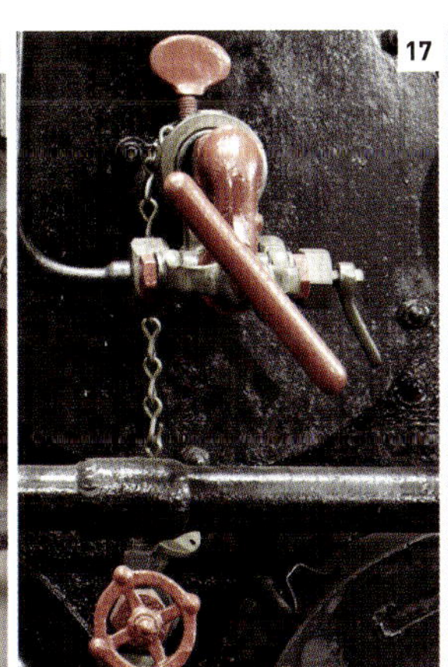

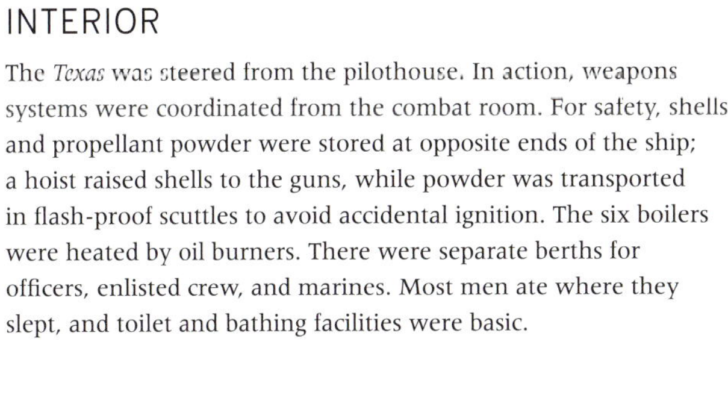

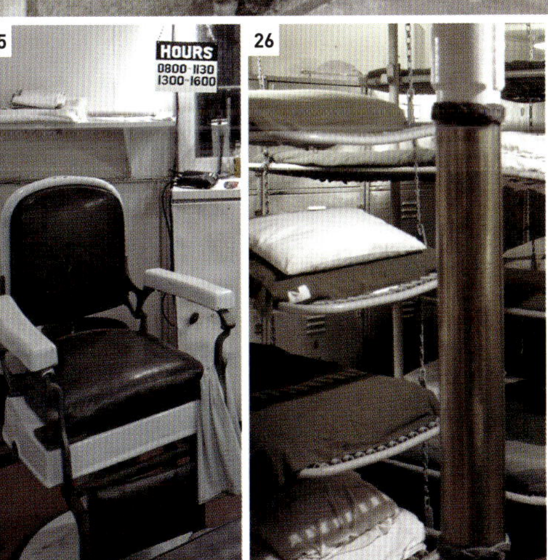

INTERIOR

The *Texas* was steered from the pilothouse. In action, weapons systems were coordinated from the combat room. For safety, shells and propellant powder were stored at opposite ends of the ship; a hoist raised shells to the guns, while powder was transported in flash-proof scuttles to avoid accidental ignition. The six boilers were heated by oil burners. There were separate berths for officers, enlisted crew, and marines. Most men ate where they slept, and toilet and bathing facilities were basic.

12. Combat room **13.** Pilothouse **14.** Chart room **15.** Below-deck 14in shell hoist **16.** Powder scuttles **17.** Oil burner nozzle detail **18.** Emergency steering position **19.** Oil-fired boiler **20.** Enlisted men's galley **21.** Bakery **22.** Cafeteria **23.** Post office **24.** Crew locker **25.** Barber's shop **26.** Marine berths

Destroyers and Escorts

Essentially coastal vessels, early destroyers displaced around 220 tons (200 tonnes), but by 1914 destroyers had grown in size, with some displacing over 1,100 tons (1,000 tonnes). Although much bigger, these ships were still fast, some with speeds in excess of 30 knots (56 km/h), and they typically carried 4-inch guns or larger, in addition to torpedoes. Shipping losses to German U-boats during World War I diverted Allied destroyers from defending the fleet to protecting convoys and hunting submarines. Built for speed and with limited range, these destroyers were not ideal for long-range duties, so specialist escort destroyers with depth charges and hydrophones were developed to counter the U-boat threat.

Bow-mounted 4 in gun

Derrick and lifeboat

△ HMS Hornet

Date 1911 **Origin** UK
Displacement 1,109 tons (1,006 tonnes)
Length 246 ft (75 m)
Top speed 28 knots (52 km/h)

Armed with two 4 in guns, two 12-pounders, and a pair of torpedo tubes, *Hornet* was one of 23 *Acheron*-class destroyers built for the British Royal Navy. *Hornet* served throughout World War I, screening battle squadrons and carrying out anti-submarine work. In 1918, it survived serious damage inflicted by fire from Austro-Hungarian destroyers.

△ SMS S19

Date 1913 **Origin** Germany
Displacement 768.3 tons (697 tonnes)
Length 233 ft (71 m)
Top speed 32 knots (59.3 km/h)

This torpedo boat of the Imperial German Navy was designed to be smaller than previous iterations. It fought in the Battle of Jutland in 1916, and survived World War I to be kept in reserve until 1931.

△ Novik

Date 1913 **Origin** Russia
Displacement 3,450 tons (3,129 tonnes)
Length 361 ft (110 m)
Top speed 25 knots (46 km/h)

The *Novik* was a German-built Russian armored cruiser. It was damaged and scuttled during the Russo-Japanese War (1904–05), but subsequently salvaged, repaired, and heavily modified for the Japanese Navy. It served Japan from 1906 to 1913 as the *Suzuya*, albeit with reduced performance.

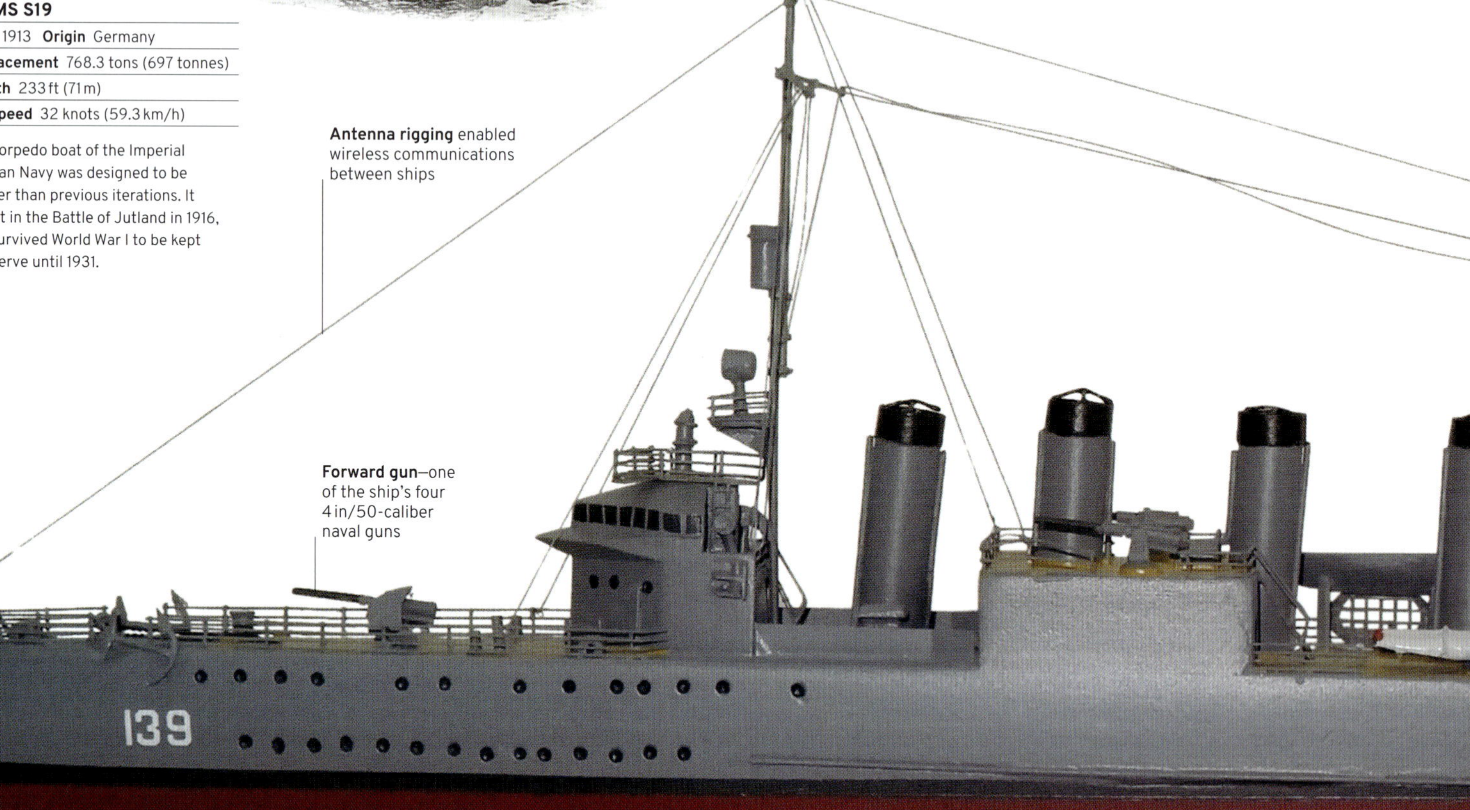

△ Bisson

Date 1913 **Origin** France	
Displacement 882 tons (800 tonnes)	
Length 256 ft (78 m)	
Top speed 30 knots (56 km/h)	

Six *Bisson*-class destroyers were constructed for the French Navy. *Bisson*, the lead ship of the class, was commissioned in September 1913. It was armed with two 100 mm guns, four 65 mm guns, and two twin 450 mm torpedo tubes. *Bisson* saw action in World War I, and served until 1933.

▽ HMAS Geranium

Date 1915 (Royal Navy) **Origin** UK	
Displacement 1,400 tons (1,270 tonnes)	
Length 268 ft (81.6 m)	
Top speed 16.5 knots (30.6 km/h)	

Built for use in World War I, this *Arabis*-class sloop (the term was used in this era for specialized convoy-defense ships) was a minesweeper used by Britain's Royal Navy until 1919, when it was transferred to the Royal Australian Navy.

△ SMS V43

Date 1915 **Origin** Germany	
Displacement 1,219 tons (1,106 tonnes)	
Length 261 ft (79.5 m)	
Top speed 33.5 knots (62 km/h)	

This *V25*-class *Großes Torpedoboot* (Large Torpedo Boat) survived numerous wartime engagements, but was one of the many German warships scuttled at Scapa Flow on June 21, 1919. British crews managed to beach and save the sinking *V43*, however, and it ended its service in 1921 as a target ship.

△ Kerch

Date 1917 **Origin** Russia	
Displacement 1,485 tons (1,347 tonnes)	
Length 304 ft (92.5 m)	
Top speed 31 knots (57 km/h)	

The *Kerch* belonged to the *Fidonisy*-class of Russian destroyer. It was built from October 1915, launched in May 1916, and commissioned in June 1917. In June 1918, however, it was scuttled by its crew to prevent it falling into German hands as part of the Treaty of Brest-Litovsk.

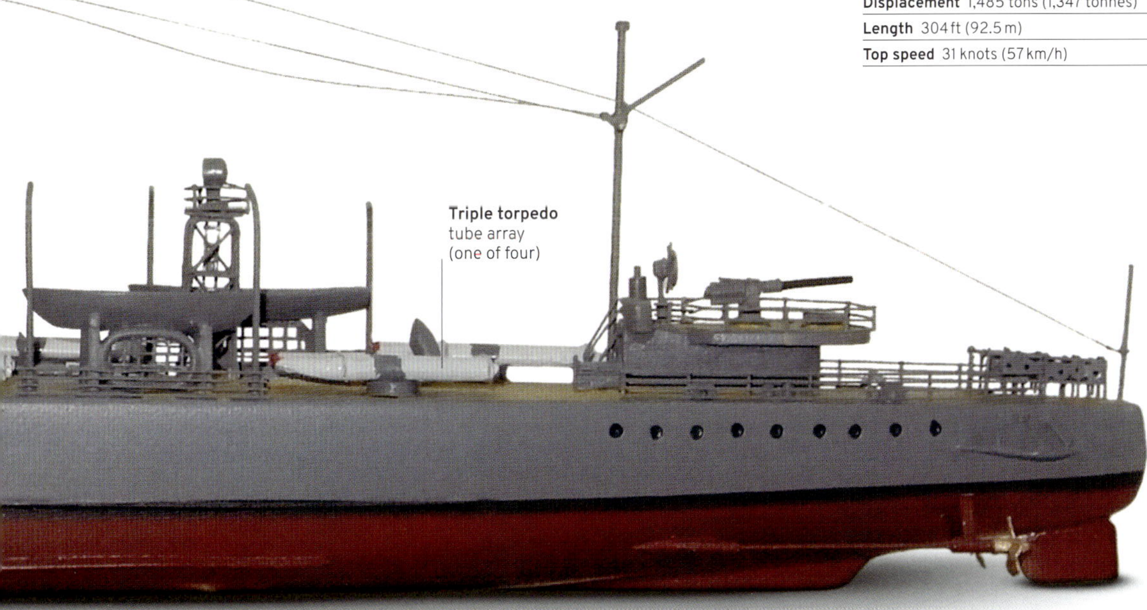

◁ USS Ward

Date 1918 **Origin** USA	
Displacement 1,397 tons (1,267 tonnes)	
Length 314 ft (95.8 m)	
Top speed 35 knots (65 km/h)	

USS *Ward*, a *Wickes*-class destroyer, was commissioned in July 1918, having been built in just over three months. It achieved fame in World War II by sinking a Japanese midget submarine at Pearl Harbor just prior to the air attack on December 7, 1941. *Ward* sank after kamikaze attacks in 1944.

Submarine Warfare in World War I

More than 5,000 Allied ships were sunk by German submarines during World War I. In September 1915, complaints from a neutral US after the sinking of passenger liners and the loss of its citizens' lives caused Germany to cease its unrestricted sinking of ships. The potential to starve Britain into submission spurred the German navy to argue for a resumption of unrestricted attacks in 1917. The German high command understood that allowing such attacks would bring the US into the conflict. Assessing that they could defeat Britain and France before the American military could influence events, they recommenced attacks. The Allies responded with new convoy tactics that limited the effectiveness of the submarines and prevented the Germans from achieving their aims. Nevertheless, the potential of submarine warfare to have strategic results on a conflict had been realized, and it would be used again in World War II.

One of the 15 UC-1 Class submarines built by Germany early in World War I surfaces. These submarines were used solely to deploy mines.

World War I Submarines

On September 5, 1914, the German submarine *U-21* sank the British cruiser HMS *Pathfinder* off eastern Scotland—the first warship ever sunk by a submarine-fired torpedo. Although the ease with which capital ships could be sunk by submarines had been predicted before World War I, Allied naval commanders sometimes disastrously failed to shield large warships with destroyer screens. Fear of submarines came to inhibit the operation of surface fleets, and the Royal Navy's Grand Fleet spent much of the war out of German U-boat range. The most effective role for U-boats, however, was as commerce raiders: attacks on merchant shipping almost succeeded in crippling Britain's war effort. The Allies eventually adopted an effective solution—a system of protected merchant convoys.

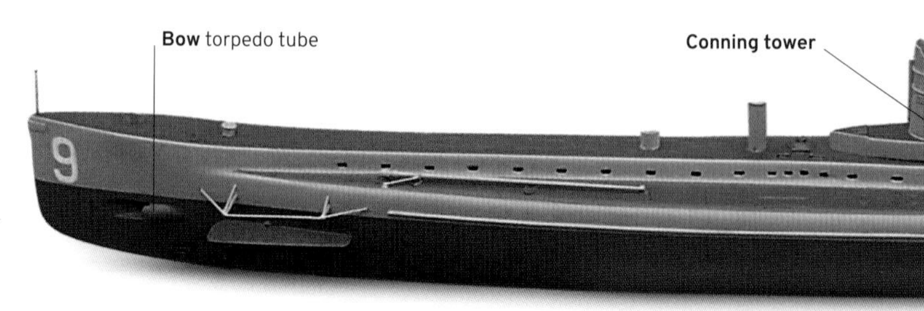

△ **SM U-9**

Date 1910 **Origin** Germany
Displacement 543 tons (493 tonnes)
Length 188 ft (57.4 m)
Top speed 14 knots (26 km/h)

Like all pre-1912 U-boats, the four Type *U-9* coastal submarines (of which *U-9* was the lead boat) had both electric motors and gasoline engines, rather than diesels. In September 1914, in one of the most famous submarine actions, *U-9* sank the British armored cruisers *Hogue*, *Aboukir*, and *Cressy* in the same engagement.

△ **SM U-10**

Date 1911 **Origin** Germany
Displacement 543 tons (493 tonnes)
Length 188 ft (57.4 m)
Top speed 14 knots (26 km/h)

Armed with four torpedo tubes, two in the bow, two in the stern, this Type *U-9* submarine took part in Germany's Atlantic campaign against merchant vessels. It disappeared in 1916 while traveling from Latvia to the Swedish coast, and was presumed sunk.

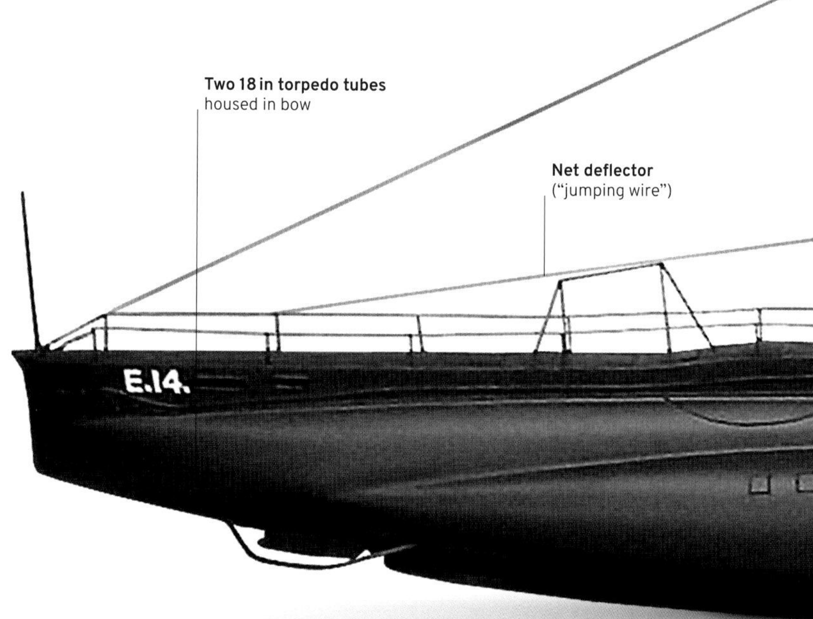

△ **RN E-class submarine**

Date 1915 **Origin** UK
Displacement Approx. 744 tons (675 tonnes)
Length Approx. 180 ft (55 m)
Top speed 15 knots (28 km/h)

The 56 E-class boats—the backbone of Britain's World War I submarine fleet—were ocean-going vessels with a range of 3,000 nautical miles (5,556 km). The first Royal Navy submarines with internal watertight bulkheads, they had five torpedo tubes: two fore, one aft, and a pair of transverse tubes amidships to fire side-on. Six were built as minelayers; these had just fore and aft torpedo tubes to accommodate 20 mines.

△ **SM U-35**

Date 1914 **Origin** Germany
Displacement 755 tons (685 tonnes)
Length 212 ft (64.7 m)
Top speed 16.4 knots (30 km/h)

One of 11 German *U-31*-class submarines, *U-35* operated in the Mediterranean during World War I and became the most successful U-boat of the war, sinking 220 Allied merchant vessels, 3 warships, and 3 auxiliary ships. The submarine survived to the end of the war, after which it was transferred to the UK; it was broken up in 1920.

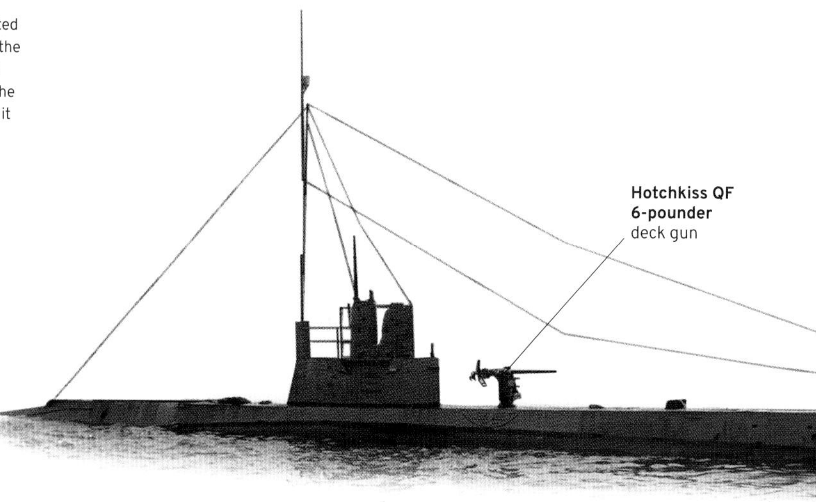

▷ **H-class submarine**

Date 1915 **Origin** UK
Displacement 407–474 tons (369–430 tonnes)
Length 150–170 ft (46–52 m)
Top speed 11.5–13 knots (21–24 km/h)

Over 40 H-class submarines were built for the British Royal Navy between 1915 and 1919. Most entered service too late to have any impact on the war. HMS *H4*, shown here, sank the German submarine *UB-52* in 1918. H-class submarines remained in service as training vessels, some until the end of World War II.

Funnel for venting gasoline engine exhaust (lowered for submerged travel)

Radio mast

Periscope

Conning tower

Single 18 in torpedo tube housed in stern

△ Bars-class submarine

Date 1915 **Origin** Russia
Displacement 728 tons (660 tonnes)
Length 223 ft (68 m)
Top speed 18 knots (33 km/h)

A total of 24 *Bars*-class submarines were built between 1914 and 1917. Three were lost in action during World War I. Surviving boats were taken over by the Soviets after the Bolshevik Revolution; later modernized, some remained in service until the 1930s.

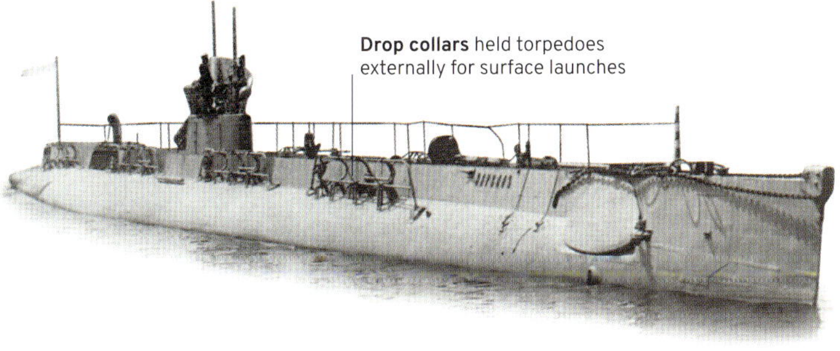

Drop collars held torpedoes externally for surface launches

△ Narval-class submarine

Date 1915 **Origin** Russia
Displacement 696 tons (631 tonnes)
Length 230 ft (70 m)
Top speed 9.5 knots (17.5 km/h)

The three *Narval*-class vessels of the Black Sea Fleet were the largest Russian submarines of the war; with crash-diving tanks for faster diving, watertight bulkheads, and ballast tanks filled by natural water flow (rather than by pumps), they were also the most advanced. As well as internal torpedo tubes, they had external "drop collars" for surface torpedo launches.

▽ L-class submarine

Date 1916–1923 **Origin** USA
Displacement Approx. 504 tons (457 tonnes)
Length Approx. 165 ft (50 m)
Top speed 14 knots (26 km/h)

The US built 11 L-class coastal defense submarines between 1914 and 1917. Some vessels had a semi-retractable deck gun. Wartime service showed the boats to be underpowered and not suited to long North Atlantic patrols. After the war, they were used for trials of torpedoes and hydrophone systems, before being decommissioned in the early 1920s.

Canvas surround was erected around conning tower for extended surface travel

Bow carried a pair of torpedo tubes; two more were located in the stern

1918–1945

THE BATTLEFIELD REDEFINED

CC221044

The Era of Maneuver

Aftermath of battle
A disabled US M4 Sherman medium tank stands on the island of Iwo Jima, March 1945. Its sides clearly show shell impacts, and the tank has lost its right track.

The changes in vehicle technology between 1919 and 1945 were immense. In every theater—land, sea, and air—military vehicle design and performance were upgraded dramatically, giving rise to entirely new approaches to warfare.

World War II is regarded as one of the greatest tragedies in human history, with unimaginable loss of life in theaters around the world. However, it also represents a six-year period of unmatched and rapid innovation in military technology, particularly in the case of vehicles. The wave of technological revolutions had begun in the interwar period, aided by continuing improvements in engine design, materials science, mechanical and electric engineering, aerodynamics, and fluid mechanics.

The path to war

The development of military vehicles during the interwar period was erratic, heavily dependent upon economics and politics. During the 1920s, postwar austerity restrained the spending of many national armed forces, while Germany's military research and development was hampered under the tight restrictions imposed by the 1919 Treaty of Versailles. On the seas, warship construction was limited by the Washington Naval Treaty of 1922. However, there was still future-looking innovation. Important steps forward in this era included the development of tanks with rotating gun turrets; improved generations of armored cars; the first half-track prototypes; the first aircraft carriers; and the progressive shift from biplanes to all-metal monoplanes. As new vehicle types emerged, they required fresh tactics to go with them. Land-warfare innovators such as J. F. C. Fuller (UK) and Heinz Guderian (Germany) outlined bold visions of armored warfare, while William "Billy" Mitchell (US) and Giulio Douhet (Italy) predicted futures in which air power would be dominant, both strategically and tactically. The world's navies began discussions about future sea warfare, including topics such as improved interservice cooperation, and the roles of submarines and aircraft carriers.

All these technologies and ideas became more relevant during the 1930s, when the world found itself rushing to rearm, facilitated by new efficiencies in industrial production. The propaganda material of this era projected the idea that martial spirit was synonymous with advanced military technologies,

Timeline
The interwar period and World War II transformed the tactical influence of military vehicles. Land armies focused on motorization, mechanization, and armored vehicles; navies invested in aircraft carriers and submarines; and air forces created new generations of monoplanes, including the first jet fighters.

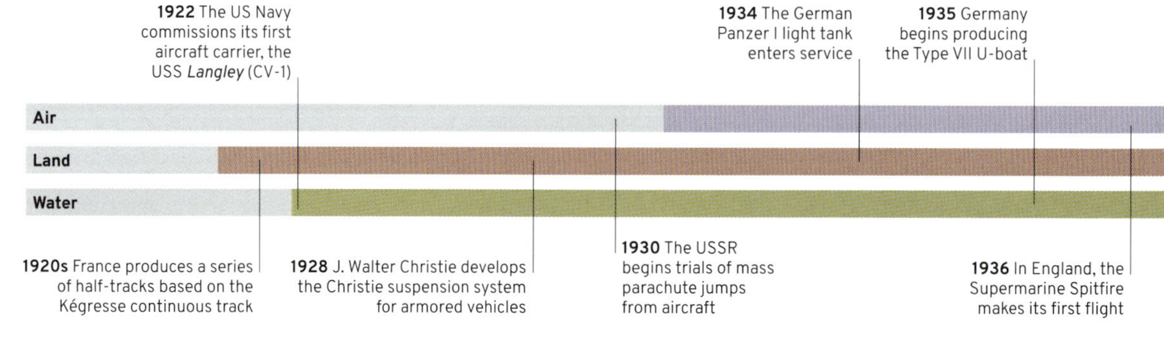

particularly vehicles such as tanks and combat aircraft. It was clear that the idea of warfare had changed. Static warfare based around trenches and fixed positions was now largely a thing of the past. Warfare's future clearly lay with mobility and maneuver.

A new era

World War II saw major contrasts in the scale, capability, and destructive effect of vehicular warfare compared to its predecessor. In terms of ground warfare, infantry and artillery were still center stage as they had been in the previous conflict, but tactically armor led the way in Europe, while amphibious landing craft did the same in the Pacific. Supply was now dependent on trucks instead of horses, particularly on the well-equipped Allied side from 1942. At sea, navies retained battleships and cruisers, but it was submarines, aircraft carriers, and merchant ships that were most influential in the naval war. In the air, biplanes had almost disappeared, replaced by high-performance monoplanes, in types ranging from light reconnaissance aircraft to long-range heavy bombers and even the first generations of jet aircraft. The pressures of total war brought constant innovation and improvement at an unprecedented speed.

The consequences of these changes were far-reaching. War was now, quite literally, faster. While World War I biplanes flew at speeds of about 110 mph (177 km/h), a monoplane fighter such as a P-51D Mustang flew at 437 mph (703 km/h). Likewise, a T-34 tank ran at 33 mph (53 km/h), instead of the walking pace of a tank in the previous war. Fighting was also conducted across greater distances. US and British strategic bombers regularly made bomb runs from the UK to Germany; from late 1944, American B-29 Superfortress bombers attacked Tokyo from Guam, a round-trip of 3,100 miles (5,000 km).

Last of the biplanes
Britain's Fairey Swordfish was one of the few biplanes to see combat in World War II. These slow-moving, carrier-launched torpedo bombers sunk or damaged Axis capital ships.

Naval war was now fought as vigorously in the air and underwater as it was on the surface. Submarines patrolled further, faster, and with more lethal weaponry, including the first generations of programmable torpedoes. A US *Lexington*-class aircraft carrier such as the USS *Saratoga* (CV-3) could carry 78 combat aircraft, the equivalent of roughly six squadrons. Naval warfare and maritime logistics were also transformed by industry. When US shipyards reached their peak output, for example, some were building an individual "Liberty" merchant vessel every four-and-a-half days.

World War II was as much a clash of machines as it was of personnel. Manning these machines required immense courage and skill, since the continued reliance upon direct-fire weaponry meant that soldiers, sailors, and airmen still fought within visual range of their enemies. Communications were also key: having assembled vast fleets of military vehicles, strategists and commanders still needed to control and coordinate them. The new age of combined-arms warfare (multiple types of military force working together) was made possible by equal advances in wireless communications, command-and-control processes, and even administrative staff work.

TALKING POINT

Deploying the atomic bombs

The two atomic bombs dropped on Japan in August 1945 were delivered by the most advanced aircraft in the US arsenal at that time, the B-29 Superfortress. This gleaming, four-engine bomber had several highly advanced features: fully pressurized crew compartments; a high-aspect-ratio wing design that gave excellent performance at both high and low altitudes; remote-controlled gun turrets; and advanced avionics. It also had an astonishing range of 4,100 miles (6,598 km) and a bomb capacity of 20,000 lb (9,072 kg), which made it the only US aircraft capable of carrying the atomic loads: the single "Fat Man" bomb released above the city of Nagasaki on August 9 weighed 10,800 lb (4,909 kg).

Enola Gay, a Boeing B-29 Superfortress, dropped the first of the atomic bombs, nicknamed "Little Boy," which detonated over the city of Hiroshima on August 6, 1945.

> "Two fundamental lessons... **never to check momentum;** never to resume mere pushing."
>
> CAPTAIN SIR BASIL LIDDEL HART, BRITISH SOLDIER, STRATEGIST, AND MILITARY HISTORIAN, *THOUGHTS ON WAR*, 1944

1939 Germany's Heinkel He 178 is the first turbojet-powered aircraft to take to the air

1939 Germany launches the battleship *Bismarck*

1940 The USSR introduces the T-34 medium tank

1940 Japan launches the *Yamato*-class battleships *Yamato* and *Musashi*

1941 Production of the US GMC CCKW military truck and Willys MB Jeep begins

1941 US shipyards begin producing "Liberty" merchant ships

1942 Avro Lancaster bombers enter service with the British Royal Air Force (RAF)

1942 The Allies utilize a range of specialist landing craft to invade North Africa

1944 Germany deploys the Me 262, history's first operational jet fighter

▽ Peerless Armored Car

Date 1919 **Origin** UK

Weight 7.7 tons (7 tonnes)

Engine Peerless 4-cylinder gasoline, 40 hp (30 kW)

Main armament 2 x .303 Hotchkiss Mark I machine guns

Pairing a Peerless truck chassis with an Austin-built armored body was not a great success: this British Army vehicle was big, cumbersome, and slow—and uncomfortable to ride in, due to its solid-rubber tires. Transferred to the Territorial Army, it was retained until the late 1930s.

▷ Rolls-Royce Armored Car

Date 1920 **Origin** UK

Weight 4.7 tons (4.3 tonnes)

Engine Rolls-Royce 6-cylinder gasoline, 80 hp (60 kW)

Main armament .303 Vickers machine gun

A modernization of the Royal Navy's 1914 Pattern Rolls-Royce, the 1920 Pattern armored car served with the British Army and Royal Air Force around the world, including in Ireland, Egypt, Iraq, and Shanghai. Some modified 1920 and 1924 Pattern cars took part in the North African Desert Campaign in 1940–41.

△ Lanchester Armored Car

Date 1931 **Origin** UK

Weight 7.8 tons (7.1 tonnes)

Engine Lanchester 6-cylinder gasoline, 90 hp (67 kW)

Main armament .50 Vickers machine gun

Larger and heavier than its namesake of World War I, this armored car had two additional .303 Vickers machine guns, four driven wheels at the rear, and a second, rear-facing driver's space at the back. Of the 39 examples built, 10 replaced the Vickers hull gun with a radio. Some vehicles survived to fight the Japanese in Malaya in 1941–42.

△ Sd Kfz 231 6 rad Armored Car

Date 1932 **Origin** Germany

Weight 6 tons (5.4 tonnes)

Engine Magirus M206 gasoline, 70 hp (52 kW)

Main armament 2 cm KwK 30 L/55 cannon

Germany's six-wheeled Sd Kfz 231 was based on a number of different 6x4 truck chassis. Its crew of four included a second driver, who faced rearward. Used in Austria, Poland, Czechoslovakia, and France, poor off-road mobility led to its withdrawal in 1940. A total of 151 were built; the one seen here is a replica.

◁ Stridsvagn fm/31

Date 1935 **Origin** Sweden

Weight 12.9 tons (11.7 tonnes)

Engine Maybach DSO 8 gasoline, 150 hp (112 kW)

Main armament 37 mm Bofors m/38 gun

To overcome the short life span of tracks on early tanks, some countries experimented with tanks that also carried a set of wheels for road runs and to reduce track wear. Sweden's unique Stridsvagn fm/31 could raise or lower its wheels in 30 seconds. The 1930s brought improvements in the longevity of tracks, rendering such complex "convertibles" unnecessary.

Interwar Armored Cars

Wheeled military vehicles retained some advantages over tanks, whose tracks could soon wear out and cost much more to build and maintain. Armored cars could often be equipped with similar firepower and protection to tanks, and they were typically more reliable and quieter—and usually faster, except across the roughest ground. These qualities made armored cars ideal as patrol vehicles or for reconnaissance duties ahead of advancing tank forces.

◁ **Leyland Armored Car**

Date 1937 **Origin** Ireland
Weight 14.6 tons (13.2 tonnes)
Engine Ford V8 type 317 gasoline, 155 hp (116 kW)
Main armament 20 mm Madsen cannon

This vehicle was an amalgamation of a 6x4 Leyland truck chassis, armor salvaged from Peerless cars, and a turret made by Landsverk of Sweden. The four examples built served with the Irish army alongside eight similar Swedish L-180s; in 1957, the front armor was rebuilt, and they were re-engined.

△ **Automitrailleuse de Découverte (AMD) Panhard modèle 1935**

Date 1937 **Origin** France
Weight 9 tons (8.2 tonnes)
Engine Panhard ISK 4-cylinder gasoline, 105 hp (78 kW)
Main armament 25 mm Hotchkiss SA 35 cannon

The quiet, fast AMD 35 was popular with crews, despite poor off-road performance. This reconnaissance vehicle had a second, rear-facing driver, who also acted as a radio operator. Production continued after France surrendered in 1940, and after the war's end in 1945; over 1,100 AMD 35s were built.

▽ **Crossley-Chevrolet Armored Car**

Date 1939 **Origin** UK
Weight 5.6 tons (5.1 tonnes)
Engine Chevrolet 6-cylinder gasoline, 78 hp (58 kW)
Main armament 2 x Vickers .303 machine guns

Crossley armored cars were first built in the 1920s and used for patrols by the British Army in India and the North West Frontier. The vehicles were built to "Indian Pattern," which included a domed turret with a "clamshell" cupola and an asbestos lining to limit temperatures inside. By 1939, the cars, now seriously in need of upgrading, were given a new Chevrolet chassis.

△ **Pansarbil m/40 (Lynx)**

Date 1939 **Origin** Sweden
Weight 7.8 tons (7.1 tonnes)
Engine Volvo 6-cylinder gasoline, 135 hp (101 kW)
Main armament 20 mm Bofors m/40 cannon

Both front and rear wheels of Sweden's symmetrical Lynx could steer, and its forward and reverse speeds were identical. It was operated by a six-man crew of front and rear drivers and gunners. Built for Danish export, only three of the initial 18 vehicles were delivered before Germany invaded Denmark in 1940. Sweden kept the other 15 and ordered 30 more.

Light, Medium, and Heavy Tanks

Advances in automotive and military technology in the 1920s and 1930s made tanks more reliable and capable. Most light tanks of the time carried machine guns, while medium and heavy tanks emphasized armor and firepower over mobility. A key development was American engineer J. Walter Christie's suspension system: each tank wheel had independent suspension—a "helicoil" spring mounted inside the hull—which improved agility and speed over broken ground. Tank development in Germany during this era was theoretically forbidden by the Treaty of Versailles.

Pistol port

Riveted armor on hull

▽ Leichter Kampfwagen LK II

Date 1918 **Origin** Germany
Engine Daimler-Benz 4-cylinder, 60 hp (45 kW)
Weight 9.7 tons (8.8 tonnes)
Main armament 57 mm Maxim-Nordenfelt

This light German tank was designed in the last year of World War I but never made it into production. Sweden secretly bought parts for 10 tanks, which were illegally imported labeled as tractor components. Assembled, they became the four-man m/21—the very first Swedish tank.

Armored skirt protects running gear

△ Vickers Mark E, 6 Ton

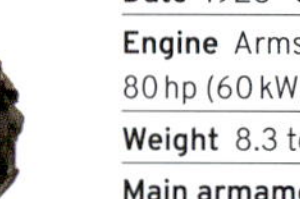

Date 1928 **Origin** UK
Engine Armstrong-Siddeley 4-cylinder gasoline, 80 hp (60 kW)
Weight 8.3 tons (7.5 tonnes)
Main armament QF 3-pounder gun

Although only 150 Mark Es were built, the tank was an export success. Vickers made sales to 12 countries, including Finland, Thailand, and Bolivia, with Poland buying 38 tanks—the largest single order. The Mark E's design was also highly influential, being the starting point for the development of the Polish 7TP and Soviet T-26 tanks. The Mark E had two variants: Type A was fitted with two machine-gun turrets; Type B, shown here, had just one.

▽ Leichttraktor Vs.Kfz.31

Date 1930 **Origin** Germany
Engine Daimler-Benz gasoline, 100 hp (75 kW)
Weight 10.7 tons (9.7 tonnes)
Main armament 3.7 cm KwK 36 L/45 gun

To circumvent post-World War I restrictions, Germany worked covertly with the Soviet Union's Kama Tank School in Russia to gain experience of designing, building, and operating tanks. It built a small number of tanks, including the Vs.Kfz.31, described as a "light tractor" to maintain secrecy.

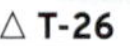

△ T-26

Date 1931 **Origin** USSR
Engine T-26 4-cylinder gasoline, 91 hp (68 kW)
Weight 10.4 tons (9.4 tonnes)
Main armament .45 mm 20K Model 1934 L/46 gun

More T-26s were produced than any other tank of the interwar era: 12,000 in all, including 2,000 twin-turreted versions and 1,700 variants. The tank's weaknesses quickly became apparent when it was first exposed to combat during the Spanish Civil War of 1936–39. Despite upgrades, it was outclassed by 1939. Some T-26s continued operating in the Far East until 1945.

▷ Christie M1931

Date 1931 **Origin** USA

Engine Liberty V12 gasoline, 338 hp (252 kW)

Weight 11.8 tons (10.7 tonnes)

Main armament .50 Browning M2 machine gun

The J. Walter Christie-designed M1931 could achieve high speeds, even on rough ground, thanks to its flexible suspension and light armor. It could run either on tracks or its wheels alone. It was purchased by the US Army, which had rejected its predecessor, the turretless M1928. The Soviet Union bought two tanks and used them to develop its BT series and the T-34.

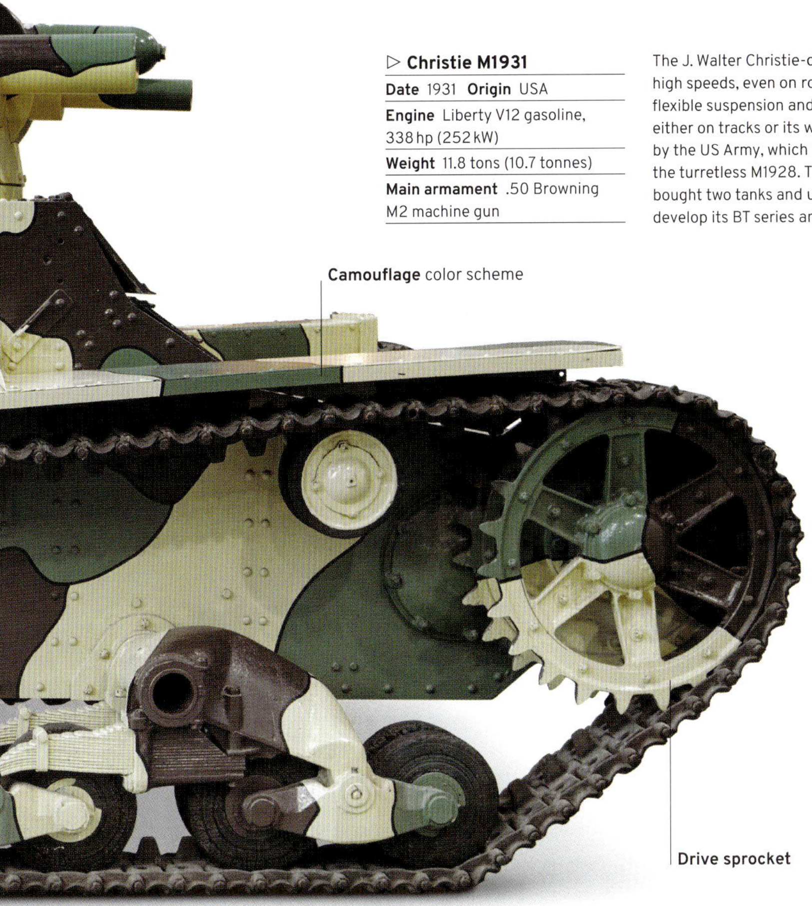

△ Light Tank M2A3

Date 1936 **Origin** USA

Engine Continental R-670-9A gasoline, 250 hp (186 kW)

Weight 10.7 tons (9.7 tonnes)

Main armament .50 Browning M2 machine gun

Only machine guns were considered necessary for the infantry support role of tanks in the M2 series. The M2A3 had twin turrets, one with a .50 machine gun, the other with a .30. The war in Europe showed that extra firepower was vital, so the M2A4, the version that went into combat with US forces, was given a 37 mm gun.

△ T-35

Date 1936 **Origin** USSR

Engine Mikulin M17T gasoline, 650 hp (485 kW)

Weight 50.4 tons (45.7 tonnes)

Main armament 76.2 mm Model 1927/32 gun

The only five-turret tank ever to enter service was the T-35. One turret was equipped with a 76.2 mm gun, two with 45 mm 20K guns, and two with DT machine guns. Just 61 examples of this slow, unreliable heavy tank were built; most were lost when Germany invaded the Soviet Union.

Driver's mirror gives view behind tank

△ Vickers Light Tank Mark VIB

Date 1937 **Origin** UK

Weight 5.8 tons (5.3 tonnes)

Engine Meadows ESTB 6-cylinder gasoline, 88 hp (66 kW)

Main armament .50 Vickers machine gun

The two-man crew of Vickers' Mark IV light tank was increased to three on the Mark V by the introduction of a two-man turret armed with .50 and .303 machine guns. The Mark VI added a radio. Nearly 1,000 Mark VIBs—the most common variant—were built, but combat in France, North Africa, and Greece showed the tanks to be inadequate.

◁ Medium Tank M2A1

Date 1939 **Origin** USA

Weight 25.8 tons (23.4 tonnes)

Engine Wright Continental R-975 gasoline, 400 hp (298 kW)

Main armament 37 mm M3 L/56.6 gun

Designed to support infantry, the M2 carried six .30 machine guns arranged to allow all-round fire. In 1939, the M2 became the first US medium tank to enter production, but by 1940 it was obsolete. However, the M2's Vertical Volute Spring Suspension (VVSS) system and R-975 engine were reused on its M3 and M4 successors.

Vickers Medium Mark II

With greater mobility and range than the tanks of World War I, the Vickers Medium was designed to fight on the move. The mainstay of the Royal Tank Corps from 1923 to 1935, the Medium—Marks I, II, and III—was the first British tank to enter service with a rotating turret and sprung suspension.

THE MEDIUM MARK I was the first variant to enter service, in 1923. Its turret was equipped with a 3-pounder main gun and Hotchkiss light machine guns. Two Vickers machine guns, one on either side of the hull, completed its weaponry. The Mark II* replaced the Hotchkiss turret guns with a coaxial Vickers machine gun. In addition to the gun tanks, the Medium was also produced in command-post and bridge-laying versions. Vickers Mediums formed the core of the British Army's Experimental Mechanised Force, which was set up in 1927 to explore how vehicles might be used in combat. After maneuvers on Salisbury Plain showed the potential of armored formations, the mechanization of the British Army continued into and throughout the 1930s.

The Vickers Medium's importance went beyond its influence on battlefield tactics: it was also an export success, being sold to numerous countries, including Russia, which bought 15. The lone Medium purchased by Japan became the model for the country's own Type 89 tank design.

FRONT VIEW

REAR VIEW

SPECIFICATIONS	
Name	Tank, Vickers Medium Mark II*
Date	1927
Origin	UK
Production	56
Engine	Armstrong Siddeley V8, 90 hp (67 kW)
Weight	13.7 tons (12.4 tonnes)
Main armament	3-pounder
Secondary armament	3 x Vickers .303 machine guns
Crew	5
Armor thickness	$\frac{1}{4}$–$\frac{3}{10}$ in (6.35–8 mm)

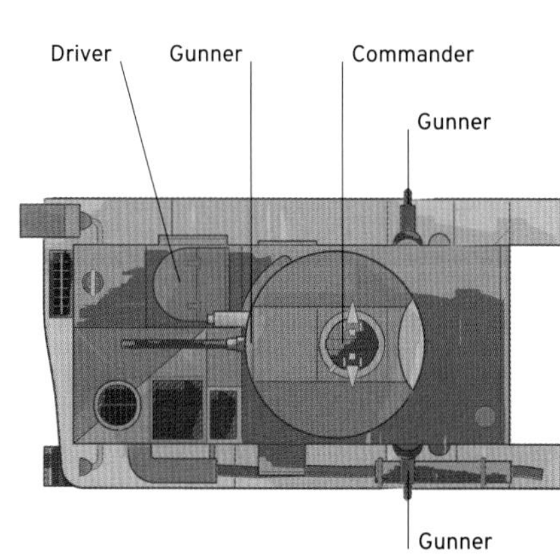

Battlefield adaptation
The Medium's main gun could tackle contemporary tanks, but it was ineffective against field fortifications, and the thin armor was vulnerable to anti-tank guns. In response, a more powerfully armed close-support version of the tank was built.

Training vehicle
Mark IIs were used to train drivers in the early years of World War II. Identifying marks indicate that this was one such tank.

Horseless cavalry
A World War II propaganda poster uses Medium tanks to emphasize how much the British Army had changed since World War I. By the 1940s, British cavalry regiments were mostly mechanized.

3-pounder main gun

Vickers .303 machine gun, one on either side of the hull

Regimental HQ tank tactical symbol

Metal track with cast links

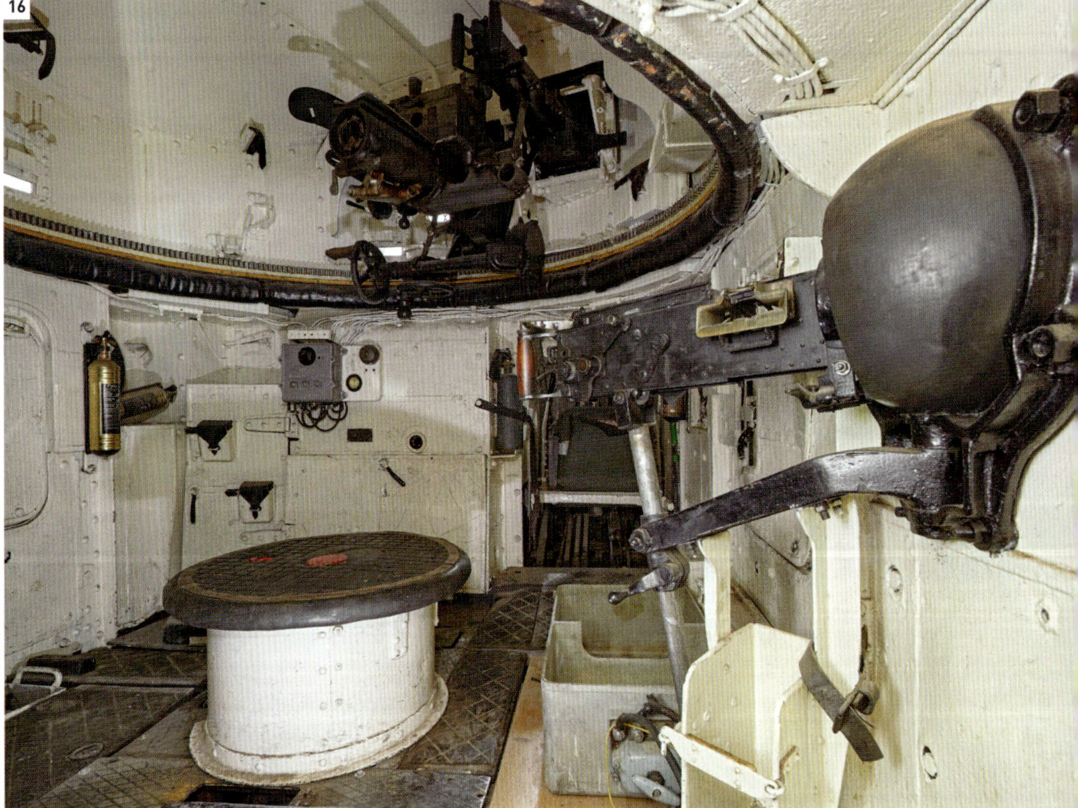

INTERIOR

Crew space inside the tank was relatively generous. The commander and main gunner occupied the turret, while the driver sat forward, beside the engine. Two more gunners, one on each side, operated the Vickers .303 hull machine guns, completing the five-man crew.

15. View through rear door **16.** Fighting compartment interior **17.** 3-pounder gun breach **18.** Vickers .303 machine gun **19.** Fire extinguisher **20.** Coaxial Vickers machine gun **21.** Hull machine-gun position **22.** Gun elevation wheel **23.** Turret traverse wheel **24.** Driver's position from above **25.** Driver's controls **26.** Manufacturer's date plate **27.** Engine oil gauge

EXTERIOR

The riveted armor-plate construction—just 0.25 in (6.35 mm) thick at the front—gave little protection against anything other than bullets. To compensate, crews of the Royal Tank Corps, formed in 1923, became expert at firing the 3-pounder gun while on the move, making it difficult for enemy gunners to target the fast, highly mobile Mediums.

1. HQ Command tank tactical sign **2.** Headlight **3.** Light shroud **4.** Driver's hatch **5.** Engine air intake **6.** Coaxial Vickers machine-gun mount **7.** Hull wall ball-mount Vickers machine gun **8.** Turret vision port **9.** Main armament sight aperture **10.** "Miter"-type commander's hatch **11.** Track tensioner **12.** Track return roller **13.** Exhaust **14.** Drive sprocket

The Age of Monoplanes

The lowest drag and highest efficiency for an aircraft is achieved with a monoplane (single-winged) design. Monoplane aircraft also have the advantage of being easier to build than biplanes. During World War I, a few monoplane aircraft saw action, such as Germany's Fokker Eindecker fighter, but it was not until the interwar period, when more powerful engines became available, that monoplane designs came to dominate. The greater power provided by the new engines generated sufficient airspeed and lift that a second wing—despite the additional surface area it gave—was unnecessary. Extra power also enabled more weight to be carried, which in turn facilitated new construction techniques, such as using riveted, thin metal sheets. By the late 1930s, most nations with a modern air force had introduced fast, low-wing monoplane fighters. When World War II broke out, the mass production of monoplanes such as the Hawker Hurricane and Messerschmitt Bf 109 became a priority for combatant nations.

British pilots of Fighter Command's No.111 Squadron make a practice "scramble" to board their Hawker Hurricane Mk.I aircraft from their base at RAF Northolt, London, on August 26, 1939.

△ **Bristol Bulldog**

Date 1929 **Origin** UK

Engine 440–490 hp (328–365 kW) Bristol Jupiter VII supercharged air-cooled 9-cylinder radial

Top speed 178 mph (287 km/h)

The Bristol Bulldog was the RAF's foremost interwar fighter. Fast, armed with twin guns, and with light bomb capability, Frank Barnwell's design was also cheap to maintain.

▽ **Polikarpov Po-2**

Date 1930 **Origin** USSR

Engine 125 hp (93 kW) Shvetsov M-11D air-cooled 5-cylinder radial

Top speed 94 mph (152 km/h)

Employed by the Soviets as trainers, night bombers, and reconnaissance and liaison aircraft in World War II, Nikolai Polikarpov's Po-2s proved difficult to shoot down. Over 40,000 Po-2s are thought to have been built.

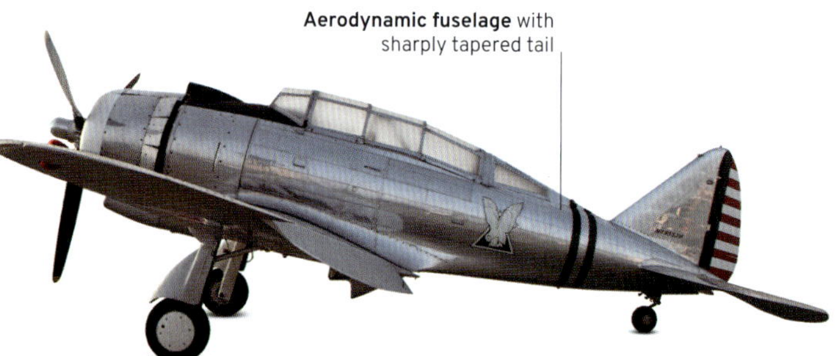

Aerodynamic fuselage with sharply tapered tail

△ **Seversky P-35/AT-12 Guardsman**

Date 1935 **Origin** USA

Engine 1,050 hp (783 kW) Pratt & Whitney R-1830-45 Twin Wasp air-cooled 14-cylinder radial

Top speed 290 mph (467 km/h)

The single-seat P-35 fighter was advanced for its time, with all-metal construction, retractable undercarriage, and an enclosed cockpit. This two-seat AT-12 was a trainer variant.

▷ **Dewoitine D27**

Date 1930 **Origin** France

Engine 425 hp (317 kW) Gnome-Rhone Jupiter VII air-cooled 9-cylinder radial

Top speed 194 mph (312 km/h)

Having moved to Switzerland in 1927, French aero-engineer Émile Dewoitine built 66 parasol-wing monoplane D27 fighters for the Swiss Air Force. The D27 was also built in Romania and Yugoslavia.

The Warplane Evolves

At the start of the 1930s, military aircraft still looked much like the fighting biplanes of late World War I. However, the decade saw rapid developments in warplane technology—especially from 1935, as war loomed again. Advanced monoplane wing designs, all-metal construction, monocoque fuselages, and enclosed cockpits became standard.

△ **Hawker Hurricane Mk1**

Date 1936 **Origin** UK

Engine 1,030 hp (768 kW) Rolls-Royce Merlin supercharged liquid-cooled V12

Top speed 328 mph (528 km/h)

Credited with 60 percent of RAF victories during World War II's Battle of Britain, Sydney Camm's Hurricane served in interceptor, fighter-bomber, night-fighter, and ground-attack roles.

△ Gloster Gladiator

Date 1936 **Origin** UK

Engine 830 hp (619 kW) Bristol Mercury IX air-cooled 9-cylinder radial

Top speed 255 mph (410 km/h)

The last biplane fighter to see frontline action with the RAF, the Gladiator took part in the 1940 defense of Malta. Though outdated, it served in the air forces of China, Finland, and numerous other countries.

△ Supermarine Spitfire MK1a

Date 1936 **Origin** UK

Engine 1,030–1,175 hp (768–876 kW) Rolls-Royce Merlin supercharged liquid-cooled V12

Top speed 360 mph (580 km/h)

Designer R. J. Mitchell's Spitfire, which first took to the skies in 1936, played a huge part in the Allies' aerial success during World War II. In all, 20,351 Spitfires were built, in 13 main variants.

△ Westland Lysander

Date 1936 **Origin** UK

Engine 810 hp (604 kW) Bristol Mercury XX supercharged air-cooled 9-cylinder radial

Top speed 212 mph (341 km/h)

During World War II, the Lysander earned a reputation for carrying out daring army missions, landing in fields at night behind enemy lines to insert or retrieve agents. A total of 1,786 were built.

△ Curtiss P-40 Warhawk

Date 1938 **Origin** USA

Engine 1,040 hp (776 kW) Allison V-1710 supercharged liquid-cooled V12

Top speed 360 mph (580 km/h)

In service throughout World War II, the Warhawk was respected for its agility, but it was not the fastest aircraft of its kind. Durable and cheap to make, the Warhawk served with 28 air forces. Production totaled 13,738.

▽ Messerschmitt Bf 109E

Date 1938 **Origin** Germany

Engine 1,000 hp (746 kW) DB601A supercharged liquid-cooled inverted V12

Top speed 355 mph (572 km/h)

Light, fast, and agile in flight—although tricky in takeoff—the all-metal Bf 109E was the foremost German fighter of its day. First flown in 1935, the early Bf 109 models saw combat during the Spanish Civil War.

World War II: Mass Mobility on Land

World War II was primarily a conflict of maneuvers. Armored fighting vehicles (AFVs) such as tanks and self-propelled guns paved the way for mechanized infantry units that went into battle in their own protected vehicles, particularly half-tracks. Elsewhere, trucks and light infantry vehicles delivered logistics and broader troop movement.

The mass mobility of World War II reflected two key trends. The first was the continuing improvement of the internal combustion engine, and the performance and reliability of the vehicles it powered. The other element was mass production: a great acceleration in manufacturing output that enabled military vehicles to be produced in enormous numbers. This surge in the number of vehicles resulted in a transformation of land warfare tactics, offering unprecedented possibilities for maneuvers and logistics.

Armor

The AFVs of World War I, primarily tanks and armored cars, had been an adjunct to infantry and artillery whose combat role was still very much evolving. In World War II, by contrast, AFVs were central to the maneuver-warfare tactics that were used on many fronts. Germany pioneered this form of warfare, having developed its Panzer arm technologically and tactically in the 1920s and 1930s to be the leading element of its newly mobile army. Wehrmacht Panzer units proved the efficacy of the tactics in the campaigns of 1939–41, spurring efforts by the rest of world to catch up or develop their own visions for armor. Tanks, self-propelled guns, and AFVs of all varieties subsequently proliferated at a scale unimaginable in World War I. At the Battle of Kursk in July–August 1943, for example, the Soviets and Germans fielded approximately 6,000 tanks.

Tank production
US factory workers assemble M3 Lee tanks during the early 1940s. The most mass-produced American tank was the M4 Sherman—more than 50,000 were made between 1942 and 1945.

The downside to this revolution in mobile armor was that AFVs placed a huge logistical burden on armies. By the last two years of the war, a US armored division required between 1,100 and 1,650 tons (1,000 and 1,500 tonnes) of supplies every day. The logistically robust Americans could cope with this demand, but the Axis forces were more stretched and increasingly struggled to maintain large armored units in the field.

Armored column
US-supplied M4 Sherman tanks of the 2nd French Armored Division form up in a powerful column ready for the advance through France during the summer of 1944. Supply trucks under camouflage netting line up beside them to deliver logistics.

Logistics

Horses were still used in significant numbers for logistical roles during World War II, particularly on the Eastern Front, but trucks and light vehicles changed the way armies moved their personnel and supplies. New generations of military trucks, such as the GMC CCKW-352 (US), Opel Blitz (Germany), and Bedford QL (UK), proved rugged and reliable workhorses. Crucial to their impact were the volumes in which they could be produced, and it was here that the Allies established an advantage. Germany produced around 346,000 trucks between 1939 and 1945, and Japan 166,000; Britain made 480,000 and the Soviet Union 197,000, but the US, which became an industrial behemoth during the war years, rolled out in excess of 2.3 million trucks. American vehicles provided through the Lend-Lease scheme became central to the wider Allied war effort; the Soviet Union alone received 400,000 US trucks, more than double its own total.

The Allies also dwarfed the Axis in the manufacture of AFVs: Germany produced 46,857 tanks and SP guns during the war, against the 88,410 manufactured by the US and 105,251

Logistics in action
A heavy US truck draws a mobile field kitchen through the bow doors of a Landing Ship, Tank (LST), during embarkation at an English port for the invasion of Normandy in June 1944.

> “The **higher** the concentration of tanks, the **faster, greater,** and more sweeping will be the **success.**”
>
> GENERALOBERST HEINZ GUDERIAN, IN *PANZER MARCSH*! (1937)

by the Soviet Union. Some historians have argued that American, Soviet, and British factories won the war.

Specialist vehicles

The motorization of armies spawned many specialist vehicles, including a wide array of engineering types largely dedicated to keeping the fleets of AFVs and trucks on the road. They included vehicles that could lay bridges and temporary roads, fill ditches and demolish obstacles, or recover disabled vehicles for return to repair depots.

Motor vehicles also performed a host of support and combat duties. They became mobile command posts, ambulances, radio trucks, workshops, flamethrowers, and antiaircraft platforms.

However, not all soldiers traveled into battle on vehicles. Even in the US Army, only five of many dozens of infantry divisions were classified as motorized divisions, although the supply chain was fully motorized. The humble infantryman, as ever, would travel long distances on his own two feet.

TALKING POINT

Blitzkrieg

A combined-arms approach to warfare was developed between the wars by German military thinkers such as Oswald Lutz, Erwin Rommel, and Heinz Guderian. Backed by mechanized infantry and air power, armored vanguards would make fast, deep breakthroughs at frontline weak points, bypass strongholds, and cause disruption in the enemy's rear.

The strategy, called *Blitzkrieg* (Lightning War) in the West and *Bewegungskrieg* (War of Movement) in Germany, worked well in Poland and Western Europe in 1939–40, but from June 1941 German forces became logistically overstretched across the vast distances of the Soviet Union.

Mock battle: Panzers and infantry take part in a demonstration of combined-arms warfare at the Nuremberg Nazi Party parade grounds in 1938.

Logistics Trains

The US, Britain, and Germany mass-produced freight locomotives during World War II. Inexpensively built yet powerful, these engines provided vital logistical support. In wartime, they transported countless troops and huge quantities of equipment, ammunition, and raw materials; in the war's aftermath, large numbers ran on European national railroads, either as replacements for lost stock or as war reparations. Many locomotives built for the United States Army Transportation Corps (USATC) were sent to Asia under lease-lend agreements and, after the war, by the UN Relief and Rehabilitation Administration (UNRAA).

△ LMS Stanier 8F

Date 1935 **Origin** UK
Wheel arrangement 2-8-0
Cylinders 2
Boiler pressure 225 psi (15.82 kg/sq cm)
Driving wheel diameter $56\frac{1}{4}$in (1,430 mm)
Top speed 60 mph (97 km/h)

The London, Midland & Scottish Railway's 8F was the standard British freight locomotive during the early part of World War II. Designed by William Stanier, it was deployed by the War Department in Egypt, Palestine, Iran, and Italy. Of the 852 built, 25 were sold to Turkey in 1941. LMS 8Fs stayed in British service until 1968, and in Turkey even into the 1980s.

△ Class V36 Shunter

Date 1937 **Origin** Germany
Wheel arrangement 0-6-0
Transmission Hydraulic
Engine Deutsche Werke/MAK diesel
Total power output 360 hp (268 kW)
Top speed 34 mph (55 km/h)

Class V36 diesels performed shunting duties for the Wehrmacht (German armed forces). Although fitted with four axles, they only had three pairs of driving wheels. After the war, the engines were used extensively in Europe and North Africa.

◁ USATC S100

Date 1942 **Origin** USA
Wheel arrangement 0-6-0
Cylinders 2
Boiler pressure 210 psi (14.8 kg/sq cm)
Driving wheel diameter 54 in (1,372 mm)
Top speed 31 mph (50 km/h)

Nearly 400 S100s built for the USATC were transported to Britain and used in Europe after the Allied invasion of France in June 1944; 15 were later bought as shunters by Britain's Southern Railway.

◁ USATC S160

Date 1942 **Origin** USA
Wheel arrangement 2-8-0
Cylinders 2
Boiler pressure 225 psi (15.82 kg/sq cm)
Driving wheel diameter 57 in (1,448 mm)
Top speed 40 mph (65 km/h)

The USATC commissioned 2,120 "austerity" (cheaper) versions of the Consolidation-type heavy freight locomotive; 800 were shipped to Britain for use in Europe after D-Day. S160s saw postwar service on many European railways, as well as in North Africa, China, India, and North and South Korea.

▷ DR Class 52 "Kriegslok"

Date 1942 **Origin** Germany
Wheel arrangement 2-10-0
Cylinders 2
Boiler pressure 232 psi (16.3 kg/sq cm)
Driving wheel diameter 55 in (1,400 mm)
Top speed 50 mph (80 km/h)

Deutsche Reichsbahn built about 7,000 of these heavy freight locomotives in World War II, primarily for Eastern Front service. A few working engines still operate in Bosnia today, and many others have been preserved, including this Class 52 No. 52.8184-5 rebuild.

△ Armored Car

Date 1942 **Origin** Germany	
Type	4-wheel
Capacity	130 (whole train)
Construction	Armor-plated steel
Railway	Wehrmacht

Railcars equipped with gun turrets, as on this replica, formed part of German BP42 armored trains that operated in the Balkans and Russia. Driven by an armor-clad Class 57 0-10-0 steam engine in the center, the trains comprised infantry, antiaircraft, and artillery wagons.

△ SR Class Q1

Date 1942 **Origin** UK	
Wheel arrangement	0-6-0
Cylinders	2 (inside)
Boiler pressure	230 psi (16.17 kg/sq cm)
Driving wheel diameter	61 in (1,549 mm)
Top speed	75 mph (120 km/h)

Shown here is No. C1, the first of a series of 40 wartime economy freight locomotives made for Britain's Southern Railway. Oliver Bulleid's lightweight design enabled the Class Q1 engines to operate over most of the company's rail network, and they remained in service on the Southern Region of British Railways until the 1960s.

▷ Indian Class AWE

Date 1943 **Origin** USA	
Wheel arrangement	2-8-2
Cylinders	2
Boiler pressure	210 psi (14.76 kg/sq cm)
Driving wheel diameter	$61\frac{1}{2}$ in (1,562 mm)
Top speed	62 mph (100 km/h)

The USATC commissioned Baldwin Locomotive Works to build a number of huge locomotives with 7-ft- (2,134-mm-) diameter boilers for hauling heavy freight trains in India. Forty of them became Indian Railways Class AWE engines. No. 22907 *Virat*, shown here, has been restored to working order at the Rewari Steam Loco Shed.

△ WD Austerity

Date 1943 **Origin** UK	
Wheel arrangement	2-8-0
Cylinders	2
Boiler pressure	225 psi (15.82 kg/sq cm)
Driving wheel diameter	$56\frac{1}{2}$ in (1,435 mm)
Top speed	45 mph (72 km/h)

This austerity version of the LMS 8F freighter, designed by R. A. Riddles, was ordered by Britain's War Department—hence the designation "WD." After D-Day, many were put to work in mainland Europe. Of 935 engines built, 733 saw postwar service with British Railways; others operated in the Netherlands, Hong Kong, and Sweden.

Bren gun
mounted on sidecar

△ **Norton Big Four SWD**

Date 1938 **Origin** UK

Engine 633 cc, side-valve single-cylinder

Top speed 65 mph (105 km/h)

Norton's sidecar outfit—a personnel, ammunition, and gun carrier—had good mobility over uneven terrain, since both its rear and sidecar wheel were driven.

◁ **Velocette MAC-MDD**

Date 1940 **Origin** UK

Engine 349 cc, ohv single-cylinder

Top speed 75 mph (120 km/h)

The MAC-MDD was militarized for a canceled French army order that was subsequently taken over by the British. It was succeeded by the improved MAP, used by the RAF.

△ **Harley-Davidson Model U US Navy version**

Date 1940 **Origin** USA

Engine 1,213 cc, side-valve V-twin

Top speed 75 mph (120 km/h)

Supplied in limited numbers to the US Army, and later the US Navy (for shore patrol), during World War II, Harley's U range had a higher specification and bigger capacity than its WLA models.

◁ **Zündapp KS750**

Date 1941 **Origin** Germany

Engine 751 cc, ohv flat-twin

Top speed 59 mph (95 km/h)

The KS750 had eight forward gears and two reverse, plus a driven sidecar wheel that permitted cross-country travel. It carried three soldiers plus weaponry.

▽ **Triumph 3TW**

Date 1940 **Origin** UK

Engine 349 cc, ohv parallel-twin

Top speed 70 mph (113 km/h)

This light, nippy army motorcycle never entered service, since the only batch made was destroyed when Triumph's Coventry factory was bombed in 1940.

Military Motorcycles

In the military, motorcycles were most often used for delivering messages and orders, especially when no other means of communication was available. Despatch riders needed robust, reliable machines that could handle difficult terrain and—because some riders were inexperienced—were simple to use. Military motorcycles were typically no-frills versions of existing civilian models fitted with accessories to suit their military use, such as racks, special lighting equipment, sump guards, and, in some cases, even gun mountings or holsters.

▽ Matchless G3/L North Africa version

Date 1941 **Origin** UK
Engine 347 cc, ohv single-cylinder
Top speed 70 mph (113 km/h)

The G3/L's hydraulically damped telescopic forks were a significant improvement on other British military motorcycles. This example is painted for desert service.

▽ Harley-Davidson WLA

Date 1942 **Origin** USA
Engine 739 cc, side-valve V-twin
Top speed 65 mph (105 km/h)

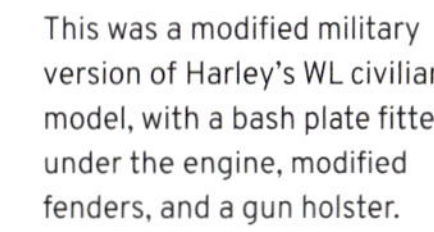

This was a modified military version of Harley's WL civilian model, with a bash plate fitted under the engine, modified fenders, and a gun holster.

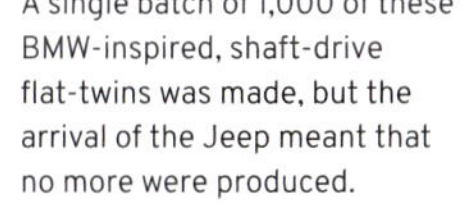

▽ Harley-Davidson XA

Date 1942 **Origin** USA
Engine 738 cc, side-valve flat-twin
Top speed 65 mph (105 km/h)

A single batch of 1,000 of these BMW-inspired, shaft-drive flat-twins was made, but the arrival of the Jeep meant that no more were produced.

△ Triumph 3HW

Date 1941 **Origin** UK
Engine 343 cc, ohv single-cylinder
Top speed 70 mph (115 km/h)

After its Coventry site was bombed, Triumph built a new factory at nearby Meriden, where it made more than 30,000 military 3HWs, based on its civilian Tiger 80.

△ Harley-Davidson WLC

Date 1942 **Origin** USA
Engine 739 cc, side-valve V-twin
Top speed 65 mph (105 km/h)

The WLC was a version of Harley's WLA made for the Canadian military. Harley supplied around 90,000 bikes to Allied forces during World War II.

△ NSU Kettenkrad HK 101

Date 1940 **Origin** Germany
Engine 1,478 cc, ohv in-line four
Top speed 44 mph (70 km/h)

Widely used in Germany's 1941 Russian campaign, the handlebar-steered Kettenkrad resembled a motorcycle/half-track hybrid. It carried troops and loads over rough terrain.

Harley-Davidson WLC

Rugged, practical, and utterly dependable, Harley-Davidson's WL military motorcycles were some of World War II's finest mechanical workhorses. Most of these 739cc V-twins were used by the US armed forces in WLA form, but a significant number, designated WLCs, were adopted by the Canadian military. Thanks to the simplicity of Harley's side-valve engine, the WLC, and its US cousin, the WLA, were well able to withstand the demands of wartime operation.

IN 1937, Milwaukee-based Harley-Davidson launched its W-series of motorcycles with V-twin engines (two cylinders in a V-configuration sharing a common crankshaft). Three years later, it turned its attention to manufacturing motorcycles for the US Army. The W-series bikes were an obvious choice for military adaptation due to the uncomplicated nature of their side-valve power plants. Among the specifications for the army's WLA variant were drab olive-camouflage paint, blackout lighting, longer forks for rough-terrain riding, and—on some examples—a rifle holster on the front forks.

When British manufacturers Norton and BSA found themselves struggling to meet the demand for military bikes from Britain and Canada, Harley stepped in to bridge the gap. The WLC, a close variant of the WLA, was produced for Canadian forces between 1941 and 1944. It was used at the Normandy landings and in many other key conflict zones across Europe. By the war's end, more than 80,000 WLA and WLC bikes had been deployed by the Allies, with both versions recognized as valuable combat motorcycles. Many continued to be used by civilians in the postwar years.

Toolbox holds spanners and other repair equipment

Rear marker light mounted on fender

Rear rack for attaching panniers

Olive-drab paint with nonreflective matte finish

Blackout bike
A "blackout kit" was carried by Canadian Army riders of the WLC. It contained shrouds that could be fitted to the front and rear lights to direct light downward in blackout conditions. Small marker lights were mounted on the front and rear fenders to compensate.

SPECIFICATIONS	
Model	Harley-Davidson WLC, 1942
Assembly	Milwaukee, USA
Production	More than 80,000
Construction	Tubular cradle frame
Engine	739 cc, side valve V-twin
Power output	23 hp (17 kW)
Transmission	Three-speed
Suspension	Leading-link front forks, rigid rear
Brakes	Drums, front and rear
Maximum speed	65 mph (105 km/h)

FRONT VIEW

REAR VIEW

Dash panel sits on top of fuel tank

Large saddle compensates for lack of rear suspension

Marker light for use in blackouts

Raised fenders stop mud from clogging the wheels

Crash bars protect both rider and machine in the event of an accident

BIKE

Adaptations to transform Harley-Davidson's civilian W Series of "flathead" V-twins into WL military bikes included revising Harley's traditional leading-link forks to give greater ground clearance, as well as adding footboards and protective crash bars. The Canadian WLC variant also differed in having an alternative throttle-lever position, an auxiliary clutch hand lever, and interchangeable wheels.

1. Identification number **2.** Horn **3.** Fork spring **4.** Speedometer **5.** Gear change **6.** Headlamp mask revealing only a small rectangle of light **7.** Kick-starter **8.** Rear sprocket **9.** Front marker lamp **10.** Data plate attached to top of tank **11.** Clutch control **12.** Front fork ride-adjuster knob **13.** Canadian emblem displayed on either side of tank **14.** Rear lights **15.** Fuel filler

1

2

3

8

9

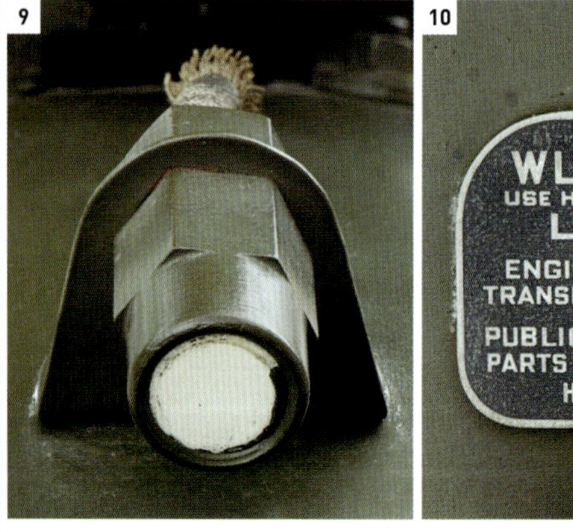

10

16

ENGINE

Ease of maintenance in combat conditions, due to the absence of moving parts in the cylinder head, was key to the military success of Harley's side-valve (or "flathead") V-twin engine. Reliability was enhanced by an oil-bath air filter to keep out dust, grit, or sand, and an upgraded lubrication system.

16. Rugged side-valve engine **17.** Ignition timing unit **18.** Inlet manifold **19.** Carburettor float chamber **20.** Air intake hose

Trucks, Half-tracks, and Light Vehicles

During World War II, a host of trucks, half-tracks, cars, and other light vehicles provided essential logistical support. They enabled the vast Allied and Axis-power armies to function, and allowed tanks and other armored vehicles to be as effective as they were on the battlefield. Auxiliary personnel now began to outnumber troops in frontline roles for the first time in military history. Specific models in this plethora of vehicles could come in a wide range of variants, with each version designed to suit a particular military role or situation.

△ SdKfz 251-8 Ausf C Half-track

Date 1940 **Origin** Germany
Weight 8.6 tons (7.8 tonnes)
Engine Maybach HL 42 6-cylinder 100 hp (74.6 kW) gasoline engine
Top speed 33 mph (52.5 km/h)

This half-track initially entered service with the German Army as an armored personnel carrier. It proved so successful that it spawned at least 22 variants, including the 251-8 battlefield ambulance shown here, as well as rocket-launcher, antiaircraft, and anti-tank versions.

△ M3A1 Scout Car

Date 1940 **Origin** US
Weight 4.4 tons (4.03 tonnes)
Engine Hercules JXD 6-cylinder 110 hp (82 kW) gasoline engine
Top speed 55 mph (89 km/h)

Poor off-road mobility limited the effectiveness of this light armored car, which was used to support American mechanized formations. The half-tracks that succeeded it, however, incorporated the best design features of the M3A1.

△ Austin K3

Date 1940 **Origin** UK
Weight 5.8 tons (5.3 tonnes)
Engine Straight 6-cylinder gasoline, 60 hp (45 kW)
Top speed 50 mph (80 km/h)

Around 17,000 K3s were built, most serving as supply trucks, ambulances, and fire engines. Many vehicles were abandoned at Dunkirk in 1940. Robust and reliable, K3s also saw action in North Africa.

Engine hood
Windscreen (folded forward)
Large steering wheel gave more leverage to turn the wheels
Safety straps secure the doorways
DORCAS
Wheel with four-wheel-drive transmission

△ Willys MB "Jeep"

Date 1941 **Origin** US
Weight 1.14 tons (1.04 tonnes)
Engine Willys 4-cylinder 60 hp (45 kW) gasoline engine
Top speed 55 mph (89 kph)

Rugged and highly versatile, Willys' four-wheel-drive general purpose vehicle was commonly known as a jeep. This iconic World War II vehicle had space for a crew of four.

▷ GMC CCKW 352

Date 1941 **Origin** USA	
Weight 4.4 tons (4 tonnes)	
Engine 6-cylinder petrol, 104 hp (77.5 kW)	
Top speed 45 mph (72 km/h)	

Featuring the cab of a 1930s Chevrolet, this truck and its variants were widely used by US and Allied forces in World War II. Its many roles included fuel transportation, mobile surgery, radio communications, and more.

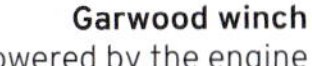

Garwood winch powered by the engine

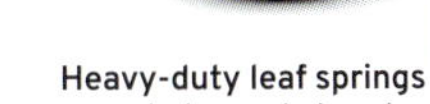

Heavy-duty leaf springs between twin axles

Desert/Normandy camouflage colors

△ Opel Blitz

Date 1942 **Origin** Germany	
Weight 2.3–3.7 tons (2.1–3.35 tonnes)	
Engine 6-cylinder gasoline, 55 hp (41 kW)	
Top speed 50 mph (80 km/h)	

The most widely used and successful of all World War II German trucks was the Blitz. Thanks to its nimble size and the ready availability of spares, it saw action in all theaters in its cargo and 88 mm-gun versions.

▽ Schwimmwagen

Date 1942 **Origin** Germany	
Weight 2,006 lb (910 kg)	
Engine 4-cylinder air-cooled 25 hp (18.4 kW) gasoline engine	
Top speed 50 mph (80 km/h); 6 mph (10 km/h) on water	

The Schwimmwagen (swimming car) was an amphibious four-wheel-drive vehicle derived from the Volkswagen. In water, it was propelled by a screw propeller at the rear, while the front wheels acted as rudders.

Fold-down windscreen

Tow hook

Watertight hull

Paddle in case of engine failure

Spare wheel

Leaf suspension

▽ M5 Half-track

Date 1942 **Origin** US	
Weight 10.2 tons (9.3 tonnes)	
Engine International Harvester RED-450-B 6-cylinder 141 hp (105 kW) gasoline engine	
Top speed 42 mph (68 km/h)	

During World War II, the US used more than 40,000 half-tracks of various specifications. These vehicles provided mobility and protection for troops in combat situations. The M5, shown here, differed little from the M3, its more famous cousin.

Rear machine gun

Haversacks slung over external rail

Fuel can

Caterpillar tracks

1-HQ4

Rise of the "Jeep"

In the early 1930s, the US Army looked at the British Army's conversion of the small Austin 7 car into a "military tourer" and saw the potential for a tough but lightweight vehicle that could act as a battlefield runabout. Underfunded at the time, the US military concentrated on civilian trucks that could be used in wartime, but nothing quite matched its requirement for a four-wheel drive "light reconnaissance vehicle" with a 0.3 ton (0.27 tonne) payload. So, in summer 1940 a group of manufacturers, including Bantam, Willys, and Ford, along with US Army engineers, put together the design that became known as the "Jeep." More than 600,000 Jeeps were made for the US Army and its allies, including 50,000 for the Soviet Red Army. General George C. Marshall, Chief of Staff of the US Army, called the Jeep "America's greatest contribution to modern warfare," and it is widely regarded as a design and engineering classic.

Columns of Jeeps head a parade of US Army troops along the Champs Élysées in Paris on August 28, 1944, to celebrate the city's liberation.

Axis Tanks

After Hitler's Nazi Party came to power in 1933, Germany flouted international restrictions and began openly building tanks. The experience gained in tank technology enabled the Germans to produce formidable tank designs in World War II, although some models were plagued by mechanical issues. The German tank manufacturers were unable to exploit the mass production methods used in Allied countries, since their vehicles were costly and time-consuming to build. Some effective tanks had been built by Italy and Japan, Germany's Axis partners, in the 1930s, but they were not improved sufficiently as the war progressed, and were soon surpassed by more advanced Allied vehicles.

△ Panzerkampfwagen I Ausf A

Date 1934 **Origin** Germany

Weight 6.1 tons (5.5 tonnes)

Engine Krupp M305 gasoline, 57 hp (43 kW)

Main armament 2 x 7.92 mm MG13 machine guns

The two-man Panzer I was designed as a training vehicle. The Ausf A model shown here, though underpowered and not really suited for combat roles, was ideal for instructing tank crews. Due to a shortage of other tanks, Panzer I variants did ultimately see action in Spain, Poland, France, Denmark, Norway, Russia, and North Africa.

△ Type 95 Ha-Go

Date 1936 **Origin** Japan

Weight 8.3 tons (7.5 tonnes)

Engine Mitsubishi 6-cylinder diesel, 110 hp (82 kW)

Main armament 37 mm Type 98 gun

Popular with crews, the Type 95's lightweight construction gave good mobility on difficult terrain, and its engine was powerful for its size. Despite success against Chinese forces in the late 1930s and in the early Japanese campaigns of 1942, the Type 95 found itself outclassed when Allied tanks entered the fray. It served on the front line until the war's end.

△ Panzerkampfwagen IV

Date 1936 **Origin** Germany

Weight 27.6 tons (25 tonnes)

Engine Maybach HL 120 TRM 12-cylinder gasoline, 224 kW (300 hp)

Main armament 75 mm KwK 40 main gun

Originally an infantry support vehicle, the five-man Panzer IV went through a series of improvements to its armor and firepower that eventually turned it into an impressive main battle tank. The Panzer IV was the only German tank to remain in service throughout World War II.

△ Panzer 38(t) Ausf E

Date 1938 **Origin** Czechoslovakia

Weight 11 tons (10 tonnes)

Engine Praga EPA gasoline, 125 hp (93 kW)

Main armament 3.7 cm KwK 38(t) L/47.8 gun

Acknowledging that the Czech Panzer 38(t) was superior to its own Panzers I and II, Germany continued 38(t) production after annexing Czechoslovakia. The 1,400-plus German 38(t)s built saw action in France, Poland, and the Soviet Union until 1942. The chassis was reused in several tank destroyers.

△ **Panzerkampfwagen III Ausf L**

Date 1939 **Origin** Germany
Weight 25.9 tons (23.5 tonnes)
Engine Maybach HL 120 TRM 12-cylinder gasoline, 300 hp (224 kW)
Main armament 50 mm KwK 39 main gun

The Panzer III was Germany's main battle tank at the start of World War II. By the end of 1941, it was clear that it could not hold its own against the Soviet T-34. It was eventually relegated to minor combat roles, but the chassis was used for other armored vehicles. This Ausf M mark had a crew of 5.

Breda 38 machine guns

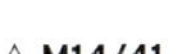

△ **M14/41**

Date 1940 **Origin** Italy
Weight 16 tons (14.5 tonnes)
Engine SPA 15T M41 diesel, 145 hp (108 kW)
Main armament 47 mm M35 L/32 gun

Lessons learned from deploying tanks in the Spanish Civil War enabled Italy to design a new generation of vehicles, which first saw action in North Africa in 1940. The well-armed M14/41 was a version of the M13/40 upgraded and optimized for desert use. The deficiency of its armor became apparent when exposed to the fire of Allied 2-pounders.

Three-man turret for commander, gunner, and loader (with driver and radio operator in hull)

◁ **Panther**

Date 1943 **Origin** Germany
Weight 51 tons (46.2 tonnes)
Engine Maybach HL230P30 V12 gasoline, 690 hp (515 kW)
Main armament 7.5 cm KwK 42 L/70 gun

First used in July 1943 at Kursk, the speedy, maneuverable Panther had a very accurate, powerful gun and strong frontal armor. It was better protected and more potent than the T-34, which it was designed to counter. Like the Tiger, it was dogged by mechanical problems, and engine fires were common.

Interleaved wheel arrangement made maintenance more difficult

Spare track links fastened to turret

Steel hawser for towing

Armor sloped variably between 25 and 50 degrees

◁ **Tiger II (King Tiger)**

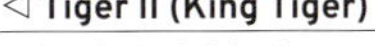

Date 1944 **Origin** Germany
Weight 76.2 tons (69.1 tonnes)
Engine Maybach HL230P30 V12 gasoline, 690 hp (515 kW)
Main armament 8.8 cm KwK 43 L/71

With an 8.8 cm gun that was a threat even at long range, and frontal armor that could resist all Allied anti-tank weapons, the Tiger II was perhaps the most powerful tank in World War II. Engine unreliability hampered its effectiveness, while low production figures—only 489 were built—limited its impact.

Tiger I

With its powerful 88 mm gun, thick frontal armor, wide tracks, and enormous size, Germany's Tiger tank gained a fearsome reputation among Allied forces on the battlefields of World War II. Although the Tiger was dogged by technical glitches, it had an immense psychological effect on its opponents, and it remains the most mythologized tank of the war.

IN MAY 1941, after German weaponry had failed to pierce the armor of British Matilda 2 and French Char B tanks, Hitler ordered the production of a heavy tank. The result was the Tiger. It resembled earlier German tanks in its boxy shape and layout but was super-sized, weighing more than two Panzer IVs. This massive tank provided a stable platform for the accurate 88 mm KwK 36 gun, for which it carried 92 rounds. During production, the engine was upgraded from 650 hp (485 kW) to 700 hp (522 kW), but engine and transmission still struggled with the vast weight, which reached 63.75 tons (57.9 tonnes) instead of the planned 55 tons (50 tonnes).

Rushed into service, the Tiger experienced a variety of teething problems that, combined with high manufacturing costs and a shortage of skilled crews, compromised its tactical effectiveness. It failed to have the desired battlefield impact: rather than punching through enemy lines as intended, it was mainly used defensively. However, its prowess was undeniable—even in this defensive role, it instilled terror in Allied tank crews.

SPECIFICATIONS	
Model	PzKpfw VI Tiger Ausf E
Date	1942
Origin	Germany
Production	1,347
Weight	63.75 tons (57.9 tonnes)
Main armament	88 mm KwK 36
Engine	Maybach HL210P45 V12 gasoline, 650 hp (485 kW)
Secondary armament	7.92 mm MG34
Armor thickness	4.75 in (120 mm) max

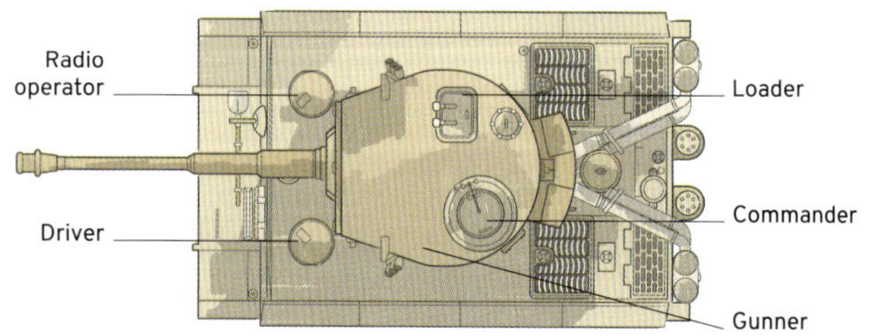

Prized capture
Tiger 131, pictured here after restoration to running order, is an early example, equipped with the original HL210P45 engine rather than the later, more powerful version. It was seized by the Allies in Tunisia in April 1943 and, being the first complete Tiger captured, taken to Britain for extensive analysis.

FRONT VIEW

REAR VIEW

131 deciphered
The number "131" reveals that this Tiger belonged to the 1st Company, the 3rd Platoon of its tank regiment, and that it was the 1st tank of its platoon.

Interleaved road wheels help to distribute weight evenly

EXTERIOR

Copying earlier German half-track designs, the road wheels are arranged in an interleaved fashion, in order to spread the immense weight of the tank. Suspension is provided by 16 torsion bars, with eight arms on either side, each arm holding three wheels. This arrangement required nine wheels to be removed in order to replace one of the inner wheels. The tank's size led to innovations such as removing outer road wheels and fitting thinner transport tracks for train travel. This tank, Tiger 131, still bears battle scars from the day of its capture.

1. National recognition symbol **2.** Driver's vision port **3.** Turret lifting lug **4.** Smoke grenade dischargers **5.** Radio operator's machine gun **6.** Track toolbox **7.** Towing cables and wire cutters on hull **8.** Feifel air filter tubes **9.** Drive sprocket and interleaved road wheels **10.** Commander's hatch **11.** Turret pistol port

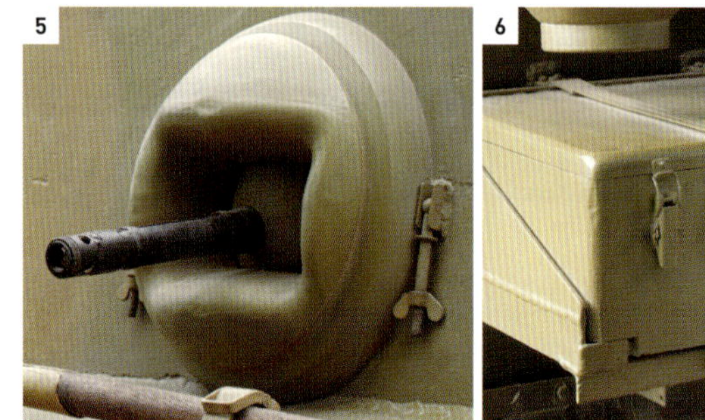

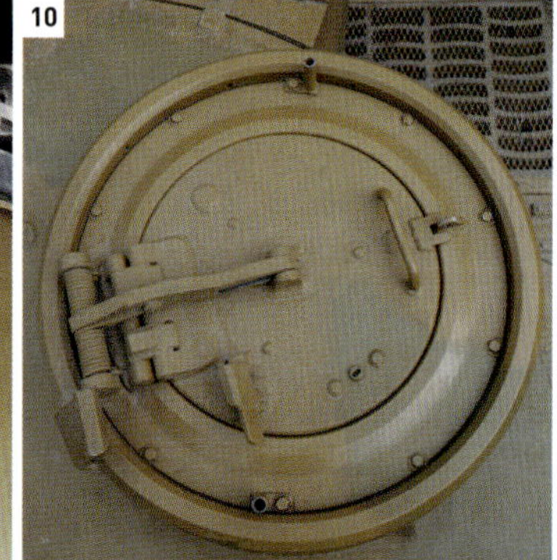

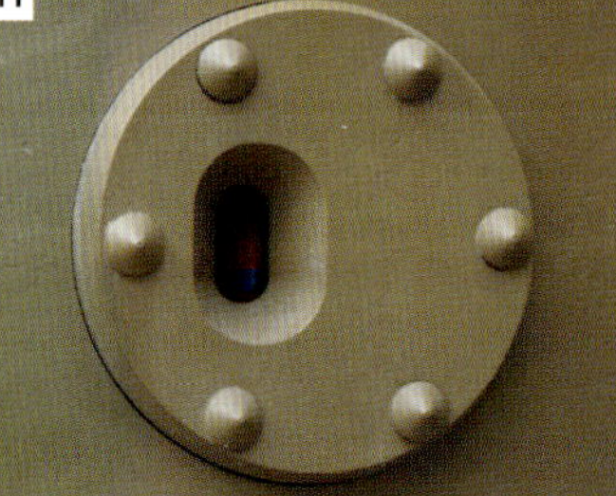

INTERIOR

The driver was stationed in the front of the main hull, to the left. On his right sat the radio operator, who operated the ball-mounted machine gun. On the turret's left-side, to the rear, sat the commander, with the gunner in front of him; the loader occupied the space to their right.

12. Looking down into commander's position **13.** Turret traverse wheel **14.** Commander's periscope **15.** Loader's position and main gun breech **16.** Driver's controls and vision port **17.** Binocular gunsight **18.** Gun recoil return gauge **19.** Turret side vision port **20.** Driver's instrument panel **21.** Barrel elevation wheel **22.** Codriver's machine gun

Allied Tanks

Although Allied tanks seldom reached the technical standard of their German counterparts, they were easier to mass produce. This was especially true of the American M4 Sherman, which played a key role in defeating German forces in Western Europe. Like other US Army tanks, it was robust and well built. In the 1930s, France produced some capable tanks, but it failed to use them effectively when Germany invaded in 1940. British tanks were often inadequate in combat situations, although later tanks such as the Comet performed well on the battlefield.

△ SOMUA S35

Date 1936 **Origin** France
Weight 21.5 tons (19.5 tonnes)
Engine SOMUA V-8 gasoline, 190 hp (142 kW)
Main armament 47 mm SA 35 L/32 gun

The three-man S35 equipped France's cavalry divisions. Its cast-steel armor gave better protection than riveted panels. The commander in the one-man turret had to load, aim, and fire the powerful gun, as well as instruct the crew.

Engine exhaust pipe
One-man turret
47 mm anti-tank gun
Metal tracks

△ Char B1 bis

Date 1936 **Origin** France
Weight 34.7 tons (31.5 tonnes)
Engine Renault 6-cylinder gasoline, 307 hp (229 kW)
Main armament 1 x 75 mm ABS 1929 SA 35 L/17.1 howitzer, 1 x 47 mm SA 35 L/32 gun

The most powerful French tank in 1940, the B1 bis mainly supported infantry. It carried a 75 mm howitzer for firing high explosives against enemy fortifications, and a turret-mounted anti-tank gun. The tank was prone to mechanical problems, and its heavy armor—up to 2⅓ in (60 mm) thick—limited both speed and range.

▷ Valentine Mark II

Date 1940 **Origin** UK
Weight 18 tons (16.3 tonnes)
Engine AEC Type 190 diesel, 131 hp (98 kW)
Main armament QF 2-pounder gun

The Valentine was the most-produced British tank of World War II, with more than 7,000 entering service. Some later versions replaced the 2-pounder gun with a 6-pounder. Used in North Africa, the Pacific, and Eastern Europe, this versatile tank spawned many specialized variants, including a bridge-layer and a flamethrower.

△ M3 Grant

Date 1941 **Origin** USA
Weight 30 tons (27.2 tonnes)
Engine Continental R-975 gasoline, 340 hp (254 kW)
Main armament 1 x 75 mm M2 gun, 1 x 37 mm M5 gun

The M3 arose from the US Army's urgent need for a tank with a 75 mm gun. Waiting for a suitable turret design would delay production, so the gun was mounted in a sponson on the M3's hull, which limited the field of fire. The M3, known as the Lee in the US, used the successful engine and suspension from the M2 medium tank. British M3s, called Grants, had a modified turret.

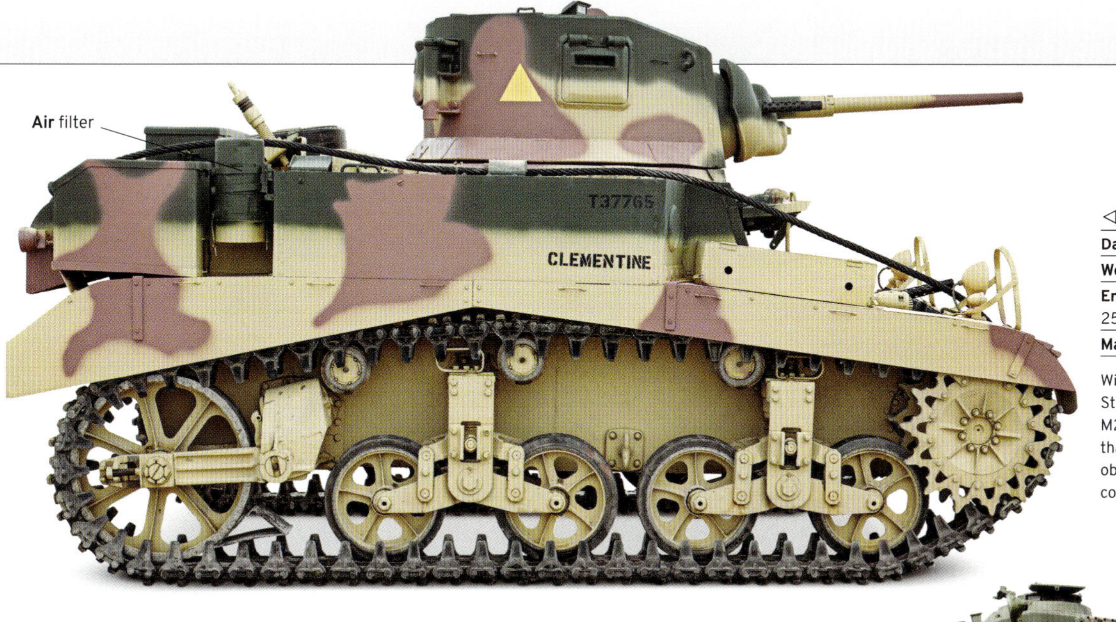

◁ M3A1 Stuart

Date 1942 **Origin** USA
Weight 14.2 tons (12.9 tonnes)
Engine Continental W-670 9A gasoline, 250 hp (186 kW)
Main armament 37 mm M6 L/56.6 gun

Widely used by the Allied powers in World War II, the Stuart was an improved version of the 37 mm-armed M2A4. It benefited from mass production techniques that made it reliable and easy to repair. Although obsolete as an offensive weapon by 1944, the Stuart continued to serve in a reconnaissance role.

Low-profile turret

VICTOR

△ Comet

Date 1944 **Origin** UK
Weight 36.9 tons (33.5 tonnes)
Engine Rolls-Royce Meteor Mark III V12 gasoline, 600 hp (447 kW)
Main armament 77 mm HV gun

Developed from the earlier Cromwell, the Comet was more heavily armored than its predecessor but equally mobile due to superior suspension. Arguably the best British tank of the war, it reached the front lines in limited numbers in early 1945, where its 77 mm gun proved effective against German Panthers and Tigers.

▽ M4A1 Sherman

Date 1942 **Origin** USA
Weight 33.4 tons (30.3 tonnes)
Engine Continental R-975 gasoline, 400 hp (298 kW)
Main armament 75 mm M3 L/40 gun

The M4 Sherman was the most important tank fielded by the Allies, equipping the armored divisions of the US and Britain. It used the chassis from the M3 topped by a turret for the 75 mm gun. The M4A1, the first standard production Sherman, had a cast hull; the tank shown here was the second ever produced and is the oldest survivor.

Pistol port

ICHAEL

T 74195

Track links

90 mm gun

Air vent

△ M26 Pershing

Date 1945 **Origin** USA
Weight 46.2 tons (41.9 tonnes)
Engine Ford GAF V8 gasoline, 500 hp (373 kW)
Main armament 90 mm M3 L/53 gun

The powerful 90 mm gun of the M26 Pershing was effective against the German Panther and Tiger, but the tank's protracted development and production meant that only 20 vehicles reached Europe in time to see combat. The Pershing used the same engine as the M4A3 Sherman variant, but its great weight left it underpowered.

M4 Sherman

Although under-armored and lacking a powerful enough gun to successfully take on the heavier German Panthers and Tigers, the Sherman was faster and had the supreme advantage of quantity through mass production. In the breakout from Normandy in 1944, American Shermans showed what they could do, sweeping across France at full tilt in large numbers, their progress halted only by supply issues.

THE M4 SHERMAN was designed in 1940 as the successor to the M3 Lee medium tank. US military strategy at the time saw tanks primarily as armored cavalry that could dash through a breach in opposing formations and cause mayhem behind enemy lines. The speedy Sherman met these criteria perfectly. It was also robust, reliable, and easy to maintain. The Sherman made its combat debut in Egypt at the Second Battle of El Alamein in October 1942, and rapidly proved well suited to the rigors of war.

Eleven different plants across the US built the Sherman, most of them with no previous experience of tank manufacture. Together, these factories produced sufficient tanks—63,181, including derivatives—to equip the US, British and Commonwealth, Russian, and other Allied armies. Shermans continued to operate in many national armies after World War II and were still serving in Paraguay as recently as 2016.

SPECIFICATIONS	
Name	M4A1 Sherman
Date	1940
Origin	USA
Production	49,234
Weight	33.3 tons (30.2 tonnes)
Main armament	75 mm M3
Engine	Wright-Continental R-975 radial gasoline, 400 hp (298 kW)
Secondary armament	.30 Browning M1919 machine guns
Armor thickness	4½ in (118mm) max

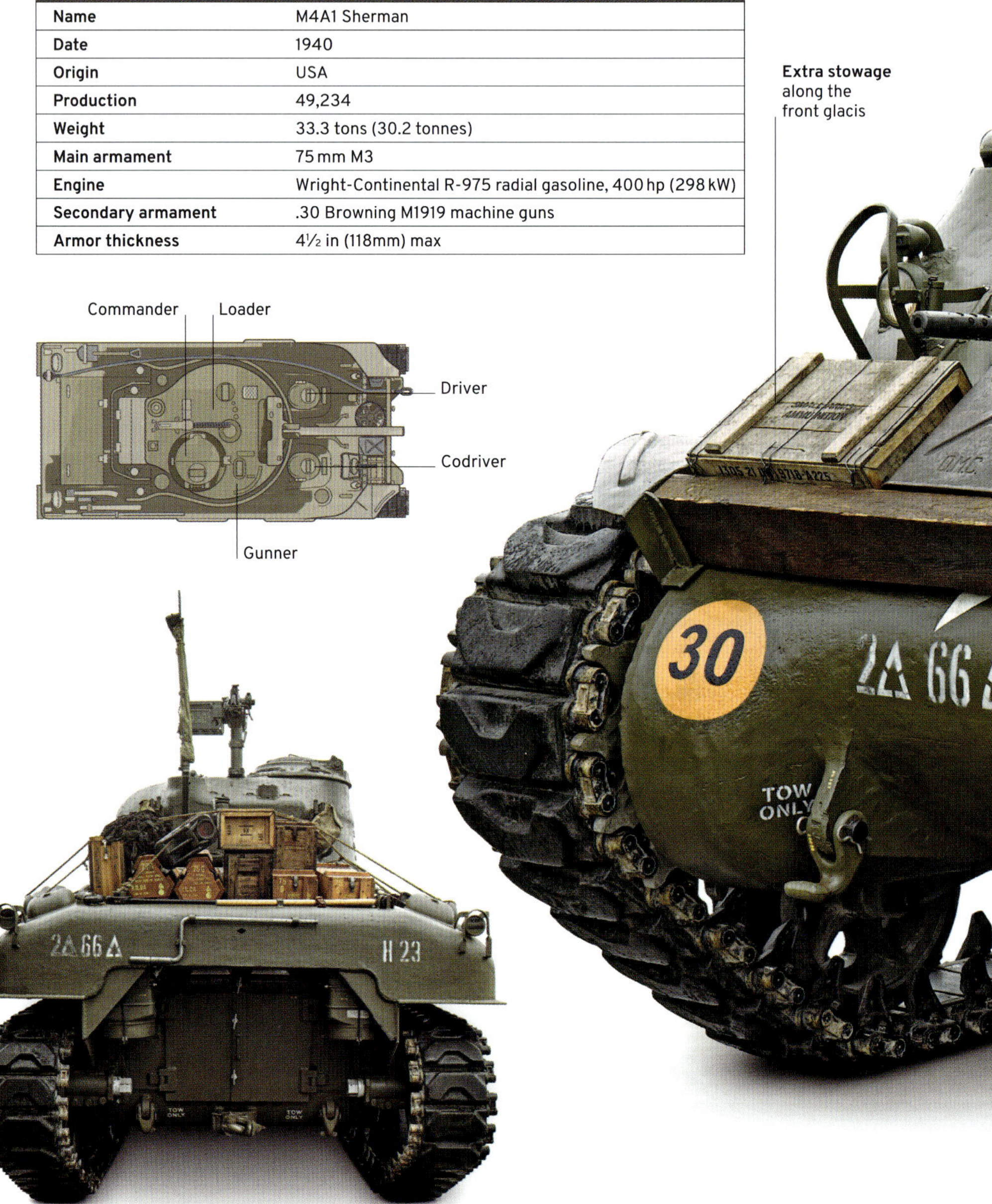

REAR VIEW

FRONT VIEW

From Ohio to France
With 11 different factories manufacturing the Sherman around four main engine types, there was considerable variation between models. This M4A1, built in 1943 by the Lima tank works of Ohio, has upgraded armor. The tank served with US forces in World War II and was subsequently used as a training vehicle by the French Army.

75 mm medium-velocity gun (later upgraded to 76 mm)

Gun mantlet

Barrel clamp

Rubber-blocked track

Additional side armor

Hull is cast rather than welded

"Havoc"
The initial letter of a tank's name indicated the company to which it belonged. This tank bears the markings H Company, 66 Armored Regiment, 2nd US Armored Division.

INTERIOR

Although later models included a second hatch, this M4A1 has the early turret design, which required commander, gunner, and loader to utilize the same hatch. Vision ports in the cupola gave the commander an all-round view of the battlefield from within the tank.

1. Looking down into the commander's position **2.** Commander's vision cupola block **3.** SCR 508 radio set **4.** Turret interior showing commander's and gunner's positions **5.** 75mm ammunition **6.** 75mm gunsight **7.** Azimuth indicator **8.** Coaxial machine gun **9.** Main gun breech **10.** Main gun elevation wheel **11.** Driver's instrument panel **12.** Driver's hatch **13.** Driver's position

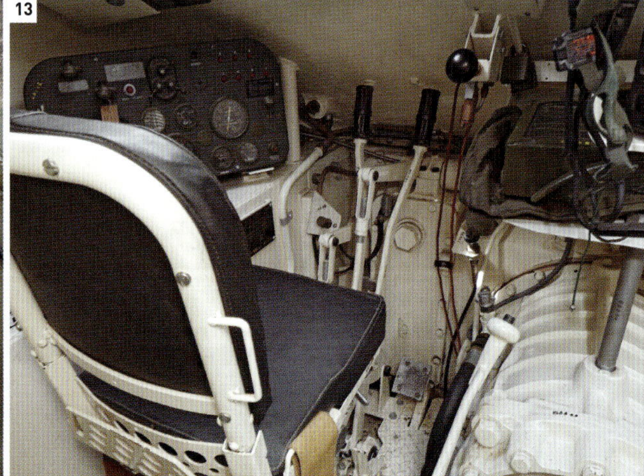

14

15

16

EXTERIOR

Analysis showed that stowed ammunition caused more fires, or "brew-ups," than the engine. Protecting ammunition was thus vital: extra side armor on the cast hull of this M4A1 helped to shield ammunition inside the tank. "Wet" ammunition storage (surrounding shell racks with water-filled jackets) was introduced on later models as an additional safeguard. Other modifications as the war progressed included wider tracks and an upgraded 76 mm gun.

17

14. Allied Forces recognition symbol **15.** Headlamp **16.** Tow hook **17.** Codriver's machine gun **18.** Armored roof fan cover **19.** Driver's periscope **20.** Driver's hatch (closed) **21.** Paired road wheels **22.** Front drive sprocket **23.** Spotlight **24.** Air filter **25.** Turret hatch and commander's cupola **26.** Engine with doors open

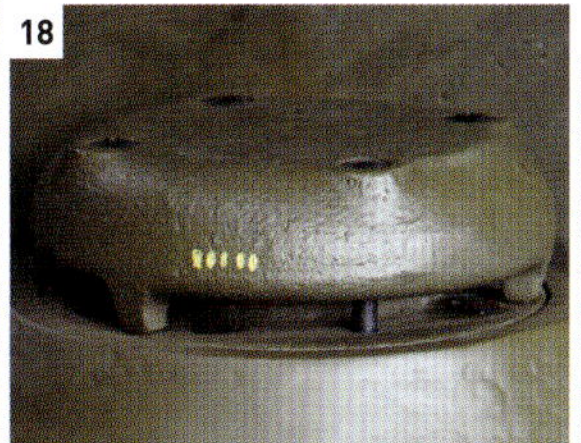
18

19

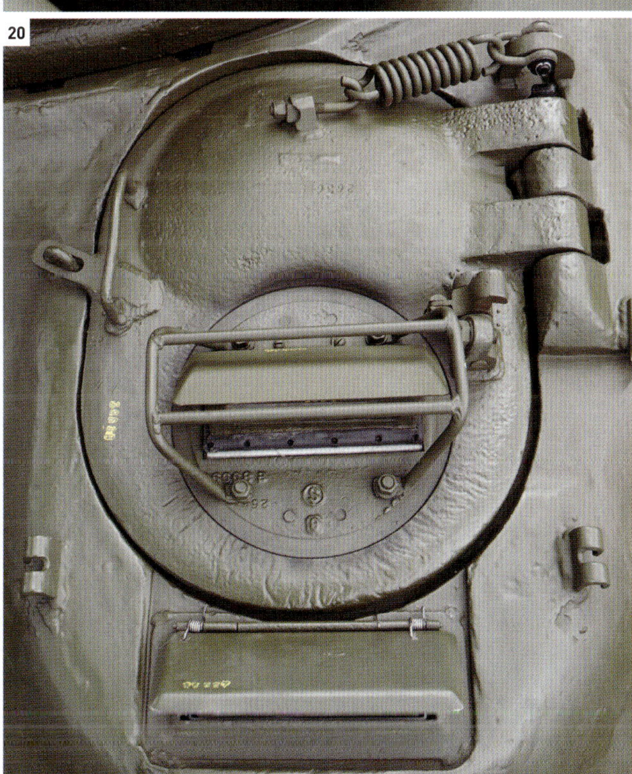
20

22

25

23

26

21

24

△ Matilda CDL

Date 1940 **Origin** UK
Weight 29.7 tons (26.9 tonnes)
Engine 2 x AEC 6-cylinder diesel, 95 hp (71 kW)
Main armament None

The Canal Defence Light (CDL) was an adapted Matilda tank with a flickering 13-million candle power searchlight in its turret to dazzle enemy forces at night. The frequency of the light's flickering intensified the blinding effect.

Vehicle body housing explosives

△ Goliath tracked mine

Date 1943 **Origin** Germany
Weight 0.45 tons (0.4 tonnes)
Engine Zundapp SZ7 gasoline, 12.5 hp (9 kW)
Main armament 220 lb (100 kg) explosive

The Goliath—a small, mobile bomb, only 5 ft 4 in (1.63 m) long and 2 ft (0.62 m) tall—was remotely controlled by an operator who remained in cover and directed the vehicle via a 2,130 ft- (650m-) long wire. Designed to destroy fortifications or clear minefields, the Goliath was vulnerable to small arms fire and rough terrain.

△ Churchill Crocodile

Date 1943 **Origin** UK
Weight 44.8 tons (40.6 tonnes)
Engine Bedford Twin-Six gasoline, 350 hp (261 kW)
Main armament Flamethrower, 75 mm QF gun

The Crocodile was a fully operational Churchill gun tank with a flamethrower mounted at the front of its hull. Fuel for the flamethrower was carried in a trailer. Flamethrower tanks like the Crocodile were highly effective against fortifications: although they attracted heavy enemy fire, their presence often persuaded defending forces to surrender.

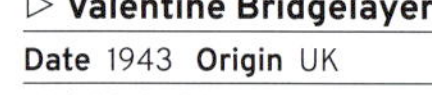

▷ Valentine Bridgelayer

Date 1943 **Origin** UK
Weight 21.9 tons (19.9 tonnes)
Engine AEC A189 gasoline, 135 hp (101 kW)
Main armament None

The bridge carried by this adapted Valentine tank could span 30 ft (9.2 m) and support 33-ton (30-tonne) vehicles. Bridge-laying tanks were first developed at the end of World War I, but did not see combat until World War II.

◁ Churchill AVRE

Date 1943 **Origin** UK
Weight 43.7 tons (39.6 tonnes)
Engine Bedford 12-cylinder gasoline, 350 hp (261 kW)
Main armament 290 mm Petard Mortar

Developed in the wake of the ill-fated 1942 Dieppe Raid, the Armoured Vehicle Royal Engineers (AVRE) provided battlefield protection and destructive power for engineers. A versatile version of the Churchill tank, the AVRE could smash fortifications with its short-range mortar.

Engineering and Specialist Vehicles

The difficulty of landing vehicles by amphibious assault was highlighted by the disastrous 1942 Dieppe Raid, when many Allied tanks failed to get off the beach. Successfully getting tanks ashore in a future invasion would thus be a challenge. Percy Hobart, British 79th Armoured Division commander, was tasked with developing vehicles to assist such landings. He based them on tank hulls, which gave the vehicles similar mobility and protection to tanks and made logistics easier. Nicknamed "Hobart's Funnies," they were used in northwest Europe, Italy, and the Far East.

Canvas flotation screen provides buoyancy

△ Valentine Mk IX Duplex Drive

Date 1943 **Origin** UK
Weight 17.6 tons (16 tonnes)
Engine GM 6046 gasoline, 375 hp (280 kW)
Main armament QF 6-pounder gun

Duplex Drive (DD) tanks were developed to provide support for the infantry during the D-Day landings. Fitted with a propeller and a canvas screen, they could "swim" from ship to shore. Valentine DDs were used to train crews in the run-up to D-Day; similarly adapted Sherman M4 DDs were used for the actual landings.

Scissors bridge folded on tank

Hydraulic arm unfolds bridge

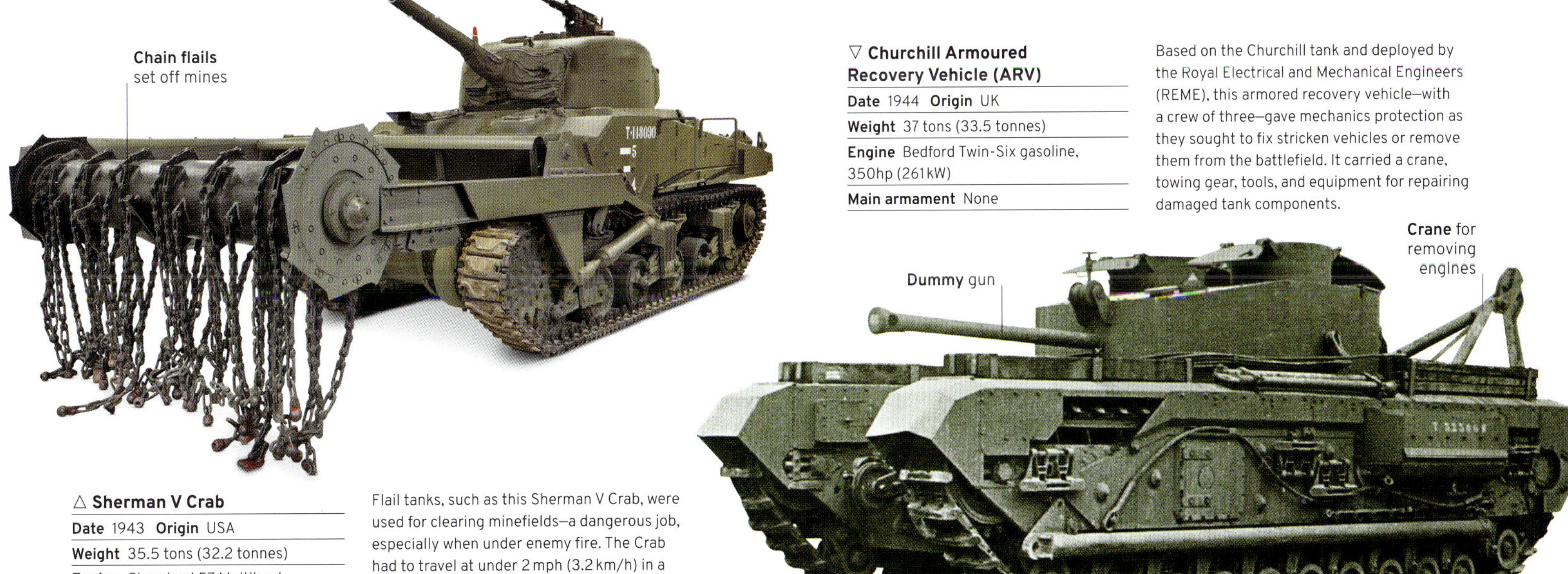

△ **Sherman V Crab**

Date 1943 **Origin** USA	
Weight 35.5 tons (32.2 tonnes)	
Engine Chrysler A57 Multibank gasoline, 425 hp (317 kW)	
Main armament 75 mm M3 L/40 gun	

Flail tanks, such as this Sherman V Crab, were used for clearing minefields—a dangerous job, especially when under enemy fire. The Crab had to travel at under 2 mph (3.2 km/h) in a straight line, while its spinning flail chains beat the ground with sufficient force to detonate any mines in the tank's path.

▽ **Churchill Armoured Recovery Vehicle (ARV)**

Date 1944 **Origin** UK	
Weight 37 tons (33.5 tonnes)	
Engine Bedford Twin-Six gasoline, 350hp (261 kW)	
Main armament None	

Based on the Churchill tank and deployed by the Royal Electrical and Mechanical Engineers (REME), this armored recovery vehicle—with a crew of three—gave mechanics protection as they sought to fix stricken vehicles or remove them from the battlefield. It carried a crane, towing gear, tools, and equipment for repairing damaged tank components.

▷ **StuG III**

Date 1940 **Origin** Germany
Weight 26.8 tons (24.3 tonnes)
Engine Maybach HL120TRM gasoline, 300 hp (224 kW)
Main armament 7.5 cm StuK 40 L/48 gun

The most-produced German armored vehicle, with over 11,000 built, the StuG or Sturmgeschütz ("assault gun") III was originally an infantry support vehicle armed with a short-barreled, low-velocity 7.5 cm L/24 gun. Its low height and armor made it ideally suited to the role of tank-destroyer, and it was soon upgraded with the longer-barreled L/48 anti-tank gun.

Drive sprocket transfers power from the engine to the tracks

▷ **M18 Hellcat**

Date 1943 **Origin** USA
Weight 19.6 tons (17.8 tonnes)
Engine Wright-Continental R-975 gasoline, 400 hp (298 kW)
Main armament 76 mm M1A2 L/52 gun

A powerful engine, very thin armor, and torsion-bar suspension helped to make the M18 Hellcat one of the fastest ever armored vehicles. Although its speed and agility met the criteria for a US tank destroyer, its lack of firepower limited its effectiveness, especially when confronted by heavier German tanks.

Allied and Axis Tank Destroyers

Tank destroyers and assault guns typically utilized the hulls of existing tank models. German and Soviet forces favored turretless designs, which made the vehicles quicker and cheaper to manufacture than conventional tanks, and enabled them to carry a larger gun and heavier armor than the tank on which they were based. American tank destroyers prioritized mobility over firepower; intended to outmaneuver enemy tanks in counterattacks, they retained the turret. In reality, all three countries used tank destroyers to support infantry and as artillery pieces.

▷ **SU-76M**

Date 1943 **Origin** USSR
Weight 11.5 tons (10.4 tonnes)
Engine 2 x GAZ-203 6-cylinder gasoline, 85 hp (63 kW) each
Main armament 76.2 mm ZiS-3Sh L/42.6 gun

Able to destroy lighter German tanks, the SU-76M was a light assault gun and mobile artillery piece based on a stretched T-70 tank chassis. With only thin armor to protect the occupants and an open top, the SU-76M's crews were rather vulnerable. Production exceeded 12,600, making it the second most-produced Soviet armored vehicle of the war, after the T-34 tank.

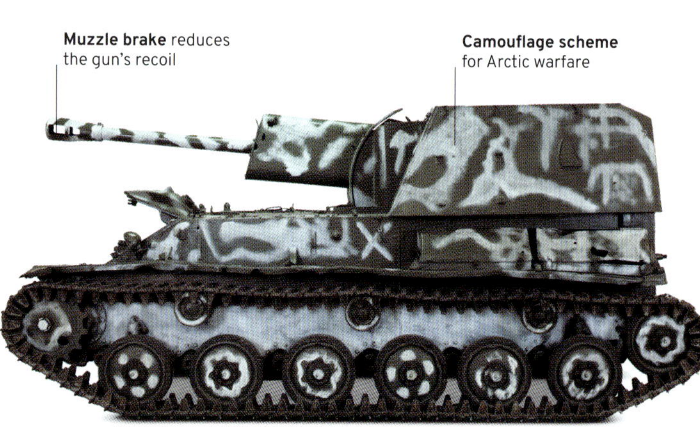

Idler wheel helps to maintain track tension

8.8 cm PaK 43/3 main gun

△ Jagdpanther

Date 1944 **Origin** Germany
Weight 51.5 tons (46.7 tonnes)
Engine Maybach HL230 P30 V12 gasoline, 690 hp (515 kW)
Main armament 8.8 cm PaK 43/3 L/71 gun

Well armored, mobile, and wielding a powerful gun, the Jagdpanther was an impressive mechanized weapon, especially when deployed in defensive or ambush roles. Based on the Panther chassis, its combat effectiveness was hampered by poor maintenance and crew training. Furthermore, only 392 examples of this forbidding tank-buster were produced—too few to affect the course of the war.

▽ SU-100

Date 1944 **Origin** USSR
Weight 34.7 tons (31.5 tonnes)
Engine Kharkiv Model V-2-34 diesel, 500 hp (373 kW)
Main armament 100 mm D-10S L/53.5 gun

Like the SU-85, from which it was developed, the SU-100 provided long-range anti-tank support to offensive formations. It also served as a backstop to defend against the heaviest German tanks. About 1,200 SU-100s were made in wartime; production and upgrades continued post war, keeping the vehicle in service around the world for decades.

External fuel tank

Commander's cupola

▽ Jagdpanzer 38(t) Hetzer

Date 1944 **Origin** Germany
Weight 17.6 tons (16 tonnes)
Engine Praga AC/2 gasoline, 150 hp (112 kW)
Main armament 7.5 cm PaK 39 L/40 gun

The Hetzer was an ideal ambush vehicle, its compact size enabling it to wait concealed on the battlefield and surprise enemy forces. Based on the hull of the Panzer 38(t), it was smaller, lighter, and cheaper than other Jagdpanzers of the late war. Crews disliked it, due to the poorly laid-out and cramped interior. A total of 2,584 Hetzers were built.

▷ ISU-152

Date 1944 **Origin** USSR
Weight 52 tons (47.2 tonnes)
Engine Kharkiv Model V-2IS diesel, 520 hp (388 kW)
Main armament 152 mm ML-20S L/29 gun-howitzer

The USSR produced a range of self-propelled guns based on the chassis of its heavy tanks. For example, the SU-152 used the KV-1S, while the ISU-152 employed the later IS chassis. A lack of 152 mm barrels called for another variation—the ISU-122, armed with a 122 mm gun. With devastating firepower, they were well suited both to urban fighting and attack support.

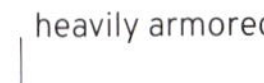

Gun mantlet is heavily armored

Spare track links carried on front of hull

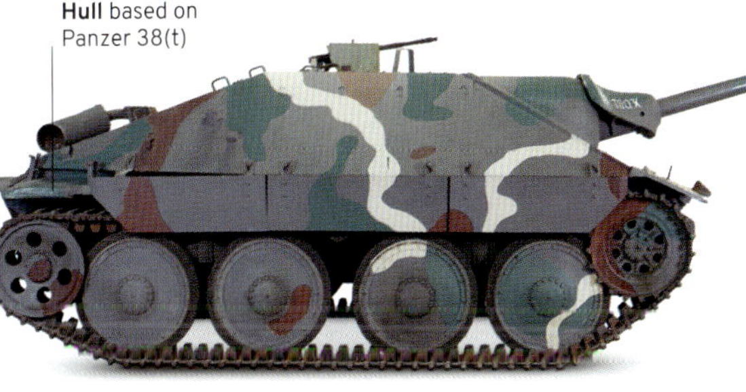

Hull based on Panzer 38(t)

12.8 cm PaK 44 main gun

▷ Jagdtiger

Date 1944 **Origin** Germany
Weight 78.4 tons (71.1 tonnes)
Engine Maybach HL230 P30 V12 gasoline, 690 hp (515 kW)
Main armament 12.8 cm PaK 44 L/55 gun

The Jagdtiger, the heaviest armored vehicle of World War II, could defeat any Allied tank in long-range combat. Using the suspension from the Tiger, Jagdtigers were prone to malfunction and were often destroyed by their crews after breakdowns.

Soviet Tanks

When German forces invaded the Soviet Union in 1941, the Soviets initially suffered heavy losses of soldiers and tanks. To safeguard manufacturing facilities, tank production shifted east, beyond the Ural Mountains; British and American tanks helped plug the gap until the new factories were up and running. To increase output, production became standardized. Consequently, the tanks were simple in design and construction, which suited the limited skills of their crews, who were often inexperienced or poorly trained.

▷ Kliment Voroshilov-1 (KV-1)

Date 1939 **Origin** Soviet Union

Weight 53.2 tons (48.3 tonnes)

Engine Kharkiv Model V-2K, 500 hp (373 kW)

Main armament 76.2 mm ZiS-5 L/41.5 gun

The heavy KV-1 proved virtually immune to German anti-tank weapons when it entered combat in 1941. It was fitted with the same gun and engine as the T-34 but had poorer mobility due to its weight. This was one of the few tanks to continue in production after the Soviet factories moved east; around 4,700 KV-1s were built in total.

152 mm howitzer for breaching fortifications

Turret is tall, heavy, and box-shaped

△ Kliment Voroshilov-2 (KV-2)

Date 1939 **Origin** Soviet Union

Weight 59.4 tons (53.9 tonnes)

Engine Kharkiv Model V-2K, 550 hp (410 kW)

Main armament 152 mm M-10T L/20 howitzer

The Soviets believed that a tank armed with an artillery piece was vital to overcome well-fortified bunkers, having struggled in Finland in 1939–40 against such installations. The KV-2 was a KV-1 hull equipped with a howitzer. It was ineffective in practice, since the tall turret made the tank heavier, slower, and easier to target. When production ended in 1941, only 334 had been built.

20 mm cannon could only penetrate light armor

▷ T-60

Date 1941 **Origin** Soviet Union

Weight 6.4 tons (5.8 tonnes)

Engine GAZ-202 6-cylinder, 70 hp (52 kW)

Main armament 20 mm TNSh cannon

The T-60 was a two-man Soviet scout tank used for reconnaissance. When the T-60 came up against German forces, it soon became evident that the tank was under-gunned and too lightly armored. Since the turret was too small to accommodate a larger gun and efforts to thicken its armor reduced its mobility, it was replaced by the T-70.

▷ T-34

Date 1941 **Origin** Soviet Union

Weight 34.6 tons (31.4 tonnes)

Engine Kharkiv Model V-2-34, 500 hp (373 kW)

Main armament 76.2 mm F-34 L/41 gun

Easy to operate due to its basic design, the T-34 was the mainstay of Red Army forces during World War II. Its relatively light weight and wide tracks were excellent for traveling cross-country over mud and snow.

45 mm armor on rear of hull

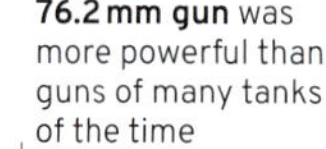

76.2 mm gun was more powerful than guns of many tanks of the time

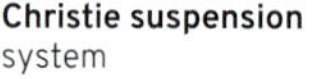

Christie suspension system

△ **T-70**

Date 1942 **Origin** Soviet Union
Weight 10.1 tons (9.2 tonnes)
Engine 2 x GAZ-202 6-cylinder, 70 hp (52 kW) each
Main armament 45 mm ZiS-19BM gun

A more heavily armed and armored successor to the T-60, the T-70 still proved no match for Germany's advanced tanks. By 1943, the Soviets had decided to relegate light tanks to secondary roles, realizing that they had no useful place on the battlefield. An assault gun, the SU-76, was developed from the chassis of the T-70.

▷ **T-34/85**

Date 1944 **Origin** Soviet Union
Weight 35.3 tons (32 tonnes)
Engine Kharkiv Model V-2-34, 500 hp (373 kW)
Main armament 85 mm ZiS S-53 L/55 gun

By late 1943, the T-34 needed a revamp: it was being outgunned by other tanks, and its crews found it difficult to work effectively in the cramped two-man turret. Both issues were resolved in the T-34/85 ("85" denoting its improved 85 mm gun). The T-34/85 enjoyed a long postwar career with the Soviets and their client states, with one used as late as 2015 in Yemen.

▽ **Iosif Stalin-2 (IS-2)**

Date 1944 **Origin** Soviet Union
Weight 49.3 tons (44.7 tonnes)
Engine Kharkiv Model V-2IS, 520 hp (388 kW)
Main armament 122 mm D-25T L/45 gun

Galvanized by the need to counter the threat of Germany's Tiger and Panther heavy tanks, the Soviets produced the IS series—a development of the KV-1, with a new transmission and hull. When it entered service in 1944, the IS-2 replaced both the IS-1 and the 85 mm-armed KV-85. Organized into several heavy tank regiments, IS-2s were used to spearhead attacks on German positions.

△ **Iosif Stalin-3M (IS-3M)**

Date 1945 **Origin** Soviet Union
Weight 51.3 tons (46.5 tonnes)
Engine Kharkiv Model V-2IS, 600 hp (447 kW)
Main armament 122 mm D-25T L/45 gun

Rapidly developed and rushed into service because of shortcomings in the IS-2's speed and armor, the IS-3 arrived too late to play a part in World War II. The IS-3 itself suffered from mechanical problems, but these were corrected in the improved IS-3M. The IS-3's sloping sides gave better protection, and this feature was adopted for subsequent postwar Soviet tanks.

T-34/85

The powerfully armed and well-protected T-34 was called the "best tank in the world" by German General Paul Ludwig Ewald von Kleist when his forces first encountered it in the summer of 1941. Speedy and nimble, hardy and easy to repair, and with a design suited to mass production, this medium tank and its variants were used in huge numbers.

MIKHAIL KOSHKIN'S design for the T-34 embodied lessons learned fighting the Japanese at Khalkhin Gol in 1939. His tank had thicker armor and a larger gun than its predecessors, the BT series, and a diesel engine that was less of a fire risk than earlier gasoline engines, which had been vulnerable to incendiary devices. The first tanks rolled out of the factory in September 1940.

The T-34's armor of homogenous rolled and welded nickel steel offered good protection, while its 76 mm high-velocity main gun—which was fired by the tank commander in the two-man turret—proved effective at armor penetration. In 1944, the up-gunned T-34/85 came into service, mounting an 85 mm gun in an enlarged turret. Although crews were not always sufficiently trained, their bravery and the Red Army's growing awareness of how to use its tanks most effectively enabled T-34s to defeat more technically advanced adversaries.

Modifications made manufacturing quicker and cheaper, reducing the unit cost from 269,500 to 135,000 roubles. The need for simplicity was partly driven by production having to move to eastern Russia due to German advances. After the war, the tank was made in Czechoslovakia and Poland. Tens of thousands of T-34s saw service worldwide.

SPECIFICATIONS	
Name	T-34/85
Date	1940
Origin	Soviet Union
Production	84,700
Engine	Model V-2-34 V12, 500 hp (373 kW)
Weight	35.3 tons (32 tonnes)
Main armament	85 mm ZiS-53
Secondary armament	2 x 7.62 mm DT machine guns
Armor thickness	2.4 in (60 mm max)

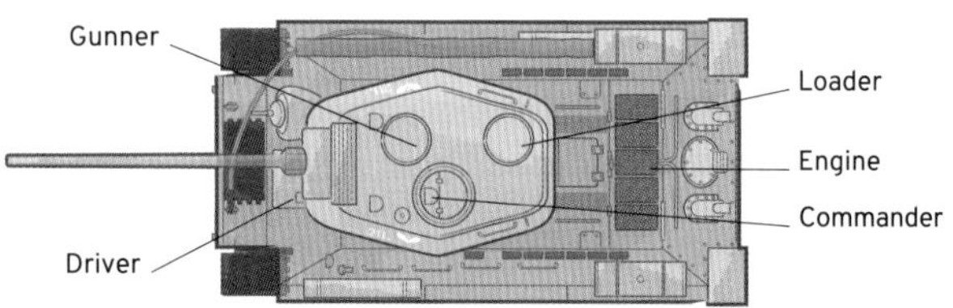

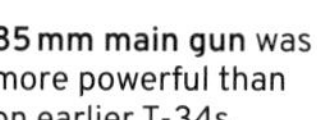

85 mm main gun was more powerful than on earlier T-34s

Coaxial machine gun operated by the codriver

Upgraded model
The up-gunned T-34/85's larger turret had space for three men—commander, gunner, and loader—allowing the functions of commander and gunner to be separated.

FRONT VIEW

REAR VIEW

Commander's cupola, added to later models

211и

Battalion number
This T-34/85 was deployed in the second company (2) of the first battalion and was the command tank (11) of the first platoon. The small Russian letter on the right ("I" in English) is the initial of the first battalion's commander, Ivanov.

Fuel drum

Rubber-rimmed road wheels

Idler wheel set at the front

EXTERIOR

Although the finish on early T-34s was good, standards fell when manufacture of the tanks relocated east, to improvised factories beyond the Urals. The Red Army's leaders acknowledged that crude cast marks on the turret had little impact on the tank's fighting ability, so any time spent removing them would only lengthen the production process and increase costs.

1. Regimental insignia of 4th Guards Tank Corps **2.** Driver's hatch (closed) **3.** Codriver's machine gun **4.** Spare track links **5.** Road wheels **6.** Exhaust **7.** Fuel cap **8.** Commander's (right) and gunner's (left) hatches **9.** Axle joint **10.** Commander's periscope **11.** Fuel drum **12.** Engine bay

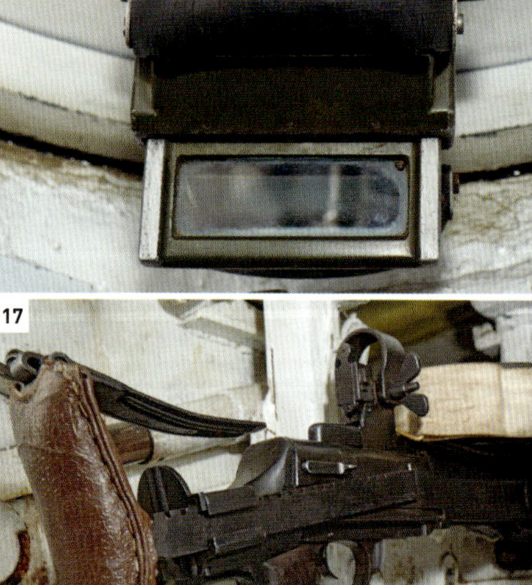

INTERIOR

Since tanks in wartime had an estimated service life of just a few months, the Soviets classified them as disposable munitions, alongside weapons such as hand grenades and shells. Consequently, little importance was given to crew comfort in the design of the T-34, and the interior of the tank was extremely basic but functional. The enlarged turret on the upgraded T-34/85 was slightly more spacious than that on earlier variants.

13. Looking down into commander's position **14.** Spare shells **15.** Commander's position showing main gun breech **16.** Gunner's periscope **17.** Coaxial machine gun **18.** Radio **19.** Main gun breech (open) **20.** Fire extinguisher release **21.** Barrel elevation handle **22.** Turret traverse handle **23.** Instrument panel **24.** Pressure pump **25.** Escape hatch **26.** Gear lever **27.** Instrument dials **28.** Driver's position

▷ **Universal Carrier, Mark II**

Date 1939 **Origin** UK

Weight 4.4 tons (4 tonnes)

Engine Ford flathead V8 gasoline, 85 hp (63 kW)

Main armament .303 Bren machine gun

The Universal Carrier descended from British Carden-Loyd vehicles of the interwar era. It was effectively an amalgamation of several carrier developments into one "universal" design. This versatile vehicle was used to transport troops, weaponry, supplies, and artillery observation equipment, with some variants being made into gun platforms. Popular with infantry, it was one of the most-produced armored vehicles in history.

Idler wheel at front of track

Armored vision port gave view to the side

Fuel cans

◁ **Daimler Mark II "Dingo"**

Date 1940 **Origin** UK

Weight 3.3 tons (3 tonnes)

Engine Daimler 6HV gasoline, 55 hp (41 kW)

Main armament None

Nicknamed the "Dingo," this small, popular, two-person scout car was highly mobile, thanks to the design of its transmission—shared with the Daimler Armored Car—which offered five speeds, both forward and reverse. Early Dingos had a sliding armored roof and four-wheel steering; both features were omitted on later versions, although the solid rubber tires were retained. Around 6,600 Dingos were made before production ended in 1945.

Machine-gun mount

▷ **Humber Scout Car**

Date 1942 **Origin** UK

Weight 3.9 tons (3.5 tonnes)

Engine Humber 5-cylinder gasoline, 87 hp (65 kW)

Main armament .303 Bren machine gun

While the standard British scout car in World War II was Daimler's "Dingo," other companies were commissioned to produce similar vehicles to meet wartime demand. Humber made around 4,300 such vehicles. In the latter stages of World War II, Humbers were mainly allocated to armored units, with Dingos generally being used by the infantry.

Canvas canopy

△ **CT15TA Armored Truck**

Date 1943 **Origin** Canada

Weight 5.1 tons (4.6 tonnes)

Engine General Motors 270 gasoline, 100 hp (75 kW)

Main armament None

The CT15TA was based on the Canadian Military Pattern truck chassis. With a crew of two, it was used as a troop carrier and an ambulance, as well as a load carrier, but it was never intended as a vehicle for front-line combat.

Armored Cars and Troop Carriers

World War II saw the widespread use of scout cars and armored cars for reconnaissance and to provide support to infantry. Although fully tracked armored infantry carriers were less common than half-tracks, the seemingly ubiquitous Universal Carrier fulfilled a multitude of support and combat roles for the Allies. Toward the end of the war, the highly successful tank-based Ram Kangaroo at last gave Allied infantry units the same mobility as their tank counterparts.

▷ Praying Mantis

Date 1943 **Origin** UK

Weight 5.8 tons (5.3 tonnes)

Engine Ford flathead V8 gasoline, 85 hp (64 kW)

Main armament 2 x .303 Bren machine guns

The Praying Mantis's body could be hydraulically raised over cover, allowing the two-man crew lying prone inside to fire at targets. This quirky attempt at a very-low-profile vehicle proved a failure, being difficult to operate and liable to make its occupants feel nauseous.

Compartment for driver and machine gunner

Running gear—like the engine—was from the Universal Carrier

▽ M8 Greyhound

Date 1943 **Origin** USA

Weight 8.2 tons (7.4 tonnes)

Engine Hercules JXD gasoline, 110 hp (82 kW)

Main armament 37 mm M6 L/56.6 gun

The M8 was originally designed as a wheeled tank destroyer, but it soon became a reconnaissance vehicle because of its light armament. Its six-wheel drive gave it a high speed on roads, but its suspension limited it across country. The vehicle was open-topped and thinly armored.

△ Ram Kangaroo

Date 1944 **Origin** Canada

Weight 27.5 tons (24.9 tonnes)

Engine Wright-Continental R-975 gasoline, 400 hp (298 kW)

Main armament .30 Browning M1919 machine gun

Kangaroos were armored personnel carriers made from converted tanks. Most were based on the Canadian Ram tank. This example could carry 11 soldiers. Kangaroos were widely used late in the war, as they allowed infantry to advance at the same pace as tanks, providing a high level of mobility and protection.

△ Sd Kfz 234/3 Schwerer Panzerspahwagen, 8-rad

Date 1944 **Origin** Germany

Weight 12.9 tons (11.7 tonnes)

Engine Tatra 103 diesel, 220 hp (164 kW)

Main armament 7.5 cm Kwk 51 L/24 gun

The Sd Kfz 234 was developed in the latter stages of World War II to replace the Sd Kfz 231 armored car. It was equipped with a more powerful engine than its forerunner, thicker armor, and advanced suspension and steering that gave greater mobility. The four variants, including one with a turret, carried different armaments. This open-topped 234/3, equipped with a 7.5 cm gun, provided fire support to more lightly armed versions.

Aerial Combat Takes Center Stage

Collectively, the combatant nations produced and fielded more than 700,000 military aircraft during World War II. The battle for the skies became as intense as the battle for supremacy on land, and air power gradually extended its strategic influence over all theaters of war, including the world's seas and oceans.

Combat aviation went through radical technological changes in the 1920s and 1930s. Biplanes were superseded by faster, stronger, cantilever-winged monoplanes with greater range and combat capabilities. New types of military aircraft were developed: two-engined medium bombers and four-engined medium-heavy bombers; dive-bombers; torpedo bombers; high-performance fighters; transport aircraft; military seaplanes, and others. What the burgeoning air forces also needed was a tactical doctrine to guide their efforts.

Tactical positions

At the beginning of World War II, it was the Germans who appeared to take the lead in air combat tactics. During the campaigns in Poland and Western Europe in 1939–40, German fighters such as the Bf 109 established air superiority, while Junkers Ju 87 Stuka dive-bombers acted as flying artillery in support of armor and infantry, and medium bombers such as the Heinkel He 111 delivered area bombardments against cities, troop concentrations, and logistics centers. For a time, the tactics worked well, but the Germans did not adapt their approach as circumstances changed. Crucially, the Luftwaffe failed to

Daylight bombing
Flying in close formation to concentrate bomb strikes, US B-24 Liberator heavy bombers of the 15th Air Force hit the oil refinery at Pardubice, eastern Bohemia, on August 24, 1944.

Carrier operations
A Grumman F6F Hellcat prepares to take off from the flight deck of the USS *Yorktown*. During the battle for the Pacific, Hellcats shot down more than 5,200 enemy aircraft.

develop an effective long-range heavy bomber or an accompanying strategy, so it was unable to inflict decisive damage on distant industrial targets.

Long-range bombing

The same was not true of the Allies. Britain and, later, the US not only fielded endless squadrons of nimble fighters and formidable ground-attack aircraft, but they also produced large numbers of four-engined bombers, such as the British Avro Lancaster and the American Boeing B-17 Flying Fortress. From 1942, heavy bombers enabled the Allies to unleash a joint strategic bombing campaign of unprecedented proportions against German cities, the British bombing by night and the Americans by day. By 1943, bombing raids of more than 1,000 aircraft at a time were being launched. Allied losses were initially huge, but round-trip fighter escort from P-47 Thunderbolts and P-51 Mustangs gradually reduced the toll. The Germans were compelled to devote more and more resources to producing fighters to counter the raids, resulting in an ever-greater attrition of pilots and aircraft.

The German air force also lost the battle for air superiority and for tactical ground support. This was partly due to the Allies' far greater industrial output, but also because between 1942 and 1944 the Allies developed a brilliantly flexible system of ground-attack command. By 1944, German troops and vehicles could barely move across exposed highways or open spaces for fear of air attack.

Carrier war

In the Pacific theater, the air war was radically different. The Pacific War opened with a Japanese air attack on the US Pacific Fleet at Pearl Harbor on December 7, 1941. Not only did this attack showcase the skill of the Imperial Japanese Navy Air Service (IJNAS), but it also demonstrated that aircraft carriers, from which the devastating attack was launched, were the future of naval warfare.

On the open waters of the Pacific, a struggle for supremacy began between the aircraft carriers of the United States and Japan. The fight was close until the Battle of Midway on June 4–7, 1942, in which the Americans destroyed all four of the Japanese fleet carriers: *Akagi*, *Kaga*, *Sōryū*, and *Hiryū*. It was a blow from which the Japanese Navy never recovered.

The US tapped into its enormous industrial capability to produce fleet carriers, escort carriers, and naval combat aircraft at rates far exceeding the capacity of a struggling Japan, and the attrition of Japanese aircraft and pilots became relentless. As the US regained Japanese-held territories and began to close in on the home islands, the Imperial Japanese Army Air Service (IJAAS) turned to kamikaze suicide missions. These self-sacrificing attacks could not stop the onslaught, nor could the Japanese prevent a strategic bombing campaign against the main islands that culminated in the dropping of atomic bombs on Hiroshima and Nagasaki in August 1945.

> "I do not **personally** regard... the cities of Germany as **worth the bones** of one British Grenadier."
>
> SIR ARTHUR HARRIS, MARSHAL OF THE RAF, SUPPORTING THE STRATEGIC BOMBING OF GERMANY, IN A LETTER OF MARCH 29, 1945

TALKING POINT

Japan's last resort

The Japanese kamikaze campaign was an improvised effort to turn the tide of the Pacific War. The word kamikaze refers to the "divine wind," the storm that supposedly saved Japan from Mongolian invasion in 1281. From 1944, extreme nationalism merged with warrior *bushido* and Shinto spirituality to persuade hundreds of young pilots to voluntarily fly bomb-laden aircraft into enemy ships, killing themselves in the destruction of their target. Kamikaze was a desperate response to US air superiority and the increasing inexperience of Japanese pilots. It did not reverse American dominance, but it did inflict serious damage. The US lost 34 ships sunk, many more damaged, and 5,000 sailors killed from kamikaze waves, the worst attacks coming around the Philippines and Okinawa in 1944–45.

A recruitment poster seeks new aviators for the Imperial Japanese Navy. As the war progressed, inexperienced pilots were sent on suicide missions in crude aircraft.

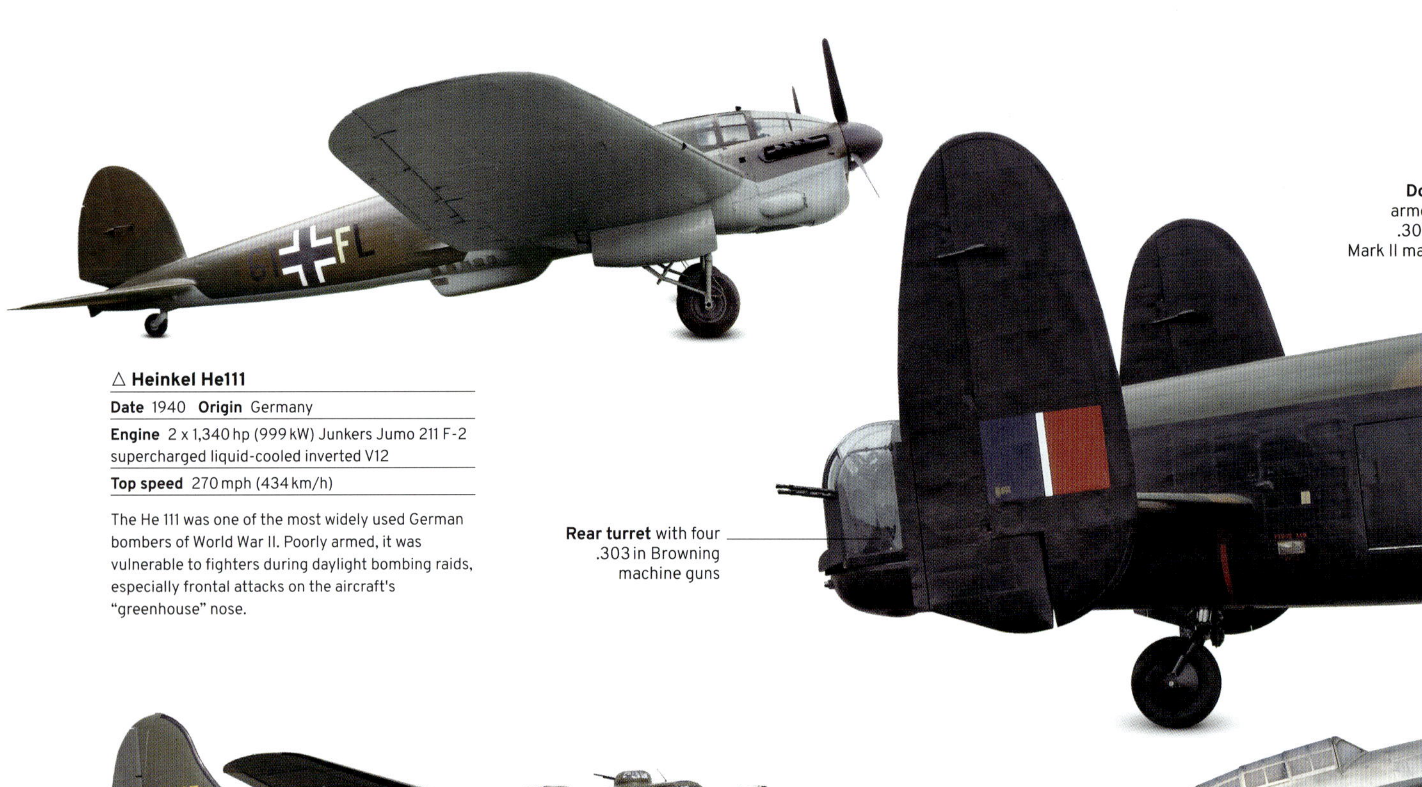

△ **Heinkel He111**

Date 1940 **Origin** Germany

Engine 2 x 1,340 hp (999 kW) Junkers Jumo 211 F-2 supercharged liquid-cooled inverted V12

Top speed 270 mph (434 km/h)

The He 111 was one of the most widely used German bombers of World War II. Poorly armed, it was vulnerable to fighters during daylight bombing raids, especially frontal attacks on the aircraft's "greenhouse" nose.

△ **B-17G Flying Fortress**

Date 1940 **Origin** USA

Engine 4 x 1,200 hp (895 kW) Wright R-1820-97 Cyclone turbocharged air-cooled 9-cylinder radial

Top speed 287 mph (462 km/h)

The USAAF used the B-17 for precision daytime raids in World War II. The heavy defensive armament—vital for daylight operations—compromised the B-17's bomb capacity, reducing it to half that of the Avro Lancaster.

△ **Yokosuka D4Y3 Model 33 "Judy"**

Date 1940 **Origin** Japan

Engine 1,075 hp (802 kW) Mitsubishi Kinsei air-cooled 14-cylinder radial

Top speed 342 mph (550 km/h)

Few World War II dive-bombers could rival the speed of the carrier-borne D4Y, which was also used for kamikaze attacks and reconnaissance missions, and as a night fighter. Design issues restricted production to just 2,038 aircraft.

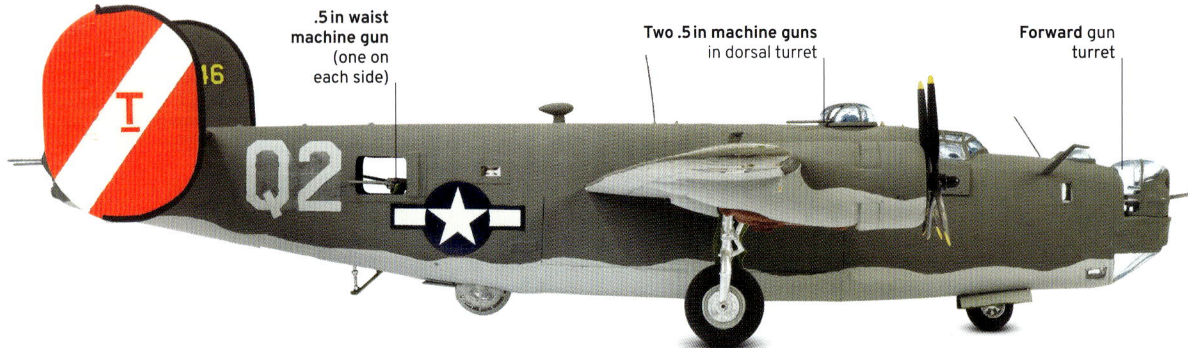

◁ **Consolidated B-24 Liberator**

Date 1941 **Origin** USA

Engine 4 x 1,200 hp (895 kW) Pratt & Whitney R-1830-65 Twin Wasp turbosupercharged air-cooled 14-cylinder radial

Top speed 290 mph (467 km/h)

More than 18,400 B-24s were built for Allied forces. The B-24 surpassed the B-17 in range, speed, and bomb capacity, and it was lighter too. However, it was unpopular with aircrews, being harder to fly than the B-17 and more likely to catch fire or crash when hit.

Bombers

Two types of bomber aircraft emerged in World War II: "tactical" bombers that struck at battlefield targets, and "strategic" bombers that flew long-range missions to destroy infrastructure or drop bombs onto industrial cities to disrupt manufacturing. The development of more powerful engines, radar-based guidance systems, and predictive bombsights made strategic bombers more effective. By 1944, the best of them could accurately deliver heavy bomb loads onto targets thousands of miles from their bases. However, they sustained huge losses—Britain's RAF Bomber Command alone lost over 8,325 aircraft during the war.

▷ **Junkers Ju 87D Stuka**

Date 1941 **Origin** Germany

Engine 1,400 hp (1,044 kW) Junkers Jumo 211J V12

Top speed 240 mph (390 km/h)

The Ju 87 Sturzkampfflugzeug first saw combat in Spain in 1937, and later became a key element of German blitzkrieg tactics. Its wailing siren had a terrifying effect as it dived to attack ground targets.

Bombardier's position

Rolls-Royce Merlin engines

Bomb bay doors (open)

Landing gear retracts hydraulically into recesses within the inner engine nacelles

△ **Avro Lancaster**

Date 1941 **Origin** UK	
Engine 4 x 1,280 hp (954 kW) Rolls-Royce Merlin XX supercharged liquid-cooled V12	
Top speed 285 mph (460 km/h)	

The Lancaster, the RAF's main heavy bomber, had a huge bomb capacity of 14,000 lb (6,350 kg). It excelled as a night bomber, its four Rolls-Royce Merlin engines carrying the plane and its bomb load to targets in Germany and beyond.

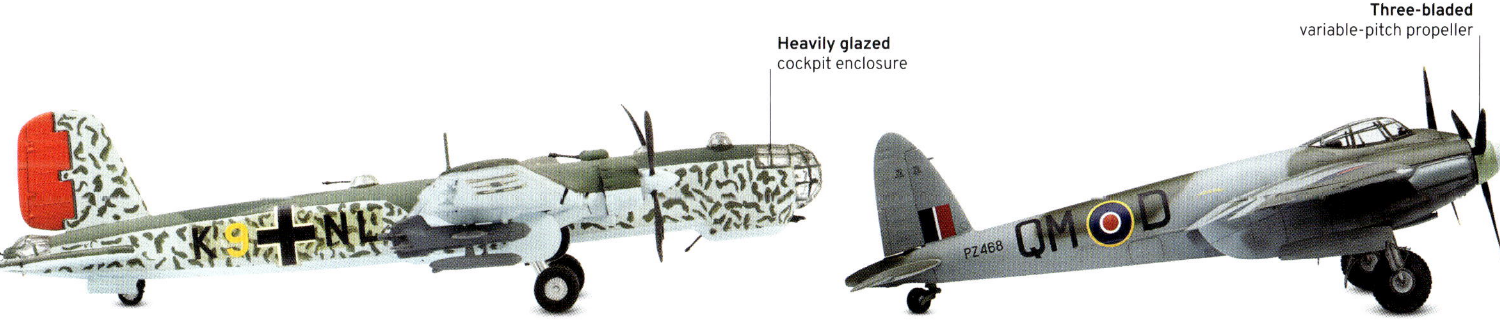

△ **Heinkel He 177 Grief**

Date 1942 **Origin** Germany	
Engine Two 2,600 hp (1,939 kW) Daimler-Benz DB 610 W-24s	
Top speed 350 mph (565 km/h)	

Germany's only purpose-built long-range heavy bomber of World War II, the Heinkel 117 had a troubled service history. It was beset by structural problems, an overcomplicated engine, and the stipulation that it should also be able to function as a dive-bomber—a role it never successfully fulfilled.

△ **De Havilland Mosquito B.16**

Date 1942 **Origin** UK	
Engine Two 1,710 hp (1,275 kW) Rolls-Royce Merlin 76 V12s	
Top speed 415 mph (670 km/h)	

Made mostly of lightweight plywood, the Mosquito was fast and agile enough to outrun most enemy fighters. Serving in bomber, day- and night-fighter, anti-ship, and reconnaissance roles, it became one of the most successful RAF aircraft of World War II.

△ **Boeing B-29A Superfortress**

Date 1944 **Origin** US	
Engine Four 2,200 hp (1,640 kW) Wright R-3350-23 Duplex Cyclone radials	
Top speed 357 mph (575 km/h)	

The state-of-the-art Superfortress—the biggest, most capable Allied strategic bomber—had a pressurized fuselage and remotely controlled guns. In June 1944, Superfortresses began raids against targets in Japan, first from a base in China and later from the Mariana Islands. The aircraft is most famous for dropping nuclear bombs on the Japanese cities of Hiroshima and Nagasaki in August 1945.

Boeing B–17

Bristling with guns, able to defend itself against enemy fighters, and highly resistant to battle damage, the Boeing B-17 justified its name of "Flying Fortress." This extraordinary warplane, which could fly at an altitude of over 30,000 ft (9,000 m), became a symbol of the United States' ability to take the war to Germany, and massed ranks of Flying Fortresses took on most of the daylight bombing campaign.

WHILE ITS BOMB LOAD was comparable to that carried by the much smaller and faster de Havilland Mosquito, vast formations of B-17s could deliver a staggering tonnage of explosives. The B-17 was built in fewer numbers than the Consolidated B-24 Liberator, its contemporary, but a system of mass production ensured that for every Flying Fortress lost, US factories produced more than two new aircraft. Despite cramped, uncomfortable conditions, hours in freezing temperatures, and often altitude sickness caused by the unpressurized cabin, the crew had to remain alert and ready to battle the Luftwaffe's fighters once over enemy territory. The immensely strong B-17 gained a reputation for being able to withstand a great deal of punishment and still get its crew back to base; because of this, the dependable Flying Fortress won the abiding affection of those who flew in it.

SPECIFICATIONS	
Model	Boeing B-17G Flying Fortress, 1940
Origin	USA
Production	12,731
Construction	Aluminum and steel
Weight	55,000 lb (24,948 kg) loaded
Wingspan	103 ft 9 in (31.6 m)
Engine	4 x 1,200 hp (895 kW) Wright R-1820-97 Cyclone turbocharged air-cooled 9-cylinder radial
Length	74 ft 4 in (22.7 m)
Top speed	287 mph (462 km/h)

Large fin stabilizes the bomber in flight

Waist gunner positions, one on either side, offer protection to the B-17's flanks

FRONT VIEW

REAR VIEW

Fighting machine
Originally known as "Sally B," this 1945 aircraft is the last remaining airworthy B-17 in Europe. It featured in the 1990 film *Memphis Belle*: the artwork added for the film is still visible on one side of the nose; the paintwork on the other side has now been restored to its "Sally B" design.

Large wings aid performance at high altitude

Top turret equipped with a pair of 0.5 in machine guns

Nose section houses the bombardier and defensive armament

Retractable undercarriage

Wright Cyclone engine, noted for being rugged and reliable

EXTERIOR

Built to be tough and envisaged from the outset as a kind of "aerial battleship," Boeing's B-17 was part of a new generation of all-metal monoplanes with enclosed cockpits. Reporting on the prototype, a journalist noted that it resembled a "flying fortress"—the name immediately struck a chord with Boeing, who trademarked it.

1. Waist machine-gun position **2.** Transparent Plexiglas nose **3.** Wright Cyclone radial engine with Hamilton Standard hydromatic propeller **4.** Chin guns remotely controlled by bombardier **5.** Sperry swiveling ball turret **6.** Gunsight for tail-gunner's station **7.** Mainwheel with oleo suspension

INTERIOR

With so much of the B-17's interior allocated to bombs and fuel, crew space was at a premium: the only place where a crew member could stand fully upright was the radio operator's station. Both bombardier and navigator had to crouch to reach their seats in the bomber's nose, while the tail gunner had to crawl to get to his remote position at the very rear of the aircraft. The ball-turret gunner, beneath the fuselage, had to be small enough to fit into his notoriously cramped station. On the flight deck sat the pilot and copilot, with the flight engineer above and behind them.

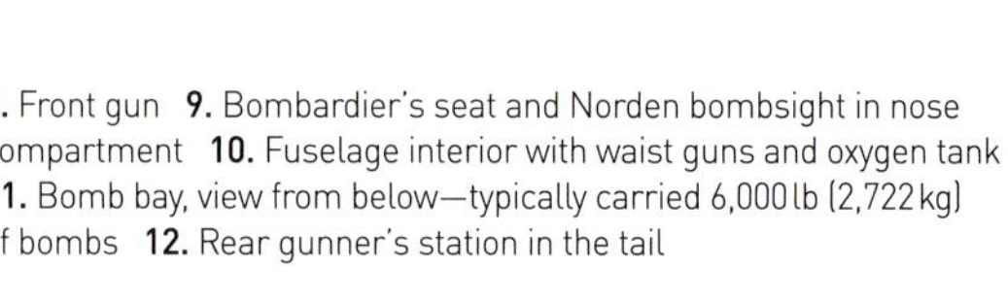

8. Front gun **9.** Bombardier's seat and Norden bombsight in nose compartment **10.** Fuselage interior with waist guns and oxygen tank **11.** Bomb bay, view from below—typically carried 6,000 lb (2,722 kg) of bombs **12.** Rear gunner's station in the tail

COCKPIT

Spacious and efficient, the B-17's "office" provided excellent visibility to the front and sides. The central console, between pilot and copilot, held the throttle controls, fuel switches, and controls for the fuel mixture and propeller-pitch. Behind this, located in the central panel, were the basic flight instruments—altimeter, airspeed indicator, turn-and-bank indicator, and rate-of-climb indicator. The pilot sat in the left-hand seat, with the copilot to his right. It was the copilot's responsibility to monitor the engine controls, which were on the right-hand side of the central panel.

13. The "office"—the B-17 flight deck **14.** Propeller-feathering controls **15.** Panel containing flight and engine instruments **16.** Copilot's control stick featuring Boeing logo **17.** Propeller pitch controls **18.** Throttle controls

Rudder painted with tricolor national markings

△ Dewoitine D.520

Date 1940 **Origin** France

Engine 935 hp (687.6 kW) Hispano-Suiza 12Y 45 in-line V12

Top speed 330 mph (535 km/h)

With a service ceiling of 34,500 ft (10,500 m) and a range of 950 miles (1,530 km), the D.520 was the most capable French fighter aircraft of World War II. It proved a match for Germany's Bf 109E, but only 400 had been produced before France surrendered in June 1940.

Metal skin fastened with rivets

△ Supermarine Spitfire MkII

Date 1940 **Origin** UK

Engine 1,150 hp (858 kW) Rolls-Royce Merlin 45 supercharged liquid-cooled V12

Top speed 357 mph (575 km/h)

The MkII played a key role in the Battle of Britain, its light weight and aerodynamic profile giving the Spitfire superiority over opponents. Later variants remained in service until well after the end of World War II.

▷ Focke-Wulf Fw 190

Date 1941 **Origin** Germany

Engine 1,940 hp (1,447 kW) BMW 801S supercharged air-cooled 14-cylinder radial

Top speed 408 mph (658 km/h)

Designed by Kurt Tank, the Fw-190—the first important fighter of World War II with a radial engine—remained technically superior until confronted by the Spitfire Mk IX. More than 20,000 of all variants were built.

Each wing housed a pair of 20 mm cannons and one or two machine guns

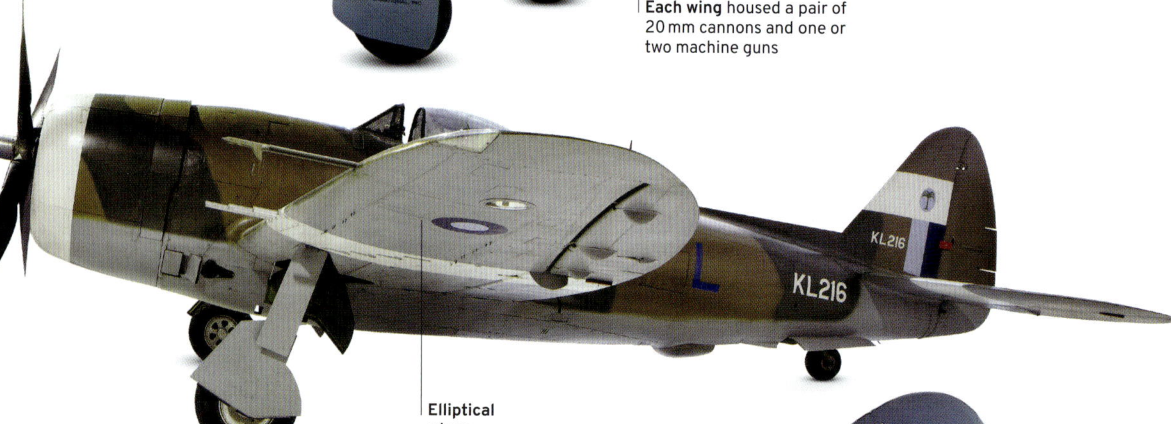

Elliptical wings

△ Republic P-47 Thunderbolt

Date 1942 **Origin** US

Engine 2,535 hp (1,890.3 kW) Pratt & Whitney R-2800-59W Double Wasp radial

Top speed 435 mph (700 km/h)

The Thunderbolt, nicknamed the "Jug" for its bulky shape, was an effective ground-attack fighter-bomber. Its ability to survive damage and its exceptional high-altitude performance, being able to out-dive any German aircraft, earned it the respect of pilots.

Fin and rudder designed to maximize maneuverability

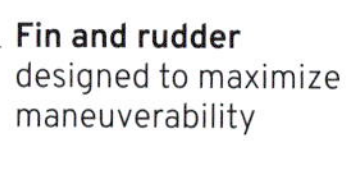

Retractable tail wheel

Fighter Planes

By the outbreak of World War II, the most able fighters could reach speeds exceeding 348 mph (560 km/h) and climb to 34,000 ft (10,360 m). Some combatant nations, such as Japan, initially favored lightweight, lightly armored planes, believing that maneuverability was all-important; others focused on protection and firepower. It was the latter that proved more effective. Such fighters were also easier to adapt to the ground-attack role, which became increasingly important as the war progressed.

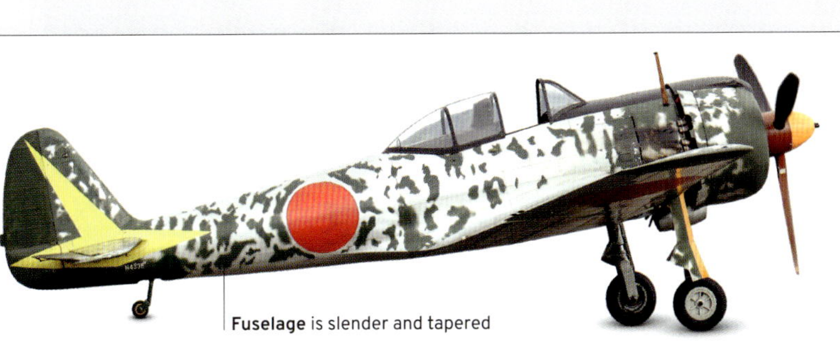

△ **Nakajima Ki-43 Hayabusa "Oscar"**

Date 1942 **Origin** Japan

Engine 1,150 hp (845.8 kW) Nakajima Ha-115 14-cylinder radial

Top speed 330 mph (530 km/h)

Although slow by contemporary standards and poorly armed, the Hayabusa (Peregrine Falcon) was well-regarded by pilots for its maneuverability and superb climb rate, made possible by a weight of just 2.5 tons (2.3 tonnes). It was superior to opposing fighters in the war's early stages, but later suffered as Allied planes acquired heavier firepower.

△ **North American P-51 Mustang**

Date 1943 **Origin** US

Engine 1,590 hp (1,185.6 kW) Packard Merlin V-1650-7 V12

Top speed 438 mph (705 km/h)

The highly aerodynamic P-51 Mustang was produced in response to a request from the UK. It initially underachieved, but once refitted with a Packard-built Rolls-Royce Merlin engine, it played a huge part in the Allied air success. The Mustang became a mainstay of the USAAF, in both long-range escort and fighter-bomber roles.

Each wing could carry four 3in rockets or a single 500 lb (226.8 kg) bomb

△ **Hawker Tempest Mk II**

Date 1944 **Origin** UK

Engine 2,590 hp (1,931.3 kW) Bristol Centaurus V radial

Top speed 432 mph (695 km/h)

The fast, agile Tempest was the last and best of Britain's World War II piston-engined fighters. Used intelligently by skilled pilots, the Tempest could even take on Germany's jet-powered Messerschmitts and Arados. It also performed superbly as a ground-attack aircraft.

Two 30 mm cannons housed in wing roots

Air intake for engine

◁ **Yakovlev Yak-3**

Date 1944 **Origin** Soviet Union

Engine 1,300 hp (969.4 kW) Klimov VK-105PF-2 V12

Top speed 410 mph (655 km/h)

Easy and cheap to maintain, the small, light, agile Yak-3's high power-to-weight ratio made it a formidable adversary in dogfights. Many pilots who flew the Mustang, the Spitfire, and the Yak-3 rated the Yak as the superior aircraft.

Supermarine Spitfire

Designed by R. J. Mitchell, creator of Supermarine's Schneider Trophy-winning racing floatplanes of the 1920s and early 1930s, the Spitfire is arguably the most famous aircraft of all time. Along with the Hawker Hurricane, this elegant, iconic fighter was instrumental in fending off the Luftwaffe during the Battle of Britain in 1940. Continuously modified and improved, the Spitfire remained in production throughout World War II.

MITCHELL'S SPITFIRE epitomized stressed-skin construction. Rather than fabric covering a wooden or metal frame, Mitchell used an eggshell-thin, aluminum-alloy outer surface to carry much of the load imposed on the aircraft. The striking elliptical wing shape was chosen for practical rather than aesthetic reasons, because it offered low drag yet still allowed room for eight 0.303-in Browning machine guns (later a combination of guns and 20-mm cannon) and the retracted undercarriage.

Superb handling characteristics ensured the Spitfire's immediate success. When flown to its limits in dogfights, the Spitfire could shake off a pursuer with a flick and half-roll and a quick pull out of the subsequent dive. It had the edge over the German Messerschmitt Bf 109 in speed, climb, and turning circle, although the Me 109 outperformed it at altitudes above 20,000 ft (6,000 m) and in steep dives.

The basic design of the Spitfire lent itself to continued development. By the time Mitchell's successor, Joseph Smith, had produced the final Spitfire variant—the Mk24—in 1946, the aircraft possessed more than twice the horsepower of the prototype, and its maximum weight had increased by the equivalent of 30 passengers.

Aerial mast for high frequency (HF) radio

Rudder is fabric-covered and horn-balanced

RAF roundel type A1 with wide yellow outer ring

Rear fuselage is elliptical-section stressed skin

Fin flash aids identification, helping to avoid "friendly fire" incidences

Squadron markings

Distinguished veteran
This MkIIa Spitfire, P7350, entered service in August 1940 and took part in the Battle of Britain. Currently operated by the Battle of Britain Memorial Flight, it is the oldest substantially original Spitfire still flying.

Demarcation between upper camouflage and "Sky" undersurfaces

SPECIFICATIONS	
Model	Supermarine Spitfire MkII, 1940
Origin	UK
Production	20,351
Construction	Aluminum alloy stressed-skin
Maximum weight	6,172 lb (2,799 kg)
Engine	1,150 hp (858 kW) Rolls-Royce Merlin XII supercharged liquid-cooled V12
Wingspan	36 ft 10 in (11.23 m)
Length	29 ft 11 in (9.12 m)
Range	405 miles (651 km)
Top speed	357 mph (575 km/h)

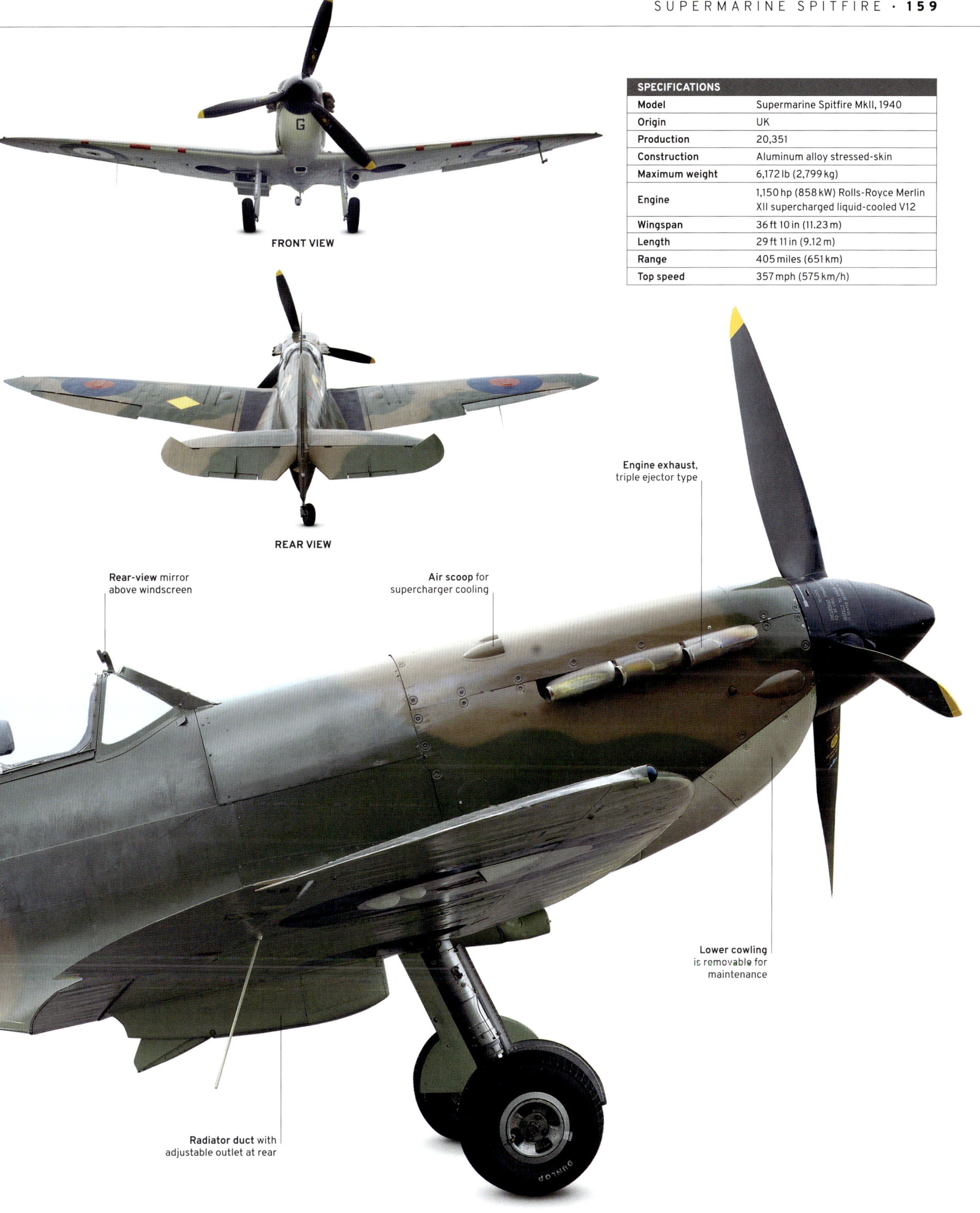

FRONT VIEW

REAR VIEW

Rear-view mirror above windscreen

Air scoop for supercharger cooling

Engine exhaust, triple ejector type

Lower cowling is removable for maintenance

Radiator duct with adjustable outlet at rear

EXTERIOR

In a dogfight, speed can determine which pilot lives or dies, so the Spitfire's design tried to squeeze as many miles per hour as possible from the aircraft. Since streamlined surfaces reduce drag, flush-rivets were used on the wings—and, on later versions, on the fuselage too—to make the skin smoother. Adding ejector exhausts and a "Meredith Duct" around the radiator also increased speed by augmenting the main thrust from the propeller.

1. Ejector engine exhausts **2.** Carburettor air intake **3.** Pitot head measures airspeed **4.** Radiator air intake **5.** Tailplane fairing **6.** Cartridge ejection chutes under wing **7.** Fabric patch over machine-gun port to reduce drag (rounds break fabric when gun fires) **8.** Starboard navigation light **9.** Cockpit door with escape crowbar **10.** Typical stenciling **11.** IFF (Identification Friend or Foe) aerial grommet **12.** Rudder trim-tab actuator **13.** Taillight **14.** Stencil for electrical bonding

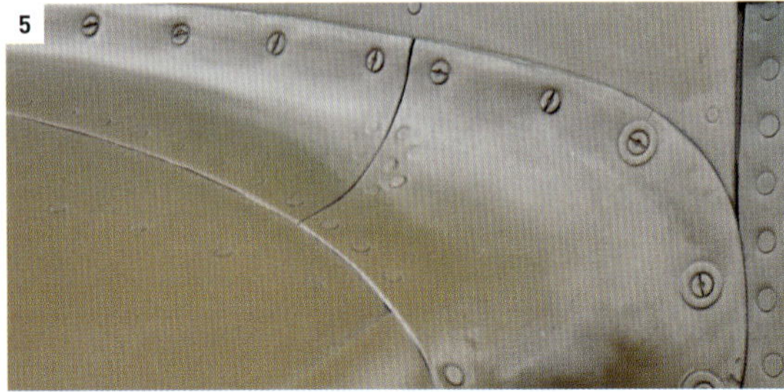

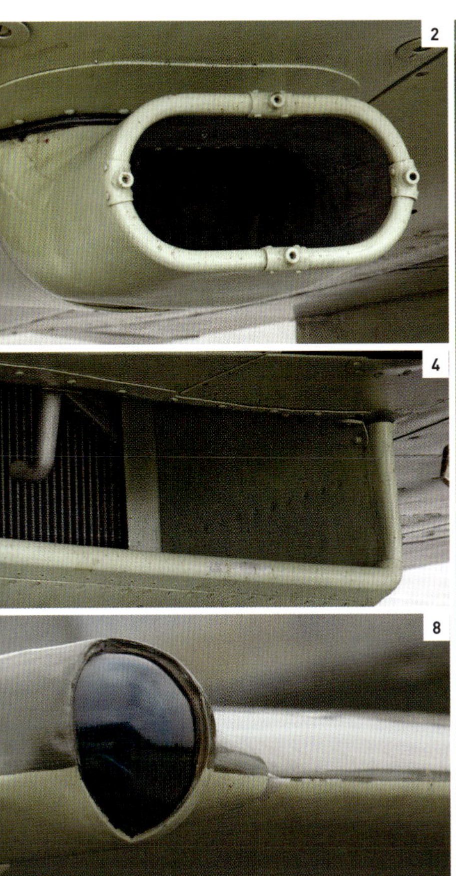

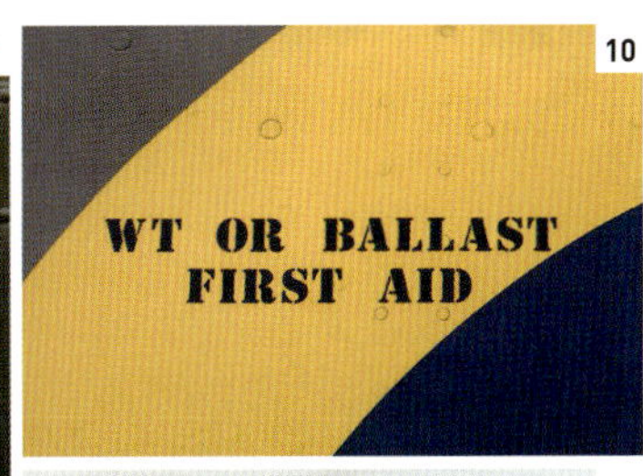

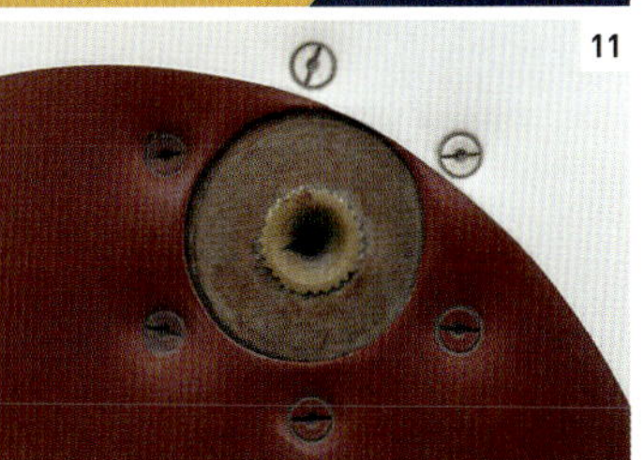

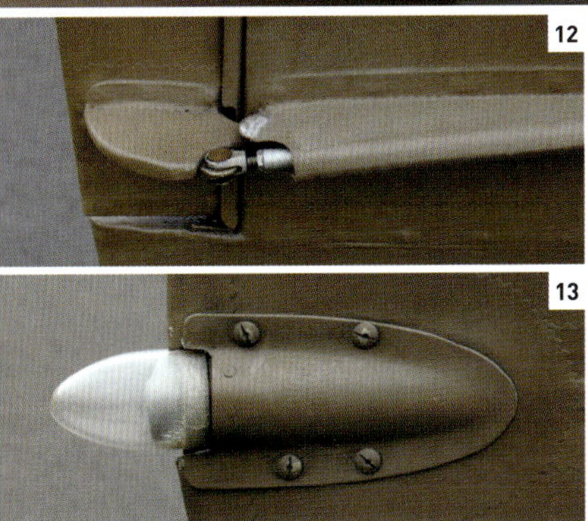

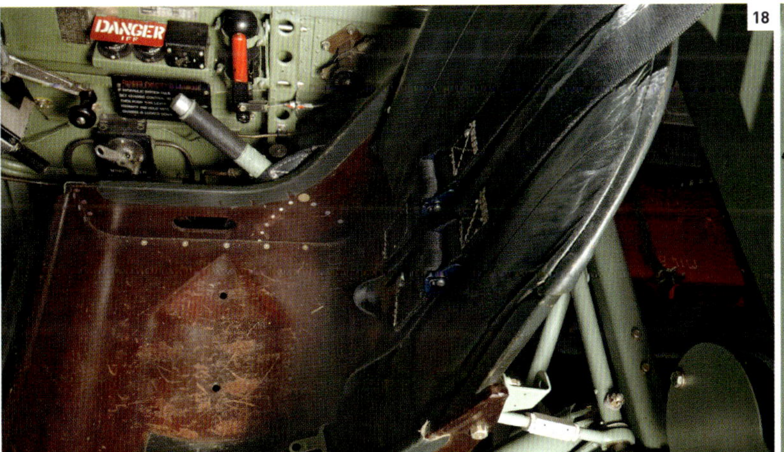

COCKPIT

Behind the control column was the "Basic Six" instrument panel (typical of most RAF aircraft of the time), comprising airspeed indicator, artificial horizon, vertical speed indicator, altimeter, heading indicator, and turn-and-slip indicator. To the right were the engine instruments; to the left, oxygen, undercarriage, and flap controls, and other instruments. The cockpit had no floor—just rudder pedals on which to rest the feet, with structure and systems beneath.

15. Instrument panel (with modern avionics in place of gunsight) **16.** Control column, with gun button at top **17.** Undercarriage selector **18.** Pilot's bucket seat with height adjustment lever **19.** Gun-camera indicator **20.** Headrest and armor **21.** Rudder pedal

HH229
BT879

The Gliders of World War II

The use of airborne forces brought a new dimension to warfare, allowing troop and equipment landings behind enemy lines. Adverse weather conditions, however, could disperse parachutists over a wide area, leaving them isolated and vulnerable to attack. The glider provided a way to land groups of troops together and deliver a greater load of equipment. Towed by transport aircraft or heavy bombers, gliders, once released, were silent in their approach to a landing zone, enabling them to lead precision attacks, such as the German capture of Fort Ében-Émael in Belgium in 1940 and the British capture of the Orne River and Cael Canal crossings on the morning of D-Day in June 1944. Considered a one-use item, gliders were made of wood and could suffer major damage with rough landings, but they were relatively cheap to make and glider-borne infantry were quicker to train than paratroopers.

Glider pilots and airborne infantry receive instruction from RAF trainers, using troop-carrying Hotspur gliders, near Oxford in October 1942.

▷ **Messerschmitt Me262 Schwalbe**

Date 1942 **Origin** Germany

Engine 2 x 1,980 lb (898 kg) thrust Junkers Jumo 004 B-1 turbojets

Top speed 559 mph (900 km/h)

The first turbojet-powered combat fighter, the Me 262 quickly made an impact against the Allies' daylight bombing raids. However, it was hampered by a lack of dive brakes, as well as its engines' short life and inherent unreliability.

△ **de Havilland DH100 Vampire FB 6**

Date 1943 **Origin** UK

Engine 3,350 lb (1,520 kg) thrust de Havilland Goblin 3 turbojet

Top speed 548 mph (882 km/h)

First flown in 1943, the Vampire did not enter service until 1946. It was the RAF's second jet fighter, and the first made by British aircraft manufacturer de Havilland. Unusually, a large amount of wood (plywood and balsa) was used in its construction. The twin tail boom arrangement kept the tailplane clear of the exhaust.

△ **Messerschmitt Me 163 Komet**

Date 1944 **Origin** Germany

Engine 3,750 lb (1,700 kg) Walter HWK 109-509A-2 liquid-fuel rocket

Top speed 600 mph (960 km/h)

The Komet was the sole rocket-powered fighter aircraft to see active service. With limited fuel, it could only make one or two firing passes at high-altitude bombers before having to glide back to base.

△ **Heinkel He162**

Date 1944 **Origin** Germany

Engine 1,760 lb (798 kg) thrust BMW 003 turbojet

Top speed 562 mph (905 km/h)

Intended to be cheap and simple enough to be flown by inexperienced pilots, the He162 was nicknamed the "Volksjager" (People's Fighter). A few He162s saw combat before the war's end; having been rushed through production, more were lost through design flaws than were shot down.

◁ **Lockheed P-80A Shooting Star**

Date 1944 **Origin** USA

Engine 4,600 lb (2,087 kg) thrust Allison J33-9 turbojet

Top speed 558 mph (898 km/h)

The first US jet fighter to see combat, the Shooting Star arrived in Europe too late for World War II service but, redesignated as the F-80, it featured extensively in the Korean War. Soon obsolete as a fighter, it was developed into the T-33 jet trainer, which remained in service until the 1970s with both the US Air Force and Navy.

Early Jets

Jet engines made their first appearance in aircraft in the latter stages of World War II. The advent of jet-propulsion technology required entirely new designs for combat aircraft. The new jet planes, which not only looked radically different from their piston-powered predecessors but also had significantly higher top speeds, changed aerial combat forever. Within a decade, piston-engined fighters had largely disappeared; most other propeller-driven military aircraft would soon go the same way.

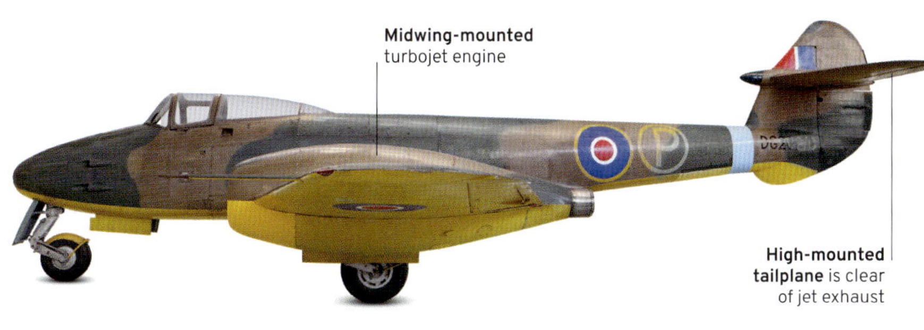

△ Gloster Meteor

Date 1944 **Origin** UK
Engine 2 x 3,500 lb (1,590 kg) Rolls-Royce Derwent turbojets
Top speed 600 mph (965 km/h)

This was the only Allied jet to enter combat in World War II, and it later served in Korea. It set new world records for speed, rate-of-climb, and endurance. The last Meteor variant was withdrawn as late as 1965.

△ Arado Ar 234B-2

Date 1944 **Origin** Germany
Engine 2 x 1,103 lb (500 kg) thrust Junkers Jumo 004B-1 turbojets
Top speed 461 mph (742 km/h)

Germany's Ar 234 was the world's first jet bomber and reconnaissance aircraft. It was so fast that it easily outran Allied piston-engined fighters. To save weight, it was initially given a dolly and skid-type undercarriage; this proved impractical in service, so wheels were fitted instead.

Machine guns located in the nose

Straight wings spanned 36 ft 5 in (11.10 m)

△ Republic F-84C Thunderjet

Date 1946 **Origin** USA
Engine 5,560 lb (2,522 kg) thrust Allison J-35 turbojet
Top speed 622 mph (1,000 km/h)

Republic developed the F-84 as a jet-powered successor to its P-47 Thunderbolt. As the company's first jet, it had a long and difficult gestation period. Despite this, the Thunderjet evolved into a highly competent fighter-bomber that saw frontline action in Korea. It was also the first plane flown by the Thunderbirds—the US Air Force aerobatic team.

Sea Battles in World War II

The naval war fought between 1939 and 1945 signaled the end of the era of the big-gun battleship. In its place came more technologically advanced submarines and aircraft carriers—the navy that could dominate the spaces above and below the waves could dominate the sea's surface.

British submarine
An S-class submarine moves through ice-covered waters off the east coast of England in 1940. In September 1939, when war began, Britain had 60 submarines in service.

The navies of World War II included history's greatest battleships, in terms of physical size and firepower. However, despite their awesome gunnery and fearsome silhouettes, many were sunk by submarines or aircraft, or both.

On October 14, 1939, the British battleship HMS *Royal Oak*—a veteran of World War I—was torpedoed and sunk by the German submarine U-47 at Scapa Flow in Orkney, Scotland. Three battleships—the USS *Arizona*, *Oklahoma*, and *Utah*—were among the American losses from Japanese air attack at Pearl Harbor on December 7, 1941. Three days later, Japanese aircraft sank the British battleship *Prince of Wales* and battle cruiser *Repulse* off the east coast of Malaya. The German battleship *Tirpitz* was capsized at anchor in Norway on November 12, 1944, by British Lancaster bombers equipped with 12,000 lb (5,400 kg) "Tallboy" bombs.

The largest, most heavily armed battleships that ever floated—the Japanese *Yamato* and *Musashi*—were both bombed to destruction by US Navy carrier aircraft in 1944–45. By the end of the war, battleships had become regarded as liabilities.

Naval theaters

The nature of the naval war changed according to the theater of operations. In the confines of the Mediterranean Sea, the war between 1941 and 1943 was primarily that of Allied and Axis shipping trying to resupply operations to North Africa and other coastal territories, harried by enemy air forces and submarines. Beyond the far north of Europe, from 1941 the Allied Arctic convoys—merchant ships with naval escorts—made freezing supply runs fraught with peril between Britain and the USSR through ice-choked seas, under heavy attack by German aircraft and U-boats.

The Atlantic theater was defined by the battle between German U-boats and Allied convoys bringing vital supplies from the US to Europe. At several key "happy times," as they were known in Germany, between 1940 and 1942, the U-boats were sinking Allied ships at a rapid rate, often faster than they could be built. From 1943, however, Allied anti-submarine technologies and tactics improved to the extent that by 1945 the German navy's U-boat arm had a 70 percent crew fatality rate.

Although the undersea threat also had a profound impact in the Pacific theater, where US Navy submarines alone accounted for more than 50 percent of Japanese merchant losses, the ocean was, above all, the domain of the aircraft carrier. Ship-launched aviation projected power across the vast Pacific distances, well beyond the reach of naval guns. Between 1942 and 1945, the US built 17 large fleet

Carrier power
The USS *Hornet* (CV-8), with five of its aircraft on deck, lies at anchor in the Pacific. The ship, a *Yorktown*-class carrier, was sunk in the Battle of the Santa Cruz Islands on October 27, 1942.

"The only thing that ever **really frightened** me during the war was the **U-boat peril.**"

WINSTON CHURCHILL, FROM HIS WORLD WAR II MEMOIRS

carriers, while Japan produced just six. By war's end, the US Navy also had around 37,000 aircraft, more than 10 times the Japanese number.

Coming ashore

Amphibious landings were another critical element of the sea war—an aspect of naval combat mastered by the Allies, who could not defeat Japan or Germany without putting troops and equipment on hostile shores. The Pacific theater was essentially one great "island-hopping" campaign, while in Europe the operations at Sicily in July 1943 and Normandy in June 1944 delivered the largest amphibious landings in history and the springboard to ultimate victory.

Heavy fire
The USS *Iowa* (BB-61) fires its massive 16-in (406-mm) main guns across the Pacific around 1944. The guns were used mainly for shore bombardments of Japanese-held coastlines in preparation for amphibious landings.

TALKING POINT

Arctic convoys

Following the German invasion of the USSR in June 1941, the Allies sought to provide the beleaguered Soviets with essential war supplies via merchant convoys sailing from Britain and Iceland through the Arctic Ocean to the ports of Murmansk and Archangel. The supplies included trucks, aircraft, tanks, radios, tractors, railway engines, and even boots. Storms, pack ice, and subzero temperatures made the two-way journey highly dangerous, and if a sailor entered the water, life expectancy was about five minutes. In June 1942, convoy PQ17 lost 23 out of its 34 ships to German aircraft and U-boats on its way to the USSR. Out of all the Allied convoy campaigns the Arctic had the highest loss rate, 17 times greater than in the Atlantic, with nearly 3,000 sailors losing their lives.

A sailor on the British light cruiser HMS *Sheffield* operates an ice-covered signal projector in 1941. Ice buildup was a serious problem for the Arctic convoy ships.

Battleships and Cruisers

Major navies entered World War II focused on developing ever bigger, more capable battleships, with Germany's *Tirpitz* and *Bismarck*, the US's *Iowa*, and Japan's *Yamato* and *Musashi* all under construction at the war's start. Fast and powerfully armed, these huge ships were extraordinary fighting vessels. Such big-gun vessels undoubtedly played a key role in the war at sea; nevertheless, they also proved vulnerable to air attack, and aircraft carriers soon eclipsed them as the most valuable type of warship. Cruisers—typically described as "light" if armed with 6 in guns, and "heavy" if they mounted anything larger—took part in surface engagements and escorted carrier and battleship groups. To combat the aerial threat, antiaircraft cruisers emerged, with high-angle guns to protect against bombers.

△ **HMS Rodney**

Date 1927 **Origin** UK
Displacement 50,624 tons (45,925 tonnes)
Length 710 ft (216.4 m)
Top speed 23 knots (43 km/h)

An unconventional arrangement of their main armament—all nine 16 in guns were located forward, in three triple turrets—characterized *Rodney* and its sister ship *Nelson*. HMS *Rodney* played a key role in the sinking of the *Bismarck* in 1941 and bombarded coastal defences during the D-Day landings of 1944.

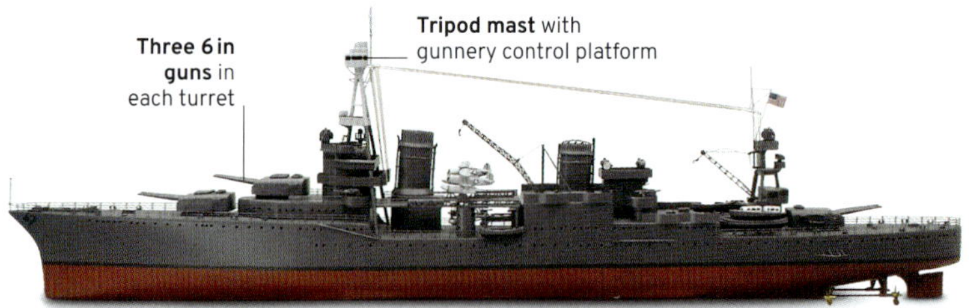

△ **USS Northampton**

Date 1930 **Origin** USA
Displacement 12,790 tons (11,603 tonnes)
Length 600¼ ft (183 m)
Top speed 32.5 knots (60 km/h)

The six *Northampton*-class armored heavy cruisers saw much action in World War II. Three of the ships were lost, including *Northampton* itself, which was sunk by Japanese torpedoes during the short, hectic Battle of Tassafaronga on the night of November 30, 1942.

△ **Takao**

Date 1932 **Origin** Japan
Displacement 14,314 tons (12,985 tonnes)
Length 668½ ft (203.8 m)
Top speed 35.5 knots (66 km/h)

Built in the interwar years, the four *Takao*-class ships were upgraded prior to World War II. These ships were the largest, most effective of Japan's wartime heavy cruisers. Three were sunk at the Battle of the Philippine Sea in 1944; *Takao* was damaged, but survived—unrepaired—until the war's end.

▷ **Bismarck**

Date 1940 **Origin** Germany
Displacement 57,008 tons (51,717 tonnes)
Length 814 ft (248 m)
Top speed 29 knots (54 km/h)

Bismarck and its sister ship *Tirpitz* posed such a threat that the British Navy deployed significant resources to keep them contained. In 1941, on *Bismarck*'s sole offensive operation, it sank the battleship HMS *Hood*. Pursued and attacked by British ships and aircraft, *Bismarck* was sunk by a combination of shellfire, torpedo strikes, and scuttling. *Tirpitz* survived until 1944.

△ **Vittorio Veneto**

Date 1940 **Origin** Italy
Displacement 50,434 tons (45,742 tonnes)
Length 780 ft (237.8 m)
Top speed 30 knots (56 km/h)

During its five-year construction, the design specification for *Vittorio Veneto* altered significantly. One of only three fast Italian battleships to serve with the Italian navy during World War II, *Vittorio Veneto* carried its nine main guns in triple turrets, two forward and one aft.

▽ **Yamato**

Date 1941 **Origin** Japan
Displacement 71,113 tonnes (78,389 tons)
Length 263 m (863 ft)
Top speed 27 knots (50 km/h)

Despite being the largest and most powerfully armed battleships ever built, *Yamato* and its sister ship *Musashi* proved vulnerable to air attack: both were sunk by carrier-launched US aircraft. *Shinano*, the third *Yamato*-class ship, was modified into an aircraft carrier during construction, but was sunk by the US submarine *Archerfish* while en route for fitting out.

▽ USS North Carolina

Date 1941 **Origin** USA
Displacement 49,706 tons (45,093 tonnes)
Length 729 ft (222.1 m)
Top speed 28 knots (52 km/h)

Marking a significant departure in US battleship design, *North Carolina* and its sister ship *Washington* were bigger, faster, and armed with more powerful guns than those laid down at the end of World War I. Nicknamed "The Showboat," *North Carolina* won 15 battle stars. It is now preserved at Wilmington in its home state.

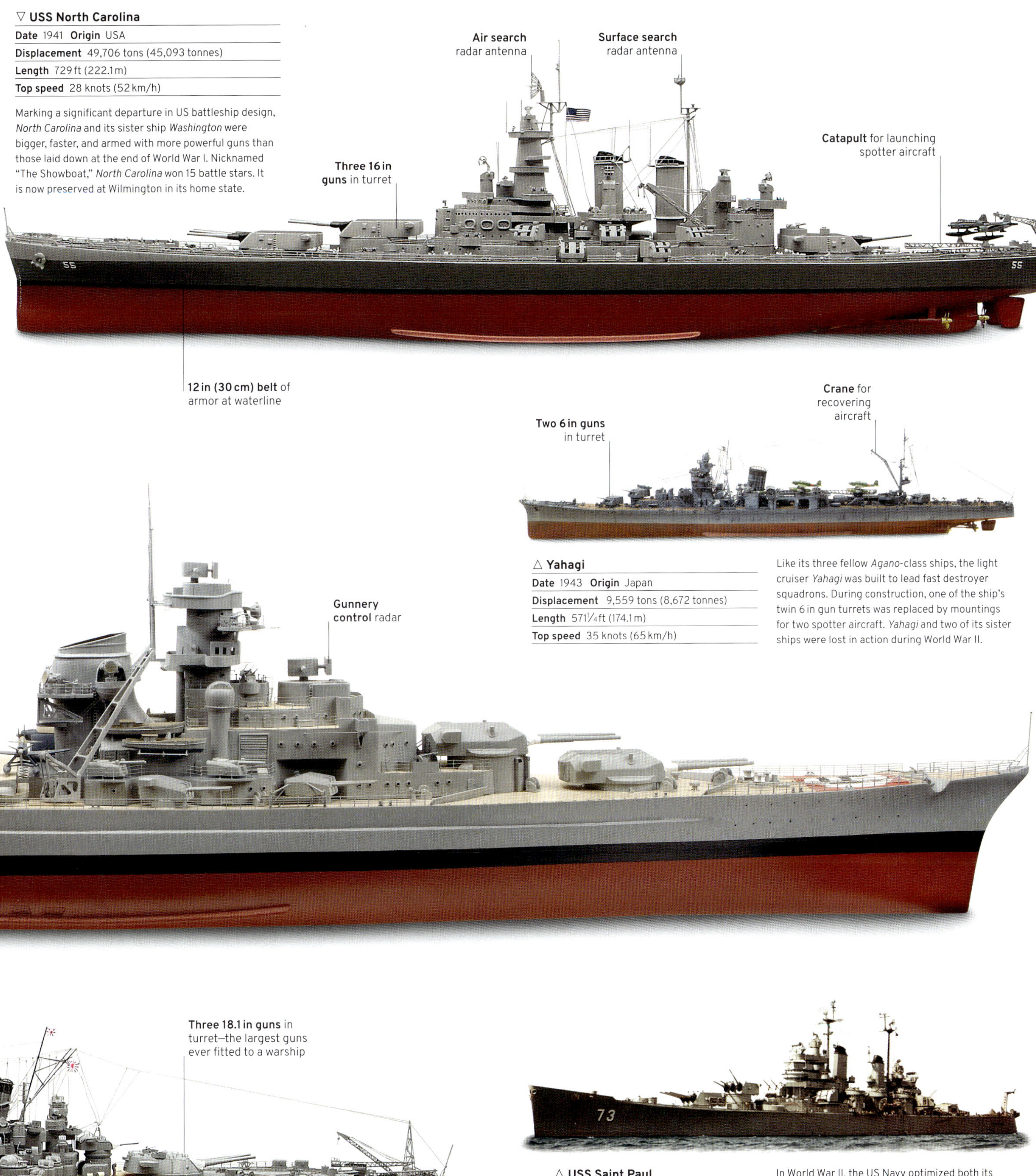

△ Yahagi

Date 1943 **Origin** Japan
Displacement 9,559 tons (8,672 tonnes)
Length 571¼ ft (174.1 m)
Top speed 35 knots (65 km/h)

Like its three fellow *Agano*-class ships, the light cruiser *Yahagi* was built to lead fast destroyer squadrons. During construction, one of the ship's twin 6 in gun turrets was replaced by mountings for two spotter aircraft. *Yahagi* and two of its sister ships were lost in action during World War II.

△ USS Saint Paul

Date 1945 **Origin** USA
Displacement 17,600 tons (15,966 tonnes)
Length 673½ ft (205.3 m)
Top speed 33 knots (61 km/h)

In World War II, the US Navy optimized both its light and heavy cruisers for antiaircraft duties. *Baltimore*-class heavy cruisers, such as the USS *Saint Paul*, were mainly used to protect carrier battle groups from air attack. *Saint Paul* later saw action during the Korean and Vietnam wars.

HMS Belfast

Ordered from Belfast shipbuilders Harland & Wolf in 1936 and launched in 1938, HMS *Belfast* was part of the British Royal Navy's response to the threat of Japan's *Mogami*-class cruisers. This light cruiser saw varied action during World War II, from escorting Arctic convoys and fighting German battleships, to bombarding the D-Day beaches and deployment to the Far East. HMS *Belfast* later took part in the Korean War, finishing its naval service years as an accommodation ship before being retired in 1963.

To prevent a naval arms race, definitions for warship types and limitations on their numbers were agreed in international treaties during the interwar years. As a category, cruisers fitted between larger battleships and smaller destroyers. By World War II, the roles of cruisers included scouting for the main fleet, attacking enemy ships and merchant vessels, and—having greater speed but less protection than battleships—cruising the wider oceans.

The 1930 London Naval Conference defined the light cruiser as having guns of less than 6.1 in (155 mm) and a displacement not exceeding 11,200 tons (10,160 tonnes). However, as *Town*-class cruisers, *Belfast* and its sister ship *Edinburgh* weighed 11,648 tons (10,567 tonnes)—the size restriction was ignored because Germany and Japan had failed to sign subsequent naval treaties.

In November 1939, just months after being commissioned, *Belfast* triggered a German mine. The subsequent rebuild turned *Belfast* into arguably the Royal Navy's most powerful cruiser. For the D-Day invasion of Normandy on June 6, 1944, *Belfast* was part of Bombardment Force E, supporting British and Canadian landings on Gold and Juno beaches; it remained there until the ground campaign moved out of range of her guns. The ship performed a similar role during the Korean War, firing over 8,000 rounds from her twelve 6 inch guns at land targets.

SPECIFICATIONS	
Model	HMS *Belfast*
Commissioned	1939
Class and type	*Town*-class light cruiser
Displacement	12,936 tons (11,735 tonnes)
Length	614 ft (187 m)
Propulsion	4 x Parsons geared steam turbines
Armament	12 x 6 in guns
Armor	4½ in (114 mm) max.
Maximum speed	32 knots (59 km/h)

Draft marks indicate depth of the ship below the waterline

Turret (one of four) housing three 6 in guns

Unique ID
Moored on the Thames River in London, HMS *Belfast* is now a museum ship. *Belfast*'s unique Royal Navy pennant number—C (for Cruiser) 35—is painted on its hull. Pennant numbers are used for identification.

EXTERIOR

Like many warships, *Belfast* was upgraded and improved during her service life. Although now partially returned to her wartime D-Day configuration, much of *Belfast*'s postwar refitting is still in evidence, including an enclosed bridge—constructed in 1956 as part of a modernization program—to protect against nuclear, biological, and chemical (NBC) attack.

1. Name on hull **2.** Ship's bell **3.** Life buoy **4.** Upper decks and bridge **5.** Lattice mast with communications antennas and radar equipment **6.** 40mm Bofors antiaircraft guns and fire control (port side) **7.** Radar director for 6in guns **8.** 40mm Bofors antiaircraft guns and fire control (starboard side) **9.** Forward 6in gun turrets

11

12

13

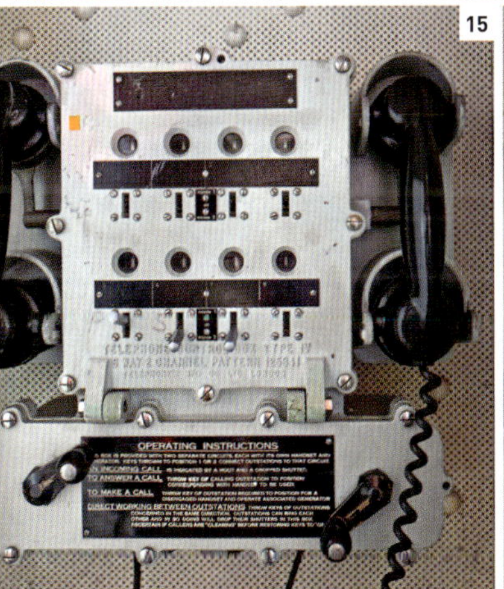
15

16

17

19

INTERIOR

Navigational, tactical, communication, and gunnery control systems were situated on the upper decks. Essential crew facilities included berths, a galley, bakery, and laundry, and a medical center with sick bay, dental surgery, dispensary, and examination room. The mid-part of the lower decks was enclosed by a thick "box" of cemented armor to protect the boilers and turbines. Each gun turret was served by its own shell room in the hold; shells from a revolving carousel were hoisted up to the turret.

10. Compass platform (part of bridge) **11.** Heating drainage controls **12.** Engine **13.** Shell room with 6in munitions **14.** Radar screen **15.** Telephone control box **16.** Laundry room **17.** Pressure gauges **18.** Fire-hose reel **19.** Sick bay

Destroyers and Escorts in World War II

During World War I, the primary function of destroyers had been to defend the battle fleet against attack from similar ships or torpedo boats, and to hunt submarines. For much of the interwar period, the size and numbers of naval vessels—including destroyers—were limited by international naval treaties, such as the Washington Treaty of 1922 and the London Treaty of 1930, although some nations exploited loopholes. By the late 1930s, Japan and Germany had rejected such restrictions. In World War II, with the concept of the battle fleet now obsolete, destroyers required a new role. Now larger, up-gunned, and armed with depth charges, they were employed—along with a new generation of smaller escorts, including corvettes—to guard convoys of merchant ships against attack from submarines and aircraft.

△ F-class escort ship

Date 1936 **Origin** Germany	
Displacement	785 tons (712 tonnes)
Length	249 ft (75.9 m)
Top speed	28 knots (52 km/h)

The ten German F-class ships built in the 1930s were conceived as fast fleet and convoy escorts that could also carry out anti-submarine and minesweeping duties. Unreliable power plants and poor performance in rough seas saw them withdrawn from frontline service later in the war.

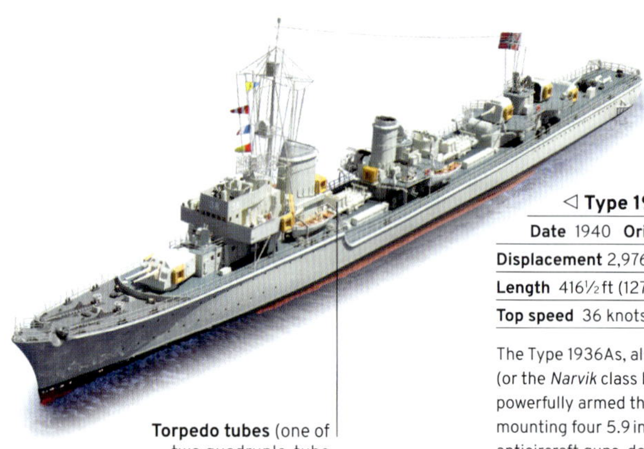

◁ Type 1936A destroyer

Date 1940 **Origin** Germany	
Displacement	2,976 tons (2,700 tonnes)
Length	416½ ft (127 m)
Top speed	36 knots (67 km/h)

The Type 1936As, also called the Z23 class (or the *Narvik* class by the Allies), were more powerfully armed than most destroyers, mounting four 5.9 in main guns. As well as antiaircraft guns, depth charges, and torpedoes, they could carry up to 60 mines.

△ HMS Acanthus

Date 1940 **Origin** UK	
Displacement	1,394 tons (1,265 tonnes)
Length	205 ft (62.5 m)
Top speed	16.5 knots (31 km/h)

Based on the design of commercial whale-catchers and powered by piston engines rather than turbines, *Flower*-class corvettes such as HMS *Acanthus* were the smallest purpose-built convoy escorts. *Acanthus* was armed with a single main gun, machine guns, and depth charges.

△ HMS Avon Vale

Date 1941 **Origin** UK	
Displacement	1,820 tons (1,651 tonnes)
Length	280 ft (85.3 m)
Top speed	27 knots (50 km/h)

This multi-role British ship was designed to defend merchant convoys against attacks by both submarines and aircraft. *Avon Vale* was the first of the second group of *Hunt*-class destroyer-escorts built for the Royal Navy during the early years of World War II.

▷ Suzutsuki

Date 1942 **Origin** Japan	
Displacement	4,144 tons (3,759 tonnes)
Length	440¼ ft (134.2 m)
Top speed	33 knots (61 km/h)

Suzutsuki and its 11 *Akizuki*-class companions were built as fast, antiaircraft escorts for carrier battle groups. The later addition of torpedo tubes and depth-charge launchers turned it into a general-purpose destroyer. *Suzutsuki* survived the war, along with five of the other *Akizuki*s.

▷ **USS Parker**

Date 1942 **Origin** USA
Displacement 2,682 tons (2,433 tonnes)
Length 348½ ft (106.2 m)
Top speed 35 knots (65 km/h)

Parker was one of the later examples of the US Navy's *Benson/Gleaves*-class destroyers, which were the last to be designed before World War II. *Parker*'s weaponry was reduced from five to four 5 in guns in single turrets, with light antiaircraft guns installed in place of the fifth turret.

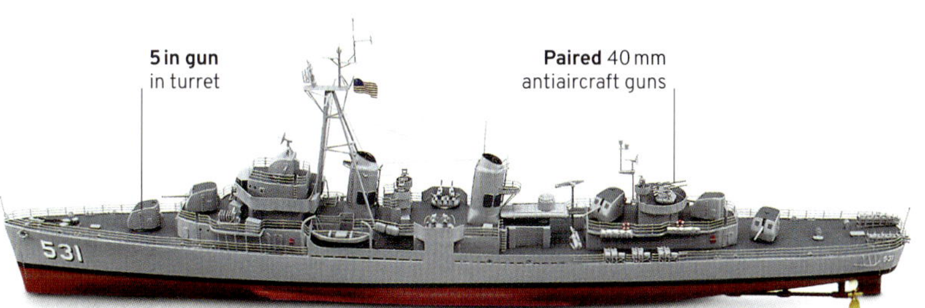

△ **USS Hazelwood**

Date 1943 **Origin** USA
Displacement 3,276 tons (2,972 tonnes)
Length 376½ ft (114.7 m)
Top speed 38 knots (70 km/h)

Designed in 1939 and built up until 1944, *Fletcher*-class destroyers such as the *Hazelwood* were the first to be built by the US without adhering to the limitations of the naval treaties. In all, 175 ships were produced. The *Hazelwood* and many other World War II survivors were reactivated out of reserve during the Korean War.

▽ **Buckley-class destroyer escort**

Date 1943 **Origin** USA
Displacement 1,874 tons (1,700 tonnes)
Length 306 ft (93 m)
Top speed 24 knots (44 km/h)

The US Navy's 102 *Buckley*-class vessels were prefabricated at US factories, then assembled on shipyard slipways. A further 46 were delivered to the Royal Navy, which classed them as frigates. *Buckleys* escorted convoys and engaged in anti-submarine warfare.

◁ **Type D escort ship**

Date 1944 **Origin** Japan
Displacement 829 tons (752 tonnes)
Length 228 ft (69.5 m)
Top speed 17.5 knots (32.5 km/h)

In 1943, Japan began mass producing escort ships to protect its convoys from Allied attacks. While simple in design, to aid speedy construction, Type Ds were robust, showing a surprising survival rate when struck by torpedoes or mines. However, they were not as effective against Allied aircraft and submarines.

World War II Submarines

During World War II, when Germany's surface fleet was severely hampered by Hitler's prejudice against it, the Kriegsmarine's U-boats accounted for the bulk of German naval successes. Attacking escorted Atlantic convoys in "wolf packs" and sinking around 2,000 merchant vessels, the U-boats came close to bringing Britain to its knees. Improved technology, tactics, air cover, and intelligence eventually allowed the Allies to turn the tide decisively against the U-boats. In the Pacific, Allied submarines, primarily those of the US Navy, preyed on Japanese merchant vessels in order to weaken the economy of Japan. They also targeted troop transports and warships, landed raiding parties, and participated in evacuations.

△ **RN T-class (1937–44)**

Date 1938–45 **Origin** UK
Displacement 1,478 tons (1,341 tonnes)
Length 275 ft (83.8 m)
Top speed 15.5 knots (29 km/h)

More than 50 T-class (or *Triton*-class) boats were built for Britain's Royal Navy in three groups between 1937 and 1944. The design saw considerable improvements, with the maximum dive depth of 300 ft (91 m) increasing to 350 ft (106 m) in the last group. Later builds remained in service until the 1960s.

▷ **German Type VIIC**

Date 1940–44 **Origin** Germany
Displacement 839 tons (761 tonnes)
Length 220 ft (67.1 m)
Top speed 17 knots (31 km/h)

Type VIIs formed the backbone of Germany's submarine force. From ports in western France they harried Atlantic convoys and came close to shutting down the shipping routes that brought Britain much-needed supplies from North America. Around 660 Type VIIs were completed—more than any other submarine in history—with Type VIIC variants predominating.

▽ **USS Gato**

Date 1941 **Origin** USA
Displacement 1,707 tons (1,549 tonnes)
Length 311½ ft (95 m)
Top speed 20 knots (37 km/h)

Gato was the lead vessel of one of three closely related classes of "fleet boats" that accounted for most of the US Navy's wartime submarines (the other two classes being *Balao* and *Tench*). The vessels were modified extensively during and after the war. In the postwar years, *Gato* was used as a training boat until the 1960s. Many *Gato*-class boats were transferred to other navies in the 1970s, some remaining in service to the 1990s.

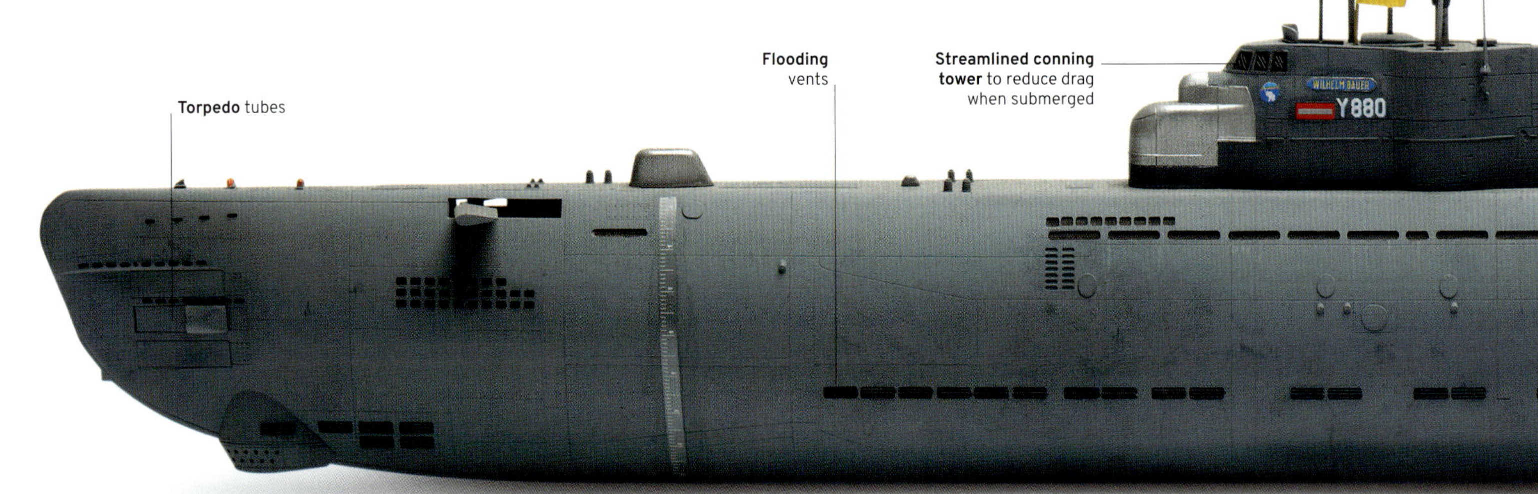

◁ **RN X-craft**

Date 1942–45	**Origin** UK
Displacement 30 tons (27.2 tonnes)	
Length 51½ft (15.7m)	
Top speed 6 knots (11km/h)	

With a crew of four, which included a diver, this midget submarine carried a pair of 2-ton mines, called "side-charges," along the sides of its hull. The mines were released to lie on the seabed below their intended targets. Just 23 X-craft were built for the British Royal Navy.

△ **I-400**

Date 1944	**Origin** Japan
Displacement 5,852 tons (5,309 tonnes)	
Length 410¼ft (122m)	
Top speed 18.7 knots (35km/h)	

Air strikes could be launched from the deck of this *Sen Toku*-class submarine aircraft carrier. Eighteen such boats were ordered by Japan to attack locks on the Panama Canal linking the Atlantic and the Pacific oceans; just three were built, one being converted into a tanker during construction. Not until the US Navy's *George Washington*-class nuclear-powered submarines appeared in the 1960s was their size surpassed.

◁ **Wilhelm Bauer**

Date 1945	**Origin** Germany
Displacement 1,786 tons (1,620 tonnes)	
Length 251½ft (76.7m)	
Top speed 15.6 knots (29km/h)	

Originally U-2540, *Wilhelm Bauer* was a Type XXI—the war's most advanced submarine design. Many features introduced on the Type XXI are still found on modern submarines. Around 120 XXIs were commissioned, but none saw combat before the war's end. *Wilhelm Bauer* was scuttled in May 1945. Raised 12 years later and recommissioned, it is now a museum ship at Bremerhaven.

U-995 Submarine

For much of World War II, German U-boats—especially Type VIICs, the most numerous Axis submarines—were the scourge of Allied transatlantic convoys. Built at the Blohm and Voss yard in Hamburg and commissioned in September 1943, U-995 sank two warships and three merchant vessels on its nine patrols. U-995 was an upgraded Type VIIC, known as a VIIC/41, with a stronger pressure hull that enabled it to dive deeper than its predecessor.

SPECIFICATIONS	
Name	U-995
Commissioned	1943
Type	Type VIIC/41 submarine
Displacement	837 tons (759 tonnes)
Length	220 ft (67 m)
Propulsion	2 x 2,800–3,200 hp (2,088–2,386 kW) diesel; submerged: 2 x 750 hp (559 kW) electric
Armament	5 x torpedo tubes (14 torpedoes carried)
Top speed	17.7 knots (32.8 km/h)

Bridge, used for surface navigation and signaling; immediately below it is the conning tower, from where the ship was commanded during submerged attacks

Anti-submarine net deflector

Antiaircraft guns

Adolf Hitler backed the idea of a powerful German navy, but only in 1939 did he approve Plan Z, a project to build ten battleships and four aircraft carriers by 1948. As a result, the war came too soon for the German navy. Its U-boat submarine fleet, led by Admiral Karl Dönitz, was not ready. Dönitz estimated he needed 300 U-boats to successfully campaign against Allied shipping, targeting mainly the supply convoys that crossed the Atlantic, but he had just 46 operational vessels when war began.

To build up U-boat numbers, construction was accelerated. Although 568 Type VIIC U-boats—the "standard" boat—were built from 1940 to 1945, there were never enough in service at any one time to dominate the sea-lanes, despite experimenting with "wolf packs"—groups of submarines fighting together. Hitler also distracted the U-boats from their key task of sinking convoys by ordering them to patrol the Norwegian coast in case of invasion and to support the Italians in the Mediterranean Sea and Germany's Afrika Korps in North Africa.

In late 1940, with the use of captured bases on the western French coastline, the U-boats had their first "happy period," sinking significant quantities of British shipping. However, revised convoy tactics and the breaking of the German navy's Enigma codes in May 1941 led to higher level of U-boat detection by the Allies. Another "happy period" occurred after the US's entry into the war at the end of 1941, with ships sunk off the US coast and in the Caribbean. By spring 1943, air cover, better intelligence, the increased use of sonar and radar detection, and, once again, improved tactics, had led to fewer Allied losses and more U-boat sinkings.

U-995 was one of the 1,181 submarines that served with the German navy during World War II, of which 785, around two-thirds, were lost. In total, just under 3,000 Allied ships, warships, and merchant vessels were sunk by German U-boats.

Sole survivor
At the war's end, U-995 was one of 156 U-boats that surrendered; 116 were scuttled by the Royal Navy, but 30 were divided between Britain, the US, and the USSR for reuse. Britain gave U-995 to the Norwegian navy in 1948, and it served as the *Kaura* until 1965. Now a museum ship at Laboe, near Kiel, Germany, it is the only surviving Type VIIC U-boat.

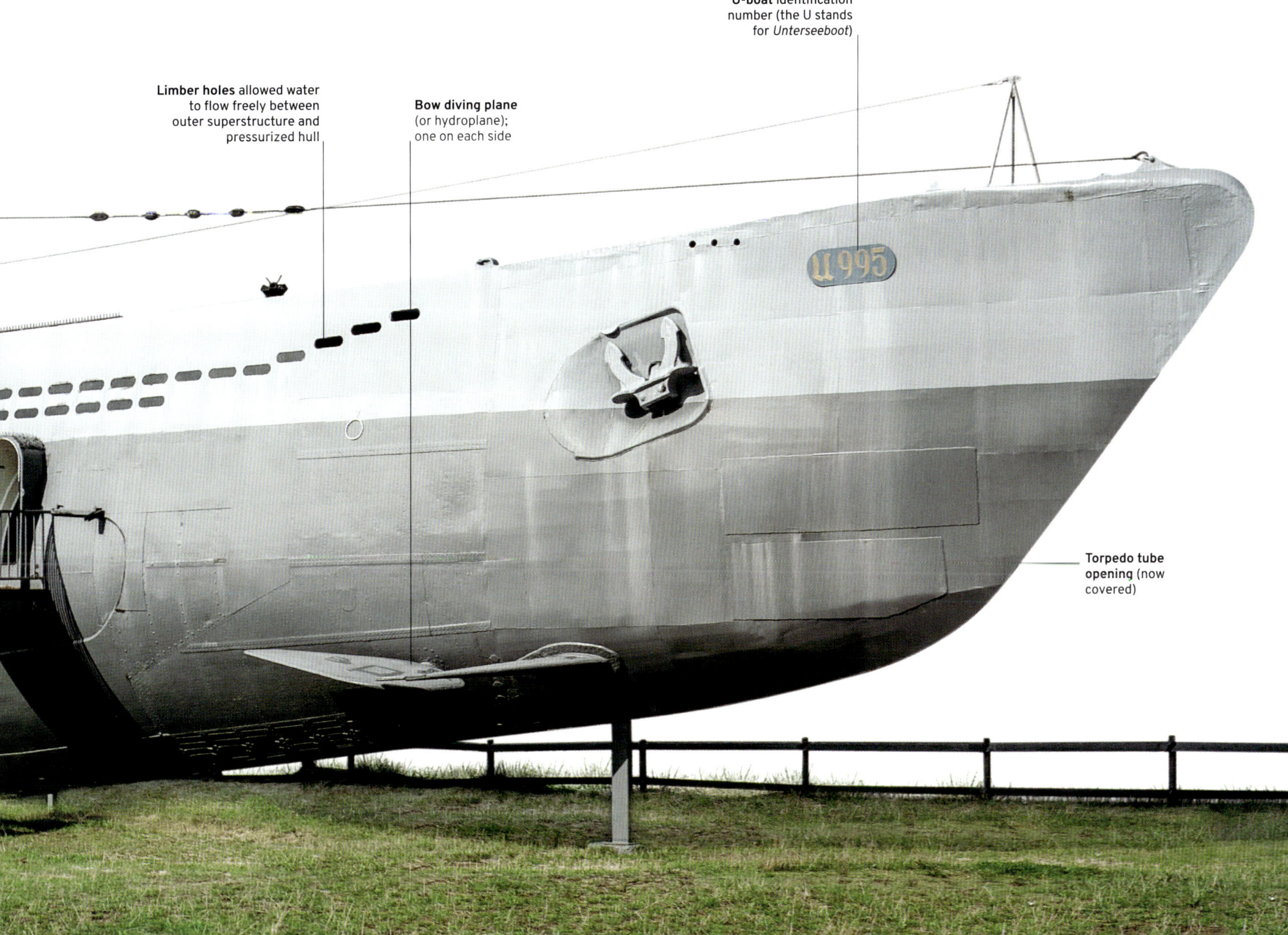

U-boat identification number (the U stands for *Unterseeboot*)

Limber holes allowed water to flow freely between outer superstructure and pressurized hull

Bow diving plane (or hydroplane); one on each side

Torpedo tube opening (now covered)

EXTERIOR

U-995's distinctive external features are the bridge and conning tower, guns, and bulging saddle tanks (external ballast tanks outside of the pressure hull). It typically traveled on the surface, mainly at night, to use the greater speed of its diesel engines and to charge the batteries needed by its electric motors when submerged. Antiaircraft guns, important for protection should the U-boat be surprised on the surface, could also be used against smaller vessels if an expensive torpedo was considered wasteful.

1. Flak 38 20mm antiaircraft guns **2.** Identification number **3.** Circular radio direction finder between attack periscope (left) and observation periscope (right), ship's logo beneath **4.** Stern view of twin rudders and twin propellers **5.** 3.7cm Flak M42U antiaircraft gun **6.** Radar antenna **7.** Starboard movable diving plane behind fixed fin **8.** Anchor **9.** Port saddle tank

INTERIOR

The rear was dominated by the electric motors and diesel engines. In the center, beneath the conning tower, was the control room, the ship's operational hub. Up front was the main torpedo room, with access to four tubes (there was a further tube at the stern). With a crew of up to 52, depending on the type of mission, living and working conditions were cramped—many of the men slept in the forward torpedo room—so maintaining morale and discipline was vital to ensure a successful patrol. Missions could last from 3 weeks to 6 months; fresh water for washing and shaving was limited, and most crew members grew beards.

10. View from aft through bulkhead door into control room **11.** Engine order telegraph **12.** Forward torpedo room **13.** Control room interior, with chart table (left) and observation periscope (right) **14.** Electric motor room **15.** Forward torpedo launch tube hatches **16.** Diesel engine room

Aircraft Carriers

The first ships to carry aircraft operated as floating bases for seaplanes. With subsequent experimentation, particularly during and after World War I, the aircraft carrier began to develop as a distinctive type of ship, equipped with a full-length flight deck and equipment for launching and recovering aircraft. By 1939, Britain's Royal Navy had a dozen such carriers in service or under construction; the Imperial Japanese navy had a similar number, and the US Navy eight. The US Navy embraced the type most wholeheartedly in World War II, building large numbers of "fleet" carriers, and lighter, less-capable "escort" carriers—including many escort carriers for the British Royal Navy. During the war, carriers played a key role in winning crucial naval battles, keeping vital merchant shipping lanes open, and supporting amphibious landings.

△ **HMS Furious**

Date 1917 **Origin** UK
Displacement 25,635 tons (23,255 tonnes)
Length 786½ft (239.7m)
Top speed 30 knots (55km/h)

During construction, *Furious* was modified from a light battle cruiser into a carrier by removing the forward turret and adding a short flying-off deck. It was later rebuilt from the main deck up and equipped with 36 aircraft. *Furious* served with distinction during World War II. In September 1944, now showing its age, it was withdrawn from frontline service and placed in reserve.

△ **USS Saratoga**

Date 1927 **Origin** USA
Displacement 48,220 tons (43,745 tonnes)
Length 888ft (270.7m)
Top speed 33 knots (61km/h)

Saratoga and its sister ship *Lexington* were begun as battle cruisers—part of a group of six ordered by the US Navy at the end of World War I—but chosen to be completed as carriers. In exercises, the pair helped to develop US carrier tactics prior to World War II. *Saratoga* won seven battle stars during her wartime service with the US Pacific Fleet.

◁ **Akagi**

Date 1927 **Origin** Japan
Displacement 47,880 tons (43,435 tonnes)
Length 855½ft (260.7m)
Top speed 31 knots (57km/h)

Laid down as a battle cruiser, *Akagi* was finished as a carrier. Aircraft mainly took off from the lower hangar-deck levels and landed on the upper deck. Rebuilt in 1935–38 with an island superstructure and a single flight deck, *Akagi* took part in the attack on the US Pacific Fleet at Pearl Harbor in December 1941.

▽ USS Enterprise

Date 1938 **Origin** USA
Displacement 28,945 tons (26,260 tonnes)
Length 809 ft (246.6 m)
Top speed 32.5 knots (60 km/h)

A participant in nearly every Pacific carrier battle, the USS *Enterprise*—the second of three *Yorktown*-class vessels—won a record 20 battle stars. Despite such extensive involvement in combat, the *Enterprise* survived the war; however, her two sister ships, *Yorktown* and *Hornet*, were sunk in 1942.

▷ HMS Ark Royal

Date 1938 **Origin** UK
Displacement 31,045 tons (28,165 tonnes)
Length 800 ft (243.8 m)
Top speed 31 knots (57 km/h)

Ark Royal, Britain's first large, purpose-built aircraft carrier, introduced many elements—including steam catapults for launching aircraft, and hangars and a flight deck that were an integral part of the hull—that became standard on later carriers. Struck by a U-boat torpedo in the Mediterranean in 1941, having delivered aircraft to Malta, *Ark Royal* sank while being towed to Gibraltar.

◁ HMS Illustrious

Date 1940 **Origin** UK
Displacement 32,750 tons (29,710 tonnes)
Length 753½ ft (229.6 m)
Top speed 30.5 knots (56 km/h)

Illustrious was the lead ship of a class of three British fleet carriers laid down in 1937. The carrier trio served throughout the war, surviving multiple attempts to sink them. *Illustrious* pioneered armored flight and hangar decks, but at the cost of a diminished capacity to store aviation fuel—a shortcoming that was never rectified.

Two 5 in high-angle guns

△ USS Essex

Date 1942 **Origin** USA
Displacement 39,065 tons (35,440 tonnes)
Length 872 ft (265.8 m)
Top speed 32.7 knots (61 km/h)

No other group of ships played such a vital role in victory in the Pacific as the 24 *Essex*-class fleet carriers. The core of the US Navy's Fast Carrier Task Force, they all survived World War II. Rebuilt with angled flight decks, they went on to form the basis of the US postwar carrier fleet.

Bridge and flight operations control center

Wings of aircraft folded to save space

△ USS Guadalcanal

Date 1943 **Origin** USA
Displacement 12,210 tons (11,075 tonnes)
Length 512¼ ft (156 m)
Top speed 19 knots (35 km/h)

By employing mass production techniques, Henry Kaiser's shipyards could assemble ships more quickly and cheaply than other yards. Based on a freighter hull, *Guadalcanal* was built for the US Navy at Kaiser's yard in Vancouver, Canada. It was one of 50 *Casablanca*-class escort carriers.

Carrier and Maritime Strike Aircraft

The first planes to be operated from aircraft carriers were identical to those that used airfields on land, but by the mid-1920s aircraft were being specifically adapted for shipboard use. The designs of carrier- and land-based aircraft subsequently diverged, particularly during World War II, when it became apparent that carriers could be key to winning naval battles. Carrier-based aircraft included fighters to defend the mother ship and other vessels in the fleet, long-range reconnaissance aircraft, and dive-bombers and other specialist attack planes armed with torpedoes or bombs to strike targets at sea or on land.

△ de Havilland DH98 Mosquito

Date 1941 **Origin** UK

Engine 2 x 1,480 hp (1,104 kW) Rolls-Royce Merlin 21/21 + 23/23 water-cooled V12, later 2 x 1,690 hp (1,260 kW) 113 + 114

Top speed 366–415 mph (589–670 km/h)

Nicknamed the "Wooden Wonder," the Mosquito was fast, light, and highly versatile. It performed many roles during World War II, including missions against enemy shipping and submarines using rockets, bombs, and cannons.

△ Grumman F4F Wildcat

Date 1940 **Origin** USA

Engine 1,200 hp (895 kW) Pratt & Whitney R-1830-86 Twin Wasp radial

Top speed 320 mph (515 km/h)

Grumman adapted its mid-1930s F3F biplane fighter to create the F4F Wildcat, which had an improved tail, a more powerful engine, and a mid-mounted wing. Although not a match for the impressive Japanese Zero, the Wildcat proved a competent monoplane fighter.

△ Douglas SBD-5 Dauntless

Date 1942 **Origin** USA

Engine 1,200 hp (895 kW) Wright R-1820-60 Cyclone radial

Top speed 255 mph (410 km/h)

The rugged and dependable "Slow But Deadly" (SBD) sank more Japanese ships in World War II than any other American aircraft. It remained the US Navy's main dive-bomber until 1943. The SBD later evolved into the A-1 Skyraider, which was deployed in Korea and Vietnam.

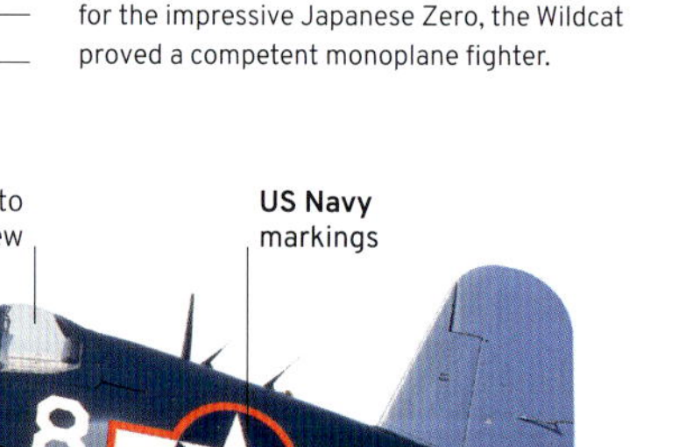

△ Vought F4U Corsair

Date 1942 **Origin** USA

Engine 2,000 hp (1,491.3 kW) Pratt & Whitney R-2800-8 radial

Top speed 416 mph (670 km/h)

The Corsair had a very powerful engine and an inverted gullwing design that allowed ground clearance for its huge propeller. It was World War II's most capable carrier-based fighter, also adept in a fighter-bomber role.

▽ Mitsubishi A6M3 Zero

Date 1942 **Origin** Japan

Engine 1,130 hp (842.6 kW) Nakajima NK1F Sakae 21 radial

Top speed 335 mph (540 km/h)

With superb agility and range, the Mitsubishi Zero (codenamed "Zeke" by the Allies) was Japan's best naval fighter; only in 1943 did Allied planes begin to surpass the Zero's combat abilities.

△ Supermarine Seafire

Date 1942 **Origin** UK

Engine 1,850 hp (1,379.5 kW) Rolls-Royce Griffon VI V12

Top speed 391 mph (630 km/h)

Seafire was a version of the Mark V Spitfire with modifications for shipborne use. It was developed to meet a shortfall in carrier aircraft supplied to the UK by the US, which also provided many carriers.

△ **Grumman F6F Hellcat**

Date 1943 **Origin** USA

Engine 2,200hp (1,641kW) Pratt & Whitney R-2800-10W Double Wasp radial

Top speed 379 mph (610 km/h)

The Hellcat's similarity to the Wildcat sometimes confused Japanese pilots. It was a costly mistake: the Hellcat was a new design, around 60 mph (95 km/h) faster than its lookalike and with better acceleration.

△ **Grumman F8F Bearcat**

Date 1945 **Origin** USA

Engine 2,400 hp (1,790 kW) Pratt & Whitney R-2800-34W Double Wasp radial

Top speed 422 mph (680 km/h)

The Bearcat—the last of World War II's "Cats"—had the same engine as the Hellcat, but it was about 20 percent lighter, giving it a 30 percent better climb rate and an extra 40 mph (70 km/h) on its top speed.

◁ **Hawker Sea Fury**

Date 1945 **Origin** UK

Engine 2,480 hp (1,849 kW) Bristol Centaurus XVIIC supercharged air-cooled 18-cylinder radial

Top speed 740 km/h (460 mph)

This "navalized" version of Hawker's canceled Fury fighter had folding wings and an arrester hook. It was highly effective, even holding its own against jet fighters in the Korean War.

The Normandy Landings

The Allied invasion of Europe that began on June 6, 1944—D-Day—was the largest amphibious operation ever attempted, landing around 156,000 troops and involving nearly 7,000 ships and other vessels, supported by almost 12,000 aircraft. Such an ambitious undertaking required a previously unmatched level of planning and preparation. Air superiority had been achieved against the Luftwaffe over France, and the German navy had been limited to a few fast attack boats in the channel ports. The objective was to successfully land enough soldiers and equipment to break through the German beach defenses and then progress inland, and this led to the development of specialized landing craft and support vessels that had to be built in quantity. Tanks were adapted to swim ashore or carry additional equipment to demolish seawalls, clear minefields, or lay bridges.

Troops of the US 2nd Infantry Division pass a German bunker as they climb a bluff above the Easy Red sector of Omaha Beach, where supply trucks gather and landing craft and other vessels bring further men and equipment.

1945–1989

THE COLD WAR

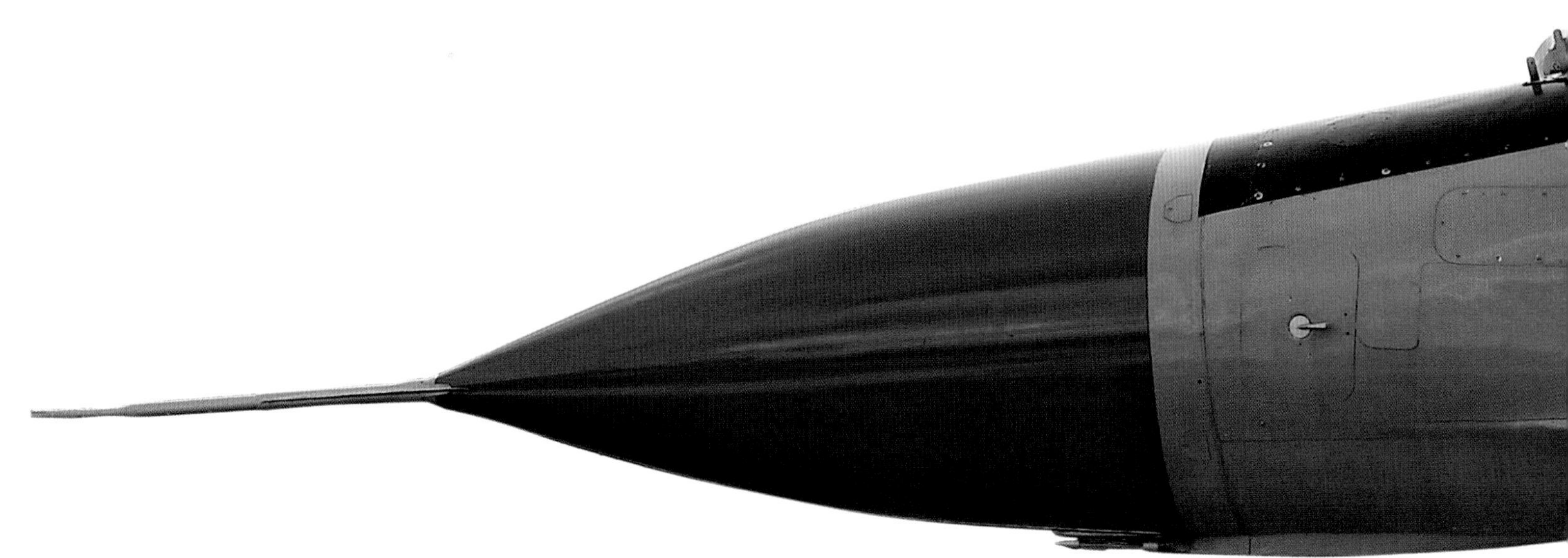

The Age of Technology

The Cold War was a nuclear standoff between the US and the Soviet Union, with numerous proxy wars fought in other nations around the world. The demands of this uncertain era and the arrival of computerization helped elevate military vehicle design to new heights.

As well as building up stockpiles of nuclear weapons, the two rival superpowers needed to develop the means of delivering the warheads to their targets. The primary instruments of nuclear warfare were initially long-range strategic bombers, which included huge aircraft such as the American B-52 Stratofortress and the Soviet Tupolev Tu-95. Over time, intercontinental ballistic missiles (ICBMs) took over the majority of the nuclear launch role, as well as submarine-launched ballistic missiles (SLBMs). However, heavy bombers remained on station on both sides of the Iron Curtain for the duration of the Cold War. The B-52 also found use in a conventional bombing role during the Vietnam War (1955–75).

TALKING POINT

Berlin Airlift

At the end of World War II, the German capital Berlin was divided into four zones of occupation: French, British, US, and Soviet. In June 1948, a breakdown in political relations resulted in the Soviet Union imposing a land blockade on Allied West Berlin. In response, the USAF and RAF began an extraordinary 11-month, nonstop resupply operation to West Berlin via airlifts. By May 1949, when the blockade was finally lifted, in excess of 200,000 flights had delivered more than 2.54 million tons (2.3 million tonnes) of food, medicines, fuel, and other vital supplies to German citizens and Allied troops in West Berlin.

Berliners watch as a Douglas C-54 Skymaster comes in to land at Templehof airfield. At the very peak of the airlift, at Easter 1949, a plane landed in West Berlin almost every minute.

The military vehicles of the Cold War were designed to operate in a nuclear age, and increasingly military vehicles of all types incorporated nuclear, biological, and chemical (NBC) protective features, intended to shield the crew from the effects of poststrike radiation or from nightmarish chemical or biological weapons. However, overall the postwar evolution of military vehicles was driven more by technological progress than by the threat of nuclear attack.

New power sources, new vehicles

The Cold War era saw great advances in rockets and jets. Successive breakthroughs in aircraft design and jet engines meant that by the 1960s, some military aircraft were flying at two or three times the speed of sound. This great leap in capability placed new demands on pilots. In World War II, if opposing fighters approached each other head-on at a distance of around 20 miles (32 km), their pilots would have had at least a minute or so before they needed to perform tactical maneuvers. With the supersonic fighters of the Cold War, at the same distance they might have around 10 seconds.

The power-plant revolution extended to other domains and technologies too. During the 1950s and 1960s, the first nuclear-powered submarines and aircraft carriers entered service, their reactor engines offering almost indefinite range and endurance. The 1960s and 1970s also witnessed the development of the first production tanks and warships powered by gas turbine engines, which gave a higher power-to-weight ratio than internal combustion engines, albeit with less fuel efficiency at lower speeds.

Different types of vehicles also came to prominence in the Cold War era. The helicopter in particular rose to prominence, and was widely used in tactical military mobility. Over a decade of involvement in the war in Vietnam, for example, the US deployed more than 11,800 helicopters, which took on a

> "Today the **kind and quality of systems** which a nation develops can **decide the battle** in advance."
>
> US AIR FORCE GENERAL BERNARD "BENNIE" SCHRIEVER

Timeline

Building on the foundations of World War II, the Cold War era saw huge increases in the range, sophistication, and power of weapons and military technology. Computerization became widespread, and new power plants, including jet engines, gas turbines, and nuclear reactors transformed propulsion.

Air / Land / Water

1947 The T-54, the USSR's new postwar medium tank, enters service

1953 The US F-100D Super Sabre becomes the first fighter capable of supersonic speed in level flight

1954 The USS *Nautilus* (SSN-571), the world's first nuclear-powered submarine, is commissioned

1955 The US Air Force introduces the B-52 Stratofortress long-range strategic bomber

1956 In the US, the Bell UH-1 Iroquois helicopter enters production

1959 Production begins of the Soviet MiG-21, the Cold War's most numerous supersonic fighter

1959 The USS *George Washington* (SSBN-598), the first nuclear-ballistic-missile submarine, is launched

1960 The M113 armored personnel carrier (APC) transforms US infantry transport broad range of utility, support, and combat roles (it was the Vietnam War that inspired the helicopter gunship concept). Land vehicles were also changing. Tank fleets were increasingly rationalized, with advanced main battle tank (MBT) types, equipped with gyro-stabilized guns and composite armor, replacing both the medium and heavy tanks of the past. Army mechanization was fast-tracked by new generations of armored personnel carriers (APCs) and infantry fighting vehicles (IFVs). IFVs could transport troops onto the battlefield, but they also had missile and gun armament to take on enemy armor, even MBTs. Military commanders of the Cold War now had far more technological force multipliers at their disposal.

Computerization and vehicles

Computers changed the capabilities of military vehicles most significantly during this era. The early computers of the 1940s and 1950s were the size of a room, but in the 1960s, developments in transistors and integrated circuits resulted in computer miniaturization, making them small enough to install in vehicles. Advances in computerization between the 1960s and 1980s transformed communications, fire control, missile and bomb guidance, aircraft performance (through fly-by-wire technologies), range finding, surveillance, threat detection, and command-and-control systems among others. Later developments included satellite communications and battlefield data transfer.

Tank standoff
With Cold War tensions high, US M48 Patton tanks face Soviet T-55s across the famous Checkpoint Charlie, the border control point connecting East and West Berlin, in October 1961.

Equipped with these new technologies, military vehicles became ever more adaptive and lethal. The gunner of an M1A1 Abrams tank of the late 1980s had a ballistic fire-control computer that nearly guaranteed a first-round hit at a range of 2 miles (3.2 km), while the pilot of an F-14 Tomcat could launch an AIM-54 air-to-air missile (AAM) at a target more than 80 miles (128 km) away. Electronic countermeasures (ECM) aircraft were able to detect and block enemy radar and radio transmissions over areas of hundreds of square miles. Even comparatively simple military trucks could now be equipped with a Global Positioning System (GPS) navigation computer, reducing the possibilities of navigational errors in confused battle spaces. Personnel also needed to adapt to this new technology: by the end of the Cold War in 1989, a level of technical skill and digital acumen in military vehicle operators had become a necessity in many of the world's armies.

US civil defense recruitment poster, 1951
The threat of global nuclear war was just as salient to civilian thinking as it was to military minds during the Cold War. Civil defense organizations sought to prepare citizens for the worst and mitigate the effects of a nuclear strike.

1966 The Soviet BMP-1, a tracked infantry fighting vehicle (IFV), enters service

1967 The *Moskva* helicopter carrier enters service with the Soviet navy

1972 The McDonnell Douglas F-15 Eagle makes its maiden flight

1973 T-72 tanks, the next generation of Soviet MBTs, are introduced by the Red Army

1975 Commission of the nuclear-powered supercarrier USS *Nimitz* (CVN-68)

1981 First flight of the Lockheed F-117 Nighthawk stealth aircraft

1981 US Army units receive the first Bradley infantry fighting vehicles (IFVs)

1983 The first of 16 Type 23 frigates is commissioned into the British Royal Navy

1985 The US M1A1 Abrams embodies a new approach to main battle tank (MBT) design

1991 *Arleigh Burke*-class destroyers enter US Navy service

Transporting Missiles

During the Cold War era, the annual November parade in Moscow served as a platform for the Soviet Union to display the strength of its armed forces both to its people and to the watching West. With the emergence of missiles as key determinants of military strategy and deterrence, missile-carrying vehicles became the most eye-catching features of these displays of military might. The Soviet Union required its missile arsenal, which ranged from surface-to-air missiles (SAMs) to huge intercontinental ballistic missiles (ICBMs), to have mobility for transportation and deployment. This inspired innovation among Soviet engineers, who began producing impressive designs for missile carriers, both wheeled and tracked, that could cope with rough, often muddy terrain, and harsh Soviet winters. These even included 16×16 wheeled configurations, which were among the largest vehicles ever built. Some missile carriers were designed for the safe transportation of these crucial weapons. Others were built as mobile launchpads for use in combat. Called transporter erector launchers (TELs), they were able to elevate to a firing position and launch one or multiple missiles.

Soviet 2k11 Krug TELs, each carrying a pair of SAMs, parade through Moscow's Red Square during the 1971 November parade.

НАРОДА

Communist Bloc Tanks

The T-54, introduced soon after World War II, was the first of a series of Soviet tanks that were mass produced and exported to Warsaw Pact countries and Communist client states during the Cold War era, with derivatives also forming the basis of China's tank force. Intended for frontline breakthroughs and advances deep into enemy territory, these mobile tanks were low in profile, making them more difficult to hit—but also cramped inside. Many are still in service around the world, a testimony to their longevity: Russia even sent old T-54s and T-55s into combat after invading Ukraine in 2022.

△ T-54

Date 1947 **Origin** USSR
Weight 39.7 tons (36 tonnes)
Engine V-54 V12 diesel, 520 hp (388 kW)
Main armament 100 mm D-10T L/53.5 rifled gun

For the T-54, designers opted for torsion bars instead of Christie suspension. The tank was armed with the 100 mm gun that had proved its value on the earlier SU-100 tank destroyer. One of the most produced tanks in history, the T-54 has seen combat in Europe, the Middle East, Africa, and Asia.

▷ T-55

Date 1958 **Origin** USSR
Weight 39.7 tons (36 tonnes)
Engine V-55 V12 diesel, 580 hp (433 kW)
Main armament 100 mm D-10T2S L/53.5 rifled gun

The T-54 was developed into the T-55 by the addition of a more powerful engine and a nuclear, biological, and chemical (NBC) warfare protection system. With Soviet T-55 production continuing until 1981, later improvements included laser range finders and new sights. Many countries operating T-55s made their own upgrades, helping to extend the tank's lifespan into the 21st century.

▽ Type 59-II

Date 1959 **Origin** China
Weight 39.7 tons (36 tonnes)
Engine 12150L V12 diesel, 520 hp (388 kW)
Main armament 105 mm L7 rifled gun

By incorporating Chinese and Western technology, the Type 59 has diverged significantly from the Soviet-era T-54 tank from which it was originally developed. This Type 59-II variant is equipped with a British-designed gun, a gun-stabilization system, and NBC protection.

▷ T-62

Date 1962 **Origin** USSR
Weight 41.9 tons (38 tonnes)
Engine V-55-5 V12 diesel, 580 hp (433 kW)
Main armament 115 mm 2A20 L/49.5 smoothbore gun

Planned as a stopgap measure, the T-62 ended up becoming the mainstay of the Red Army into the 1970s. It had a larger hull than its forerunner, the T-55, added infrared night-vision, and a more powerful 115 mm gun—the first smoothbore gun in service and the first to fire Armor Piercing Fin Stabilized Discarding Sabot (APFSDS) projectiles.

△ **Type 62**

Date 1962 **Origin** China
Weight 23.2 tons (21 tonnes)
Engine 12150L-3 V12 diesel, 430 hp (321 kW)
Main armament 85 mm Type 62-85TC rifled gun

Type 62—essentially a scaled-down version of the Type 59—was produced for use in regions of China where the large, heavy Type 59 found it difficult to operate successfully. The Type 62 had better ground pressure and mobility than the Type 59, although this came at the expense of its firepower and protection. The tank saw action during the Vietnam War.

▽ **T-64B1**

Date 1966 **Origin** USSR
Weight 43 tons (39 tonnes)
Engine 5DTF diesel, 700 hp (522 kW)
Main armament 125 mm 2A46 L/48 smoothbore gun

The T-64's advanced, complex design introduced many new features, the most notable being an autoloader for the gun. The T-64 was never exported, being built solely for the tank battalions that spearheaded the Soviet Army. The breakup of the Soviet Union left the T-64 factory in Ukraine, where the tank was further developed. The variant shown here is the T-64B1.

Twelve wheels driven by a V46 diesel engine

◁ **T-72M1**

Date 1973 **Origin** USSR
Weight 45.8 tons (41.5 tonnes)
Engine V46.6 diesel, 780 hp (582 kW)
Main armament 125 mm 2A46 L/48 smoothbore gun

Like the T-64, the three-man T-72 dispensed with a fourth crew member in favor of an automatic loader. It has received extensive upgrades over its long career: the latest models are fitted with distinctive Explosive Reactive Armor (ERA) panels and thermal hunter-killer sights. Export versions generally have less sophisticated systems and thinner armor.

Smoke grenade dischargers

Explosive Reactive Armor (ERA) on glacis plate

△ **T-80U**

Date 1976 **Origin** USSR
Weight 50.7 tons (46 tonnes)
Engine GTD-1250 gas turbine, 1,250 hp (932 kW)
Main armament 125 mm 2A46M1 L/48 smoothbore gun

An evolution of the T-64, the T-80 was deployed on Moscow streets during the attempted coup of 1991, and it has seen combat in Chechnya in 1995 and in Ukraine in the 2020s. This T-80U upgrade has a more powerful turbine than the original and a new turret protected by ERA panels.

Infrared searchlight for night operations

◁ **Type 69-II**

Date 1983 **Origin** China
Weight 40.5 tons (36.7 tonnes)
Engine 12150L-7BW V12 diesel, 580 hp (433 kW)
Main armament 100 mm smoothbore gun

Using the Type 59 as a template, Chinese manufacturers developed the Type 69 without help from the USSR. Shown here is the Type 69-II variant, which had an over-the-barrel laser range finder and an infrared searchlight next to the gun. Despite proving a significant export success, the Type 69 was not widely adopted by the Chinese military.

T-72

Designed for use if the Cold War had escalated into open conflict, the Soviet T-72 was relatively light compared to contemporary Western tanks, weighing just over 45 tons (41 tonnes). As with many Cold War-era Soviet tanks, it was believed to be less effective than its Western rivals in one-on-one encounters. However, it was fit for purpose, since Soviet commanders intended to use it in vast numbers for massed attacks that would swamp Western defenses.

Smoothbore barrel, strong enough to ram through walls

125 mm gun, larger than those of contemporary Western tanks

FRONT VIEW

REAR VIEW

Sloping armor on front of hull

THE T-72 WAS SIMPLER in design and easier to maintain than its predecessor, the expensive and complex T-64. It incorporated features from earlier Soviet tank designs, including a frying pan-shaped turret, a reliable diesel engine, and a low profile.

Fed ammunition by an autoloader, the main gun could fire up to three shots in 13 seconds. The autoloader held 22 rounds in a circular, horizontal carousel, while a further 17 rounds were stored in the hull. Without the need for a manual loader, the T-72 could now function with just a commander, gunner, and driver. This, in turn, permitted a smaller, lighter design, since less crew space was needed. Guidelines stipulated that the three crew members could be no taller than 5 ft 9 in (175 cm), to ensure they could work in the T-72's cramped interior.

Having entered service with the Red Army in the 1970s, the T-72 is still used by over 40 countries. T-72s were also manufactured in Poland and Czechoslovakia, and the Soviets themselves produced versions of the T-72 specifically for export, often with lower standards of protection.

SPECIFICATIONS	
Name	T-72M1
Date	1973
Origin	Soviet Union
Production	Over 25,000
Engine	V46.6 V12 diesel, 780 hp (581 kW)
Weight	45.7 tons (41.5 tonnes)
Main armament	125 mm 2A46M smoothbore
Secondary armament	12.7 mm NSVT machine gun
Crew	3
Armor thickness	11 in (280 mm) max

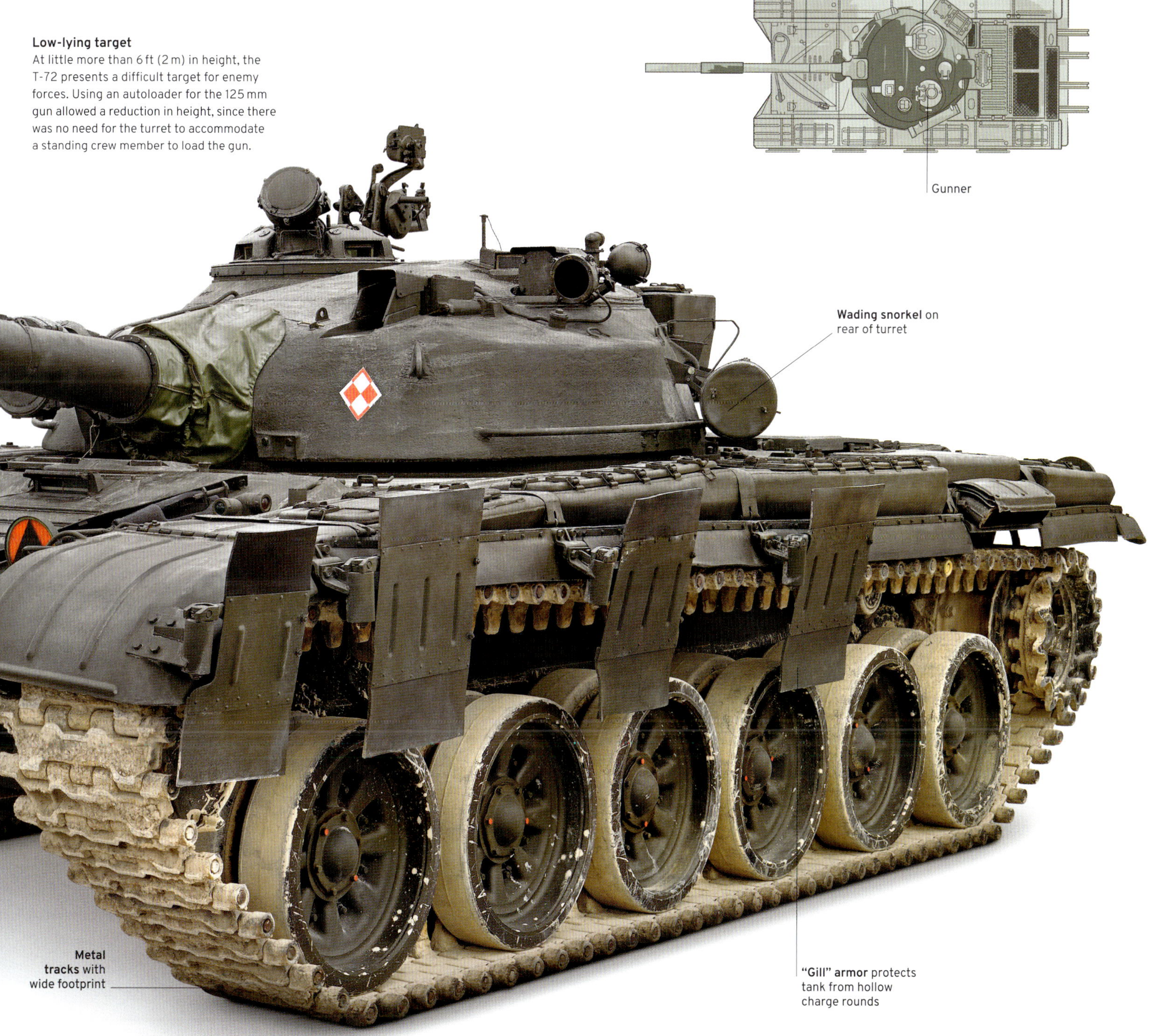

Low-lying target
At little more than 6 ft (2 m) in height, the T-72 presents a difficult target for enemy forces. Using an autoloader for the 125 mm gun allowed a reduction in height, since there was no need for the turret to accommodate a standing crew member to load the gun.

EXTERIOR

This T-72 from Polish service has been augmented along its sides by "gill" armor—rubber squares that can be angled forward to detonate or disrupt hollow charge rounds before they strike the tank's main body. In addition to the 125 mm gun, the turret originally housed a 7.62 mm PKT coaxial machine gun, while the external machine-gun bracket was mounted with an antiaircraft 12.7 mm NSVT.

1. Polish national emblem **2.** Station keeping/convoy light **3.** Main gunsight **4.** Headlamp **5.** Infrared light **6.** Machine-gun bracket **7.** Gunner's hatch (closed) **8.** Deep wading snorkel (stowed) **9.** Commander's hatch (closed) **10.** Machine-gun ammunition boxes **11.** Engine exhaust **12.** Additional "gill" armor **13.** Fuel drum brackets **14.** Rear reflector **15.** Spare track links on hull

INTERIOR

Although typically cramped and uncomfortable, the T-72's three-man crew compartment offered nuclear, biological, and chemical (NBC) protection. The tank's gunner had access to gunsights and a laser range finder for daylight fighting, as well as infrared sights for use in combat at night.

16. Looking down into commander's position **17.** Commander's sight **18.** Looking down into gunner's position **19.** Gunner's sight **20.** Commander's seat back and pistol case **21.** Gun elevation handwheel **22.** Driver's instrument panel **23.** Driver's periscope **24.** Main gun breech and autoloader **25.** Gear lever **26.** Left-hand steering lever **27.** Looking down into driver's position

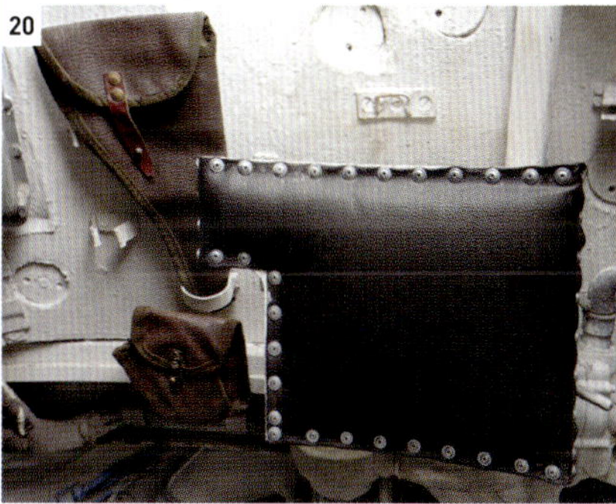

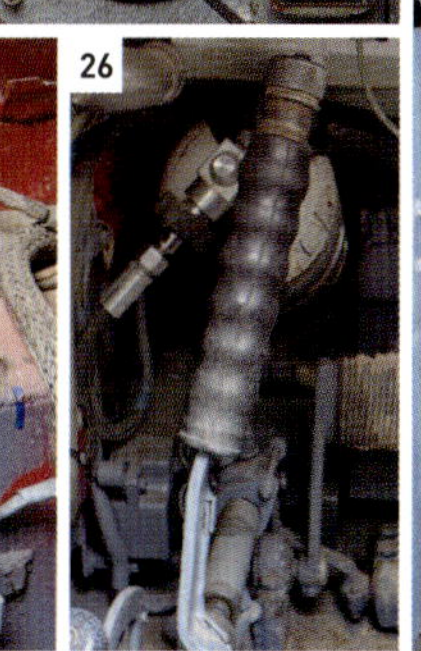

▷ **Centurion Mark 3**

Date 1948 **Origin** UK

Weight 56 tons (50.8 tonnes)

Engine Rolls-Royce Meteor Mark IVA gasoline, 650 hp (485 kW)

Main armament Ordnance QF 20-pounder gun

The Centurion Mark 3 had an automatic stabilization system that enabled it to fire its powerful 20-pounder gun accurately while on the move. More than 4,400 Centurions were built, the majority of which were Mark 3s. This highly successful tank was exported to many countries and saw combat in Korea, India, Pakistan, and Vietnam.

◁ **M41A1 Walker Bulldog**

Date 1951 **Origin** USA

Weight 25.6 tons (23.2 tonnes)

Engine Continental AOS-895-3 gasoline, 500 hp (373 kW)

Main armament 76 mm M32 L/64 gun

The M41 replaced the M24 Chaffee light tank, which had been in service since late World War II. Still light enough to be transported by air, the M41 carried a significantly more potent gun. Widely exported, the M41 saw combat with US and South Vietnamese forces; a few nations still operate the M41.

▷ **M48 Patton**

Date 1952 **Origin** USA

Weight 49.3 tons (44.7 tonnes)

Engine Continental AV-1790-5B gasoline, 810 hp (604 kW)

Main armament 90 mm M41 L/50 rifled gun

Development began on the M48 even before the M47, its predecessor, entered production. The M48 had an improved hull, turret, and suspension; later models were given an AVDS-1790 diesel engine and a 105 mm M68 gun. The M48 served with 26 nations and saw action in several conflicts; nearly 12,000 were built.

NATO Tanks

During the Cold War, NATO countries standardized many aspects of their militaries so that they could fight effectively together, but the alliance never produced a standard tank. Consequently, differing national doctrines led to contrasting designs: German Leopards, for example, emphasized mobility and were lightly armored, while British Chieftains were better protected but less mobile. A key development was composite armor, consisting of layers of different materials, to replace steel, which was vulnerable to high-explosive anti-tank (HEAT) projectiles.

◁ **AMX-13**

Date 1953 **Origin** France

Weight 16.5 tons (15 tonnes)

Engine Sofam Model 8Gxb gasoline, 250 hp (186 kW)

Main armament 75 mm SA 50 rifled gun

The AMX-13 was an air-portable light tank developed to support airborne forces. It was fitted with a front-mounted engine, an autoloader, and a two-part, oscillating turret whose entire upper section moved with the gun. The AMX-13, an export success, had many upgrades during its production, including 90 mm and 105 mm guns.

◁ **Chieftain Mark 11**

Date 1966 **Origin** UK

Weight 60.6 tons (55 tonnes)

Engine Leyland L60 multifuel, 750 hp (559 kW)

Main armament 120 mm L11A5 L/55 rifled gun

The Chieftain replaced both the Conqueror and the Centurion in 1966, with the Mark 11 the final variant, in the 1980s. It was the first tank in which the driver drove in a semi-reclined position, enabling the tank's height to be reduced. Designed to defend against attacking Soviet forces, the Chieftain prioritized firepower and armor over mobility.

▽ **Leopard 2A4**

Date 1979 **Origin** West Germany

Weight 60.9 tons (55.2 tonnes)

Engine MTU MB 873 Ka-501 diesel, 1,500 hp (1,119 kW)

Main armament 120 mm Rheinmetall 120 L/44 gun

The 120 mm smoothbore gun, which would become standard on Western tanks, was introduced on the Leopard 2. The tank's turret incorporated composite armor, which meant it did not have to be sloped to be effective. The Leopard 2 is still in production and service; the 2A4, shown here, is the most common variant.

120 mm smoothbore gun was adopted by other Western tanks

Turret armor is vertical

Chobham-armor side skirt

◁ **M1 Abrams**

Date 1980 **Origin** USA

Weight 60.1 tons (54.5 tonnes)

Engine Textron Lycoming AGT1500 gas turbine, 1,500 hp (1,119 kW)

Main armament 105 mm M68 L/52 rifled gun

A replacement for the US Army's aging M60, the M1's gas-turbine engine gave the new tank unmatched speed, but at the expense of very high fuel consumption. The M1 was clad in Chobham composite armor and equipped with a computerized fire-control system. Its armor was improved on later models, and the gun upgraded to a 120 mm smoothbore.

△ **Challenger 1**

Date 1984 **Origin** UK

Weight 68.3 tons (62 tonnes)

Engine Perkins CV12 V12 diesel, 1,200 hp (895 kW)

Main armament 120 mm L11A5 L/55 rifled gun

Designed for Iran but brought into service with the British Army when the contract was canceled, the Challenger 1 was one of the first tanks with Chobham composite armor. Inside, it resembled a late-model Chieftain, but it carried a more powerful and more reliable engine, and it had hydrogas suspension. Challenger 1s first saw combat in the Gulf War of 1990–91.

Prague Spring

Tanks have been described as coming in two guises: as liberators or oppressors. The 4,600 Soviet tanks that rumbled into Czechoslovakia during August 20–21, 1968, were classic examples of the latter. The Prague Spring—leader Alexander Dubček's liberalization of the Communist-run country in an attempt to implement "socialism with a human face"—had drawn the ire of the Soviet Union. The Soviets responded by invading Czechoslovakia, aided by four other Warsaw Pact nations. Although resistance by the outraged population was mainly nonviolent, more than 100 people died, hundreds were injured, and 300,000 fled the country. Prague, the capital, was the scene of huge protests against the occupying troops, many of whom were confused as to why they were there. Photographs of tanks facing citizen protesters were widely published in the West. They became a symbol of blunt Communist oppression, leading to taunts of "Workers of the World Unite, or I'll shoot you."

A T-62 tank, marked with a white invasion recognition cross, smashes the colonnades of Prague buildings as protesters look on during the 1968 invasion.

grafia
314

Leopard 1

First entering service in 1965, the German Leopard is without question one of the most successful tanks of the postwar era. Unlike the heavily armored German tanks of late-World War II, the Leopard's design prioritized mobility over protection. For firepower, the Leopard was equipped with perhaps the most effective tank weapon of the time—the British 105 mm L7 gun, as used in the Centurion.

THE WEST GERMAN ARMY, which was formed in 1955, was at first equipped with American tanks. Two years later, Germany and France embarked on a joint tank-development project, but the partnership ended in 1962, with France pursuing a separate path to build its AMX-30. The Germans then followed their wartime practice of selecting the best model from prototypes built by different commissioned companies (or, in this case, groups of companies). In 1963, the contract for the new Standard Panzer—the tank that subsequently became known as Leopard—was awarded to Krauss-Maffei of Munich.

The Leopard won many export orders, serving with the armies of 15 nations. From this relatively simple tank, numerous variants arose as new technologies were added, armor was augmented, and changes were made to suit individual countries' needs. On retirement, Leopards were often refurbished and sold in modified forms, including engineer-vehicle and recovery models.

SPECIFICATIONS	
Name	Leopard 1A1A2 (pictured)
Date	1965
Origin	West Germany
Production	6,486
Engine	MTU MB838 10-cylinder multifuel, 830 hp (619 kW)
Weight	46.7 tons (42.4 tonnes)
Main armament	105 mm L7A3
Secondary armament	2 x 7.62 mm MG3 machine guns
Crew	4
Armor thickness	0.4–2.8 in (10–70 mm)

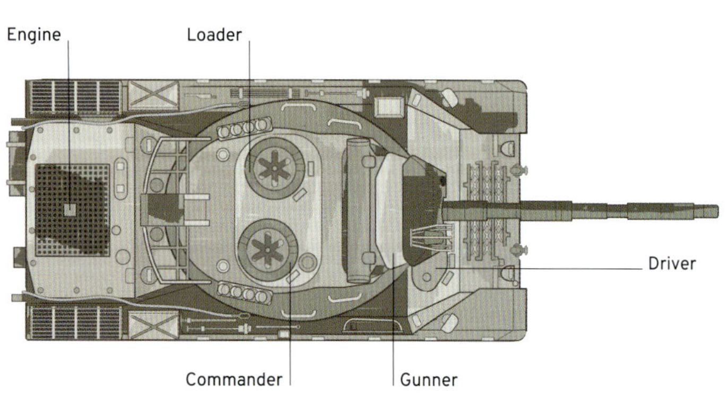

FRONT VIEW

REAR VIEW

Low-light TV/infrared night light in protective cage

Commander's hatch

Iron Cross, the German Army emblem

Upgraded Leopard
This 1980s version of the Leopard, the 1A1A2, has numerous upgraded features, including a gun-stabilization system, additional layers of turret armor, and improved gunsights and observation equipment.

Double pin tracks

INTERIOR

The engine occupied the rear of the Leopard's two interior compartments, which were separated by a fire wall. At the front was the crew area: the tank commander sat in the turret, with the gunner in front of him, the loader to his left, and the driver sitting forward and to the right.

15. Gunner's position **16.** Looking down into commander's cupola **17.** Commander's TRP 2A panoramic sight eyepiece **18.** Loader's safety switch **19.** Gunner's azimuth indicator dial **20.** Commander's hydraulic hatch controls **21.** 105mm gun breech **22.** Looking down into driver's position **23.** Gun stabilization system drift compensation box **24.** Driver's controls **25.** Intercom control panel **26.** Driver's instrument panel **27.** Gear lever **28.** Fire extinguisher system

EXTERIOR

To make the Leopard 1 as light and mobile as possible, the tank's design reduced armor to a minimum. To mitigate this vulnerability, the hull's front-most section—the glacis plate—was angled at 60 degrees to the vertical to help deflect enemy projectiles. It also effectively thickened the hull by forcing projectiles to take a longer, diagonal route through its surface.

1. National recognition symbol **2.** Headlight **3.** Ice grousers **4.** Holder for engine deck lifting tool (tool missing) **5.** Driver's periscopes **6.** Commander's TRP 2A panoramic sight head **7.** Commander's cupola (closed) **8.** Range finder aperture **9.** Rear stowage bin **10.** Drive sprocket **11.** Gun cleaning rods **12.** Smoke dischargers **13.** Spare track link **14.** Gun cradle above Leitkreuz blackout light

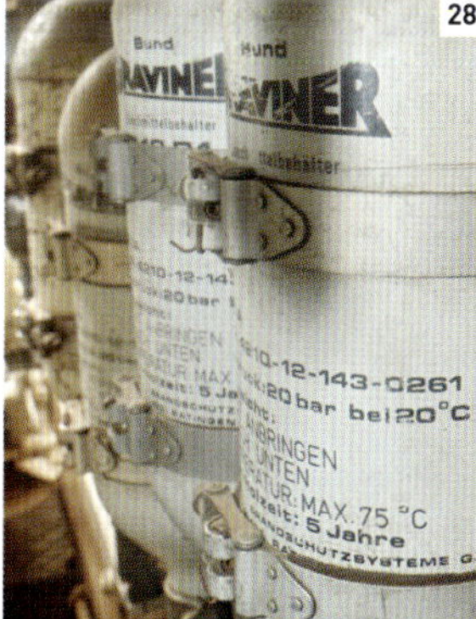

▷ BTR-152

Date 1950 **Origin** USSR

Weight 11.1 tons (10.1 tonnes)

Engine ZIS-123 gasoline, 110 hp (82 kW)

Main armament 7.62 mm SGMB machine gun

The six-wheeled BTR-152 carried 15 troops within its welded-steel body. Later models had an armored roof and a central tire-pressure regulation system. More than 12,500 BTR-152s of all variants, made for the Soviet military and for export, saw decades of service around the world.

△ FV603 Saracen

Date 1952 **Origin** UK

Weight 11.2 tons (10.2 tonnes)

Engine Rolls-Royce B80 Mk 6A gasoline, 160 hp (119 kW)

Main armament .30 Browning M1919 machine gun

Able to carry 10 troops, the Saracen was armed with a .30 Browning machine gun. Its drivetrain gave excellent mobility. There were command-vehicle and ambulance variants, and an internal security version was used in Northern Ireland. It was replaced by the FV432.

△ BTR-50P

Date 1954 **Origin** USSR

Weight 15.7 tons (14.2 tonnes)

Engine Model V6 diesel, 240 hp (179 kW)

Main armament 7.62 mm SGMB machine gun

Based on the Soviet PT-76 light tank chassis, the BTR-50P shared the amphibious capability of its parent. Originally open-topped, it could carry 20 infantrymen, who climbed in and out over the sides; early vehicles carried a ramp to allow an artillery piece to be carried on the deck. The BTR-50P spawned a huge range of variants and is still in use around the world.

◁ M113A1

Date 1960 **Origin** USA

Weight 12.1 tons (11 tonnes)

Engine Detroit Diesel 6V-53 diesel, 212 hp (158 kW)

Main armament .50 Browning M2 machine gun

The petrol engine that powered early M113s was soon replaced by a diesel. In the Vietnam War, US and South Vietnamese forces valued the mobility of their M113s, which they modified with extra machine guns and armor. More than 80,000 M113s in over 40 variants served with at least 44 countries. Many users made their own upgrades to keep the vehicles operational in the 21st century.

▷ FV432 Bulldog

Date 1963 **Origin** UK

Weight 16.8 tons (15.2 tonnes)

Engine Rolls-Royce K60 No4 Mk 4F multifuel, 240 hp (179 kW)

Main armament 7.62 mm L7 machine gun

The FV432 has been the standard British APC since the 1960s. Developed for service in Iraq and Afghanistan, the Bulldog, the latest variant, features extra armor, a new engine and transmission, and NBC (nuclear, biological, and chemical) protection. It is part of the FV430 family, which also includes mortar, ambulance, command, communications, and recovery vehicles.

△ **AAV7A1**

Date 1971 **Origin** USA

Weight 27.9 tons (25.3 tonnes)

Engine Cummins VT400 diesel, 400 hp (298 kW)

Main armament .50 Browning M2 machine gun, MK 19 40 mm Automatic Grenade Launcher

With capacity for 25 troops, the AAV7A1 (originally LVTP-7) was built as an amphibious tractor, or "amtrac," for the US Marine Corps. The latest of numerous upgrades incorporates automotive components from the M2 Bradley infantry fighting vehicle. Around 1,500 have been made, with worldwide sales.

Troop Carriers

Armored personnel carriers (APCs) are generally intended as troop transports, with infantry dismounting to fight on foot when they encounter the enemy. In widespread use throughout the Cold War, APCs often shared automotive components with their more heavily armed tank counterparts, which made them cheaper to build and easier to maintain. Some states, such as the USSR, West Germany, and the UK, split their APC fleets, using tracked infantry fighting vehicles for frontline action and wheeled vehicles to deliver reinforcements or perform defensive roles.

Pneumatic tires

△ **Véhicule de l'Avant Blindé**

Date 1976 **Origin** France

Weight 14.3 tons (13 tonnes)

Engine Renault MIDS 06-20-45 diesel, 220 hp (164 kW)

Main armament .50 Browning M2 machine gun

This amphibious armored personnel carrier can hold 10 infantry personnel. Designed to complement the tracked AMX-10P, the VAB has had a multitude of upgrades, including NBC protection. It continues in French service and has been used in UN peacekeeping roles. Variants include command-post, radar-carrier, and antiaircraft missile launcher versions.

▽ **Bv206**

Date 1980 **Origin** Sweden

Weight 7.3 tons (6.6 tonnes)

Engine Ford V6 gasoline, 136 hp (101 kW)

Main armament None

Light enough to be lifted by larger helicopters, the Bandvagn ("tracked vehicle") 206 is an articulated, all-terrain carrier. An armored version, the Bv206S, provides protection for the occupants against small arms fire, and is in service with several national armed forces in troop-carrier and ambulance roles.

△ **LAV-25**

Date 1983 **Origin** USA

Weight 14.2 tons (12.9 tonnes)

Engine Detroit Diesel 6V53T diesel, 275 hp (205 kW)

Main armament 25 mm M242 cannon

The LAV-25, a version of the MOWAG Piranha-1 adapted for the US Marine Corps, is used mainly for reconnaissance, with anti-tank, command, and recovery variants. Upgrades include improved armor, suspension, and sights. It has a crew of three and can carry six troops.

Infantry Fighting Vehicles

The thin armor, light firepower, and limited mobility of armored personnel carriers (APCs) left them vulnerable to attack. Military designers responded by developing a new generation of vehicles able to fight alongside tanks. These infantry fighting vehicles (IFVs) carried more potent guns and gave their occupants greater protection against conventional munitions and the atmospheric contamination expected on a nuclear battlefield. The Soviet BMP-1 set the template for IFV design. Western nations, concerned by this innovative vehicle, soon developed their own IFVs.

△ Schützenpanzer Lang HS.30

Date 1958 **Origin** West Germany	
Weight 16.1 tons (14.6 tonnes)	
Engine Rolls-Royce B81 Mark 80F gasoline, 220 hp (164 kW)	
Main armament 20 mm Hispano-Suiza HS.820 cannon	

The low-profile Schützenpanzer Lang had capacity for five troops, who entered and left via roof hatches. To comply with the prevailing West German military doctrine that tanks, infantry, and troop carriers were to fight alongside each other, the vehicle was more heavily armed and armored than contemporary APCs. Expensive upgrading resolved initial mechanical problems and unreliability.

△ BMP-1

Date 1966 **Origin** USSR	
Weight 14.9 tons (13.5 tonnes)	
Engine UTD 20 diesel, 300 hp (224 kW)	
Main armament 73 mm 2A28 smoothbore gun	

The first true IFV, the well-armored BMP-1 had a powerful main gun, an anti-tank missile launcher, and space for 10 troops, who could fire their weapons from inside the vehicle. However, it was cramped, vulnerable to mines, and its fuel tanks were located between the infantry's seats.

Smoke grenade dischargers

△ Marder 1

Date 1971 **Origin** West Germany	
Weight 38.6 tons (35 tonnes)	
Engine MTU MB 833 Ea-500 diesel, 600 hp (447 kW)	
Main armament 20 mm Rheinmetall Rh202 cannon	

Early versions of the Marder, the first Western IFV, had a remotely controlled machine gun over the rear entry and firing ports for six troops. Thicker armor and a MILAN anti-tank missile launcher were added later. The Marder served with German forces during the Cold War, and subsequently in Kosovo and Afghanistan; vehicles supplied to Ukraine have seen action against Russian forces.

△ AMX 10P

Date 1973 **Origin** France	
Weight 16 tons (14.5 tonnes)	
Engine Hispano-Suiza HS 115 diesel, 260 hp (194kW)	
Main armament 20 mm Nexter M693 cannon	

The AMX 10P was the inaugural French IFV. Its three-man crew and eight infantry passengers entered and exited via a ramp at the rear. Export destinations included Saudi Arabia, Singapore, and Indonesia, the latter receiving a marine-corps variant equipped with a 90 mm gun.

25 mm cannon has an effective range of 1¾ miles (3 km)

Rear stowage bin

▷ AIFV (Armored Infantry Fighting Vehicle)

Date 1977 **Origin** USA	
Weight 15.1 tons (13.7 tonnes)	
Engine Detroit Diesel 6V-53T diesel, 267 hp (199 kW)	
Main armament 25 mm Oerlikon KBA-B02 cannon	

Based on the M113 APC, the AIFV had a gun turret, improved armor, an infantry capacity of seven, and firing ports. The Netherlands, the largest user, renamed it the YPR-765. Dutch forces operated over 2,000 vehicles in several variants; some saw action in Afghanistan.

▽ M2 Bradley

Date 1983 **Origin** USA

Weight 35.4 tons (32.1 tonnes)

Engine Cummins VTA-903T diesel, 600 hp (447 kW)

Main armament 25 mm M242 cannon

Despite a long and problematic development, and initial unreliability solved by costly modification, the M2 Bradley has since shown its worth in combat, with its TOW anti-tank missile launcher proving particularly effective. The three crew members and six troops enter and leave via roof hatches. Upgrades have improved its armor, sights, and electronic systems, and added space for a seventh soldier.

△ Warrior

Date 1986 **Origin** UK

Weight 30.9 tons (28 tonnes)

Engine Perkins CV-8 TCA diesel, 550 hp (410 kW)

Main armament 30 mm L21A1 RARDEN cannon

The Warrior originally had capacity for seven troops, but this upgraded version can carry only six. Other changes included giving the seats better protection against mine blasts and improving the suspension and crew visibility. Electronic countermeasures and extra armor were added for service in the Gulf, the Balkans, and Afghanistan. Repair, recovery, and command-post variants have since been developed.

△ Type 89

Date 1989 **Origin** Japan

Weight 29.8 tons (27 tonnes)

Engine Mitsubishi 6SY31 WA diesel, 600 hp (447 kW)

Main armament 35 mm Oerlikon KDE cannon

In addition to its 35 mm cannon, the Type 89 carries a Type 79 anti-tank missile on each side of its turret. Developed during the 1980s and used solely by Japan, the Type 89 is similar to Soviet vehicles in that its seven infantry passengers enter through two rear doors; Western designs typically have a single door or ramp.

▷ BMP-3

Date 1990 **Origin** USSR

Weight 20.6 tons (18.7 tonnes)

Engine UTD 29M diesel, 500 hp (373 kW)

Main armament 1 x 100 mm 2A70 smoothbore gun, 1 x 30 mm 2A72 cannon

The Soviet-designed BMP-3 is heavily armed for an IFV. It is bigger and more spacious inside than the BMP-2 on which it is based. To get in and out, passengers must climb over the engine at the rear. Newer versions have explosive reactive armor (ERA) and active protection systems. BMP-3s have seen combat in Chechnya, Yemen, and Ukraine.

Transporting Special Forces

The birth of special forces in World War II called for transport tailored to the activities of these units, such as covert raids, behind-the-lines operations, or extracting personnel. Standard trucks, for example, might be modified to give greater range and more capacity for the bespoke weaponry and supplies of their special forces passengers, or enable them to cope with unusually challenging terrain. Likewise, the need for stealth and speed for the rapid insertion of troops led to the development of dedicated vehicles, boats, and aircraft.

Special forces became adept at adopting and adapting civilian technology. Manufacturers, in turn, gained kudos by working with special forces, and could sometimes incorporate military innovations into their products.

French naval commandos use a fast rigid inflatable boat (RIB) off the coast of Djibouti in 1985. The French military retained a base in Djibouti after the country's independence, which they used for hot-weather and desert training.

Tanks of Nonaligned Nations

In the Cold War, nonaligned nations often tried to plot a course between the two rival power blocs. Yugoslavia, for example, bought tanks from both sides; Switzerland and Sweden purchased from the West while they built up their own design and manufacturing ability; Finland bought Soviet tanks.

△ Strv 74

Date 1958 **Origin** Sweden

Weight 24.8 tons (22.5 tonnes)

Engine 2 x Scania-Vabis 603/1 diesels, 170 hp (127 kW) each

Main armament 75 mm Strv 74 rifled gun

A modification of Sweden's 1940s-vintage m/42 tank, the Strv 74 was given a new, more powerful gun housed in a large but thinly armored turret. The 225 Strv 74 conversions supplemented the Centurion in Swedish Army tank units until the late 1960s.

▽ Type 61

Date 1961 **Origin** Japan

Weight 38.6 tons (35 tonnes)

Engine Mitsubishi 12HM21WT diesel, 570 hp (425 kW)

Main armament 90 mm L/52 rifled gun

The Type 61 was Japan's first post-World War II tank. Rather than buying American tanks, which proved too large and heavy for Japanese crew and the country's terrain, a decision was taken to commission a home-grown vehicle. In all, 560 Type 61s were built; none were exported or saw combat.

▷ Vijayanta

Date 1965 **Origin** India

Weight 43 tons (39 tonnes)

Engine Leyland L60 diesel, 535 hp (399 kW)

Main armament 105 mm L7A2 L/52 rifled gun

Built in India, the Vijayanta was a licensed version of the privately developed British Vickers Mark 1 export tank. Using the same gun as the Centurion, which was already in use in India, it had the engine and transmission from the Chieftain. Some 2,200 were built.

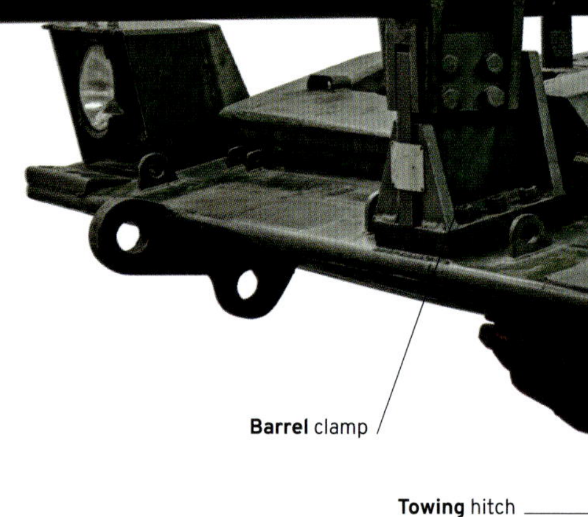

▷ Strv 103 (S-Tank)

Date 1967 **Origin** Sweden

Weight 43.7 tons (39.6 tonnes)

Engine Rolls-Royce K60 multifuel, 240hp (179 kW) and Caterpillar 553 gas turbine, 490 hp (365 kW)

Main armament 105 mm Bofors L/62 rifled gun

The Strv 103's autoloading gun—fixed within the hull—was aimed by steering and adjusting the height of the hydropneumatic suspension. A low, turretless profile and a second, rear-facing driver made the Strv 103 extremely effective as an ambush vehicle, striking at the enemy then reversing to escape.

◁ Type 74

Date 1975 **Origin** Japan

Weight 41.9 tons (38 tonnes)

Engine Mitsubishi 10ZF diesel, 720 hp (537 kW)

Main armament 105 mm L7 L/52 rifled gun

The Type 74 was Japan's response to the Soviet T-62, but a long gestation period meant it was slow to enter service. Its hydropneumatic suspension was able to raise, lower, or incline the vehicle to suit terrain being traveled over. Improved night vision systems and a laser range finder were among upgrades.

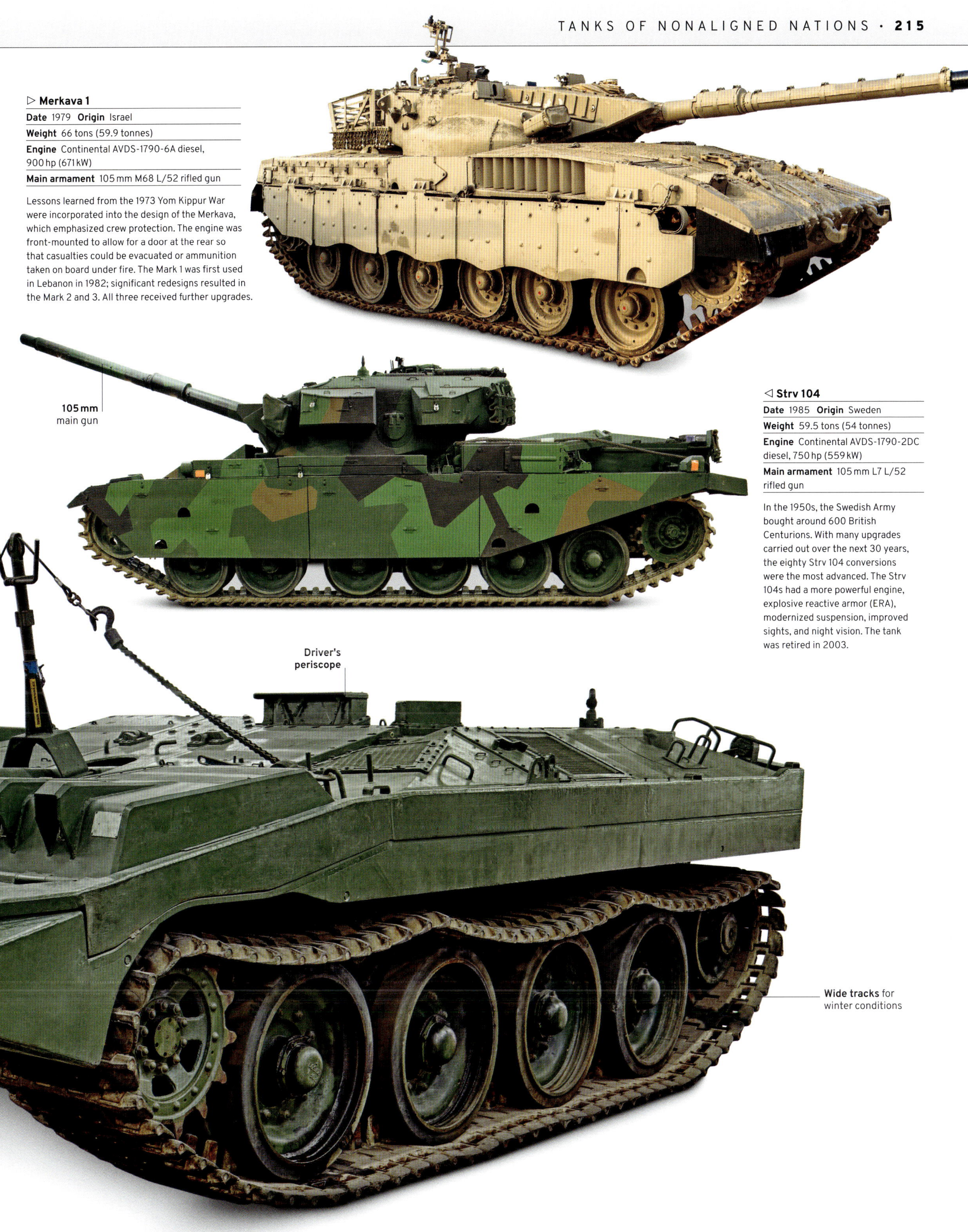

▷ **Merkava 1**

Date 1979 **Origin** Israel

Weight 66 tons (59.9 tonnes)

Engine Continental AVDS-1790-6A diesel, 900 hp (671 kW)

Main armament 105 mm M68 L/52 rifled gun

Lessons learned from the 1973 Yom Kippur War were incorporated into the design of the Merkava, which emphasized crew protection. The engine was front-mounted to allow for a door at the rear so that casualties could be evacuated or ammunition taken on board under fire. The Mark 1 was first used in Lebanon in 1982; significant redesigns resulted in the Mark 2 and 3. All three received further upgrades.

◁ **Strv 104**

Date 1985 **Origin** Sweden

Weight 59.5 tons (54 tonnes)

Engine Continental AVDS-1790-2DC diesel, 750 hp (559 kW)

Main armament 105 mm L7 L/52 rifled gun

In the 1950s, the Swedish Army bought around 600 British Centurions. With many upgrades carried out over the next 30 years, the eighty Strv 104 conversions were the most advanced. The Strv 104s had a more powerful engine, explosive reactive armor (ERA), modernized suspension, improved sights, and night vision. The tank was retired in 2003.

Cold War Land Vehicles

During the Cold War era, many armies moved to full mechanization and motorization. As the world divided its allegiances between NATO and the Warsaw Pact, and new export markets opened, it became important to standardize vehicle types, features, and performance to ensure good interoperability between armed forces. The American M35 series 2½-ton 6×6 cargo truck, for example, was adopted by more than 45 nations worldwide. The new generations of military trucks and light vehicles progressively took advantage of advances in engine design, ergonomics, and off-road capability.

△ Land Rover

Date 1948 **Origin** UK

Engine 1.6-liter four-cylinder gasoline, 50 hp (37.3 kW)

Payload 1,100 lb (c.500 kg)

The Land Rover began as a four-wheel-drive civilian utility vehicle in 1948, but it was soon adopted and repurposed by the British military. Many specialist variants emerged during the 1950s and 1960s; seen here is a standard early model.

△ M35 series 2½-ton 6×6 cargo truck

Date 1949 **Origin** USA

Engine Reo or Continental gasoline, 146 hp (108.9 kW)

Payload 9,900 lb (4,500 kg)

The M35 series trucks were produced between 1950 and 1988, during which time they experienced many combat deployments. The 6×6 configuration gave good off-road performance, while on-road these trucks could carry loads of up to about 5 tons (4.5 tonnes).

Blue flag signifies a lead vehicle in a military convoy

△ Bedford RL Recovery Vehicle

Date 1961 **Origin** UK

Engine 6-cylinder gasoline, 110 hp (82 kW)

Payload 6,614 lb (3,000 kg)

The Bedford RL—and its numerous variant forms—served as the British Army's main medium truck during the early part of the Cold War. Produced from 1953 until the early 1970s, the RL was eventually replaced by the Bedford MK/MJ. When fitted out with wrecking gear, this rugged 4×4 could recover vehicles up to its own weight.

◁ GAZ-66

Date 1964 **Origin** USSR

Engine ZMZ-66-06 V8 gasoline, 120 hp (89.5 kW)

Payload Approx. 4,410 lb (2,000 kg)

Developed by the Gorky Automobile Plant, this 4×4 was a core Warsaw Pact truck, with hundreds of thousands being built from 1964 to 1998—many are still in use around the world. The truck embodied the typical Soviet vehicle traits of reliability and simplicity, although later variants acquired "frills" such as central tire inflation.

△ **Steyr-Daimler-Puch Pinzgauer**

Date 1975 **Origin** Austria/UK

Engine 4-cylinder gasoline, 85 hp (63.4 kW)

Payload 2,200 lb (1,000 kg)

With a backbone-tube chassis and coil-sprung axles, this 4×4 (also available as a 6×6) had a top speed of 68 mph (110 km/h) and capacity for 10 passengers. A simple design and good cargo space won it popularity with European armies.

△ **Mercedes-Benz G Wagon Wolf**

Date 1979 **Origin** West Germany/Austria

Engine 2.3-liter M 102 E 23, 232 hp (173 kW)

Payload Approx. 2,200 lb (1,000 kg)

A vehicle popular with both civilian and military users, Mercedes' G-class was developed in West Germany and Austria from the early 1970s. When adopted by the Bundeswehr—the German armed forces—it acquired the "Wolf" nickname.

◁ **Humvee (High Mobility Multipurpose Wheeled Vehicle)**

Date 1985 **Origin** USA

Engine 6.2-liter Detroit Diesel V8, 215 hp (160.3 kW)

Payload 2,500 lb (1,136 kg)

The Humvee became the defining US military vehicle of the 1990s and 2000s. The Humvee has been produced in a wide range of configurations, including troop carrier, anti-tank missile platform, and ambulance variants.

Wide body profile gives good stability

Entering the Jet Age

The first operational combat jets entered service toward the end of World War II, but were too late to influence the outcome of the air war. In the 1950s and 60s, however, jet power reset the parameters of combat aircraft, greatly increasing levels of performance and lethality.

Korean War jets
Two McDonnell F2H-2 Banshee jets cruise high over Wonsan Harbor, North Korea, looking for targets during the Korean War. The Banshee's maximum speed was 580 mph (933 km/h).

On October 14, 1947, in the skies over Muroc Dry Lake in California's Mojave Desert, USAF captain Charles E. Yeager piloted an experimental Bell X-1 rocket-propelled aircraft to a speed of 700 mph (1,127 km/h). In doing so, Yeager became the first human to break the sound barrier in level flight. Yeager's adventure in speed was a seminal moment in the history of the jet age.

Going supersonic

During the second half of the 1940s, many air forces began to make the switch from piston-engined aircraft to jets, particularly in terms of their fighter complement. While the first generations of jet fighters, such as the British De Havilland Vampire and the Soviet Mikoyan-Gurevich MiG-9, were only capable of subsonic speeds, by the start of the 1950s, lessons learned from Yeager's landmark flight laid the foundations for supersonic jets to become a practical reality. The Korean War of 1950–53 saw the first clashes between transonic (close to the speed of sound) fighters, such as the North American F-86 Sabre and the Soviet MiG-15, both of which used turbojet engines and a swept-wing design.

As the 1950s progressed, increasing numbers of military aircraft acquired true supersonic capability in level flight, assisted by the adoption of newly developed afterburner technology. An afterburner is a device that injects fuel into the hot exhaust gases produced by the engine and burns it to provide additional thrust. Among these supersonic pioneers were the American F-100 Super Sabre and F-105 Thunderchief, and the Soviet MiG-19 "Farmer" and MiG-21 "Fishbed." Not only were jets now becoming very fast—some could fly at Mach 2+—but they also possessed astonishing climb rates, even with heavy ordnance loads. However, jets consumed large amounts of fuel. To prolong flights and extend ranges, effective methods of air-to-air refueling were developed, whereby fuel could be transferred in-flight from a tanker aircraft to a receiving jet.

The fast new jet fighters changed the nature of air battles, because high speeds made line-of-sight gun combat increasingly difficult. As a result, the mid-1950s saw the start of a shift toward air-to-air missiles (AAMs). Two examples were the Soviet RS-1U AAM, which "rode" a radar beam, and the American radar- and infrared-guided Hughes AIM-4F Super Falcon.

Heavy lift

The sheer power of jet engines made them ideal for heavyweight aircraft. Cold War air forces on both sides of the Iron Curtain raced to develop new strategic bombers capable of carrying massive thermonuclear devices across huge distances. The most successful of these designs was the Boeing B-52 Stratofortress, powered by eight Pratt & Whitney turbojets and with a wingspan exceeding 185 ft (56 m).

Manston Meteor
The Gloster Meteor F Mark I was Britain's first jet fighter and the Allies' only jet aircraft to perform combat missions in World War II. The RAF's 616 Squadron based at Manston in Kent, England, was the first to operate Meteors.

The B-52D variant, in service from 1956, could carry 42,000 lb (19,090 kg) of conventional or nuclear ordnance up to 8,338 miles (13,418 km) without refueling. Such was the integrity of the aircraft design that the B-52 is still operational, more than 70 years after its introduction.

Other early jet bombers included the Soviet Myasishchev M-4 "Bison" and a trio of "V-bombers" developed by Britain during the 1950s as its strategic nuclear force: the Vickers Valiant, Handley Page Victor, and Avro Vulcan. The Vulcan, with its striking delta wing, had exceptionally powerful performance. In 1960, the US introduced the Convair B-58 Hustler, the first operational bomber that could reach Mach 2.

By this time, the turbojet-powered logistical and support aircraft had also entered service. The Boeing KC-135 Stratotanker, for example, which was based on Boeing's 367-80 transport demonstrator, entered service with the USAF in 1957 as an air-to-air refueling aircraft. In almost every domain of military aviation, the switch to jet power was taking place.

Flying wing
The Northrop YB-49—a prototype jet-powered, American, heavy bomber—takes to the air for its first flight on October 21, 1947. Its "flying wing" design later led to the development of the B-2 Spirit, also known as the Stealth Bomber.

> "Flying fighters is **fun.** Flying bombers is **important.**"
>
> USAF GENERAL CURTIS EMERSON LEMAY

TALKING POINT

Wernher von Braun

German engineer Wernher von Braun (1912–77) was drawn into rocket research by a fascination with the idea of space flight. In the mid-1930s, he experimented with installing rockets in aircraft: a Heinkel He 112 he converted was the first plane to be powered by a liquid-fueled rocket engine. He also produced designs for a rocket-powered interceptor aircraft, but it was never built. In World War II, Von Braun oversaw development of the V-2 ballistic missile. His work paved the way for the rocket planes introduced by Germany in the war's latter stages. After emigrating to the US at the war's end, he became a leading figure in the US space program, rising to become director of NASA's Marshall Space Flight Center in Alabama.

Wernher von Braun sits behind his desk at the NASA Space Flight Center in 1964. A charismatic public speaker, he became a well-known scientist and engineer in the US.

▽ Mikoyan-Gurevich MiG-17

Date 1951 **Origin** USSR

Engine 5,046–7,423 lb (2,289–3,367 kg) thrust Klimov VK-1F afterburning turbojet

Top speed 711 mph (1,145 km/h)

A modification of the Mig-15, this successful transonic (near speed of sound) fighter was kept effective into the 1960s by adding an afterburner. China built its Shenyang J-5 version from 1966 to 1986.

△ Hawker Hunter F Mk1

Date 1954 **Origin** UK

Engine 7,600 lb (3,447 kg) thrust Rolls-Royce Avon 113 turbojet

Top speed 702 mph (1,130 km/h)

Aided by its compact Rolls-Royce Avon engine, the long-serving Hunter was among the best of the early jet fighters. Designed by Sydney Camm, the Hunter's prototype set a world air speed record in 1953 of 727 mph (1,171 km/h).

Thin, stubby wings had span of just 21 ft 11 in (6.9 m)

△ Lockheed F-104G Starfighter

Date 1958 **Origin** USA

Engine 16,500 lb (7,484 kg) thrust General Electric J-79 turbojet

Top speed 1,328 mph (2,125 km/h)

The first fighter capable of sustained flight at speeds in excess of Mach 2, this aircraft was known as "the missile with a man in it." The Starfighter served both as a tactical fighter and a day-night interceptor.

▽ Republic F-105D Thunderchief

Date 1958 **Origin** USA

Engine 24,500 lb (11,113 kg) thrust Pratt & Whitney J-75 turbojet

Top speed 1,372 mph (2,208 km/h)

The largest single-seat, single-engined fighter-bomber ever made, Republic's Thunderchief could fly supersonic at sea level and reach Mach 2 at altitude. The "Thud," as it was known, was at the forefront of combat during the early part of the Vietnam War.

20 mm M61 Vulcan rotary cannon for air-to-air or air-to-ground engagements

Jet Fighters

One of the legacies of World War II was a tremendous advance in the development of the jet engine. Fighters and fighter-bombers in the postwar era increasingly had to be jet-powered to be competitive, and aircraft designs were continually evolving in the quest for supersonic speeds. Ever more powerful engines and an increasing understanding of supersonic aerodynamics, fueled by Cold War paranoia and big military research and development budgets, saw top speeds rise from barely breaking the sound barrier in a dive to greater than Mach 2—twice the speed of sound—in level flight.

▽ Mikoyan-Gurevich MiG-21

Date 1959 **Origin** USSR

Engine 12,655 lb (5,740 kg) thrust Tumansky R-11F-300 turbojet

Top speed 1,385 mph (2,230 km/h)

Although somewhat lacking in range and agility, the MiG-21, codenamed "Fishbed" by NATO, was an effective Mach 2-plus fighter-interceptor. Over 10,000 were built, more than any other supersonic fighter. A few are still in use around the world.

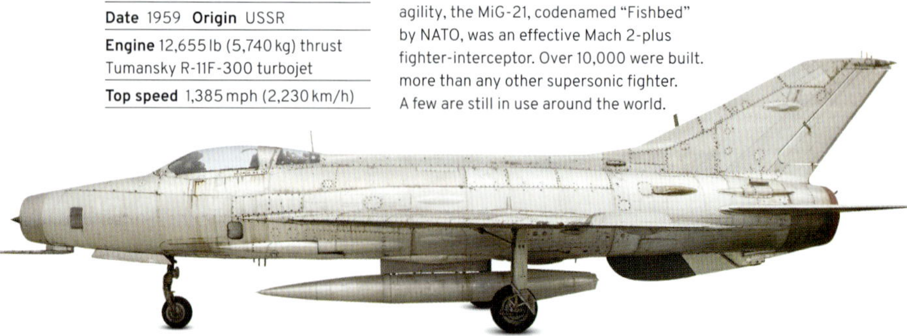

△ **Chance Vought (F-8K) F8U-2 Crusader**

Date 1960 **Origin** USA

Engine 10,700–18,000 lb (4,847–8,154 kg) thrust Pratt & Whitney J57 afterburning turbojet

Top speed 1,225 mph (1,975 km/h)

The last US fighter with guns as its primary weapons, the carrier-borne F-8 Crusader was the US Navy's principal fleet-defense fighter in the late 1950s. Its wings tilted upward to reduce takeoff and landing speeds.

Stretched fuselage of IIIE allowed for a larger avionics bay and increased fuel capacity

△ **Dassault Mirage III**

Date 1961 **Origin** France

Engine 9,436–13,668 lb (4,275–6,192 kg) thrust SNECMA Atar 9C afterburning turbojet

Top speed 1,460 mph (2,350 km/h)

The delta-winged Mirage III interceptor was introduced by the French Air Force in 1961. The stretched IIIE fighter-bomber variant is shown here. Mirage IIIs have served with 21 nations.

Wings span 34 ft 11 in (10.6 m)

▽ **English Electric Lightning F6**

Date 1968 **Origin** UK

Engine 2 x 12,530–16,000 lb (5,684–7,257 kg) thrust Rolls Royce Avon 301R turbojets

Top speed 1,500 mph (2,400 km/h)

With its stacked-engine design, the Lightning was the RAF's first supersonic jet and the only British-made Mach 2 fighter. The F1 entered service in 1960; the F6, seen here, had greater thrust and carried more fuel.

Military Transport Planes

Armies are perennially under pressure to carry out their operations faster and more efficiently, and—either for strategic or combat reasons—often on a wide geographic scale. This has led to the positioning of soldiers in bases around the globe, to establish garrisons that could be called upon in response to local events. The high cost of maintaining troops abroad prompted some nations to deposit tanks, vehicles, weaponry, and munitions in forward bases, and only transport troops to man the equipment when needed. While ships can carry larger loads, planes are a faster mode of ferrying personnel and military hardware—and speed may be a deciding factor in certain situations. Some military transporters have been converted from civilian aircraft, such as the Douglas C-47 Dakota (Skytrain), which began life as the DC-3 airliner; others, including the Lockheed C-130 Hercules, were designed specifically for military use, being able to take off from short, improvised runways and carry a heavy payload. Transport planes are costly to run and maintain, and they present large, relatively slow targets to an enemy, so no army can afford to rely on them as its sole means of moving troops and equipment.

A huge US Air Force Lockheed C-5 Galaxy transporter delivers a UH-60 Black Hawk helicopter to Latvia as part of a NATO exercise in 2017.

AIR MOBILITY COMMAND

F-86 Sabre

Just as North American's P-51 Mustang had proved its worth helping the Allies win air superiority in World War II, the F-86 Sabre, the company's next major fighter, earned its combat spurs in the Korean War. In brutal dogfights in the skies above Korea, the Sabre had the edge over the Soviet Union's state-of-the-art, swept-wing MiG-15. One of the most graceful fighters ever built, the Sabre is the epitome of the "fighter pilot's fighter."

THE SABRE'S DESIGN combined a jet engine with a swept wing—two innovations in warplane technology introduced in the latter stages of World War II by Britain and Germany respectively. The engine of this low-wing fighter was fed by a flow of air from the nose intake, with exhaust gases venting via a tailpipe in the rear of the fuselage. A prototype, the XP-86, first flew in October 1947, exceeding Mach 1 the following year.

The Sabre entered USAF service as the F-86A in early 1949. Like most of its American fighter contemporaries, it was armed with six 0.5 in machine guns, each with a firing rate of approximately 1,100 rounds per minute. Thrust into frontline action after North Korean forces, backed by the Soviet Union and China, invaded South Korea in June 1950, the Sabre fought nose-to-nose in aerial duels against the Soviet MiG-15s of the communist forces. The nimble Sabre ultimately achieved a victory-to-loss ratio over its MiG adversary of better than four to one.

35-degree sweepback on both fin and tailplane

Wing is swept back by 35 degrees

Jet pipe is built to withstand high temperatures

Lateral air brakes, one on either side of fuselage

Slotted wing flaps running from the fuselage to the ailerons extend to increase lift

SPECIFICATIONS	
Model	North American F-86A Sabre, 1949
Origin	USA
Production	554
Construction	Aluminum and steel
Maximum weight	14,108 lb (6,400 kg)
Wingspan	37 ft 1½ in (113 m)
Engine	5,200 lb (2,359 kg) thrust General Electric J47-GE-7 turbojet
Length	37 ft 6 in (11.4 m)
Range	785 miles (1,255 km)
Top speed	685 mph (1,102 km/h)

REAR VIEW

Designed for success
With its swept wing, gaping "mouth," bubble canopy, and well-proportioned overall design, the Sabre is one of the most distinctive and successful jet fighters in the history of aviation.

FRONT VIEW

Bubble canopy provides excellent all-round visibility

All-metal, flush-riveted stressed skin clads the oval-section fuselage

M-3 machine guns, with 267 rounds per gun, mounted in nose

WARNING

WARNING

F-86A Sabre

Hydraulic undercarriage is electrically controlled and sequenced

Nose-wheel door

EXTERIOR

The all-metal, flush-riveted, oval-section fuselage was aerodynamically efficient, and because the Sabre's engine was located within the fuselage and fed by a large intake in the nose, there were no drag-inducing engine pods or nacelles on the airframe. The result was a highly maneuverable aircraft. The Sabre had a rather narrow-track undercarriage, due to the main wheels needing to retract into the fuselage.

1. Painted emblem **2.** Hydraulic nose wheel **3.** Recessed step for cockpit access **4.** One of three gunports on port side **5.** V-shaped windscreen (rounded on prototype) **6.** Pitot tube mounted on starboard wing **7.** Formation light set into starboard wing tip **8.** Fuel filler—maximum capacity is 87 gallons (397 liters) **9.** Port lateral air brake **10.** Landing light (retracted) in wing **11.** Access panel for emergency engine disconnect **12.** External power receptacle and fuel filler on starboard side **13.** Fuel dump mast at rear of fuselage **14.** Stainless steel shroud for jet pipe **15.** Jet pipe

1

2

3

4

5

6

7

8
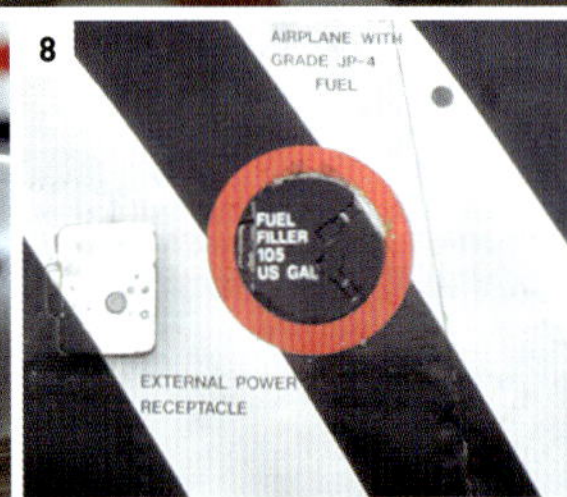

9

12
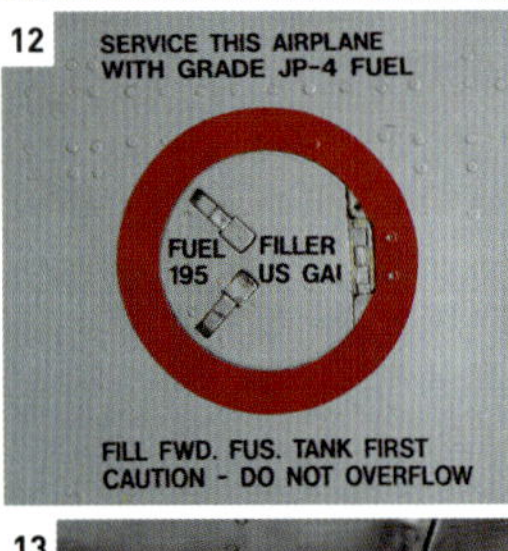

13

14

15

COCKPIT

The F-86A's bubble canopy—a holdover from North American's successful P-51 World War II fighter—gave the pilot unparalleled views in all directions. Inside the Sabre's well-designed cockpit, instruments were arranged in a neat and orderly fashion, with all flight controls placed within easy reach of the pilot. The controls for the engine, wing flaps, undercarriage, and air brakes were on panels to the pilot's left, with the radio and electrical controls to his right.

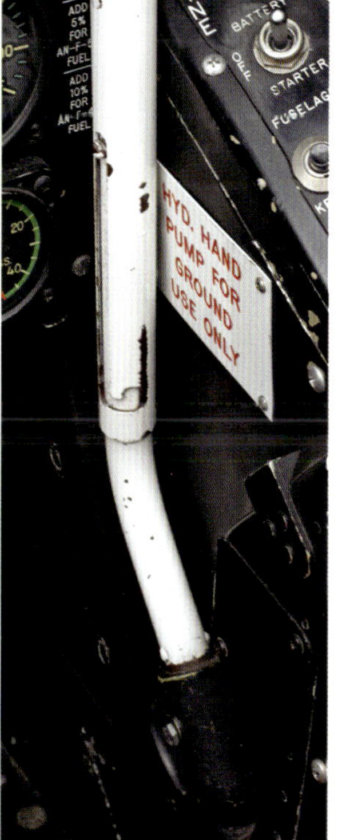

16. Cockpit view **17.** Gunsight with range (left) and span (center) selectors **18.** Flight instruments **19.** Magnetic compass **20.** Throttle and air brake controls **21.** Control column **22.** Emergency hydraulic pump

Bombers and Ground-attack Aircraft

Cold War tensions led the West to fast-track the development of jet-engined bombers and ground-attack planes. The result was some truly impressive aircraft, such as the delta-wing Vulcan, the ultra-high-altitude Canberra, and the enormous Stratofortress. At first, Soviet jet-powered bomber design lagged behind Western efforts, since only turboprops had the range to reach the US and return. However, the USSR did produce the Tu-95—the longest-range turboprop bomber ever in service, which is still operational today.

Straight wing design aided stability

Two-seat tandem cockpit

△ English Electric Canberra

Date 1951 **Origin** UK

Engine 2 x 7,400 lb (3,357 kg) thrust Rolls-Royce Avon RA7 109 turbojets

Top speed 580 mph (933 km/h)

Able to fly at high altitude and high speed, Britain's first jet bomber could evade early jet interceptors. In 1957, it set a new altitude record of 70,310 ft (21,430 m). Canberras served with many air forces.

Wing swept back at 35-degree angle

Turboprop engine

△ Tupolev Tu-95 "Bear"

Date 1956 **Origin** USSR

Engine 4 x 14,483 shp (10,800 kW) Kuznetsov NK-12M turboprops

Top speed 575 mph (925 km/h)

Combining swept-back wings and contrarotating propellers, the Tu-95 has an exceptional range, able to fly around 9,320 miles (15,000 km) fully laden without refueling. It is likely to remain in service until 2040.

Air intake for engines (two in each wing root)

△ Avro 698 Vulcan

Date 1956 **Origin** UK

Engine 4 x 17,000–20,000 lb (7,711–9,072 kg) thrust Bristol Siddeley Olympus turbojets

Top speed 646 mph (1,040 km/h)

The Vulcan, with its innovative delta-wing design, spearheaded Britain's nuclear deterrent. The aircraft delivered heavy payload capacity, high subsonic speed at altitude, and long range.

▽ Sukhoi Su-7B

Date 1961 **Origin** USSR

Engine 15,000–22,000 lb (6,800–10,000 kg) thrust Lyulka AL-7F afterburning turbojet

Top speed 1,336 mph (2,150 km/h)

The Su-7B developed from a fighter—the Su-7A—into a ground-attack version in the late 1950s. It was the first Soviet aircraft with an all-moving tailplane and movable-cone air intake.

Red star Soviet insignia

▽ **Convair B-58 Hustler**

Date 1960 **Origin** USA

Engine 4 x 9,700–15,600 lb (4,400–7,076 kg) thrust General Electric J79-GE-5A/B afterburning turbojets

Top speed 1,325 mph (2,132 km/h)

Although this delta-wing, Mach 2-capable nuclear bomber included many of the latest technological advances, crews found it difficult to fly. It was also more costly to operate than the Stratofortress and other bombers.

△ **Boeing B-52 Stratofortress**

Date 1955 **Origin** USA

Engine 8 x 12,100 lb (5,488 kg) thrust Pratt & Whitney J57 turbojets, later 17,000 lb (7,711 kg) thrust turbofans

Top speed 650 mph (1,046 km/h)

Operational since 1955, the B-52 was designed to carry nuclear warheads but evolved into a launch platform for cruise missiles and a conventional long-range bomber of awesome power. Upgraded B-52s are expected to serve into the 2040s.

▽ **Grumman A-6 Intruder**

Date 1963 **Origin** USA

Engine 2 x 9,300 lb (4,218 kg) thrust Pratt and Whitney J52-P-8B turbojets

Top speed 647 mph (1,041 km/h)

The Intruder was developed for the US Navy and Marine Corps as an all-weather long-range attack aircraft with high subsonic performance at low altitude. First flown in 1960, it entered service in 1963 and saw combat in the Vietnam War and the 1991 Gulf War.

▽ **Douglas A-4 Skyhawk**

Date 1956 **Origin** USA

Engine 7,700 lb (3,493 kg) thrust Curtiss-Wright J65, later 8,500–9,300 lb (3,856–4,218 kg) thrust Pratt & Whitney J52 turbojet

Top speed 673 mph (1,083 km/h)

The compact, agile, and ultra-light ground-attack Skyhawk was designed in the early 1950s for the US Navy and Marine Corps. Its delta wing was so small it did not need to fold for storage on carriers.

△ **Bell UH-1B Iroquois "Huey"**

Date 1959 **Origin** USA

Engine 960 shp (716 kW) Lycoming YT53-L-5 turboshaft

Top speed 135 mph (217 km/h)

A prototype of the UH-1, the US Army's first turbine helicopter, flew in 1956; the UH-1B, shown here, was larger, heavier, and twice as powerful. Largely retired from the US military, some UH-1 variants still serve with other nations' forces. Over 16,000 were built.

△ **Westland Wessex HAS3**

Date 1967 **Origin** UK

Engine 1,600 shp (1,193 kW) Napier Gazelle 18 Mk165 turboshaft

Top speed 127 mph (204 km/h)

The HAS3 was a version of the original Wessex Mk1 upgraded for anti-submarine warfare. Its revolutionary Type 195 sonar system was more expensive than the helicopter itself.

△ **Bell AH-1 Cobra**

Date 1967 **Origin** USA

Engine 1,400 shp (1,044 kW) Lycoming T53-13 turboshaft

Top speed 196 mph (315 km/h)

The world's first dedicated helicopter gunship, the agile, heavily armored Cobra, was developed for use in the Vietnam War. It combined a narrow, hard-to-hit fuselage with the dynamic components of the Huey.

△ **Messerschmitt-Bölkow-Blohm MBB Bo105CB**

Date 1970 **Origin** Germany

Engine 2 x 420 shp (313 kW) Allison 250-C20B turboshafts

Top speed 168 mph (270 km/h)

Germany's first domestically produced post-World War II helicopter, the Bo105 was also the first four-five-seat twin-engined utility design with rear-loading capability. Its composite main rotor blades and rigid titanium rotor head gave exceptional maneuverability.

△ **SA Gazelle**

Date 1973 **Origin** France

Engine 590 shp (440 kW) Turbomeca Astazou IIIA turboshaft

Top speed 193 mph (310 km/h)

Initially produced by Sud Aviation and subsequently by Aérospatiale, the compact and agile Gazelle was used for observation, liaison, and pilot training. It was the first helicopter with a fenestron, or fantail—a ducted multiblade tail.

Military Helicopters

Gas-turbine engines for helicopters were introduced in the mid-1950s. The new engines—which were lighter, more powerful, and more reliable than their piston forerunners—improved helicopter performance, lift capacity, and safety. They also opened up fresh roles for helicopters, from search and rescue (SAR) work and antisubmarine warfare (ASW) to infantry assault and medevac duties. During the Vietnam War, the first generation of pure combat helicopters emerged. Computerized fire-control and precision-guided munitions (PGMs) made these aircraft increasingly lethal as the century wore on, especially against armor.

◁ **Mil Mi-24 "HIND"**

Date 1973 **Origin** USSR

Engine 2 x 2,197 shp (1,638 kW) Isotov TV3-117 turboshafts

Top speed 193 mph (310 km/h)

The Hind—the most heavily armed attack helicopter of the Cold War, and still in service—has a rotary-barrel heavy machine gun under the nose, as well as under-wing pylons for carrying a variety of missile types.

▽ **Sikorsky UH-60 Black Hawk**

Date 1979 **Origin** USA

Engine 2 x 1,560 shp (1,163 kW) GE T700 turboshafts

Top speed 183 mph (294 km/h)

The mid-1960s-designed Black Hawk utility helicopter entered production in 1976 and active service three years later. It has been used by the US Army mainly in its troop-carrier configuration, which carries 11 soldiers. The most recent version of the Black Hawk is the UH-60M.

▷ **Boeing CH-47D Chinook**

Date 1982 **Origin** USA

Engine 2 x 3,750 shp (2,796 kW) Honeywell T55-L-712 turboshafts

Top speed 184 mph (296 km/h)

The large, tandem-rotor CH-47 Chinook is one of the heaviest-lifting Western helicopters. The CH-47D and CH-47F variants of this long-lived helicopter—dating back to the 1960s—remain in service today.

▽ **Boeing Apache AH-64**

Date 1984 **Origin** USA

Engine 2 x 2,000 shp (1,491 kW) GE T700-GE-701D turboshafts

Top speed 188 mph (303 km/h)

The Apache was the first helicopter with day-and-night, all-weather battlefield capabilities. Able to engage heavy armor and troop movements, this heavy attack helicopter has advanced defensive systems.

The Helicopter Comes of Age

Adaptable to many roles, the helicopter replaced a variety of fixed-wing military aircraft. Able to take off from and land in small spaces such as jungle clearings, it was ideal for delivering or retrieving troops or launching attacks, and, with its capacity to hover, it proved a more stable platform for firing munitions than many planes. The US produced gunships for use in the Vietnam War, while the Soviet Union developed the concept of the "flying infantry-support vehicle" to carry troops and weaponry for ground attack. One of these, the heavily armored Soviet Mil Mi-24, codenamed "Hind" by NATO, was fast in the air, able to carry a range of weapon pods, and featured titanium armor to minimize its weight. Used against mujahideen guerrillas after the Soviets occupied Afghanistan (1979–89), the Hind became the target for shoulder-launched missiles from man-portable air-defense systems (MANPADS).

Known as the "flying tank," the Soviet Mil Mi-24 was widely exported. It is seen here in Peruvian army service against guerillas and drug gangs in 1989.

AH-64 Apache

Designed to destroy tanks, armored vehicles, and air-defense units, the twin-engined AH-64 Apache employs many of the technologies that dominate the modern battlefield. Developed for the US Army by Hughes Helicopters and now produced by Boeing, the Apache was introduced in 1984. In service with a number of nations, it performed well in the Gulf War of 1991 and the invasions of Afghanistan in 2001 and Iraq in 2003.

THE APACHE'S MAIN ARMAMENT consists of up to 16 Hellfire missiles carried on the stub wings. Using target-acquisition and fire-control systems, the crew simply select targets and fire. The missiles lock on to their target and travel to their destination, which can be up to 5 miles (8 km) away, without further input from the crew. This capacity, called "fire-and-forget," allows the Apache to take evasive action immediately after it has launched its weapons. The wings can also carry a pair of rocket pods, each able to launch 19 unguided 70 mm rockets. The Apache's chain gun, under the nose, can fire 625 rounds per minute, fed from a 1,200-round magazine by an electrically driven chain mechanism.

To make the slow-flying Apache less vulnerable, the helicopter is equipped with sensors that warn of incoming threats, as well as infrared-radiation suppression systems, which impede its detection by heat-seeking enemy missiles. Decoy flares fired from near the tail by the automatic defense system confuse any missiles that do manage to target the helicopter.

SPECIFICATIONS	
Name	AH-64 Apache
Type	Attack helicopter
Length	58 ft 5 in (17.8 m)
Height	15 ft 3 in (4.64 m)
Engines	2 x GE T700-GE-701D turboshafts
Range	310 miles (500 km)
Armament	AGM-114 Hellfire missiles
Cruise speed	165 mph (265 km/h)
Maximum speed	188 mph (303 km/h)

Mast-mounted Longbow radar gives a 360-degree electronic picture of the battlefield

Rotor blade is fully articulated

Turboshaft engine is protected by armor

Stub wings

HIDAS sensors

Wing pylons allow a range of different weapons to be carried

Rocket pod

Missile launcher

Apache Longbow
The Apache is in service with a number of armed forces around the world. This is the AH1—a version of Boeing's AH-64D Apache Longbow built under licence by AugustaWestland for the British Army.

Target acquisition sensors

Flare container

EXTERIOR

The Apache's nose carries sensors for the Helicopter Integrated Defensive Aids System (HIDAS), which automatically detects and responds to enemy missiles. The main rotor blades, which attach to the hub via laminated steel straps, are easily folded or removed for transport. Wire cutters on the airframe can slice through power cables and telephone wires that might bring the aircraft down.

1. HIDAS sensors **2.** Main rotor assembly **3.** Wire cutter **4.** Decoy flare container **5.** Rocket pod **6.** M230 30mm chain gun **7.** Missile launcher (a training round is shown here)

1

2

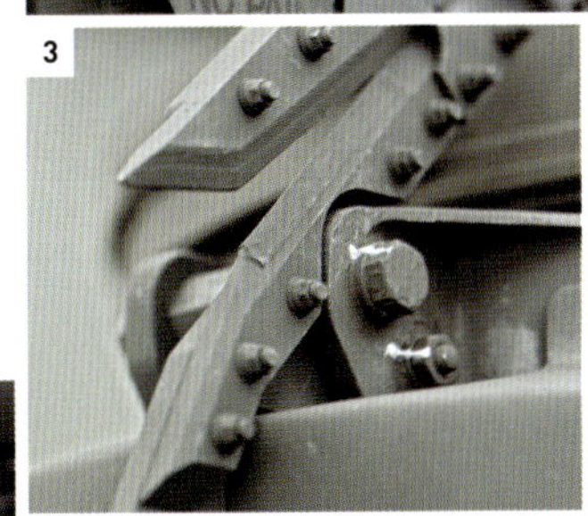
3

4

5

6

7

INTERIOR

The copilot/gunner sits in front of and below the pilot. Each crew member has a display that shows all the helicopter's systems. Both pilot and copilot are provided with flight and weapons controls in case one crew member needs to take full operation of the Apache. A "monocle" provides thermal (infrared) imaging and flight information in all conditions.

8. Control stick **9.** Canopy jettison handle **10.** Instrument panels **11.** Pilot's monocle

10

11

8

9

▷ Hawker Siddeley Harrier

Date 1970 **Origin** UK

Engine 21,500 lb (9,752 kg) thrust Rolls-Royce Pegasus 103 turbofan

Top speed 730 mph (1,176 km/h)

Equipped with vectored (directionable) thrust, the agile "Jump Jet" was the first successful vertical takeoff and landing fighter. In the hands of a skilled pilot, it could be operated from any small clearing or ship deck.

◁ Saab 37 Viggen

Date 1971 **Origin** Sweden

Engine 16,200–28,110 lb (7,348–12,750 kg) thrust Volvo RM 8A/B afterburning turbofan

Top speed 1,386 mph (2,231 km/h)

The trailblazing Viggen was the first aircraft with both afterburners and thrust reversers, and the first to have a computer with integrated circuits. Easy to maintain, it was operable from a short stretch of road.

▽ McDonnell Douglas F-15 Eagle

Date 1972 **Origin** USA

Engine 2 x 17,450–25,000 lb (7,915–11,340 kg) thrust Pratt & Whitney F100-100/-220 afterburning turbofans

Top speed 1,650+ mph (2,660+ km/h)

Built as a response to the Soviet MiG-25, the twin-engined, multi-role F-15 Eagle emerged as one of the world's foremost fighter and strike aircraft, combining advanced avionics with immense power, high performance, and maneuverability.

▽ Grumman F-14 Tomcat

Date 1974 **Origin** USA

Engine 2 x 20,900 lb (9,480 kg) thrust Pratt & Whitney TF-30-P-414A afterburning turbofans

Top speed 1,544 mph (2,485 km/h)

Developed to guard US Navy carriers against long-range anti-ship missiles and enemy aircraft, the Tomcat remained in service until 2006, thanks to multiple upgrades to its weapons, engine, and radar.

Frontline Aircraft

The introduction of turbofan engines, which produce more thrust than equivalent turbojets, provided extra power to frontline aircraft. A key advance in avionics was computerized "fly-by-wire" control, which allowed a previously unimaginable level of maneuverability. Offensive capabilities were boosted by "smart" weapons that could be guided toward their target with pinpoint accuracy, while the introduction of stealth technology on the F-117 Nighthawk was a milestone in the quest to avoid radar detection. Such innovations made developing all-new military aircraft increasingly costly.

▽ General Dynamics F-16 Fighting Falcon

Date 1974 **Origin** USA

Engine 17,155–28,600 lb (7,781–12,973 kg) thrust F110-GE-100 afterburning turbofans

Top speed 1,500 mph (2,414 km/h)

Fast and extremely agile, the lightweight F-16 was one of the first aircraft to use fly-by-wire controls. Built as an air-superiority day fighter for the USAF, the Fighting Falcon is still in production as a multi-role aircraft.

Ventral fin (port)

△ Panavia Tornado GR1

Date 1980 **Origin** UK/Germany/Italy

Engine 2 x 15,800 lb (7,167 kg) thrust Rolls-Royce Turbo Union RB199-103 turbofans

Top speed 1,452 mph (2,337 km/h)

The swing-wing, multi-role Tornado was designed to fly at a low level and penetrate enemy defenses. A joint UK, West German, and Italian development, it employed extensive fly-by-wire technology.

V-shaped tail

△ Lockheed F-117 Nighthawk

Date 1981 **Origin** USA

Engine 2 x 10,800 lb (4,989 kg) thrust General Electric F404-F1D2 turbofans

Top speed 617 mph (993 km/h)

The Nighthawk used sharply angled surfaces and a coating of radar-absorbent material to minimize its radar signature. Designed for night attacks with smart weapons, it could be flown on instruments alone.

▽ Sukhoi Su-27

Date 1984 **Origin** USSR

Engine 2 x 16,910–27,560 lb (7,670–12,500 kg) thrust Saturn/Lyulka AL-31F afterburning turbofans

Top speed 1,550 mph (2,500 km/h)

The twin-engined Su-27 has a good range, sophisticated avionics, and heavy armament. To minimize weight, large sections of this multi-role, super-maneuverable aircraft are made of titanium.

Semi-delta wing shape

Radome containing radar

Two-crew cockpit, with copilot behind pilot

Missile carried on wing pylon

Mikoyan MiG-29

Armed with the best short-range missiles of the day, the Soviet Mikoyan MiG-29 (code-named "Fulcrum" by NATO) was one of the standout fighter-bombers of the 1980s and early 1990s. Exercises showed that it was almost impossible to defeat in a low-speed dogfight, its apparent invincibility down to astonishing agility aided by a pilot's helmet that could be used to aim weapons—the first appearance of this feature on a major fighter.

THE MIG-29 REPLACED the MiG-23 as the USSR's main tactical aircraft. Designed to counter the threat of American F-15s and F-16s, the tough, cheap-to-build MiG-29 prioritized raw performance over advanced electronics. As a result, early versions of the MiG-29 lacked a fly-by-wire system—an electronic interface between pilot and flight controls—which was standard on other agile fighters of the period.

In excess of 1,600 MiG-29s have been produced, including a carrier variant, and the planes have served with more than 40 air forces around the world. The most surprising operator was the US Air Force, which ran a secret training unit equipped with MiG-29s, bought in 1997 from Moldova. The latest advanced version of the aircraft, the MiG-35, made its debut in 2007. It can be fitted with thrust-vectoring control, making it the world's most maneuverable fighter.

SPECIFICATIONS	
Model	Mikoyan-Gurevich MiG-29, 1983
Origin	USSR
Production	1650
Construction	Largely aluminum; some composites
Maximum weight	40,740 lb (18,480 kg)
Engines	2 x 18,300 lb (8,300 kg) thrust Klimov RD-33 afterburning turbofans
Wingspan	37 ft 6 in (11.43 m)
Length	57 ft 10 in (17.32 m)
Range	810–1,566 miles (1,500–2,900 km)
Top speed	1,519 mph (2,445 km/h)

Perfect blend
The MiG-29 has a mid-mounted wing with blended leading-edge root extensions (LERX). The engines are underslung and separated by a large channel. Shown here is an early 9.12 model MiG-29 operated by the Ukrainian Air Force.

Instrument landing system (ILS) aerial for communicating with ground control

Tailplane is all-moving

Starboard ventral fin

B-8W rocket pods can be fitted for the ground-attack role

FRONT VIEW

REAR VIEW

Upper wing air intake louvers feed air to the engine when on the ground to prevent debris being ingested

K-36 ejection seat operates at any speed or altitude

Infrared search and track sensor and laser ranger to track targets

Fiberglass radome protects radar antennae

Fairing for integral landing system

Air intake carries air to the engine when aircraft is in flight

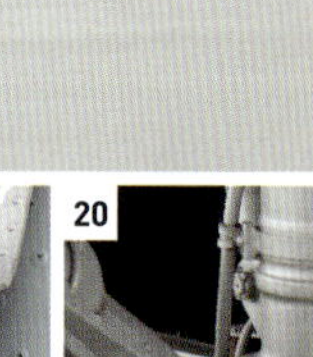

THE EXTERIOR

The muscular appearance of the MiG-29 is a product of its immensely strong airframe. The underslung engines and large leading-edge wing root extensions together contribute to the aircraft's superb high alpha performance—the ability to control the aircraft when the nose is raised at steep angles. The twin vertical tails are a legacy from the MiG-25; whereas the MiG-29's design emphasizes agility, its earlier cousin concentrated on speed.

10. Badge on tail **11.** Instrument landing system (ILS) aerial fairing **12.** Infrared search and track sensor/laser range finder **13.** Ultrahigh frequency (UHF) antenna **14.** Open cockpit compartment **15.** GSh-301 30 mm cannon muzzle apertures **16.** Landing light on leg **17.** Air intake **18.** White "06" aircraft number **19.** Light under wing **20.** Landing gear **21.** B-8W rocket pod for 20 rounds of 80 mm caliber **22.** Loading area for rocket pod at rear **23.** Variable area afterburner nozzle **24.** Port rudder

COCKPIT

There is good visibility from the roomy cockpit. The control column lacks Hands on Throttle and Stick (HOTAS) technology, whereby buttons and switches on the throttle lever and joystick enable pilots to perform vital functions without letting go of the controls. Apart from the pilot's Shchel-3UM Helmet-mounted Display (HMD), all the MiG-29's displays are analog dials—in contrast to the "glass" electronics of the American F/A-18 Hornet. The latest member of the family, the MiG-35, has three large multifunctional displays instead of analog instruments (with four displays in the rear cockpit of the MiG-35D two-seater).

1. Cockpit **2.** Radar **3.** Heading setting indicator **4.** Fuel quantity display **5.** Landing gear select and radar control panel **6.** Radar warning receiver **7.** Combined oxygen panel **8.** K-36 ejection seat headrest **9.** Control stick

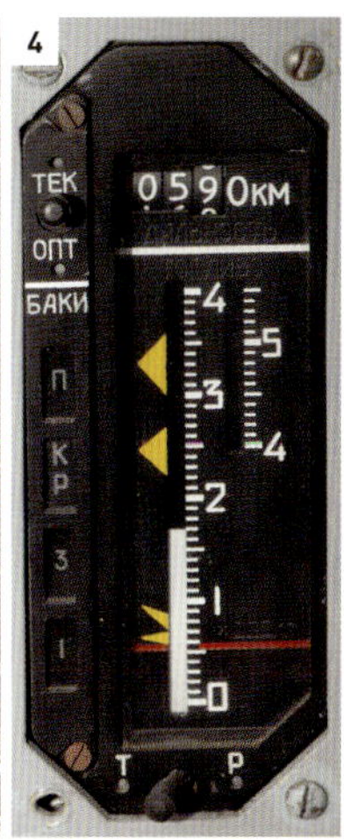

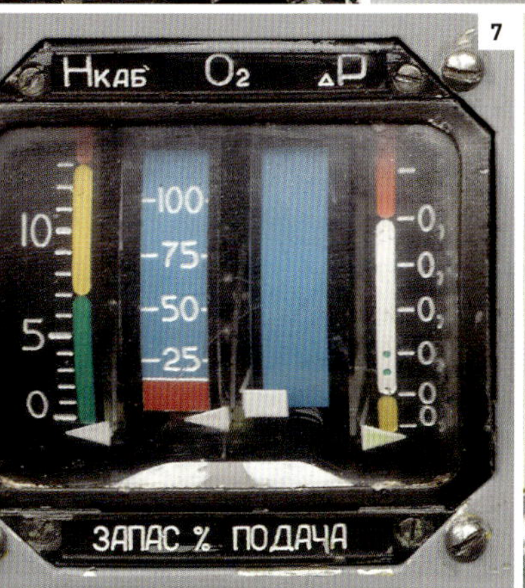

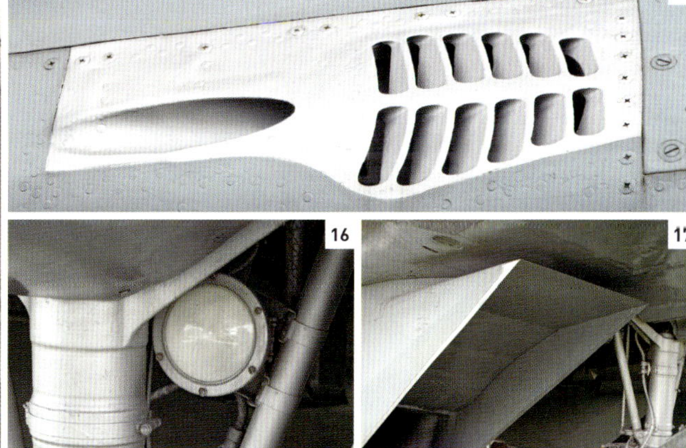

Stealth Technology

Encounters with sophisticated surface-to-air missiles in the Vietnam War convinced the US Air Force of the need to make combat aircraft less visible to radar. After lengthy development as a "black project" by Lockheed's Skunk Works, the F-117 Nighthawk—the first military aircraft to be designed around stealth technology—made its maiden flight in June 1981. Although it entered service in 1982, its existence was kept secret until 1988. The aircraft's "F" (fighter) designation is misleading: lacking any air-to-air combat capabilities, it instead carried two 2,000-lb (910-kg) laser-guided bombs. The F-117 proved a crucial weapon, participating in US operations over Panama, the Gulf (1991 and 1998), and the Balkans. It was retired in 2008.

The F-117—measuring 66 ft (20 m) long and with a wingspan of 43 ft (13 m) – had the radar footprint of a small bird. Coated with matte-black, radar-absorbent material (RAM), its angled surfaces scattered, rather than reflected, radar waves, while grilles over the engine air-intakes stopped radar bouncing back off the compressor blades. Omitting an afterburner and using long, heat-absorbent exhaust ducts reduced the aircraft's infrared signature.

A US Air Force F-117 Nighthawk flies low over the mountains of New Mexico during a training exercise.

The Changing Role of Navies

With the end of World War II, the days of large fleet engagements appeared to be over. As the Cold War intensified, however, the navies of the world found themselves with a new set of roles and responsibilities, keeping the strategic peace but also taking part in shooting wars.

The Soviet Union ended World War II comparatively weak in naval terms, certainly compared to the powerful US Navy. In July 1945, Soviet leader Joseph Stalin ordered a "still stronger and more powerful" naval service. This imperative energized naval production right through to the end of the 1960s, as the Soviet empire extended its reach over ever-greater portions of the world's oceans. The Soviets invested in new generations of surface vessels—from aircraft carriers, helicopter assault ships, and amphibious landing ships to missile-armed cruisers, destroyers, and frigates. They also built conventional and nuclear-powered submarines with ballistic-missile launch capability. By the 1970s, the Soviet navy rivaled that of the US, at least in terms of ship tonnage.

The US Navy appeared to be at a disadvantage. Its fleet strength contracted between 1964 and 1980: large numbers of World War II-era vessels were decommissioned, and funding was cut in the 1970s following the Vietnam War. However, the US Navy largely retained its technological superiority, and it substantially increased its strength during the 1980s under the "600-ship Navy" plan, which included a focus on Carrier Battle Groups (CBGs) and Marine expeditionary forces. During this decade, the underfunded Soviet navy became older and less functional.

Projecting power

At the strategic level, the Cold War was largely about power projection and deterrence. A key role of navies, in this context, was to police the sea-lanes and oceans, attempting to establish dominance over maritime trade routes and contested waters while also containing the intrusions of the opposing navy. US and Soviet submarine fleets and electronic surveillance vessels conducted a shadowy struggle to monitor and provoke their opponents. This role was helped by the increase in range and endurance provided by nuclear power plants.

Anti-submarine patrol
Maritime patrol aircraft, such as this Lockheed P-3 Orion of the Royal Dutch Navy, were a major tool used to monitor and counter the threat of nuclear-missile submarines during the Cold War period.

Although the US and Soviet navies did not engage in direct conflict, they came close to it. The Cuban Missile Crisis, in October 1962, was a tense standoff over the Soviet deployment of ballistic missiles in Cuba. The US Navy blockaded access to Cuba, in a line stretching from Florida to Puerto Rico. Only diplomacy averted naval clashes and potential nuclear war.

The numerous proxy wars from the 1950s to the 1980s meant that the US Navy made regular deployments, ranging from low-key peacekeeping to full-scale combat operations. The Korean War (1950–53) saw the US Navy providing offshore fire support to the land campaign and facilitating the massive amphibious landings at Inchon in September 1950. In March 1966, during the Vietnam War, planes from the carriers of Task Force 77 conducted around 6,500 combat sorties over North and South Vietnam and Laos, flying from the Gulf of Tonkin and South China Sea; the US Navy's riverine and coastal war in Vietnam was equally intensive. The 1980s brought the Navy into various peacekeeping and combat operations across the Middle East, and in 1982 it facilitated a major amphibious landing on the Caribbean island of Grenada. Even as the Soviet Union collapsed in 1991, US carriers provided the central air attack component of Operation Desert Storm over Kuwait and Iraq.

Submarine deterrent
The USS *Henry L. Stimson* (SSBN-655) was a *Benjamin Franklin*-class nuclear-powered submarine in service with the US Navy from 1966 to 1993. It carried 16 Polaris missiles armed with nuclear warheads.

Regional conflicts

The superpower struggle provided the wider context for naval roles between 1945 and 1991, but regional struggles also brought navies into operational use. During the 1971 India–Pakistan War, Indian Navy carrier aircraft and missile boats attacked Pakistani ships, harbors, and shore facilities. Two years later, in the Arab-Israeli Yom Kippur War, the first combat kills were made by surface-to-surface anti-ship missiles: five Syrian Arab Navy vessels were destroyed by Israeli Sa'ar-class missile boats.

The most influential naval battle of the Cold War era occurred in 1982. Argentina's amphibious invasion of the Falkland Islands (Islas Malvinas), a UK territory in the South Atlantic,

> "You seldom hear of the fleets except **when there's trouble**, and then you hear a lot."
>
> ADMIRAL JOHN. S. MCCAIN JR, COMMANDER, UNITED STATES PACIFIC COMMAND, 1968–72

prompted the British to deploy a naval task force to reclaim the islands. Prior to the invasion, Britain had been planning major cuts in naval strength; now a task force of 127 ships steamed south, centered around the carriers *Invincible* and *Hermes*.

The subsequent naval war, while ultimately a British victory, was a close-run contest. The Royal Navy established surface superiority, sinking the cruiser ARA *General Belgrano* in a torpedo attack by the nuclear-powered submarine HMS *Conqueror*. However, strike jets flying from the Argentine mainland inflicted a terrible cost on the task force at sea and during the amphibious landing: the British lost seven craft, including two Type 42 destroyers and two Type 21 frigates. While the Falklands War prompted a global rethink of naval tactics, especially in terms of air defense for ships, it also illustrated that the age of expeditionary naval warfare was not over.

Floating air base
Aircraft carriers were powerful deterrents and projectors of power. Here, a US Navy Lockheed S-3A Viking, an anti-submarine warfare (ASW) plane, launches from the USS *Forrestal*.

TALKING POINT

Intelligence Gathering

Naval surveillance was an unceasing operation during the Cold War. Its primary objective was to monitor and analyze enemy naval deployments, whether surface ships or submarines. Some of this activity was covert; both sides used state-of-the-art electronic/signals intelligence (ELINT/SIGINT) vessels disguised as merchant ships, fishing trawlers, and scientific research ships. The US Navy also deployed the Sound Surveillance System (SOSUS), a wide-area network of underwater passive hydrophones that could detect the passage of Soviet submarines in key regions of the Atlantic and Pacific oceans.

A radar operator watches his screen in 1985 aboard the HSwMS *Carlskrona*, a Swedish minelayer that has also been used for intelligence gathering.

Cold War Frigates and Destroyers

Over the near five decades of the Cold War, frigate and destroyer design went through profound changes. Deck-mounted guns were retained, but their number and significance diminished as weapons portfolios switched to new generations of anti-ship, anti-submarine, and surface-to-air missiles. From the 1960s, surface- and air-search radars became increasingly advanced, with data flowing to integrated and computerized combat information centers. Vessels such as the US Navy's *Spruance*-class destroyers and the British Type 21 *Amazon*-class frigate moved from steam-turbine to gas-turbine propulsion, which delivered a high power-to-weight ratio and faster start-up times.

▷ USS Herbert J. Thomas

Date 1945 **Origin** USA
Displacement 3,876 tons (3,516 tonnes)
Length 391 ft (119 m)
Top speed 35 knots (65 km/h)

The *Herbert J. Thomas*, one of 98 *Gearing*-class destroyers, was designed initially to provide antiaircraft and anti-submarine support for larger warships. The ship took part in both the Korean and Vietnam Wars, making effective use of its six 5-inch guns in three turrets.

Turret with two 4.5 in guns

△ HMS Diamond

Date 1952 **Origin** UK
Displacement 4,010 tons (3,637 tonnes)
Length 390 ft (119 m)
Top speed 30 knots (56 km/h)

As one of the *Daring*-class ships, *Diamond* was among the final conventional gun destroyers built for the British Royal Navy. Its guns were housed in three double turrets.

△ Kola-class frigate

Date 1951 **Origin** USSR
Displacement 2,094 tons (1,900 tonnes)
Length 315 ft (96 m)
Top speed 30 knots (56 km/h)

The Soviet *Kola*-class frigates were little different from World War II destroyers, albeit upgraded with more advanced radar and sonar equipment. Eight vessels in total were commissioned between 1951 and 1953.

▽ HMNZCS Canterbury

Date 1971 **Origin** UK
Displacement 3,349 tons (3,038 tonnes)
Length 372 ft (113.4 m)
Top speed 30 knots (56 km/h)

The *Canterbury*, one of the last *Leander*-class frigates, was built in Scotland and commissioned into the Royal New Zealand Navy. Its roles included peacekeeping in East Timor and relief efforts in the Pacific region.

Two 4.5 in guns

Flight deck for helicopter

▽ USS Pharris

Date 1974 **Origin** USA
Displacement 4,700 tons (4,264 tonnes)
Length 438 ft (133.5 m)
Top speed 27 knots (50 km/h)

Launched as a *Knox*-class destroyer, and reclassified later as a frigate, the *Pharris* was armed with anti-submarine missiles and torpedoes. The ship was commissioned into the Mexican Navy in 2000.

Missile launcher

Missile launcher

◁ **Koni-class frigate**

Date 1975 **Origin** USSR
Displacement 2,094 tons (1,900 tonnes)
Length 312 ft (95 m)
Top speed 27 knots (50 km/h)

The Soviet *Koni* class consisted of 14 anti-submarine frigates, built originally to replace the *Riga*-class ships but mostly sold for export. Type II variants included a revised superstructure to incorporate air-conditioning for use in warmer, non-European waters.

▷ **HMS Sheffield**

Date 1975 **Origin** UK
Displacement 4,872 tons (4,420 tonnes)
Length 410 ft (125 m)
Top speed 30 knots (56 km/h)

The *Sheffield*, a Type 42 guided-missile destroyer, was armed primarily with the Sea Dart missile system. The ship took part in the Falklands War of 1982, and, while on patrol, was sunk by an Exocet missile fired by an Argentinian naval aircraft.

Radar scanner
Main mast
Target-illuminating radar
Sea Dart missiles

▽ **USS Oliver Hazard Perry**

Date 1977 **Origin** USA
Displacement 4,032 tons (3,658 tonnes)
Length 445 ft (136 m)
Top speed 28 knots (52 km/h)

Built to protect military and merchant convoys, the *Oliver Hazard Perry* was the lead ship in its frigate class. It was armed with antiaircraft missiles and anti-submarine torpedoes.

Antenna for aircraft navigation aid
76 mm gun
Sikorsky helicopter

▽ **USS Nautilus**

Date 1954 **Origin** USA
Displacement 3,957 tons (3,590 tonnes)
Length 320 ft (97.5 m)
Top speed 22 knots (41 km/h)

Following the development of a successful nuclear propulsion plant by scientists and engineers at the Naval Reactors Branch of the US Atomic Energy Commission, *Nautilus* became the first operational nuclear-powered submarine in the world. In 1958, it made the first underwater transit of the North Pole. An attack submarine, *Nautilus* carried conventional torpedoes.

Bridge

Bow diving plane

▽ **George Washington-class submarine**

Date 1959 **Origin** USA
Displacement 6,744 tons (6,055 tonnes)
Length 382 ft (116.3 m)
Top speed 16 knots (30 km/h)

In service from 1959 until 1985, *George Washington*-class submarines were built to deploy the UGM-27 Polaris ballistic missile. Each submarine carried 16 of the A1 (later A3) variants of the missile in vertical launch tubes. The first Polaris test launch from a submarine was made on July 20, 1960.

Missile hatch (open)

Sail acts as a vertical stabilizer when the submarine is submerged

Streamlined shape to hull

▷ **HMS Dreadnought**

Date 1963 **Origin** UK
Displacement 3,920 tons (3,556 tonnes)
Length 266 ft (81 m)
Top speed 20 knots (37 km/h)

Equipped with six tubes for its 24 torpedoes, HMS *Dreadnought* was the British Navy's first nuclear-powered submarine. Its motive force came from an American Westinghouse S5W pressurized water reactor, which delivered 15,000 shp. Commissioned in 1963, HMS *Dreadnought* remained in service until 1980.

Nuclear-powered Submarines

Introduced in the 1950s, submarines powered by small nuclear reactors quickly proved they could surpass their diesel-electric rivals in speed, underwater endurance, and range. Some nuclear-powered submarines are attack submarines, designed to operate against surface ships or hunt down other submarines. Others, armed with nuclear ballistic missiles, are the most potent weapon systems ever developed. Lying beneath the waves, they can launch their deadly arsenal without warning, virtually immune from retaliatory action by the enemy. Their high level of concealment also gives them an invaluable second-strike capability.

▷ **Benjamin Franklin-class submarine**

Date 1965 **Origin** USA
Displacement 8,204 tons (7,443 tonnes)
Length 425 ft (130 m)
Top speed 16 knots (30 km/h)

This 12-ship class of ballistic missile submarine operated from the mid-1960s until the last vessel was decommissioned in 2002. The ships could reach dive depths of 1,312 ft (400 m) and could conduct submerged patrols lasting more than 60 days.

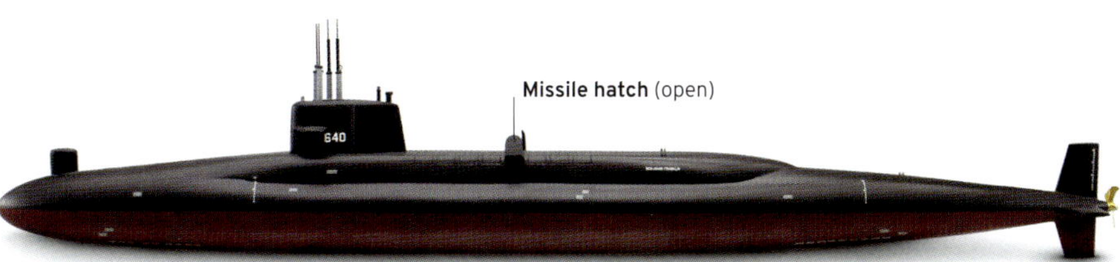

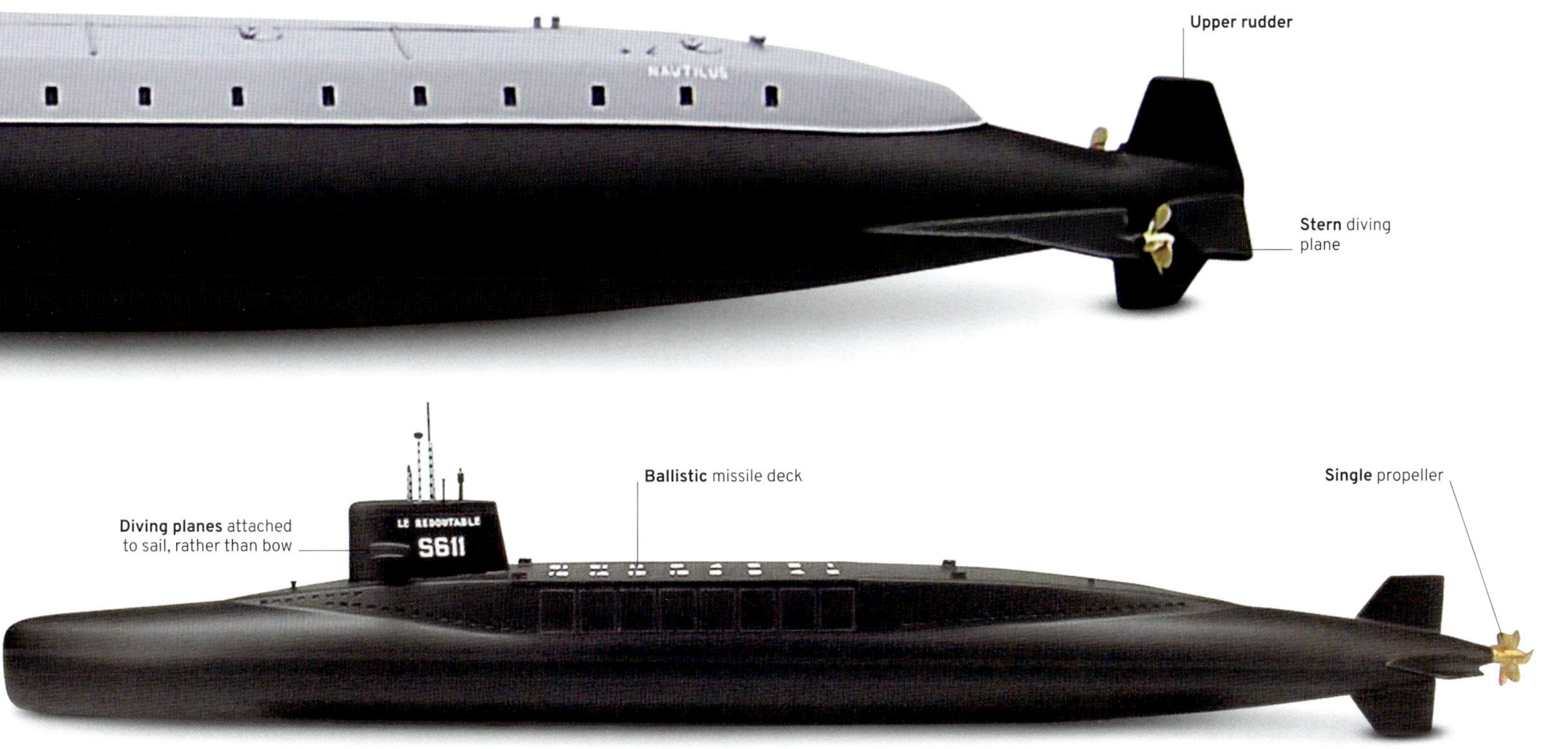

△ **Le Redoutable**

Date 1971 **Origin** France
Displacement 9,010 tons (8,174 tonnes)
Length 420 ft (128 m)
Top speed 18 knots (33 km/h)

Le Redoutable was the lead vessel of its class and France's first ballistic missile submarine. Its original complement of M1 missiles had a range of 1,243 miles (2,000 km) when carrying a 496-kiloton warhead.

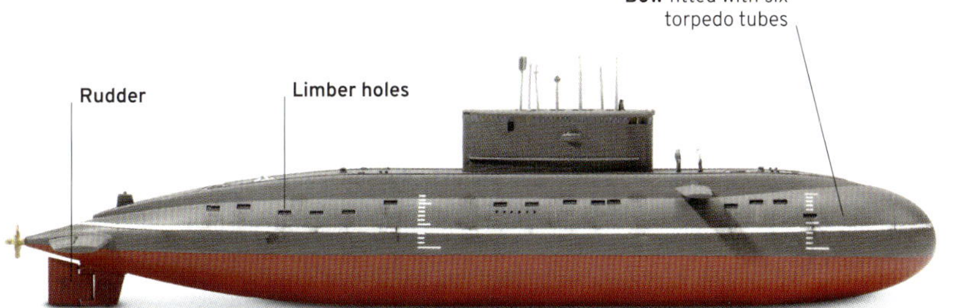

▽ **Oscar-class submarine**

Date 1975 **Origin** USSR
Displacement 16,200 tons (14,700 tons)
Length 509 ft (155 m)
Top speed 15 knots (28 km/h)

Construction of the *Oscar*-class of Soviet and Russian submarines began in 1975; the most recent of the series of 14 (to date) ships was commissioned in 2022. Modern *Oscar-II* variants are primarily designed to destroy enemy carriers using torpedoes and advanced anti-ship missiles.

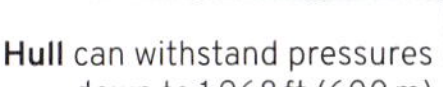

△ **Novosibirsk**

Date 1984 **Origin** USSR
Displacement 2,604 tons (2,362 tonnes)
Length 220 ft (67 m)
Top speed 15 knots (28 km/h)

A diesel-electric attack submarine of the *Kilo* class, *Novosibirsk* was armed with minelaying equipment and conventional torpedoes, as well as anti-ship and antiaircraft missiles.

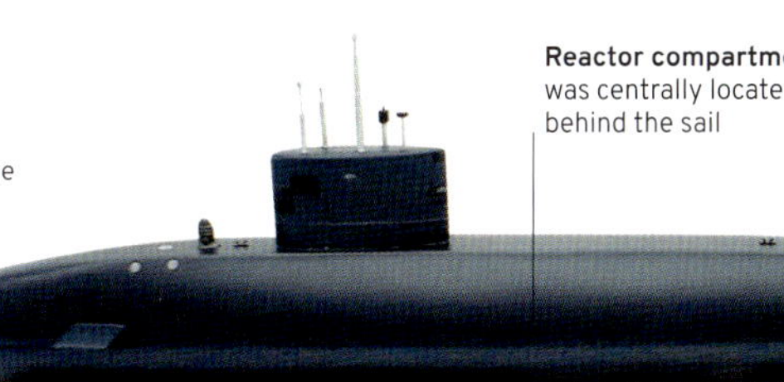

▷ **Trafalgar-class submarine**

Date 1986 **Origin** UK
Displacement 5,290 tons (4,800 tons)
Length 280 ft (85.4 m)
Top speed 20 knots (27 km/h)

The seven *Trafalgar*-class submarines, alongside the preceding *Swiftsure* class, were a core element of Britain's nuclear submarine fleet from the 1980s until 2025. Several of the vessels made combat deployments from 2001, firing Tomahawk cruise missiles at targets in Afghanistan, Iraq, and Syria.

USS Nautilus

The world's first nuclear-powered submarine, the *Nautilus* entered service in 1954, during the early stages of the Cold War. Whereas conventional submarines could submerge for 12–48 hours, the *Nautilus* was able to stay under water for two weeks or more without having to surface or refuel. Nuclear submarines would soon dominate naval strategy, either as torpedo-carrying attack vessels or as nuclear missile carriers.

POWERED BY A NUCLEAR REACTOR, the *Nautilus* had unrivaled endurance under water: in 1955, it set a new record for a submerged voyage, covering 1,381 miles (2,222 km) in 90 hours. Three years later, it became the first submarine to travel below the polar ice cap to the North Pole. In addition to its reactor, the ship's innovations included dispensing with a deck gun, an inertial navigation system (on its 1958 sub-Arctic trip), and providing each crew member with a bunk—previous submarines used a shift system for bunks.

The *Nautilus*'s armament consisted of 24 Mk14 conventional torpedoes, some of which were kept in the tubes, ready for firing, with the rest being stored on racks in the torpedo bay. The *Nautilus* was equipped with electronic countermeasures systems that detected signals from other vessels and helped foil attempts to track the submarine from its own transmissions, while sonar was used to locate ships and other submarines, follow possible targets, and avoid collisions when submerged.

The *Nautilus* was not particularly fast beneath the waves, and by 1959 it was being superseded by vessels that could achieve higher subsurface speeds and reach greater depths, thanks to improved hull designs and the use of new materials. The *Nautilus* was retired in 1980 and is now a museum.

SPECIFICATIONS	
Name	USS *Nautilus*
Commissioned	1954
Type	Nuclear submarine
Displacement	3,957 tons (3,590 tonnes)
Length	320 ft (97.5 m)
Propulsion	STR nuclear reactor
Complement	13 officers, 92 enlisted
Armament	6 torpedo tubes
Maximum speed	23 knots (43 km/h)

Radar antenna
Sail
Rudder
Hydroplane
Propeller

Submarine sail
The *Nautilus* was commanded from the bridge, located at the top of the towerlike "sail," when traveling on the surface. The sail also housed the periscopes and antennas for radio and radar.

INTERIOR

Two planesmen in the control room operated the hydroplanes to adjust the ship's angle and depth under water; the helmsman, on their right, used the rudder to adjust the course. The attack center, the heart of the submarine's role as a warship, housed controls for firing the torpedoes, two periscopes, and navigational equipment. Officers dined in the wardroom, the crew in the mess. Torpedoes were in the bow, with engines and the reactor toward the stern.

1. Control room **2.** Collision alarm **3.** Ballast tank water-level dials **4.** Hatch and vent display panel (to check closure prior to diving) **5.** Electronic countermeasures **6.** Sonar room **7.** Wardroom **8.** Galley **9.** Crew's quarters **10.** Attack center **11.** Torpedo **12.** Torpedo bay

Military Patrol Boats

For millennia, inland waterways have been used as routes for travel and trade. In wartime, they can not only act as defensive barriers but also give access to enemy positions. During the Vietnam War (1954–75), the Mekong Delta, an area with few roads but a vast network of waterways, became a key conflict zone between the Viet Cong and US and South Vietnamese forces. The US Navy established Task Forces equipped with small Patrol Boats, Riverine (PBR) and larger Patrol Craft, Fast (PCF) to stop the transportation of enemy troops and supplies, enforce nighttime curfews, defend legitimate trade, and clear mines.

Operation Giant Slingshot, beginning in late 1968, aimed to block the flow of Viet Cong fighters infiltrating into South Vietnam from Cambodia via the Mekong Delta waterways. With around 50,000 local vessels estimated to be operating on these waterways, one of the main activities of the US patrol boats was carrying out stop-and-search inspections of sampans, junks, and other river traffic to prevent the smuggling of weapons.

With gunners poised and ready for action, US Navy PCF 43 cruises along a river in Vietnam during Operation Giant Slingshot in January 1969.

1989–PRESENT

THE HIGH-TECH AGE

2A

Gulf War strike aircraft
USAF F-15 Eagle and F-16 Fighting Falcon aircraft fly over burning Iraqi oil fields during the 1991 Gulf War in a display of the Coalition's air superiority.

Present War, Future War

Since the end of the Cold War, the development of military vehicles has been influenced both by current wars and by predictions of future conflicts. In both cases, digital technology continues to reshape the battlefield.

Between January 17 and February 28, 1991, a large-scale US-led military coalition defeated the armed services of Iraq in Operation Desert Storm, the international effort to expel Iraqi occupation forces from Kuwait. The one-sided victory seemed to demonstrate the possibility of "Full Spectrum Dominance": a force being technologically superior across air, sea, land, space, and digital. The future, however, was to prove more complex.

From Gulf War to COIN war

The Gulf War was decided by aircraft, armor, ships, and artillery; there was little significant infantry fighting. The Coalition overran Iraq's largely outdated Soviet-style equipment. Ship-launched Tomahawk cruise missiles struck strategic targets with precision hundreds of miles from their launch point. Iraqi air defenses were ineffective against a massive Coalition air campaign that wiped out Iraq's command-and-control network and huge volumes of equipment and vehicles, often using new generations of precision-guided munitions (PGMs). US M1 Abrams and British Challenger I tanks outgunned Iraqi T-72s and T-64s. The Coalition forces were coordinated by a powerful digital network of surveillance and communication.

The Gulf War seemed to prove that the weapons and vehicles of the Cold War still had relevance, especially when integrated into a "network-centric battlefield." However, from 2001, the US and its allies found themselves locked into two decades of counterinsurgency (COIN) warfare, principally in Afghanistan and Iraq. Based around armed resistance by local insurgents, COIN spawned new directions in vehicle design. The focus shifted to lighter,

> "There are **two dangers**... the over-reliance on **technology** and the failure to make the most of [its] **capabilities.**"
>
> US MARINE CORPS, *WARFIGHTING*, 1997

Timeline
The Gulf War (1990–91), the War on Terror (2001–21), and the Ukraine War (2022–) tested and challenged the design of military vehicles, leading to transformational new tactics and technologies. Unmanned vehicles, stealth configurations, and the incorporation of artificial intelligence (AI) point the way to the future.

1991 The US Humvee light vehicle is used heavily in the 1991 Gulf War

1998 British Challenger 2 third-generation MBTs enter service

2005 The F-22 Raptor stealth fighter joins US Air Force squadrons

1995 The MQ-1 Predator unmanned combat aerial vehicle (UCAV) enters US service

2001 China introduces the Type 99 third-generation MBT into the People's Liberation Army (PLA)

faster types of armored fighting vehicle (AFV) more suited to urban warfare. Land vehicle designs began to reflect the distinct threats posed by improvised explosive devices (IEDs) and rocket-propelled grenades (RPGs), with mine-resistant hull shapes, up-armored light vehicles, and active armor protection systems. Aging aircraft platforms such as the Fairchild Republic A-10 Thunderbolt II ground-attack aircraft and the B-1 Lancer bomber still proved effective, and drones were also widely used for surveillance and targeting. Aircraft carriers and missile-launching ships also took part, both for offshore strike missions and as surveillance platforms.

During the same period as the Global War on Terror (GWOT), which the US initiated after attacks in the US by the al-Qaeda terrorist group in 2001, new and more advanced military vehicle technologies emerged. China made astonishingly rapid steps in modernizing its armed forces: examples included its all-weather Chengdu J-20 stealth fighter; its first domestically produced aircraft carrier (the *Shandong*); the Type 039A/B *Yuan*-class submarine; and the Type 99A main battle tank (MBT). Internationally, many more naval vessels incorporated stealth designs and some also served as mounts for directed energy weapons (DEWs), such as lasers, and experimental electromagnetic rail guns. Russia and other nations developed hypersonic, scramjet-powered missiles that could fly erratic paths to their targets, evading air defenses. In the background, warfare was changing.

New directions

In 2014, conflict broke out in eastern Ukraine between Ukraine's armed forces and Russian paramilitaries. This led to Russia's full-scale invasion of Ukraine in 2022, a conflict that has had major implications for future-warfare planning, not least for the procurement and development of military vehicles.

Some lessons learned have affirmed older technologies. During the era of COIN warfare in Afghanistan and Iraq, for example, there had been debates about the relevance of MBTs on the modern battlefield. The Ukraine conflict, however, has made extensive use of large fleets of heavy AFVs, and also of self-propelled artillery. Intense infantry combat showed the importance of infantry fighting vehicles (IFVs) for ingress and egress of the battlefield. Air power has remained influential, not least for launching long-range glide bombs beyond the range of air defenses.

The most dramatic impact in the Ukraine War was made by drones, used in their millions to perform combat missions ranging from low-level surveillance through to armor-killing "suicide" missions. The majority of these are cheap, commercial drones converted for combat use. Increasingly, military drones have autonomous capabilities, such as AI-powered targeting systems.

Unmanned, autonomous technology is the future of military vehicles. It is being tested in every domain, and at all scales. The spectrum ranges from sofa-sized "robo-mules" designed to carry an infantry squad's equipment through to full-size autonomous or semiautonomous tanks and warships. It is also likely that piloted combat aircraft will, in the future, be accompanied by autonomous "wingmen" to provide extra fighting capability.

Globally, the military world is shifting its focus from the COIN era to a new age of vehicular warfare. Future combat may well be as much about the fight between rival AI systems as it will be about battles of guns and missiles. As the digital decision-making process in warfare becomes ever faster, it points to a new generation of military vehicles in which the human being is optional—or, conceivably, even unnecessary.

TALKING POINT

Modern Communication Networks

The lethality, performance, and utility of modern military vehicles is often dependent upon their integration into advanced battlefield communications networks. Even trucks and light vehicles might carry sophisticated voice/data systems, including monitors displaying real-time situational awareness of friendly and enemy forces. Satellite datalinks enable the secure transfer and receipt of large volumes of information, and enable exceptional precision in navigation and fire control. Jamming communications is also key: many advanced armies are investing in technologies designed to deny or disrupt enemy communications, while AI is being used to make communications more resistant to this.

US soldiers fold out a vehicle-mounted antenna mast group (AMG), used as an amplifier and a communications relay for voice and data transmissions.

Preparing for war in Ukraine
A Ukrainian T-80-type tank fires its smoothbore 5 in (125 mm) main gun during a training exercise in 2024, readying itself for frontline deployment in the war against Russia.

2007 Introduction of the US V-22 Osprey tilt-rotor military transport and cargo aircraft

2007 Mine Resistant Ambush Protected (MRAP) vehicles are deployed in Iraq and Afghanistan

2010 Britain's Royal Navy commissions a new generation of nuclear submarine, HMS *Astute*

2014 The Turkish Bayraktar TB2 UCAV makes its first flight

2015 Russia begins production of the T-15 Armata advanced IFV

2016 The first US Navy *Zumwalt*-class multi-mission stealth ship is commissioned

2017 China introduces the Chengdu J-20 all-weather stealth fighter

2017 China launches its first domestically produced aircraft carrier, *Shandong* (17)

2019 The Sukhoi Su-57 becomes Russia's first stealth fighter

2020 Chinese Type 055 stealth guided-missile destroyers enter service

2022 Unmanned surface vehicles (USVs) conduct combat operations in the Ukraine War

2023 The B-21 Raider, the USAF's newest strategic bomber, makes its first flight

2024 US agencies begin tests of self-driving AFV designs

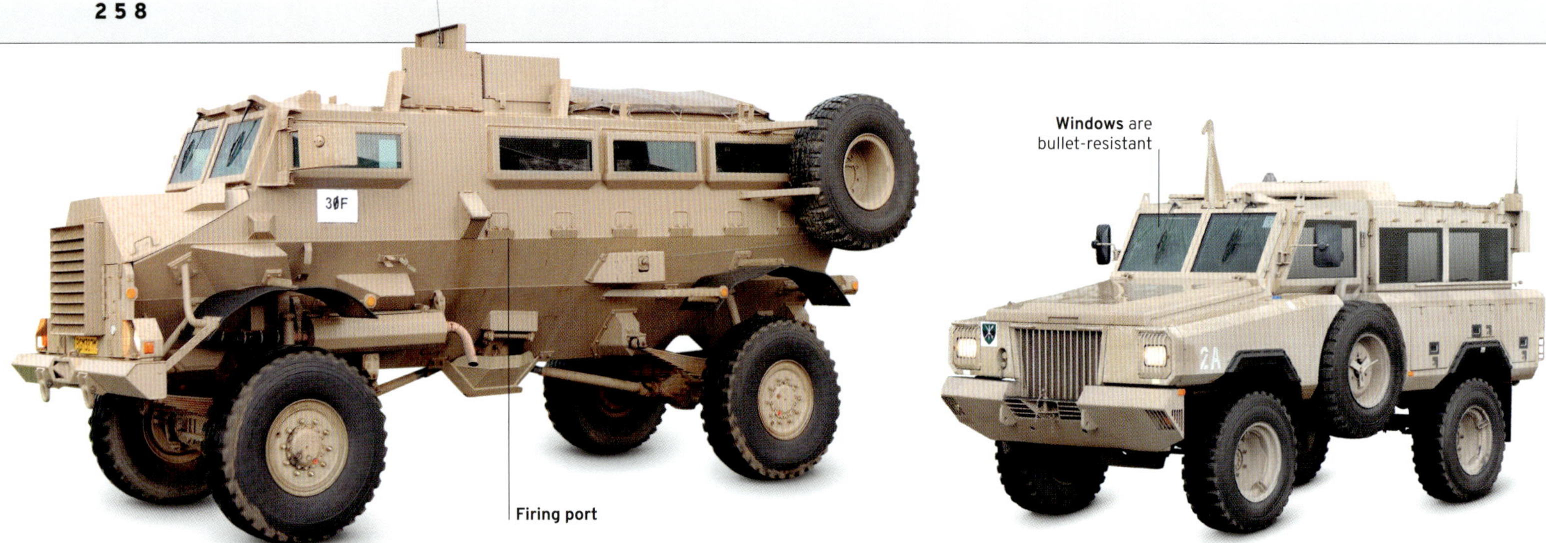

△ **Casspir**

Date 1979 **Origin** South Africa
Weight 12 tons (10.9 tonnes)
Engine Mercedes-Benz OM-352A diesel, 166 hp (124 kW)
Main armament None

With an enclosed armored body and bulletproof windows, South Africa's Casspir was designed for both riot control and fighting in the Border War. Its V-shaped underside protected against mines. This versatile, two-crew, 12-passenger vehicle was also used for recovery and mine clearance, and as a mortar carrier and tanker.

△ **Mamba**

Date 1989 **Origin** South Africa
Weight 7.5 tons (6.8 tonnes)
Engine Mercedes-Benz OM352 diesel, 123 hp (92 kW)
Main armament None

Unlike the Buffel, which it replaced, South Africa's Mamba has a roof and armored windows. Mark I Mambas were two-wheel drive and carried five troops; later models were upgraded to four-wheel drive and had capacity for nine soldiers, combining high levels of protection with a nonthreatening appearance. The Mamba's development has continued in the 21st century.

△ **Snatch Land Rover**

Date 1992 **Origin** UK
Weight 4.5 tons (4.1 tonnes)
Engine Land Rover 300Tdi diesel, 111 hp (83 kW)
Main armament None

The Snatch evolved from a series of armored Land Rovers used in Northern Ireland, notably the "Piglet," fitted with a Vehicle Protection Kit (VPK), and the Glover Webb armored patrol vehicle (APV). Deployed in Iraq and Afghanistan, the Snatch gave some protection against small arms fire and IEDs, but high crew casualties led to its withdrawal.

▽ **Mastiff**

Date 2006 **Origin** UK
Weight 26 tons (23.6 tonnes)
Engine Caterpillar C7 diesel, 330 hp (246 kW)
Main armament 7.62 mm or 12.7 mm machine gun, or 40 mm grenade launcher

The Mastiff is Britain's version of the US Army's Cougar MRAP, which saved thousands of lives in Iraq and Afghanistan. Unlike the Cougar, the Mastiff is fitted with bar armor and replaces armored side windows with armor plate.

Counterinsurgency Vehicles

The increasing use of land mines by insurgents and terrorist groups in the 1970s spawned vehicles specifically designed to protect against such devices. One solution was to raise the crew compartment higher and angle the underside to deflect the blast. The South African Border War of the 1980s saw the development of vehicles protected against both mines and direct fire. When the Improvised Explosive Device (IED) threat became a feature of war in Iraq and Afghanistan in the 21st century, these designs were the springboard for the development of Mine-resistant Ambush-protected (MRAP) vehicles.

△ **Bushmaster**

Date 2003 **Origin** Australia

Weight 17 tons (15.4 tonnes)

Engine Caterpillar 3126E diesel, 300 hp (224 kW)

Main armament Varies

The Bushmaster can provide protection for a nine-man infantry section over long distances. Its armor and mine protection made it popular in Iraq and Afghanistan, and it has mortar, command, ambulance, air-defense, and route-clearance variants. It was supplied to Ukraine after Russia's 2022 invasion.

△ **Buffalo**

Date 2003 **Origin** USA

Weight 33 tons (30 tonnes)

Engine Caterpillar C13 diesel, 440 hp (328 kW)

Main armament None

Longer and taller than other MRAPs, America's Buffalo is a transport for Explosive Ordnance Disposal (EOD) personnel. Operated from within the armored hull, its 33 ft (10 m) articulated manipulator arm can uncover and disable IEDs. The Buffalo also serves with French, Canadian, Italian, and Pakistani forces.

▽ **Foxhound**

Date 2012 **Origin** UK

Weight 9.4 tons (8.5 tonnes)

Engine Steyr M16 Monoblock 6-cylinder diesel, 210 hp (157 kW)

Main armament Varies

Britain's Foxhound—a replacement for the Snatch—carries a crew of six. Extensive use of advanced composite materials instead of metal reduces its weight, giving it unmatched maneuverability yet maintaining good blast protection.

Electronic mine-detecting system

Buffel

Entering service in 1978, South Africa's Buffel—"buffalo" in Afrikaans—was the first armored personnel carrier (APC) specifically designed to protect its occupants against landmine explosions. It spawned a new generation of mine-resistant vehicles, many of which emulated the Buffel's most innovative design features.

THE BUFFEL ORIGINATED in South Africa during the South African Border War, a series of conflicts in South West Africa (now Namibia), Angola, and Zambia between 1966 and 1990. It was a development of South Africa's Bosvark ("bushpig") vehicle, which itself was a Mercedes Benz Unimog truck modified to give a very basic level of mine protection. Like the Bosvark, the Buffel used the U416-162 Unimog chassis.

A V- or boat-shaped hull to deflect mine blasts had featured on numerous earlier vehicles, including Britain's Saracen APC. The Buffel, however, was the first vehicle to prioritize the survival of the driver and passengers in its design brief. The hull and armored sides not only offered high levels of protection in the event of mine detonations, but also shielded the passengers from small arms fire and shrapnel. The Buffel also provided good visibility to infantrymen traveling in the open-topped rear compartment.

The Buffel's revolutionary design inspired the Mine Resistant Ambush Protected (MRAP) concept in the 2000s. Many tens of thousands of MRAP vehicles were subsequently built by Coalition nations for use in Iraq and Afghanistan.

Armored windscreen protects driver

Spare tire stored on side of vehicle, away from blast zone

Mercedes 6-cylinder water-cooled diesel engine

Simple but tough
The first truly effective mine-resistant APC, the Buffel was based on the running gear of the very successful Unimog truck. This relatively simple yet incredibly tough vehicle was also produced in variants with closed infantry compartments and windows. As well as serving with South African forces, Buffels were exported to Sri Lanka and Uganda.

Infantry seats

Driver

Engine

SPECIFICATIONS	
Name	Buffel Armored Personnel Carrier
Date	1978
Origin	South Africa
Production	Approx. 2,400
Engine	Mercedes-Benz OM-352 diesel, 125 hp (93 kW)
Weight	6.7 tons (6.1 tonnes)
Main armament	None
Secondary armament	None
Crew	1 + 10
Armor thickness	Hull: unknown; windscreen: $1\frac{3}{5}$ in (40 mm) armored glass

Roll bar offers protection if vehicle overturns

FRONT VIEW

Steps for accessing rear compartment

REAR VIEW

Hull set high off the ground

EXTERIOR

Soldiers entered the passenger compartment by climbing over the hinged sides, which could be dropped down to load equipment and supplies, while a roll bar protected the troops in the event of a tip-over. A 22-gallon (100-liter) tank supplied drinking water—essential for long-range patrols in the harsh climate of southern Africa—via a tap under the rear hull.

1. Headlight grill **2.** Front tow point **3.** Cab nose flap, open **4.** Bulletproof glass windscreen **5.** Winch for raising items, including tires **6.** Main engine **7.** Main engine detail **8.** Main chassis frame **9.** Drinking water tap **10.** Rear light **11.** Suspension arms **12.** Vertical spring suspension **13.** 12.50 x 20 tires, often filled with water to absorb blasts **14.** Rear tow hook **15.** Access steps

1

2

3

4

5

6

7

8

9

10

11

12

13

14

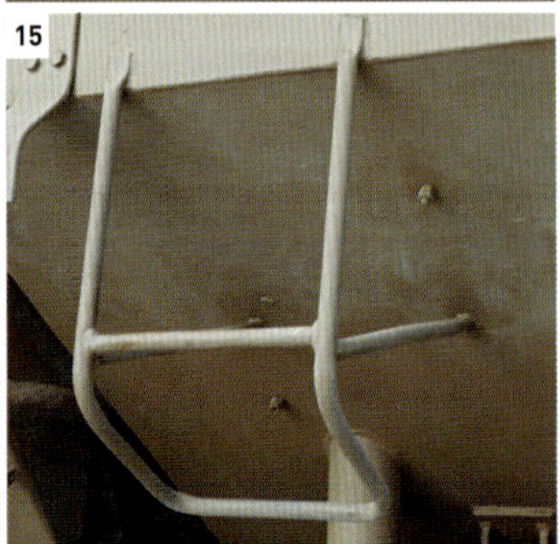

15

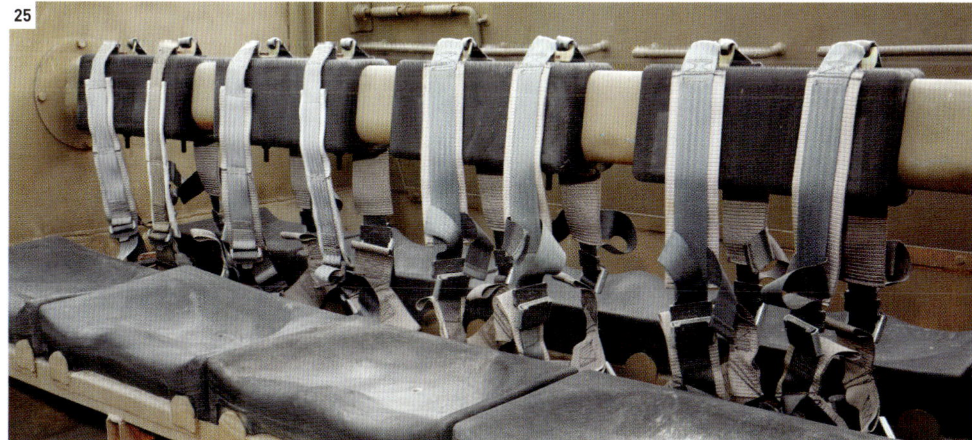

INTERIOR

The driver's position was set high off the ground behind the front axle, protected by bulletproof windows to the front and sides. In the open-topped rear troop compartment were 10 back-to-back seats, each with a four-point seat-belt harness.

16. Looking down into driver's compartment
17. Instrument panel **18.** Warning indicator lights
19. Hand and foot holds with bolt to release side panel
20. Gear and direction levers **21.** Driver's seat
22. Safety harness **23.** Choke lever **24.** Driver's panel switches **25.** Infantry seats

Modern Tank Warfare

The obsolescence of the tank has often been declared. The arrival of any new anti-tank technology has inevitably led to predictions of "the end of the tank," from the handheld anti-tank weapons of World War II and the attack helicopters of the Cold War to modern drones. However, tanks have proved amazingly resilient, even in the modern era.

Due to tanks' high cost of manufacture, and the fact that there is no civilian market, few countries now retain the ability to build them. The vast amounts of time and money needed to develop a new tank—at best, around 10 years during the Cold War—mean that it is cheaper and easier to improve, upgrade, or rebuild older models. These upgrades continue to enable tanks to cope with the latest threats.

Russia's invasion of Ukraine in 2022 has raised the profile of tanks and other armored vehicles, which are well suited to the war's tactical needs, such as the taking and holding of ground. The conflict's mass use of aerial drones and "top attack" weapons that destroy tanks' thinner upper armor from above has also presented a major threat. However, armored vehicles continue to be effective on the battlefield with modifications such as protective cages to counter these new weapons.

A Ukrainian T-64 tank fires on Russian positions in the Donetsk region of Ukraine in January 2024. Ukraine continues to modernize its T-64s.

Troop Carriers

Since 1989, the development of Armored Personnel Carriers (APCs) and Infantry Fighting Vehicles (IFVs) has been driven by technological advances and experience gained from conflicts such as the 1990–91 Gulf War and the two-decade "War on Terror." New generations of troop carriers, and upgraded older variants, have greatly increased lethality (the weapons carried) and survivability (the protection for the occupants). Improved digital fire-control systems, state-of-the-art sensors, and networked threat-detection enable rapid and often automated target engagement with the enemy. Better crew ergonomics, modular armor packages, and mine-resistant hulls have provided increased protection for crew and passengers.

△ CV90

Date 1993	**Origin** Sweden
Weight 25.1 tons (22.8 tonnes)	
Engine Scania DI 14 diesel, 550 hp (410 kW)	
Main armament 40 mm Bofors L/70 cannon	

Developed in the late 1980s, Sweden's CV90 (or Stridsfordon 90) can carry between six and eight infantry personnel. Variants include command, forward-observation, anti-aircraft, and recovery vehicles. Export models are typically armed with a 30 mm or 35 mm cannon. Swedish, Danish, and Norwegian CV90s served in Afghanistan, and vehicles donated by Sweden to Ukraine since 2022 have seen combat against Russian forces.

△ XA-185

Date 1994	**Origin** Finland
Weight 14.9 tons (13.5 tonnes)	
Engine Valmet 612 DWI diesel, 246 hp (183 kW)	
Main armament 12.7 mm NSV machine gun	

The amphibious, six-wheeled XA-180, the first XA series vehicle, was introduced in 1984. The improved XA-185, which has served in peacekeeping roles and seen action in Afghanistan and Ukraine, has a more powerful engine. Further upgrades led to the non-amphibious XA-186, XA-188, and larger XA-203. XAs have been sold to Norway, Sweden, Estonia, Latvia, and the Netherlands.

▽ Piranha III

Date 1998	**Origin** Switzerland
Weight 24.3 tons (22 tonnes)	
Engine Caterpillar C9 diesel, 400 hp (298 kW)	
Main armament Variable	

With sales to more than 12 countries, Piranha III variants range from electronic warfare, assault gun, and ambulance models to standard armored personnel carriers. Derived from the Piranha, Canada's LAV-III is used by Canadian and New Zealand armed forces. The LAV-III also forms the basis of the US Army's Stryker family of carriers and combat vehicles.

Driver's hatch

▷ **BvS10 Viking**

Date 2004 **Origin** Sweden
Weight 12.5 tons (11.3 tonnes)
Engine Cummins ISBe250 30 diesel, 275 hp (205 kW)
Main armament 40 mm CTAI CT40 cannon, 7.62 mm L7 machine gun

Steered by hydraulic rams between the two cabs, the lightly armored Viking has superb mobility on its rubber tracks, even over snow and sand. Operations in Afghanistan required extra armor to be added. The Viking was originally developed for the British Royal Marines from the smaller, unarmored Bv206.

Crew compartment

Firing port

◁ **VBCI**

Date 2008 **Origin** France
Weight 32 tons (29 tonnes)
Engine Volvo diesel, 550 hp (410 kW)
Main armament 25 mm GIAT M811 cannon

Armed with a stabilized 25 mm cannon and designed for use as an infantry fighting vehicle, the three-man, eight-wheeled French VBCI can accommodate up to nine soldiers. The VBCI has been deployed in Lebanon, Afghanistan, and Mali. France currently operates 630, of which 110 are command posts.

▷ **Schützenpanzer Puma**

Date 2010 **Origin** Germany
Weight 47.4 tons (43 tonnes)
Engine MTU MT 892 Ka-501 diesel, 1,090 hp (813 kW)
Main armament 30 mm MK30-2/ABM cannon

The successor to the impressive Marder, the Puma houses its three crew and six infantrymen together in the hull; the turret is unmanned. Its modular armor can be increased to suit a higher threat level or, for air transport, reduced to lower the weight to 34.2 tons (31 tonnes).

Smoke grenade dischargers

◁ **BMD-4M Airborne Assault Vehicle**

Date 2014 **Origin** Russia
Weight 15.4 tons (14 tonnes)
Engine UTD-29 multifuel, 500 hp (373 kW)
Main armament 1 x 100 mm 2A70 smoothbore gun, 1 x 30 mm 2A72 cannon

The lightweight yet powerfully armed BMD-4M—derived from the BMD-4, which entered service with the Russian Airborne Troops (VDV) in 2004—uses the engine and other automotive components from the earlier BMP-3 to ease costs, logistics, and maintenance. The BMD-MDM is an armored personnel carrier variant.

8x8 drive with hydropneumatic suspension

▷ **Ajax**

Date 2016 **Origin** UK
Weight 41.9 tons (38 tonnes)
Engine MTU 199 diesel, 800 hp (597 kW)
Main armament 40 mm CTAI CT40 cannon

The British Army's Ajax is an Intelligence, Surveillance, Target Acquisition, and Reconnaissance (ISTAR) vehicle with digital electronic architecture that allows it to share information with friendly forces. It is based on the ASCOD (Austrian Spanish Cooperation Development) armored fighting vehicle. Command, specialist personnel carrier, engineering, reconnaissance, repair, and recovery variants are planned.

▷ **M1A2 Abrams**

Date 1992 **Origin** USA
Weight 69.4 tons (63 tonnes)
Engine Textron Lycoming AGT1500 gas turbine, 1,500 hp (1,119 kW)
Main armament 120 mm M256 L/44 smoothbore gun

The M1A1, which entered service in 1985, had superior suspension and transmission to the M1, and was up-gunned with a 120 mm smoothbore. The M1A2 added a commander's independent thermal viewer (CITV), which enabled the tank commander to look in a different direction to the gunner. The M1A2's electronics and computer systems were enhanced following experience in the Gulf.

Solar Shield camouflage covers entire tank

Thermal imaging and gunnery sight aperture

125 mm main gun

△ **T-90S**

Date 1994 **Origin** Russia
Weight 53.6 tons (48.6 tonnes)
Engine ChTZ V92S2 V12 diesel, 1,000 hp (746 kW)
Main armament 125 mm 2A46M5 L/48 gun

Intended as a replacement for the T-72, from which it was developed, the T-90's upgraded onboard systems incorporated features from the T-80 and integrated the Shtora active protection system (APS). The largest user of the tank is India, which has 1,250 of the T-90S export version, followed by Russia, with around 550. The T-90 has seen combat in Ukraine and Syria.

△ **Challenger 2**

Date 1994 **Origin** UK
Weight 82.6 tons (74.9 tonnes)
Engine Perkins CV12 V12 diesel, 1,200 hp (895 kW)
Main armament 120 mm L30A1 L/55 rifled gun

The Challenger 2 has level 2L Dorchester armor modules on its hull and turret sides, electronic countermeasures, and heat and radar absorbent Solar Shield camouflage. Despite its name, the Challenger 2 has few parts that are compatible with the Challenger 1. Fitted with extra armor, Challenger 2s took part in the invasion of Iraq in 2003, by which time the British Army had 386.

▷ **PT 91 Twardy**

Date 1995 **Origin** Poland
Weight 50.6 tons (45.9 tonnes)
Engine PZL-Wola Type S12U multifuel, 850 hp (634 kW)
Main armament 125 mm D81TM smoothbore gun

An upgrade of the Soviet-designed, Polish made T-72M, the Twardy has a more powerful engine and transmission, additional Explosive Reactive Armor (ERA), and improved gun stabilization. Poland took delivery of 233 tanks, along with armored recovery and engineering variants; 48 Twardys were bought by Malaysia, while India ordered more than 352 of the recovery variant from Poland.

▽ **T-84**

Date 1999 **Origin** Ukraine
Weight 56 tons (51 tonnes)
Engine KMDB 6TD-4 6-cylinder diesel, 1,500 hp (,119 kW)
Main armament 125 mm KBA-3 cannon

Evolved post-1991 from the T-80UD—a Ukrainian diesel variant of the Soviet T-80 MBT—the T-84 entered service in 1999. It is armed with the 125 mm KBA-3 smoothbore cannon, fed by an automatic loader. The T-84's passive and reactive armor systems are augmented by active protection systems. In its modern Oplot variant, the T-84 outperforms many current Russian tanks in speed, survivability, and rate of fire.

Post-Cold War Tanks

At the end of the Cold War, many tanks were scrapped as nations reduced the size of their militaries. Vehicles under development in the late 1980s tended to be introduced slowly and in smaller numbers, while some existing tanks received upgrades, such as the introduction of the L/55 120 mm gun on the Leopard 2A6. Post-1989 conflicts have shown that, although heavy and difficult to deploy, tanks still have a battlefield role. In the 21st century, new vehicles have started to enter service, some with countries making their first forays into tank design.

Spaced armor at front of turret

120 mm main gun

Tracks with rubber pads

△ Leopard 2A6

Date 2001 **Origin** Germany

Weight 68.8 tons (62.4 tonnes)

Engine MTU MB 873 Ka-501 diesel, 1,500 hp (1,119 kW)

Main armament 120 mm Rheinmetall 120 L/55 smoothbore gun

The 2A6 is substantially upgraded compared to the 2A4 of the Cold War era. The turret, now electrically driven rather than hydraulically powered, has distinctive wedge-shaped spaced armor, and it carries a more powerful L/55 gun. The gunner's sight has been relocated to the turret roof.

△ Merkava Mark 4

Date 2004 **Origin** Israel

Weight 71.27 tons (65 tonnes)

Engine MTU 883 V12 diesel, 1,500 hp (1,119 kW)

Main armament 120 mm IMI MG253 L/44 smoothbore gun

Like its Merkava forerunners, the Mark 4 prioritizes crew safety, with features such as automatic fire suppression, nuclear, biological, and chemical (NBC) warfare defense, and the Trophy active protection system (APS), which counters anti-tank threats. Electronic aids, such as a battle management system and automatic target tracking, enhance the tank's combat effectiveness. The Mark 4 has seen combat in Lebanon and Gaza.

△ T-14 Armata

Date 2015 **Origin** Russia

Weight Unknown

Engine ChTZ 12N360 V12 diesel, 1,500+ hp (1,119+ kW)

Main armament 125 mm 2A82-1M smoothbore gun

Based on the Armata Universal Combat Platform—a versatile platform for a range of armored vehicles—the T-14 is much longer and taller than previous Soviet and Russian tanks. The crew of three sit at the front, while the unmanned turret houses the gun, autoloader, and sights, and both a hard- and a soft-kill APS.

125 mm KBA-3 smoothbore cannon

Radio antenna

120 mm main gun

◁ Altay

Date 2016 **Origin** Turkey

Weight 71.7 tons (65 tonnes)

Engine MTU MT 883 Ka-501 diesel, 1,500 hp (1,119 kW)

Main armament 120 mm L/55 smoothbore gun

A milestone for the Turkish armaments industry, the Altay is the country's first domestically designed tank. It is based on the South Korean K2 Black Panther but is mostly being developed and built by Turkish companies, including the sights and advanced fire-control system. Production is expected to total 1,000.

M1A2 Abrams

The Abrams was designed when engaging Soviet-bloc tanks in Europe was thought to be the most likely combat scenario. Since then, this American tank has seen action in very different locations and environments, yet time and again the Abrams has proved itself in battle. Made in large numbers—around 11,000 to date—the Abrams now equips seven national armies

AT THE TIME WORK BEGAN ON THE ABRAMS, the West displayed an ambivalent attitude toward tanks—the dilemma of potentially needing them and seeing other nations developing their own tanks, versus tightening military budgets and the restrictions they imposed on Western tank production and technology.

Viewed as a replacement for the M60, the first Abrams model carried a version of the British L7 105 mm gun, with ammunition stored separately in a blow-out compartment to protect the crew. The tank's small gas turbine engine was incredibly powerful but proved twice as thirsty as a diesel equivalent. After an American team was shown the latest British developments in Chobham armor in 1973, the tank was redesigned to adopt the new protection system. An upgrade of the laminate armor incorporating depleted uranium was later fitted to the M1A1 model, doubling the level of protection. The M1A1's armament was upgraded to the 120 mm German smoothbore gun, which gave it a huge advantage over Iraqi tanks in the 1991 Gulf War.

Improvements to the M1A2 model included a Commander's Independent Thermal Viewer, enhanced digital equipment, and a new fire control system. Street fighting in the Iraq War led to the development of the Tank Urban Survival Kit (TUSK) in 2006, which gives the tank better protection in built-up areas. With these upgrades, the Abrams will undoubtedly continue to be a powerful presence on the battlefield for decades to come.

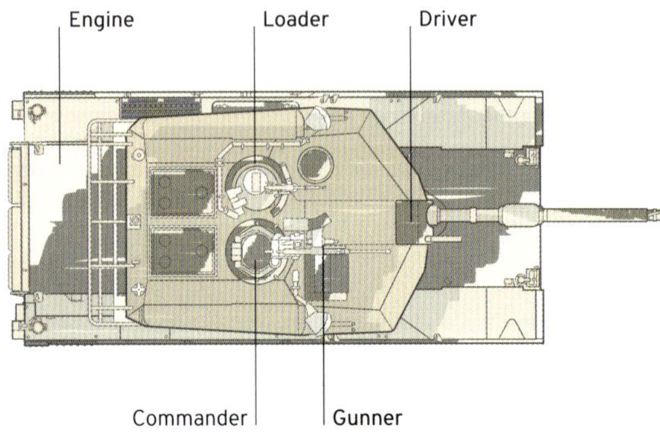

SPECIFICATIONS	
Name	M1A2 Abrams
Date	1992
Origin	USA
Production	Approx. 1,500
Engine	Textron Lycoming AGT1500 gas turbine, 1,500 hp (1,119 kW)
Weight	69.4 tons (63 tonnes)
Main armament	120 mm M256 smoothbore
Secondary armament	.50 Browning M2HB, 2 x 7.62 mm M240 MGs
Crew	4
Armor thickness	Unknown

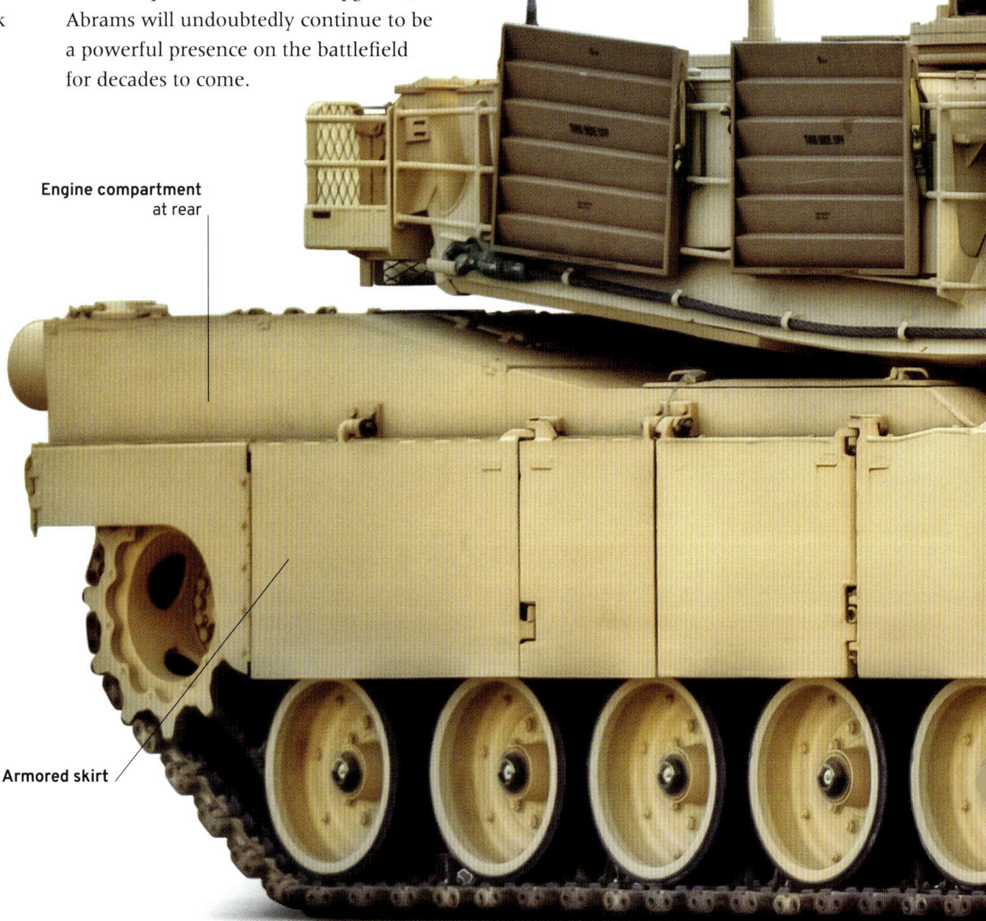

FRONT VIEW

REAR VIEW

Machine-gun mount

Hi-tech destroyer
The M1A2 SEPv2 (System Enhancement Package), the latest incarnation of the Abrams, includes a Thermal Management System and upgrades to communications, display screens, sights, and other electronic systems. It also has an added auxiliary power unit.

Fume extractor

Depleted uranium armor on front of turret

Driver's hatch

Badge of excellence
At the front, in black, is the badge of the US Army Maneuver Center of Excellence, at Fort Benning, Georgia, which unites the Infantry and Armor Schools under one command. The full-color badge (left) replaces the black with blue, yellow, and red segments—the traditional colors of the infantry, cavalry, and artillery.

Tank badge

Rubber pads on tracks

INTERIOR

The M1A2's interior is lined with Kevlar, which protects the crew against spalling (splinters caused by the explosion of enemy projectiles). Ammunition is kept in armored compartments, which feature blow-out panels. These minimize any damage should ammunition "cook off" in the heat of an explosion by ensuring that the force of the blast is directed away from the crew compartment.

1. Commander's station, looking right **2.** Driver's station, looking forward **3.** Driver's steering and throttle T-bar control **4.** Gunner's station **5.** Gunner's primary sight eyepiece **6.** Mounting for coaxial 7.62 machine gun (not fitted) **7.** Gunner's control handles **8.** Top of main gun breech (closed) **9.** Loader's station, looking left **10.** Main gun breech (closed), showing case deflector tray **11.** Bottom of main gun breech (open)

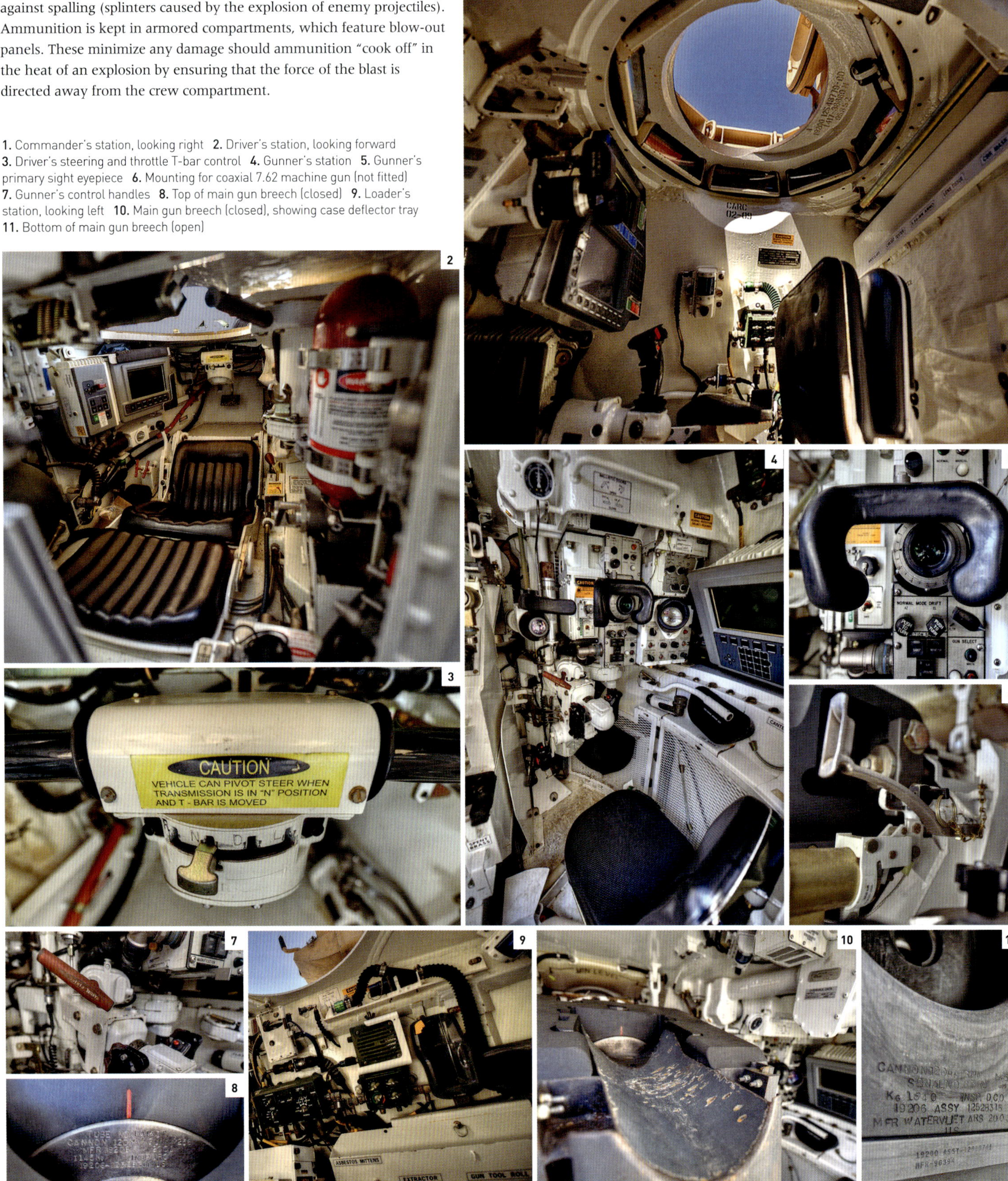

EXTERIOR

The M1A2 is one of the world's heaviest main battle tanks. The vast weight is partly due to the formidable composite armor, which is augmented by depleted uranium mesh on the turret and the front of the hull. This extraordinary armor is very effective against most current anti-tank weapons.

12. Towing eye **13.** Road wheel hub **14.** Road wheels and track **15.** Commander's (left) and loader's hatches **16.** Commander's cupola **17.** Track with rubber pads **18.** Loader's 7.62mm M240 machine gun **19.** Common Remotely Operated Weapons Station sights **20.** Nuclear, biological, and chemical protection system vent **21.** Vapor Compression System Unit, part of the Thermal Management System **22.** Infantry phone **23.** Drive sprocket

Amphibious Warfare

The disembarkation of forces on an occupied coastline, such as the 1944 D-Day landings in Normandy, is a high-risk procedure. Many such amphibious assaults are complex "combined operations" using land, naval, and air assets in a coordinated way. Conditions such as weather, geography, and the nature of enemy defenses further complicate the event.

For centuries, boats had been used to ferry soldiers and marines ashore, but in the wake of World War I and the Allies' disastrous experience of landing at Gallipoli in Turkey, the first dedicated landing craft were designed. World War II saw the production of a plethora of landing craft variations, along with amphibious vehicles and adaptations that allowed land vehicles to float or "wade" to help troops ashore. Today, many countries insist that their vehicles are amphibious and able to cross rivers and lakes, if not the open sea, while hovercraft—also known as Landing Craft Air Cushion (LCAC)—are able to access coastlines unreachable with conventional landing craft.

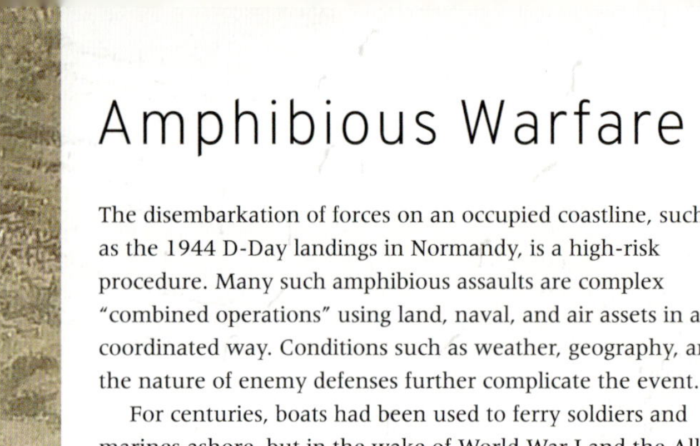

A US LCAC takes armor from ship to shore as part of the Bold Alligator amphibious assault exercise at Camp Lejeune, North Carolina, US, in 2017.

Warships in the Digital Age

From "stealth" hull profiles to autonomous pilots, the next generations of surface warships are designed to optimize lethality, survivability, and economy. The result is smaller and lighter vessels offering navies more tactical flexibility. At the same time, debates continue about the future of the biggest vessels, particularly aircraft carriers.

New generation
The USS *Zumwalt* was initially intended to provide fire support for ground forces. However, its proposed gun system was deemed too expensive and the ship was sent for refit with missile launchers for surface combat.

In October 2016, the USS *Zumwalt*, a new guided missile destroyer, was commissioned into service with the US Navy. The *Zumwalt*'s appearance was strikingly different to that of existing US Navy surface vessels: it had strange, angular hull lines that sloped inward from the waterline, a pyramid-like superstructure, and a deck curiously free from the usual guns and equipment. The *Zumwalt* was part of the world's very first generation of "stealth" warships.

Stealth and signatures

When applied to warships, the term "stealth" refers to a profile and layout deliberately designed to minimize the ship's radar signature. This approach is backed by key tactical aspirations: a stealth warship might evade detection by electronic surveillance altogether, or its signature might be so reduced that the operators of enemy sensors confuse the ship with a minor civilian vessel. Despite the fact that the USS *Zumwalt* is 600 ft (183 m) long, its radar signature as it appears on a screen is described as resembling that of a small fishing boat. Such ships are harder to spot visually and when using sonar detection. Their stealth characteristics also mean that the vessels are less vulnerable to the tracking systems on anti-ship missiles, increasing their survivability. Stealth principles are now embedding themselves in many naval fleets. Examples include Swedish *Visby*-class corvettes, Chinese Type 055 guided-missile destroyers, French *La Fayette*-class frigates, and Japanese *Mogami*-class frigates.

Multiple hulls

Stealth is just one of many recent innovations in the design of warships. Another is the exploration of trimaran (or double-outrigger) hulls for use in littoral combat ships—vessels intended to operate extremely close to enemy coastlines. A trimaran hull features a main hull plus small outrigger hulls attached to either side of the boat by lateral beams. The main advantage of this configuration is that it considerably reduces the vessel's draft compared to that of a monohull (single-hulled) design, so the craft can operate in much shallower waters. Trimarans also have good seakeeping—the ability to remain stable under rough conditions at sea—without the need for heavy weighting at the bottom, as in a typical monohull vessel.

Weapons and systems

The future armaments of warships are also beginning to take shape, with new forms of offensive and defensive weaponry currently in development. Until comparatively recently, the US Navy was funding research into electromagnetic rail guns as potential replacements for conventional guns. These weapons use electromagnetic forces to accelerate and launch inert rounds at astonishing speeds of around 4,500 mph (7,240 km/h), the projectiles relying on extreme kinetic energy alone to deliver their destructive effects. The rail gun offers the possibility of warships without vulnerable explosive magazines on board, but severe issues with the power supply and barrel caused the US program to be canceled in 2021. Several other navies have pursued rail gun technologies, however, so the weapon may yet appear on future warships.

Two major new fields in the design of naval weapons are hypersonic anti-ship missiles and directed-energy weapons (DEWs). The former are missiles that fly at Mach 5+, their extreme speed making them, with current technologies, almost impossible to defeat once they are in their final approach to target. Directed-energy weapons, by contrast, are weapons that fire laser or radio-frequency (RF) energy to destroy incoming threats, such as drones, small attack boats, and missiles.

An operational example of a DEW is the American High Energy Laser with Integrated Optical-dazzler and Surveillance (HELIOS). This has been integrated into the US Navy's influential Aegis Combat System, which tracks and engages multiple targets simultaneously. Several international navies have purchased Aegis, while others have developed systems with similar capabilities.

Ships without crews

One of the new frontiers of naval design is unmanned surface vehicles (USVs) and unmanned underwater vehicles (UUVs)—ships and submarines that are piloted remotely. Unmanned ships offer navies a number of important advantages. By operating without crews on board, they can be sent into dangerous situations without risk to human life, and they have almost unlimited endurance. Furthermore, without the need for crew quarters or stores, the ships can be smaller and cheaper to produce and the running costs are correspondingly lower. It is also easier to build such ships in "modular" formats, so they can be adapted quickly to new roles.

Uncrewed ship
This unmanned surface vehicle (USV) was developed by American company Leidos. Such vessels are becoming common in the US Navy. Note the trimaran hull design—ideal for littoral operations requiring shallow-draft vessels.

Cutting-edge carrier
Led by the USS *Gerald R. Ford*, US Navy ships sail in formation in the Mediterranean in 2023. The *Gerald R. Ford*-class is the most advanced US carrier type today. One of its key features is the Electromagnetic Aircraft Launch System (EMALS) for launching aircraft.

At present, most unmanned vessels in service are small littoral or support craft. However, the recent war in Ukraine has revealed their offensive potential. Ukrainian USVs packed with explosives were used in multiple assaults on Russian vessels, sinking or seriously damaging several ships, including the *Tarantul-III*-class missile corvette *Ivanovets* and the *Ropucha*-class landing ship *Olenegorsky Gornyak*. With the growing application of AI, the capabilities of unmanned warships will continue to expand, potentially transforming even small navies into advanced maritime fighting forces

> "**Transforming ourselves** and our great institution for the **dangerous decades** ahead is our imperative."
>
> ADMIRAL VERNON E. CLARK, US NAVY CHIEF OF NAVAL OPERATIONS, 2000–05

TALKING POINT

AI and Navies

Already many of the world's navies are testing AI-powered digital systems aboard warships. The advantages of AI for navies include the rapid acceleration in threat detection and defensive response, with the AI able to process thousands of sensor inputs in fractions of a second; greater speed and accuracy in the analysis of electronic data; improved coordination of fighting forces across a network; and more efficient management of supply, maintenance, and administration. The ultimate goal is to use AI to outperform by orders of magnitude enemies without AI or with inferior AI systems. The key question, however, is whether AI will support sailors or, in the long run, replace them.

The Combat Information Center (CIC) of a modern US Navy carrier is the tactical focal point for command-and-control decisions during aircraft operations.

▽ **Charles de Gaulle**

Date 2001 **Origin** France

Displacement 46,848 tons (42,500 tonnes)

Length 858 ft (261.5 m)

Top speed 27 knots (50 km/h)

Construction of this nuclear-powered carrier started in 1989, but work stopped on four occasions due to financial issues. Commissioned in May 2001, five years late, the ship sailed to the Indian Ocean in November, where it flew missions into Afghanistan in support of the US-led Operation Enduring Freedom.

▽ **USS Ronald Reagan**

Date 2003 **Origin** USA

Displacement 113,600 tons (103,056 tonnes)

Length 1,092 ft (332 m)

Top speed 30 knots (56 km/h)

Carrying up to 60 aircraft and with a crew of 5,000, this *Nimitz*-class aircraft carrier is one of the largest ships afloat. The *Ronald Reagan* has spent much of its service career to date with the US Seventh Fleet, which is based in Japan.

▽ **Cavour**

Date 2008 **Origin** Italy

Displacement 29,873 tons (27,100 tonnes)

Length 801 ft (244 m)

Top speed 29 knots (54 km/h)

Originally equipped with Harrier jump jets, the *Cavour* now has a complement of F35 Lightnings. When acting as a support or amphibious landing ship, it can carry 24 tanks or other vehicles and 325 marines, and deploy heavy transport helicopters. The large hangar area was ideal for the role *Cavour* played in relief operations after the 2010 Haiti earthquake.

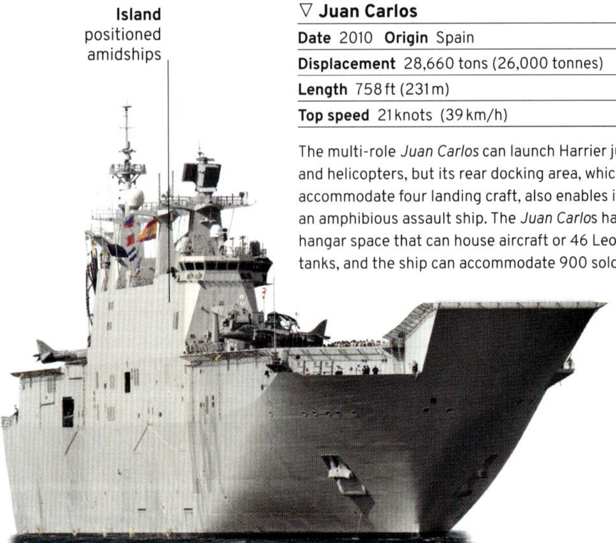

▽ **Juan Carlos**

Date 2010 **Origin** Spain

Displacement 28,660 tons (26,000 tonnes)

Length 758 ft (231 m)

Top speed 21 knots (39 km/h)

The multi-role *Juan Carlos* can launch Harrier jump jets and helicopters, but its rear docking area, which can accommodate four landing craft, also enables it to act as an amphibious assault ship. The *Juan Carlos* has a large hangar space that can house aircraft or 46 Leopard tanks, and the ship can accommodate 900 soldiers.

▽ **USS Gerald R. Ford**

Date 2017 **Origin** USA

Displacement 112,000 tons (101,600 tonnes)

Length 1,106 ft (337 m)

Top speed over 30 knots (56 km/h)

On entering service, the US$13.5 billion *Gerald R. Ford* was the largest warship ever built, carrying up to 90 aircraft and a ship's complement of over 4,500. Among the new technologies it introduced was an electromagnetic aircraft launch system (EMALS). It always travels in a carrier strike group, which includes a cruiser, two destroyers or frigates, and a supply ship.

21st-century Aircraft Carriers

An aircraft carrier provides a mobile, seaborne air base. The most substantial carriers are the largest and most complex weapon systems ever built. Carriers are able to launch fast jets and helicopters for aerial missions or boats for amphibious assaults, and their facilities can be used for rescue and disaster recovery operations. While carriers are phenomenally costly naval vessels, they are also symbols of modern power and seen as symbolic of a nation's strategic international influence.

Elevator moves aircraft between the deck and hangar

▽ **JS Kaga**

Date 2017 **Origin** Japan
Displacement 30,240 tons (27,443 tonnes)
Length 814 ft (248 m)
Top speed over 30 knots (56 km/h)

Designed as a helicopter carrier but converted to carry aircraft such as the F35 Lightning, the *Kaga* and its sister ship the *Izumo* were the first aircraft carriers built by Japan since the end of World War II. They are part of a general buildup of Japanese military forces due to rising Sino-Japanese tensions in the Pacific region.

Twin islands (forward island controls ship functions, aft island controls flight operations)

◁ **HMS Prince of Wales**

Date 2019 **Origin** UK
Displacement 88,800 tons (80,600 tonnes)
Length 932 ft (284 m)
Top speed 32 knots (59 km/h)

The *Prince of Wales* is the second *Queen Elizabeth*-class carrier and currently flagship of the fleet. Able to carry 48 F35 Lightning II aircraft, it can also accommodate 250 marines as well as attack and transport helicopters. The ship's nine decks have a combined floor area of 19,136 square yards (16,000 square meters).

Island is located aft, giving more room for aircraft on deck

Flight deck has an electromagnetic aircraft launch system (EMALS) and advanced arresting gear (AAG)

E-2D Advanced Hawkeye airborne early warning and control system (AWACS) aircraft

Main flight deck has 14-degree "ski jump" for takeoff

◁ **INS Vikrant**

Date 2022 **Origin** India
Displacement 49,600 tons (45,000 tonnes)
Length 861 ft (262.5 m)
Top speed 30 knots (56 km/h)

India has decided to deploy a three-carrier fleet: one vessel each for sea service east and west of the country, and one in reserve. The *Vikrant* can host up to 36 aircraft, both fixed-wing and rotary. It is the first carrier built in India, at a cost of US$3.1 billion.

USS George Washington

Commissioned in 1992 and boasting a flight deck covering 4.5 acres (1.8 hectares)—roughly the size of two-and-a-half soccer pitches—the USS *George Washington* is one of the US Navy's 10 *Nimitz*-class "supercarriers." The largest military vessels ever to take to the seas, these enormous aircraft carriers are the ultimate symbols of modern naval power.

SUPERCARRIERS SUCH AS the *George Washington*, the sixth US *Nimitz* class carrier, function as mobile strike platforms that can operate from anywhere in international waters. The *George Washington* can accommodate 85 aircraft, including fighter, strike, and transport planes, airborne early warning (AEW) aircraft, and helicopters.

The ship's dominant feature is the "island" superstructure. This command-and-control center, located on the starboard side, houses the bridge and primary flight-control area. From here, officers monitor activities below. During flight operations, when four aircraft can be launched per minute, the deck is bustling with activity, with jets taking off and landing, and being refueled, maneuvered, and armed. Launch is aided by four catapults, two in the bows and two at the forward end of the angled deck: the landing deck is angled to port, to allow other activities to take place while aircraft return to the ship. When landing, a plane's tailhook must catch one of four high-tensile steel arrestor wires running across the flight deck. These decelerate the aircraft rapidly, bringing it to a halt within two seconds. A pilot increases the throttle when touching down, so that if the aircraft fails to catch the arrestor wires it still has sufficient speed to take off again and attempt another landing—a practice known as "touch and go."

Most aircraft are stored in the vast internal hangar, which stretches for much of the ship's length. Below deck are living quarters for the ship's personnel—the *George Washington* is a floating home for around 6,000 service men and women.

Floating battle station
Although designed primarily to offer an offensive strike capability via its jets, the *George Washington* is equipped with its own defenses, such as antiaircraft and antimissile weapon systems, and rapid-fire 20 mm guns.

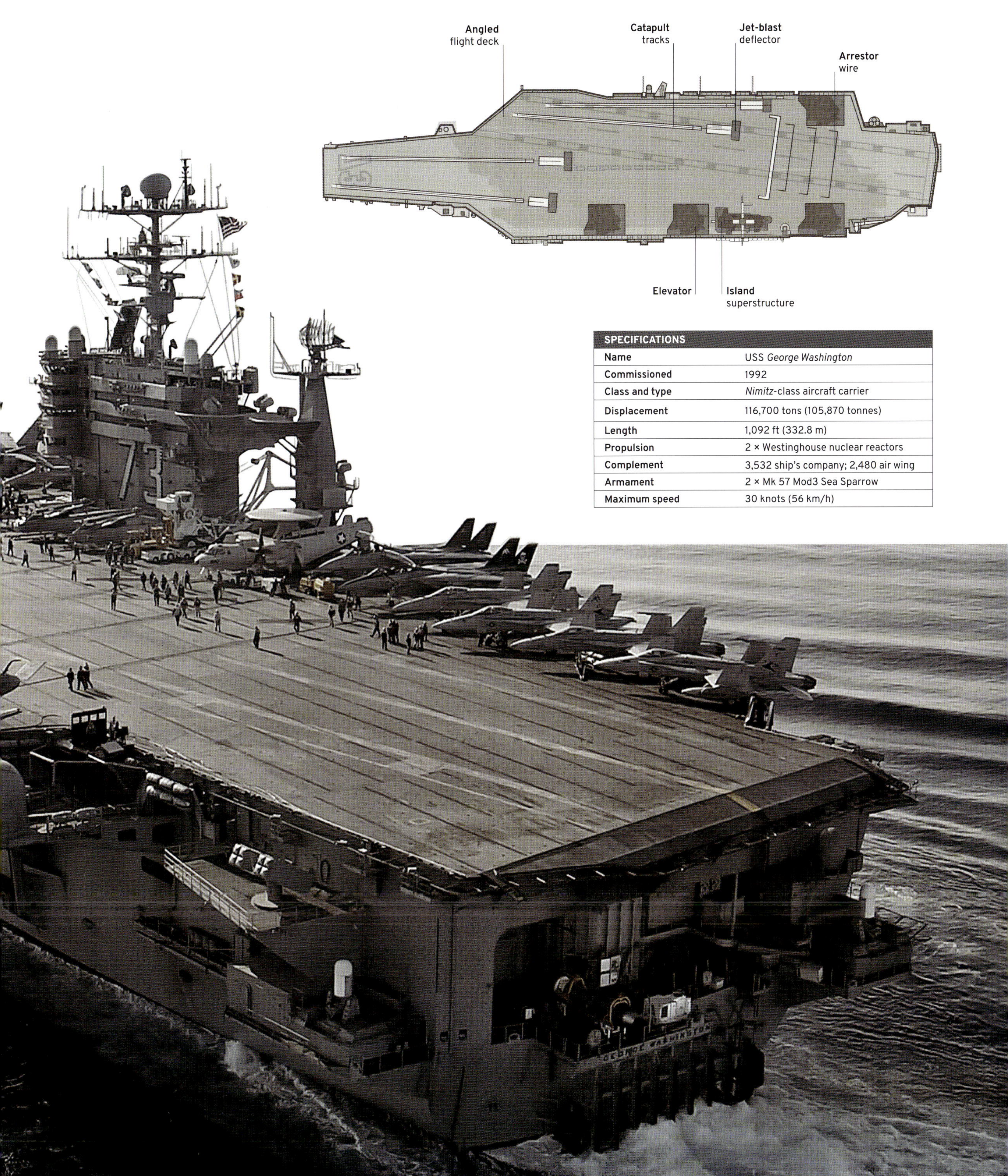

SPECIFICATIONS	
Name	USS *George Washington*
Commissioned	1992
Class and type	*Nimitz*-class aircraft carrier
Displacement	116,700 tons (105,870 tonnes)
Length	1,092 ft (332.8 m)
Propulsion	2 × Westinghouse nuclear reactors
Complement	3,532 ship's company; 2,480 air wing
Armament	2 × Mk 57 Mod3 Sea Sparrow
Maximum speed	30 knots (56 km/h)

INTERIOR

The control rooms for the ship and for flying operations are based both in the island superstructure and below deck. In addition to the aircraft hangar, where aircraft are serviced and stored, the below-deck areas include the catapult and arrestor-gear machinery, 44 magazines, the nuclear power plant, and the engine room. Facilities for the thousands of crew and air wing personnel include messes, berths, medical facilities, and a gym.

1. Catapult mechanism instrument panel **2.** Bridge **3.** Hangar **4.** Propeller shaft **5.** Operating room **6.** Arrestor-gear piston **7.** Operations room **8.** Reactor controls **9.** No. 3 Pump room (sends aviation fuel to the flight deck) **10.** Primary flight control **11.** Engine bay (with F-14 Tomcat engine in foreground) **12.** Bakery **13.** Briefing room

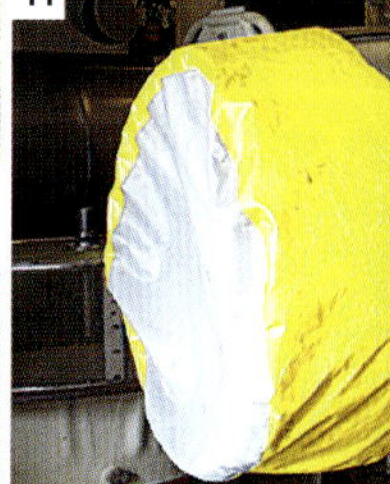

4

5

12

13

21

EXTERIOR

Four hydraulic elevators raise aircraft to the flight deck. The catapult shuttle, which launches the aircraft, attaches to a plane's undercarriage and is propelled along a track set into the flight deck by a steam-powered piston. During takeoff, deflector shields prevent engine exhaust gases from causing damage or injury. Arrestor wires toward the stern halt jets as they land. Much of the ship's electronics, including radar and satellite communications equipment, is based on the island, which has the ship's number painted on its sides.

14. Preparing for take off **15.** Catapult observation pod (retracts below flight deck) **16.** Catapult shuttle **17.** Shuttle track **18.** Jet-blast deflector **19.** Grumman F-14 Tomcat landing **20.** Hydraulic elevator **21.** Island superstructure **22.** Aircraft weaponry **23.** Helicopter maintenance

22

23

◁ **USS Arleigh Burke**

Date 1991 **Origin** USA
Displacement 9,218 tons (8,362 tonnes)
Length 505 ft (154 m)
Top speed 30 knots (56 km/h)

A guided-missile destroyer, the *Arleigh Burke* is the lead ship of its class, incorporating stealth technology and the advanced AEGIS integrated total combat system. Armament includes Tomahawk cruise missiles.

▷ **HMS Lancaster**

Date 1992 **Origin** UK
Displacement 5,401 tons (4,900 tonnes)
Length 436 ft (133 m)
Top speed 28 knots (52 km/h)

A Type-43 frigate that carries Sting Ray anti-submarine torpedoes, Sea Ceptor antiaircraft and Harpoon anti-ship missiles, and a Wildcat helicopter, *Lancaster* has advanced attack and defense capabilities.

▽ **HMCS Vancouver**

Date 1993 **Origin** Canada
Displacement 5,258 tons (4,770 tonnes)
Length 440 ft (134 m)
Top speed 30 knots (56 km/h)

A multi-role frigate, the *Vancouver* is the second *Halifax*-class series vessel of the Canadian Navy, built to deal with surface, aerial, and submarine threats, using missiles, torpedoes, and guns. It can also carry a Sikorsky helicopter.

Modern Destroyers and Frigates

While aircraft carriers and submarines are the most important weapons and key strategic deterrents of today's major naval forces, smaller escort vessels still have an important part to play. Since the Cold War, the distinction between destroyers and frigates has become less fixed, with both the (larger) destroyer and the (smaller) frigate favoring increasingly sophisticated guided-missile systems over guns as their main armament. Modern escort vessels may concentrate on either antiaircraft or anti-submarine warfare but are usually equipped for both.

△ **Brandenburg-class frigate**

Date 1994 **Origin** Germany
Displacement 4,949 tons (4,490 tonnes)
Length 456 ft (139 m)
Top speed 29 knots (54 km/h)

The German *Brandenburg*-class frigates were built to perform a range of patrol and combat duties, including anti-submarine warfare, air defense, and flight coordination. Armed with torpedoes and Sea Sparrow and Harpoon missiles, each vessel also carries two Sea Lynx helicopters and powerful electronic countermeasures.

▽ Brahmaputra-class frigate

Date 2000	**Origin** India
Displacement	4,244 tons (3,850 tonnes)
Length	415 ft (126.5 m)
Top speed	30 knots (56 km/h)

The three *Brahmaputra*-class guided-missile frigates, built in India for the Indian Navy, are a development of earlier *Godavari*-class ships. Their enhanced weaponry includes Kh-35 (SS-N-25 Switchblade) anti-ship missiles and Israeli-made Barak surface-to-air missiles.

△ Type 054A frigate

Date 2008	**Origin** China
Displacement	4,368 tons (3,963 tonnes)
Length	440 ft (134 m)
Top speed	27 knots (50 km/h)

More than 30 Type 054A guided-missile frigates have been commissioned into China's People's Liberation Army Navy (PLAN). They employ stealth technology and advanced radar and electronic warfare systems, and can carry HQ-16 surface-to-air missiles and YJ-83 anti-ship cruise missiles, as well as anti-submarine rockets.

▽ Admiral Gorshkov class

Date 2018	**Origin** Russia
Displacement	5,952 tons (5,400 tonnes)
Length	443 ft (135 m)
Top speed	30 knots (56 km/h)

Also known as Project 22350, the *Admiral Gorshkov* class of frigates is one of the latest generations of Russian naval surface vessels. It incorporates stealth design and technologies and has a powerful array of armament, including Kalibr land-attack cruise missiles, Oniks anti-ship missiles, and Otvet anti-submarine missiles.

Nuclear-powered Submarines

With their armament of submarine-launched ballistic missiles (SLBMs), nuclear-powered submarines are arguably the most powerful weapon system ever developed. Hidden deep beneath the waves, they are able to fire their highly destructive weapons without warning and are virtually immune from retaliatory action by the enemy. The submarines' high level of concealment also provides them with an invaluable capability to retaliate to a first nuclear strike and so act as an effective deterrent. More conventional attack submarines, powered either by nuclear reactors or diesel-electric motors, operate against surface vessels or hunt down other submarines.

△ Project 971 Shchuka-B (Akula-class)
Date 1984 **Origin** USSR
Displacement 8,140 tons (7,385 tonnes) (Akula I)
Length 362 ft (110.3 m)
Top speed 10 knots (19 km/h)

First deployed in 1986, this attack submarine type (designated *Akula*-class by NATO) was advanced for the time and underwent a series of upgrades lasting until the early 2000s. It features a double-hull system and eight torpedo tubes; seven original models were built, of which three are believed to still be in service.

▷ USS Maryland (SSBN-738)
Date 1992 **Origin** USA
Displacement 16,764 tons (15,208 tonnes)
Length 560 ft (171 m)
Top speed 18 knots (33 km/h)

One of 14 *Ohio*-class ballistic missile submarines, *Maryland* is at the forefront of the US Navy's nuclear deterrent. It can carry up to 20 Trident missiles, with multiple warheads per missile and a range of 4,573 miles (7,360 km).

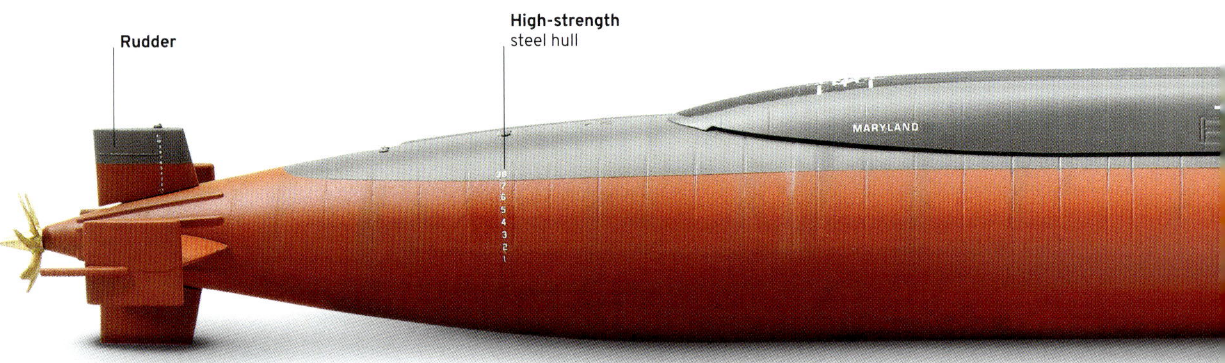

◁ HMS Vanguard (S28)
Date 1993 **Origin** UK
Displacement 17,527 tons (15,900 tonnes) submerged
Length 492 ft (150 m)
Top speed 25 knots (46 km/h) submerged

The lead vessel of its class, the *Vanguard*—the tenth Royal Navy ship to have that name—is armed with 16 Trident SLBMs, each capable of carrying up to 12 warheads. The submarine also has four tubes for Spearfish guided torpedoes.

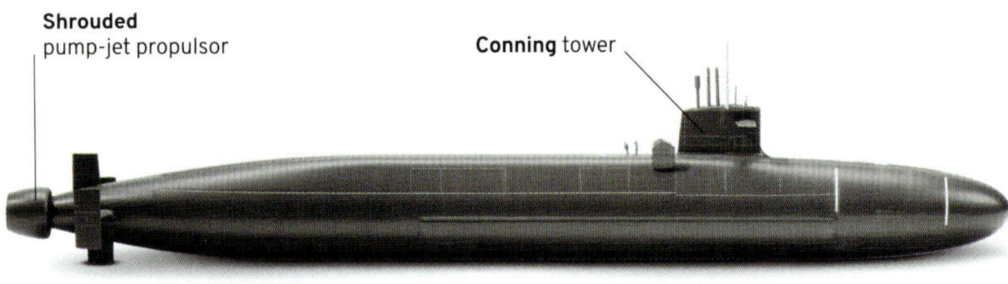

△ Le Triomphant (S616)
Date 1997 **Origin** France
Displacement 13,933 tons (12,640 tonnes)
Length 453 ft (138 m)
Top speed 20 knots (37 km/h)

Le Triomphant is armed with 16 M51 SLBMs, each with up to ten warheads and a range of around 4,970 miles (8,000 km), and also has four torpedo tubes. It is the lead vessel of its class, which replaced the French navy's *Le Redoutable* class.

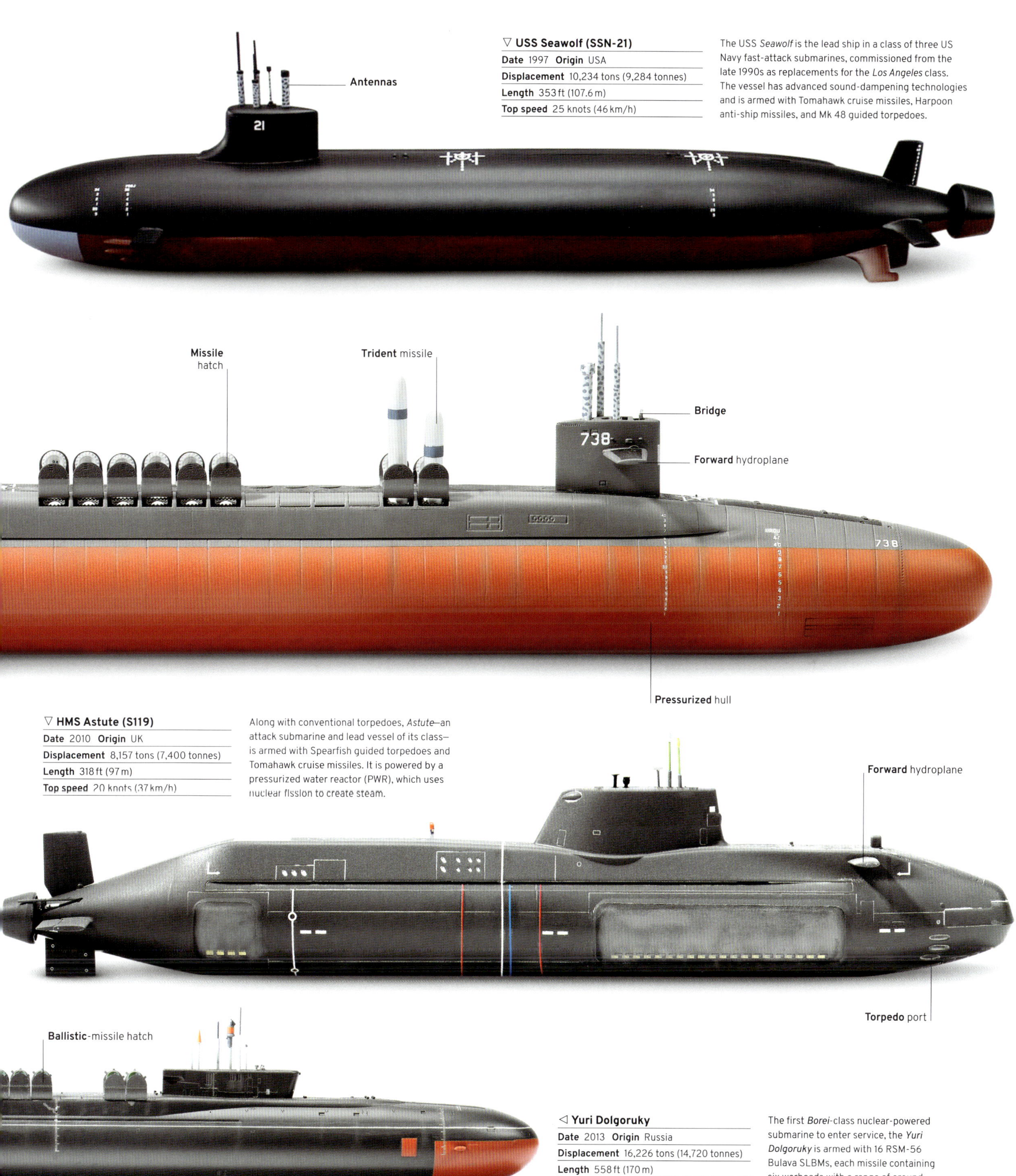

▽ **USS Seawolf (SSN-21)**

Date 1997 **Origin** USA
Displacement 10,234 tons (9,284 tonnes)
Length 353 ft (107.6 m)
Top speed 25 knots (46 km/h)

The USS *Seawolf* is the lead ship in a class of three US Navy fast-attack submarines, commissioned from the late 1990s as replacements for the *Los Angeles* class. The vessel has advanced sound-dampening technologies and is armed with Tomahawk cruise missiles, Harpoon anti-ship missiles, and Mk 48 guided torpedoes.

▽ **HMS Astute (S119)**

Date 2010 **Origin** UK
Displacement 8,157 tons (7,400 tonnes)
Length 318 ft (97 m)
Top speed 20 knots (37 km/h)

Along with conventional torpedoes, *Astute*—an attack submarine and lead vessel of its class—is armed with Spearfish guided torpedoes and Tomahawk cruise missiles. It is powered by a pressurized water reactor (PWR), which uses nuclear fission to create steam.

◁ **Yuri Dolgoruky**

Date 2013 **Origin** Russia
Displacement 16,226 tons (14,720 tonnes)
Length 558 ft (170 m)
Top speed 15 knots (28 km/h)

The first *Borei*-class nuclear-powered submarine to enter service, the *Yuri Dolgoruky* is armed with 16 RSM-56 Bulava SLBMs, each missile containing six warheads with a range of around 5,157 miles (8,300 km).

Tech in the Sky and Beyond

Autonomous, pilotless aircraft have already made a dramatic impact on the battlefield, and they may soon come to dominate air-to-air combat as well. Even further into the skies, governments are racing to establish space as a new frontier for military vehicles. The stakes are high as it seems increasingly likely that space will be a key theater of war in future conflicts.

Militarization of space
A US Military Atlas V rocket carrying the Navy Mobile User Objective System 2 satellite launches from Cape Canaveral, Florida. The satellite, one of a constellation of five, is used mainly for defense communications purposes.

In 1903, the *Wright Flyer*, built by American brothers Orville and Wilbur Wright, made the first flight by a powered, controlled, heavier-than-air aircraft; aloft for 12 seconds, it traveled just 120 ft (37 m). Only a century later, there were aircraft that could exceed the speed of sound by many times, aircraft that could fly around the world or near the edge of space, aircraft able to lift tanks, and even aircraft that did not need pilots.

AI, autonomy, and drones

Around two decades on from the centenary of the *Wright Flyer*'s short "hop," digital technology—in particular artificial intelligence (AI)—is opening up new horizons in aviation, and it promises to transform air combat. In 2020, for example, the USAF ran tests in which human fighter pilots flew against AI pilots in five simulator combats. The AI won all five engagements. In September 2023, over Edwards Air Force Base in California, two real F-16s fought a nonlethal dogfight, one piloted by a human and one by AI, with the jets reaching speeds of 1,200 mph (1,931 km/h) and coming within 1,968 ft (600 m) of each other. The outcome remains confidential, but it appears that the AI-controlled F-16—known as the X-62A VISTA (Variable In-flight Simulator Test Aircraft)—performed well.

Autonomous aircraft are now an accepted part of the future in military aviation. They offer all the advantages of uncrewed aircraft, such as 24-hour endurance, more space for ordnance and equipment, and the ability to withstand g-forces that would render a human pilot unconscious. To these, AI adds ultrafast data processing and decision-making, since the technology can draw on millions of tactical rehearsals to calculate the optimal maneuvers for victory.

By 2024, the USAF was looking to sign its first contracts for autonomous fighters, and many other countries are near to doing the same. A key concept is Manned-Unmanned Teaming (MUM-T), which foresees piloted and unmanned AI aircraft working seamlessly together, the latter acting as AI-powered "wingmen."

The Ukraine War, which began in 2022, has seen advances in the development of semiautonomous and fully autonomous unmanned aerial vehicles (UAVs), popularly known as drones. The battlefield arms race has begun to shift toward the possibility of AI-controlled swarms of attack drones flexibly executing their mission profile, individually selecting targets through image-recognition software, and destroying them with onboard weaponry. Current advanced drones such as the Helsing HX-2 have onboard AI that allows for dynamic adaptation to new threats and targets. Autonomous military aircraft is a future that has already arrived.

Cutting-edge fighter
The Lockheed Martin F-22A Raptor was at the forefront of fighter design on its introduction in 2005. Its features include stealth technology, super-maneuverability, and supercruise (supersonic flight without afterburners).

Space wars

Military technology now extends beyond Earth's atmosphere. Orbiting satellites fulfil a range of roles in support of the military, including communications, missile-launch early warning; space situational awareness (SSA); intelligence, surveillance, and reconnaissance (ISR); navigation; and meteorological forecasting. Correspondingly, satellites are now of vital military importance. America's Global Positioning System (GPS) satellite network, for example, delivers accurate positioning information to aid navigation, and is also used to direct many precision-guided munitions (PGMs). GPS can track the positions of friendly and enemy forces, facilitate secure data exchange (through high-precision timing), support supply chain

> "The potential for **autonomous air-to-air combat** has been imaginable for decades, but the reality has remained a **distant dream up until now.**"
>
> US SECRETARY OF THE AIR FORCE FRANK KENDALL, 2021–25

High-performance UAV
The Northrop Grumman MQ-4C Triton is a high-altitude, long-endurance unmanned UAV used by the US Navy and Australian Air Force for surveillance and reconnaissance. It can stay aloft for around 30 hours.

management, time-stamp electronic warfare, and underpin both nuclear and conventional command and control. Any disruption to the network of GPS satellites would have a severe impact on military operations 12,400 miles (20,000 km) below. Other countries have developed their own geolocation satellite networks as alternatives to GPS: China, for example, has the sophisticated BeiDou Navigation Satellite System, while Russia has its aging GLONASS.

Attempts at disrupting geolocation satellites have already been made, and defense analysts and space authorities have noted satellites being moved into "threatening" positions in relation to other satellites, in order to interfere with their signals or orbits. Development is underway of military satellites with "advanced maneuvering capability" that will be able to intercept their orbital rivals. There is also evidence that some countries are developing powerful conventional, nuclear, or directed-energy weapons (DEWs) that could destroy or disable dozens of satellites in an instant, leaving enemies without space-based positioning, timing, or observation. Such actions could also bring civilian life to a standstill, because many digital activities, from banking to navigation, rely on satellites.

The militarization of space, much like the use of AI in weapons technology, is still in its early days. Given the limits of physics and rocket propulsion, futuristic visions of dogfighting spacecraft are unlikely to become reality, and most military space vehicles are likely to be satellites. Exactly how these satellites will be used, what technology they will carry, and how they will interact with each other remain to be seen, but there is no doubt that they will be pivotal in the 21st-century arms race.

TALKING POINT

Driverless Land Vehicles

Driverless vehicles may come to dominate land warfare as well as aerial combat. Unmanned ground vehicles (UGVs) are remotely or autonomously driven military vehicles. Remote-control UGVs, which date back to World War II, have largely been experimental or peripheral, or used as expendable bomb-disposal tools. Today, however, UGVs with improved power supplies, powerful digital suites, advanced robotics, and AI are being adopted by armies. UGVs can perform reconnaissance, surveillance, mine clearance, medevac, and supply duties. Increasing numbers are being mounted with machine guns or missile launchers. Armed UGVs are not standard, but they seem likely to become so one day.

Mounting a .50-caliber heavy machine gun, the tracked Titan Strike UGV—shown here on exercise—can deliver mobile suppressive fire in support of infantry units.

High-tech Fighters

The latest generations of fighter aircraft vie for supremacy in digital technology as well as in terms of airframes, maneuverability, and weaponry. Those developed since 2010 feature cutting-edge characteristics: a stealth design with reduced radar cross section (RCS) and infrared-signature management; advanced avionics and target sensors; high maneuverability, often through thrust vectoring; electronic warfare systems (EWS); network-centric warfare (NCW) capabilities, with improved situational awareness (SA) and information sharing. The next generations of fighters are increasingly likely to be piloted by artificial intelligence (AI), either as fully autonomous (pilotless) aircraft or with a human-in-the-loop approach—either an onboard pilot or a ground controller.

▽ Dassault Mirage 2000D

Date 1995 **Origin** France

Engine 14,300–21,400 lb (6,486–9,707 kg) thrust SNECMA M53-P2 afterburning turbofan

Top speed 1,453 mph (2,338 km/h)

France's Mirage 2000D (the "D" stands for *diversifié*) is a two-seater multi-role fighter and ground-attack aircraft. It is designed for long-range precision strikes and close air-support missions.

△ Boeing F/A-18E Super Hornet

Date 1999 **Origin** USA

Engine 2 x 13,000–22,000 lb (5,897–9,979 kg) thrust General Electric F414-GE-400 afterburning turbofans

Top speed 1,190 mph (1,915 km/h)

Heavier than its F/A-18 Hornet predecessor—and with a greater range—the single-seater F/Z-18E is a multi-role strike fighter. The aircraft can carry a variety of weapons, including missiles and precision-guided bombs.

Electro-Optical Targeting System (EOTS)

Thrust-vectoring capability

△ Sukhoi Su-30 MkI

Date 2002 **Origin** Russia

Engine 2 x 19,842–27,558 lb (9,000–12,500 kg) thrust Lyulka-Saturn AL-31FP vectoring turbofans

Top speed 1,320 mph (2,124 km/h)

This highly agile and sophisticated version of the Su-30, carrying both air-to-air and air-to-surface missiles, was developed jointly by Russia and India and is made for the Indian Air Force (IAF). More than 250 have been built, forming the backbone of the IAF.

▽ BAe Harrier GR.9A

Date 2004 **Origin** UK

Engine 23,800 lb (10,795 kg) thrust Rolls-Royce Pegasus Mk107 turbofan

Top speed 662 mph (1,065 km/h)

The GR.9A was the final version of BAe's vertical takeoff aircraft, fitted with a more powerful Pegasus engine, and avionics and weapons upgrades. It was withdrawn from service in 2010 on cost grounds.

Underwing hardpoints

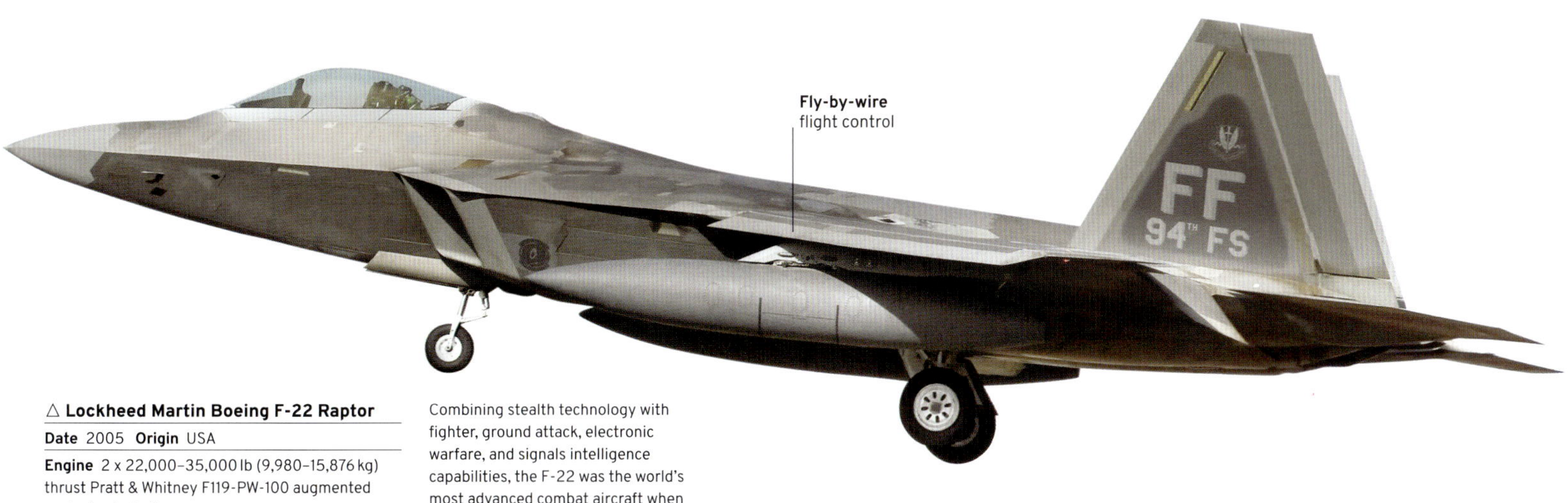

△ Lockheed Martin Boeing F-22 Raptor
Date 2005 **Origin** USA
Engine 2 x 22,000–35,000 lb (9,980–15,876 kg) thrust Pratt & Whitney F119-PW-100 augmented vectoring turbofans
Top speed 1,500 mph (2,414 km/h)

Combining stealth technology with fighter, ground attack, electronic warfare, and signals intelligence capabilities, the F-22 was the world's most advanced combat aircraft when it went into service. Production ended in 2012, with 187 jets operational.

Radar-absorbent materials

LF

△ Lockheed Martin F-35 Lightning II
Date 2015 **Origin** USA
Engine 1 × 43,000 lb (19,505 kg) thrust Pratt & Whitney F135-PW-100 afterburning turbofan
Top speed 1,200 mph (1,930 km/h)

Like many modern fighters, the F-35 is a multi-role aircraft, capable of ground attack as well as air superiority and interception missions, helped by advanced sensor technologies. It also includes variants designed for aircraft carrier operations.

△ Chengdu J-20
Date 2017 **Origin** China
Engine 2 × 32,000 lb (14,515 kg) thrust Shenyang WS-10C afterburning turbofans
Top speed 1,324 mph (2,130 km/h)

The Chengdu J-20 is an advanced all-weather stealth fighter. Its latest variants include thrust-vectoring control, advanced EWS, and the ability to collaborate with AI-controlled unmanned combat air vehicles (UCAVs).

△ Sukhoi Su-57
Date 2020 **Origin** Russia
Engine 2 x 33,000 lb (15,000 kg) NPO Lyulka-Saturn *izdeliye* 117 augmented turbofans
Top speed 1,327 mph (2,135 km/h)

A multi-role stealth fighter, the Su-57 is designed for extreme maneuverability and has a large weapons payload. It is intended as the first of a family of similar aircraft.

Eurofighter Typhoon

The Typhoon is an advanced tactical fighter and one of the world's most exceptional military aircraft. Fast, agile, and bristling with sensors and weapons, this state-of-the-art aircraft makes a formidable opponent in dogfights. Considered by many to be second only to the F-22 Raptor in overall air-to-air combat capabilities, the Eurofighter Typhoon enjoys an advantage over the F-22 in aerial battles at close quarters.

THE EUROFIGHTER TYPHOON, the product of a collaboration between the UK, Germany, Italy, and Spain, took its maiden flight in 1994. Its canard delta configuration, with foreplanes (small wings) ahead of the main wings, typifies modern European fighters. Key to its extraordinary aerial performance is a lightweight construction—82 percent of the aircraft's surface is made of composite materials—combined with powerful turbofan engines.

Able to perform both fighter and bomber roles, the Typhoon first saw combat in 2011, using Enhanced Paveway II bombs against loyalist forces in Libya. Its maneuverability, acceleration, and climb rate surpass those of the F-15 Eagle and the F-16 Fighting Falcon, and make it a close rival to the F-22 Raptor. The Typhoon serves with five European nations—including those that developed it—and four Arabian Gulf states.

Carbon-fiber tail fin

Heat exchanger air intake

Adjustable petals of engine-nozzle

Towable radar decoy can be used to counter radar-guided missiles

External fuel tank mounted on wing

SPECIFICATIONS	
Model	Eurofighter Typhoon FGR4, 2007
Origin	UK, Germany, Italy, and Spain
Production	600+
Construction	Carbon-fiber composites, lightweight alloys, titanium, glass reinforced plastics
Wingspan	35 ft 10 in (10.95 m)
Length	52 ft 5 in (15.96 m)
Maximum weight	52,000 lb (23,500 kg)
Engines	2 x 20,000 lb (9,060 kg) thrust EJ200 turbofans
Range	2,350 miles (3,790 km) ferry range
Top speed	1,320 mph (2,124 km/h)

FRONT VIEW

REAR VIEW

Best in service
The Typhoon is the largest, most powerful, and fastest modern European fighter in service. Compared to the other Eurocanards—the Saab Gripen and the Dassault Rafale—it has larger wings and canards.

RAF roundel with No.29 Squadron "colors"

Forward fuselage strake improves airflow

Bubble canopy gives good all-round visibility

Fiberglass reinforced plastic dome encloses radar

Louvers for bleed air spill

Movable canard helps to control pitch and keep the aircraft stable

Nose wheel retracts rearward

EXTERIOR

A composite construction, and the fact that the engine face lies hidden deep within the fuselage, make the Typhoon relatively difficult to detect by radar. The wide horizontal spacing between the wings and the canard foreplanes allows more control torque to be exerted, which is one reason why the Typhoon has unparalleled agility at higher speeds. The variable lip of the "smiling" chin-mounted intake smooths the flow of air into the engine at higher angles-of-attack—the vertical angle of the aircraft relative to the direction of flight.

1. No.29 Squadron badge **2.** Air data sensors **3.** Canard foreplane (fully deflected) **4.** Port main undercarriage wheel **5.** Maintenance data panel (MDP) **6.** Cap on main body fuel tank **7.** Cap on wing-mounted fuel tank **8.** Low-visibility RAF roundel with No.29 Squadron "colors" **9.** Canopy release **10.** Laser warning receiver (LWR) **11.** Integrated tip stub launcher (ITPSL) including chaff dispenser **12.** Nozzle petals **13.** Engine bleed-air primary heat exchanger **14.** Navigation light **15.** Air conditioning system heat exchanger exhaust **16.** EJ200 afterburner section **17.** Missile approach warning system (MAWS) "sausage"

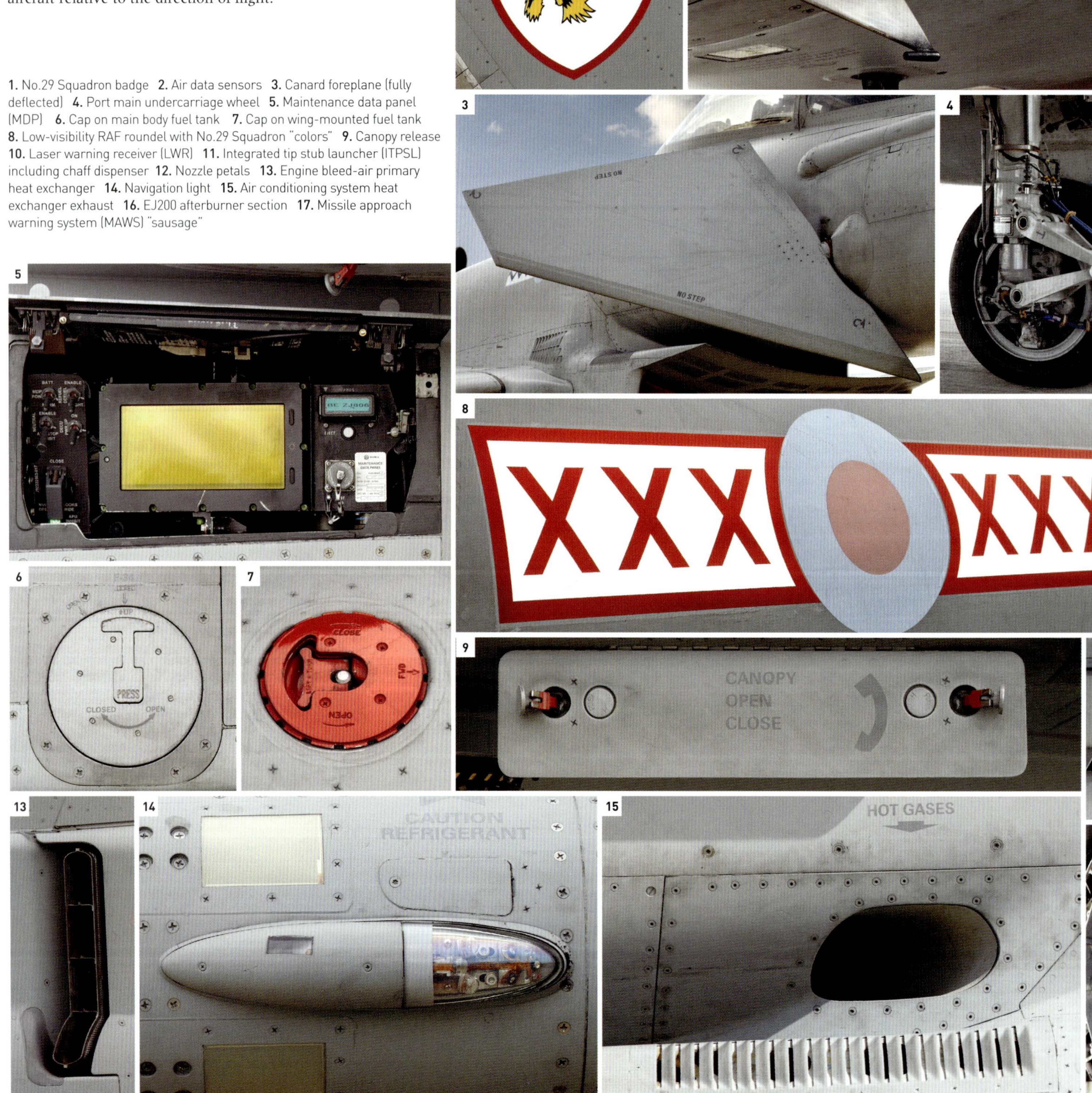

COCKPIT

Although it has a central control column rather than a sidestick, which is unusual for a modern Western fighter, the Typhoon is easy to fly and operate thanks to its pilot-aircraft interface. The pilot has voice control and the most advanced helmet in service: data presented on the visor can be used to designate targets. A wide-angle head-up display (HUD) and three large multifunctional displays (MFDs) enhance the ease of interacting with the Typhoon's systems.

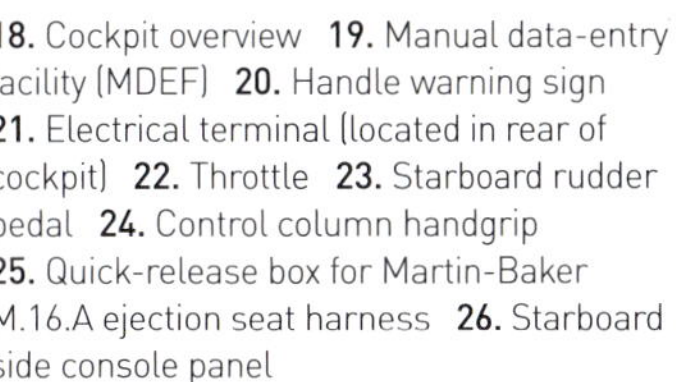

18. Cockpit overview **19.** Manual data-entry facility (MDEF) **20.** Handle warning sign **21.** Electrical terminal (located in rear of cockpit) **22.** Throttle **23.** Starboard rudder pedal **24.** Control column handgrip **25.** Quick-release box for Martin-Baker M.16.A ejection seat harness **26.** Starboard side console panel

18

19

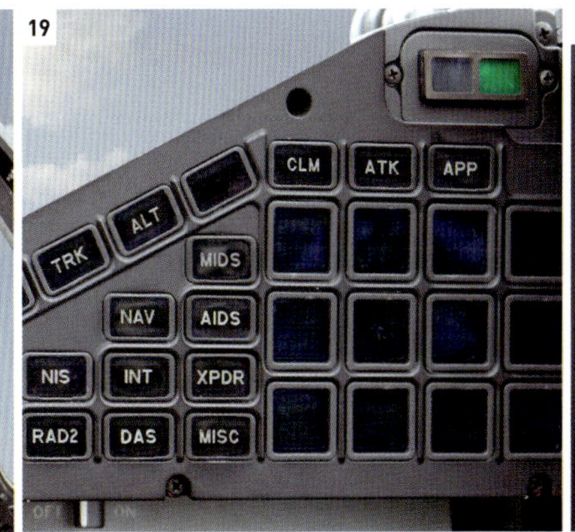

20

DO NOT PULL
DANGER
HANDLE

21

10

11

12

16

17

22

23

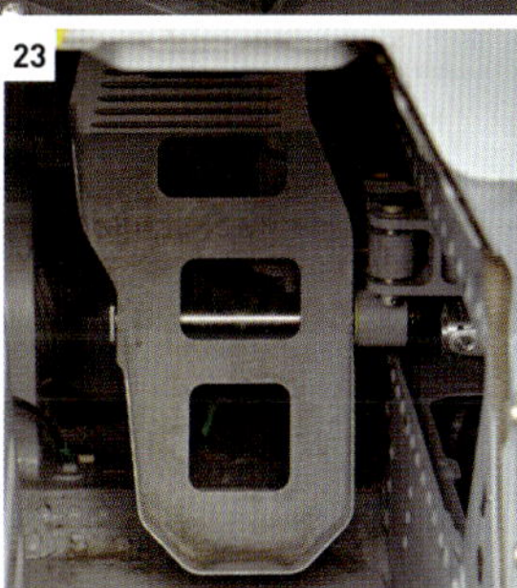

24

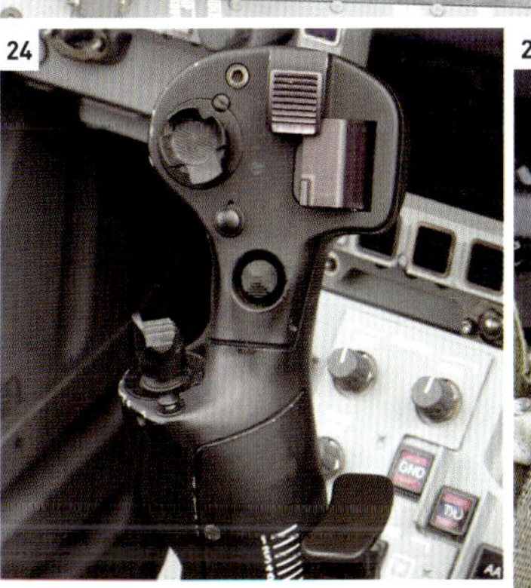

25

26

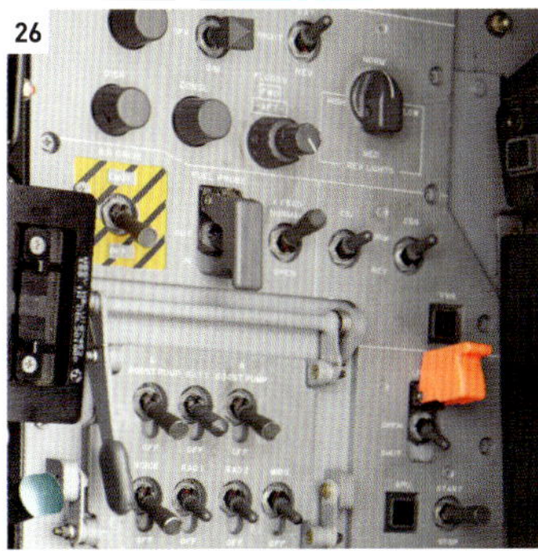

Drones in Modern Warfare

Unmanned aerial vehicles (UAVs) were first built during World War I on an experimental basis, although they never saw active service. By the 1930s, UAVs were being used as training targets, and in the Vietnam War they were deployed in large numbers for reconnaissance. Since then many nations have been developing UAVs, or "drones," for military and other purposes. The conflict in Ukraine, after Russia's invasion of 2022, saw rapid expansion in the use of drones, not only for the constant monitoring of enemy forces, but also as a new, relatively cheap weapon that could be mass produced. Commercial drones were converted, then manufactured in large quantities, to carry and drop bombs or deliver an explosive charge by crashing into a target. In response, electronic countermeasures were developed to disrupt the control signals of those flying the drones. This cat-and-mouse game of measure and countermeasure has meant that the technology of drones and the way they operate continue to change at an increasing tempo.

A Ukrainian soldier prepares a Vampire unmanned combat aerial vehicle (UCAV) for launch in February 2024. It can carry a 33 lb (15 kg) payload.

Drones

Unmanned aerial vehicles (UAVs) acquired the name "drones" (as in a drone bee) from the DH.82B Queen Bee, an unpiloted, radio-controlled target aircraft developed in Britain in the mid-1930s, although the origins of such vehicles date back to World War I. The role of UAVs diversified in the 1960s and 1970s, when they were mainly used for surveillance. It was from the 1990s, however, that UAVs revealed their full potential, not only as high-endurance reconnaissance platforms, but also as combat weapons delivering precision-guided munitions (PGMs) and, today, as single-use "suicide" drones.

▷ Northrop Grumman RQ-4 Global Hawk

Date 2001 **Origin** USA

Engine 7,600 lb (3,447 kg) thrust Rolls-Royce F137-RR-100 turbofan

Top speed 357 mph (575 km/h)

Able to survey through sandstorm and cloud, the Global Hawk was widely used in Iraq and Afghanistan. It can operate at high altitude for more than 30 hours, with a range of 14,155 miles (22,780 km).

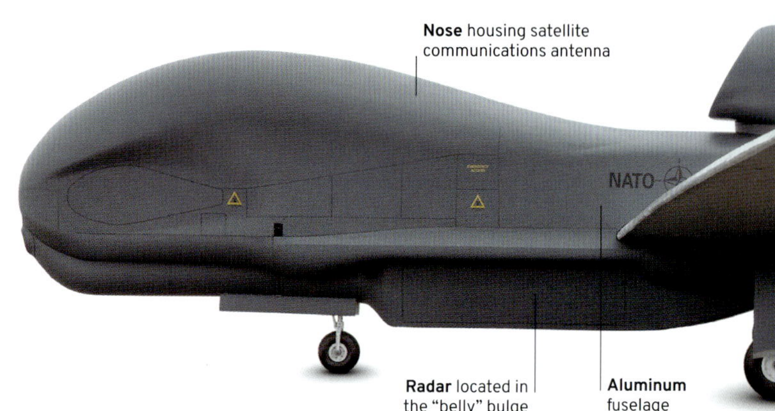

Nose housing satellite communications antenna

Radar located in the "belly" bulge

Aluminum fuselage

▽ General Atomics MQ-9 Reaper

Date 2007 **Origin** USA

Engine 900 hp (671 kW) Honeywell TPE331-10 turboprop

Top speed 288 mph (463 km/h)

The Reaper came into service with the US Air Force as the world's most advanced, and lethal, UAV. Turboprop powered, it is operated by a remote crew of two and carries a weaponry payload of 3,750 lb (1,701 kg), including up to eight Hellfire air-to-ground missiles.

C-band antenna for line-of-sight communication with ground control

Inverted-V tail with twin booms

Dome holds the aircraft's satellite communications system

Wingspan of 66 ft (20 m)

△ BAE Systems Mantis

Date 2009 **Origin** UK

Engine 2 x 380 hp (283 kW) Rolls-Royce M250B-17 turboshafts

Top speed 345 mph (556 km/h)

Designed to explore the military potential of UAVs, Mantis can fly itself and plot its own route, relaying data back to its base station via satellite. Capable of long-range missions, it has an endurance of at least 24 hours.

V-tail reduces radar and infrared signature

△ STC Orlan-10

Date 2010 **Origin** Russia

Engine 0.95 hp (0.71 kW) Saito Manufacturing FA-62B 1-cylinder 4-stroke

Top speed 93 mph (150 km/h)

The Orlan-10 has become one of Russia's most important reconnaissance drones, used in Ukraine, Syria, Libya, and Azerbaijan. It operates at fairly low altitudes of up to 16,404 ft (5,000 m), but can fly for 16 hours at a distance of up to 373 miles (600 km) from the command station.

Twin tail booms

△ Selex Galileo Falco Evo

Date 2012 **Origin** Italy

Engine 65–80 hp (48–60 kW) gasoline

Top speed 134 mph (216 km/h)

Built originally for the Pakistan Air Force, this surveillance UAV has an operational time of 20 hours and a ceiling of 19,685 ft (6,000 m). It can carry a range of sensors and electronic warfare systems.

▽ Bayraktar TB2

Date 2015 **Origin** Türkiye

Engine 100 hp (75 kW) TM-100 gasoline 2-stroke

Top speed 138 mph (222 km/h)

The Turkish Bayraktar TB2 is a combat-proven UAV, deployed in Syria, Libya, Azerbaijan, Ukraine, and parts of Africa. The drone has an operational altitude of 16,000 ft (4,877 m) and can carry a variety of precision-guided missiles.

T-shaped tail unit

Turboshaft engine delivering power to a propellor

▽ Ukrainian quadcopter

Date 2023 **Origin** Ukraine

Engine 4 electrically powered rotors

Top speed Unknown

Typical of the budget combat drones used in the Ukraine War, this Ukrainian quadcopter marries commercial drone technology with a shaped-charge high-explosive anti-tank (HEAT) warhead. The controller simply flies the drone into an enemy target to detonate the explosives.

Warhead tied to the body of the drone

MQ-9 Reaper

Part of the new wave of unmanned aerial vehicles (UAVs) that is changing the dynamics of modern warfare, the General Atomics Reaper can be deployed for surveillance and reconnaissance of ground targets. With a lengthy "loiter time," it is able to remain on station or provide an overwatch capacity to convoys or advancing ground forces. If required, it can fire precision-guided weapons at targets. The MQ-9 Reaper has a "crew" of two that operate it remotely—even from thousands of miles away.

Developed from General Atomics' Predator UAV, the Reaper first flew in 2001 and entered service with the US Air Force in 2007. A 950 hp (708 kW) turboprop engine gives the Reaper a cruising speed of 200 mph (310 km/h). When carrying extra fuel tanks, it can cover 1,610 miles (2,590 km) and linger over a target area for 30 hours, or 23 hours with a full weapons load.

Up to six pylons can mount laser-guided bombs, such as the GBU-12 Paveway II; air-to-ground missiles, like the AGM-114 Hellfire II; and the AIM 9 Sidewinder air-to-air missile. The Reaper can also carry Joint Direct Attack Munitions (JDAMs), which are standard bombs augmented to turn them into precision-guided weapons. Sensors may also be added to the pylons, depending on the nature of the mission.

The Reaper system can be transported in a container to a suitable launch site. It is controlled during its flight by a pilot and a sensor operator who may be many miles away in a home headquarters; their flight control adjustments, relayed by satellite, take 1.2 seconds. Extensively used by the US in Afghanistan and Iraq, the Reaper has also taken part in anti-pirate operations, carried out border-monitoring duties, and assisted search and rescue missions.

SPECIFICATIONS	
Model	MQ-9 Reaper
Origin	USA
Production	2007–
Maximum weight	2.4 tons (2.2 tonnes); full load 5.8 tons (5.3 tonnes)
Engines	Honeywell TPE331-10GD 950 hp (708 kW) turboprop
Wingspan	66 ft (20 m)
Length	36 ft (11 m)
Range	Standard 1,150 miles (1,850 km); extended 1,610 miles (2,590 km)
Top speed	300 mph (480 km/h)

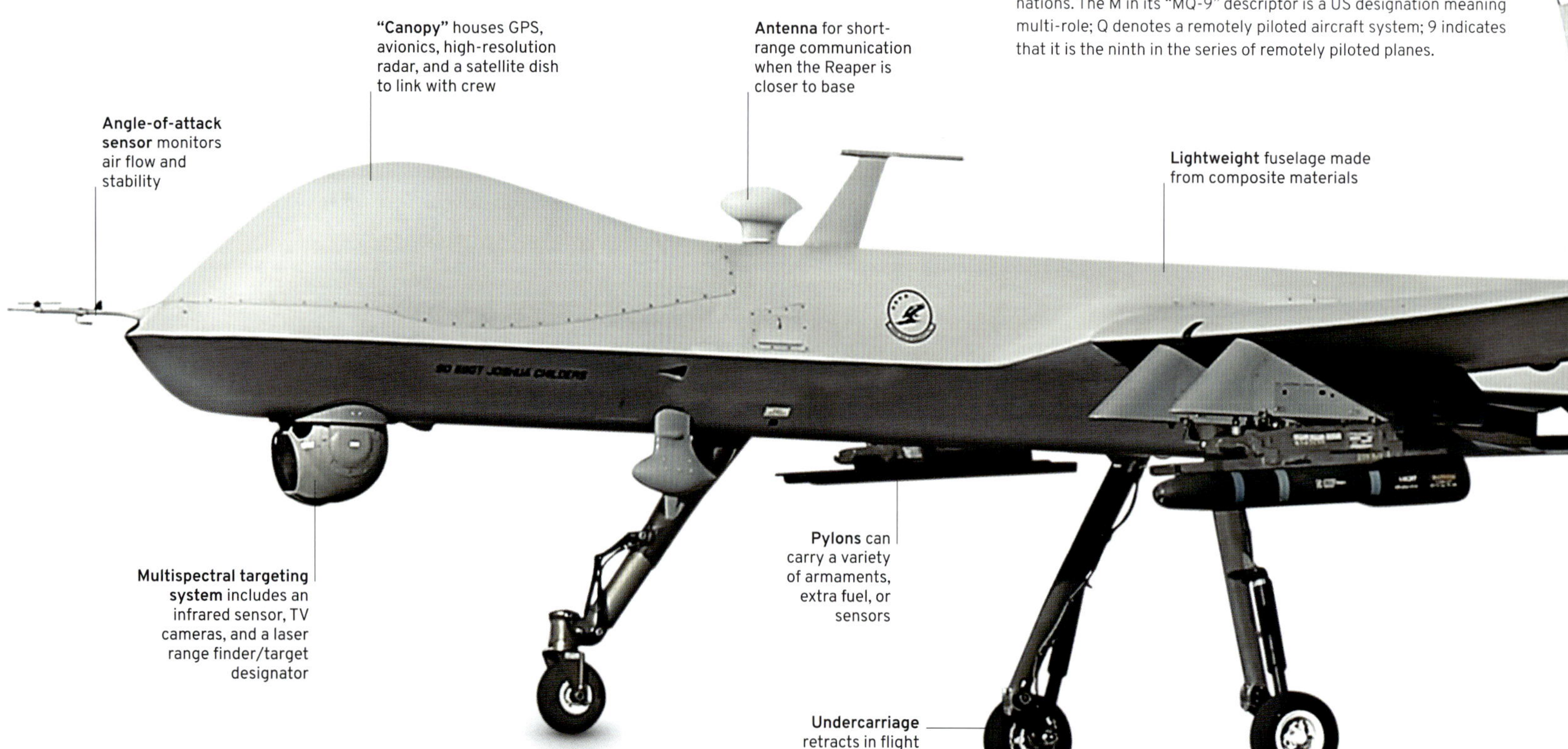

Remotely piloted aircraft
First used by the US Air Force, the Reaper now also serves with other nations. The M in its "MQ-9" descriptor is a US designation meaning multi-role; Q denotes a remotely piloted aircraft system; 9 indicates that it is the ninth in the series of remotely piloted planes.

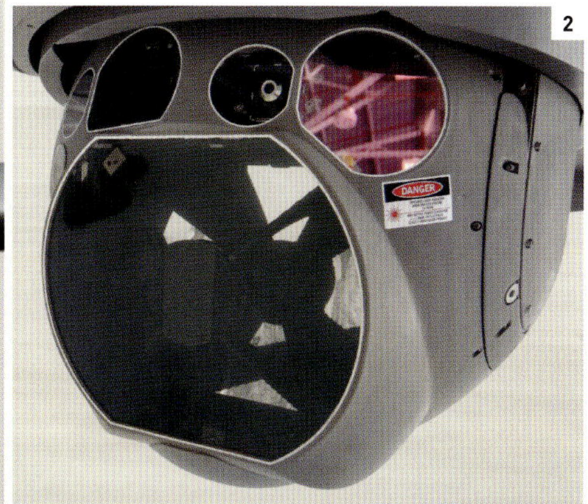

EXTERIOR

Although the MQ-9 Reaper's wingspan of 66 ft (20 m) is larger than that of many jet fighters, the aircraft can be disassembled and stored in a single container for shipment. Among the sensors on the MX-15 gimbal mount is a camera that it is claimed can read a car number plate from 2 miles (3.2 km) away. The Reaper has a two-tone gray paint scheme, darker on its upper surfaces, lighter underneath.

1. Nose: angle-of-attack sensor (above), camera (below) **2.** Multispectral targeting system **3.** Extended range fuel tank **4.** Propeller **5.** Pylons with GBU-12 Paveway II (left) and AGM-114 Hellfire (right) **6.** Dorsally mounted engine vent **7.** Wingtip winglets (on some models)

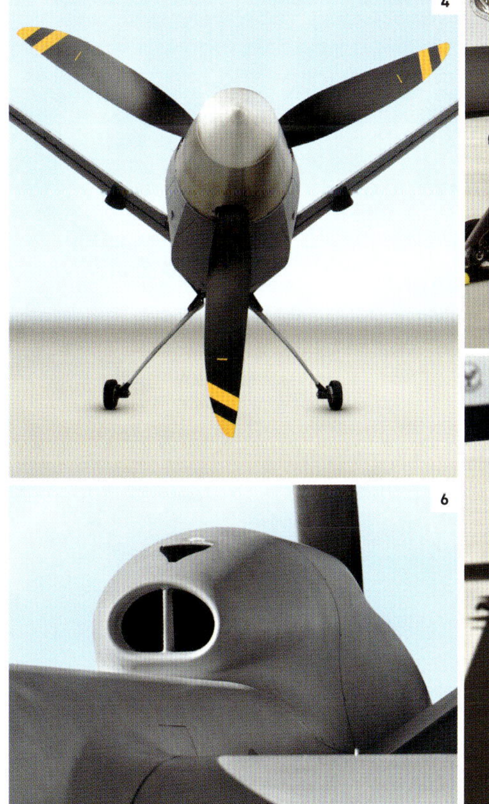

Seafaring Technology

Throughout history, the sea has provided a means of transporting goods around the world and finding fresh markets for trade. It also became a means for countries to spread their influence and acquire colonies by force. In times of war, ships built for trading journeys could be fitted with defensive weapons or converted to warships. Eventually, rivalries between powers such as Spain and Britain led to the establishment of permanent navies of purpose-built warships. Guns of bigger size and range led warships to increase in tonnage, and then to take on armor protection and new forms of propulsion. In the industrial era, warship technology became an even more urgent race to surpass rivals in speed, armor, and weaponry. Innovative technologies—such as submarines, mines, or aircraft that could be launched at sea, and radar and satellite surveillance—frequently threatened to make warships vulnerable, but in these cases counter-technologies were soon developed to limit or negate these threats. In the 21st century, as with many other areas of warfare, a new generation of unmanned craft is just starting to be deployed.

Talking point

Merchant ships in warfare

The expense of maintaining ships full-time for exclusively military purposes meant that for centuries merchant vessels were brought into military use when necessary, and military ships were sometimes converted to carry cargo or act in a dual role. During World War I and World War II, Britain's merchant navy had up to 200,000 sailors and carried supplies and troops all over the world. In recent times, civilian ships have been used for the ocean transport of large military forces during the Falklands War (1982), the Gulf War (1991), and the Iraq War (2003–11).

Trireme

Warships with banked rows of oars, each oar worked by an individual rower, were developed in the Mediterranean. Both the Greeks and the Phoenicians have been cited as the possible originators. Triremes—fighting vessels boasting three tiers of oars on each side—were in use by the 7th century BCE. Large numbers of oars freed triremes from dependency on the wind, allowing them to be more maneuverable in battle and to quickly build up speed for ramming attacks. A typical Athenian trireme had 170 oarsmen, which were usually citizens carrying out their military service.

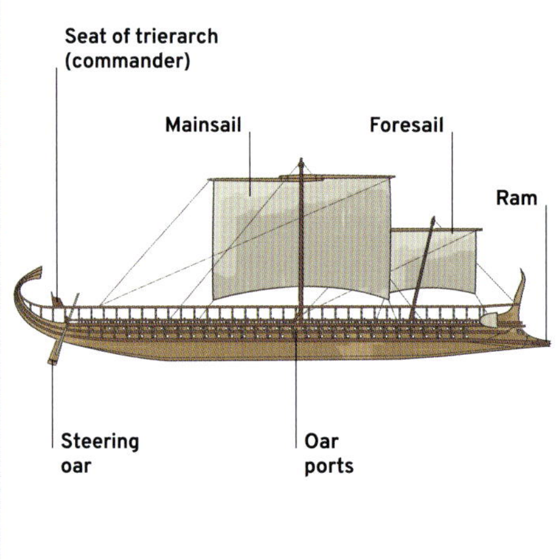

Longship

Scandinavian longships varied in detail due to variations in local materials and in the skills of builders. However, they all followed a general design: all were wooden, clinker built (with overlapping wooden hull planks), and had positions for oarsmen along each side, as well as a sail on a single mast for wind propulsion. Their shallow draft allowed them to travel up estuaries and inland along rivers. Viking longships made lengthy sea voyages, reaching Greenland and the North American mainland. The longship's design was so effective that it lasted for more than 1,500 years. The last longship was defeated in battle in 1429.

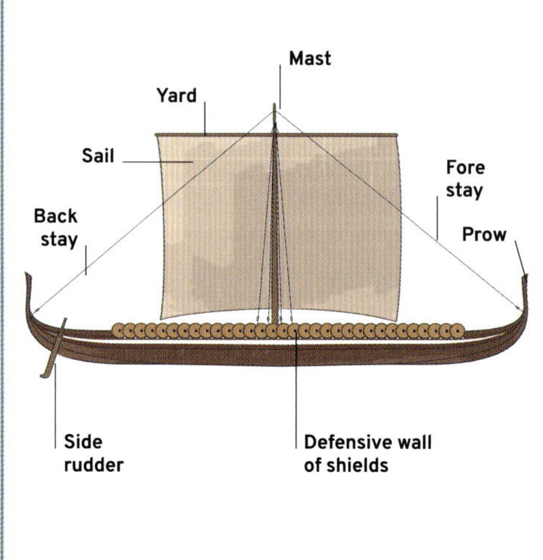

Galley

Developed from earlier Mediterranean vessels, the galley style of ship was built from antiquity through to the early 19th century. Galleys had a shallow draft and a narrow keel, and sat low in the water. While they had sails, galleys could also be powered by oars arranged in one or more banks. Galleys were used as trading vessels or warships—often as both on the same voyage, since ships had to protect themselves from pirates. Maritime powers such as Venice built fleets of galleys, with some vessels having a crew of up to 1,000. Castle-like structures were added on the rear to house weaponry and soldiers.

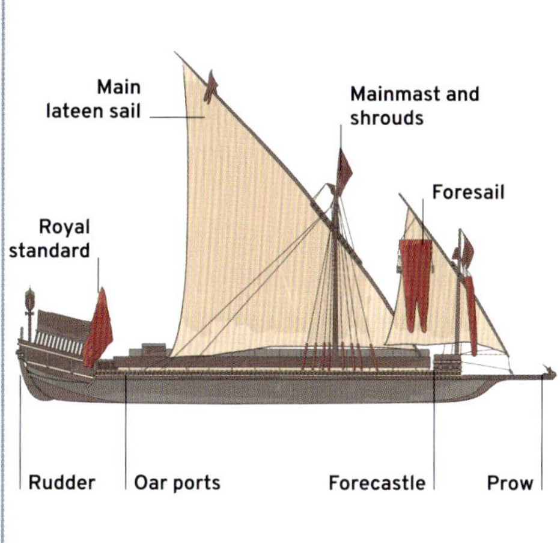

Ship of the line

Ships of the line were purpose-built, heavily armed, sail-powered battleships. They were introduced as the British Royal Navy and the Dutch navy devised tactics whereby ships would line up and fire a devastating broadside at the enemy. In such encounters, the ships with the most cannon to fire and with guns of greater size and range would have an advantage, and this led to ships of the line carrying up to 140 cannon. In the age of sail, from the 17th century to the mid-19th century, the number of ships of the line a nation possessed became an indicator of its naval power.

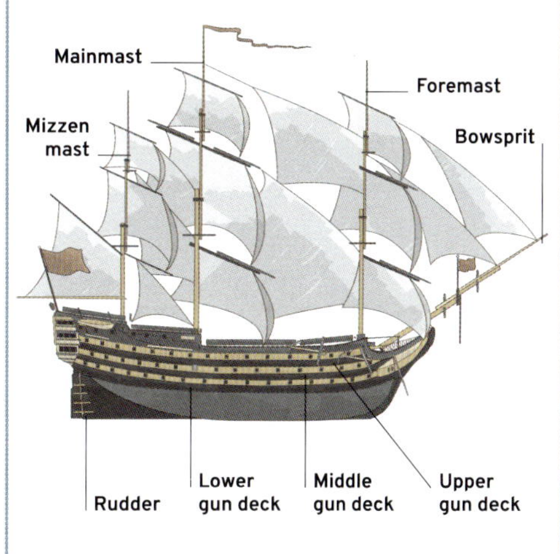

Pre-dreadnought

Steam-powered warships began to appear in the 1830s, and new "ironclad" ships saw action in the American Civil War of 1861–65. The design of Britain's *Majestic* class, launched in the 1890s, set a template for battleships that was mimicked by other navies. The ships had armor protection, coal-fired boilers, and sizable (12 in) guns in rotating, deck-mounted turrets. A naval arms race saw countries such as Japan and Russia commissioning similar battleships from British dockyards. This type of battleship, now known as a pre-dreadnought, became redundant after the launch of HMS *Dreadnought* in 1906.

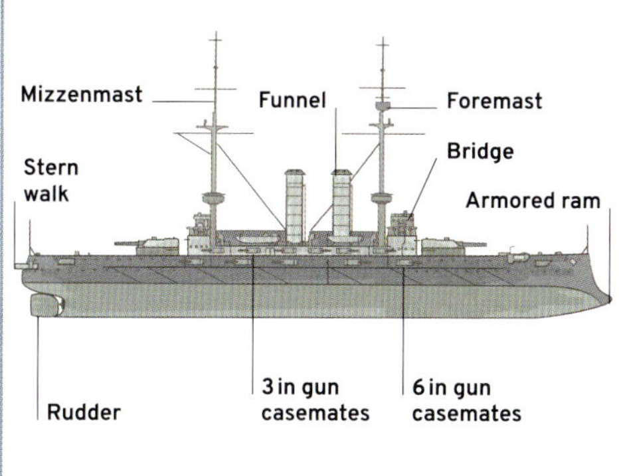

World War I battleship

With new steam turbines that gave it unprecedented speed, and an all "big gun" arrangement of ten 12 in guns in armored turrets, HMS *Dreadnought*, commissioned in 1906, was a revolutionary battleship. Britain and Germany engaged in a race to develop ships of "dreadnought" specification, and other countries soon felt compelled to follow suit. Although the fleet actions of dreadnoughts in World War I were limited to the inconclusive Battle of Jutland (1916), Allied dreadnoughts saw some success in restricting the activity of the German fleet and blockading Germany from foreign supplies.

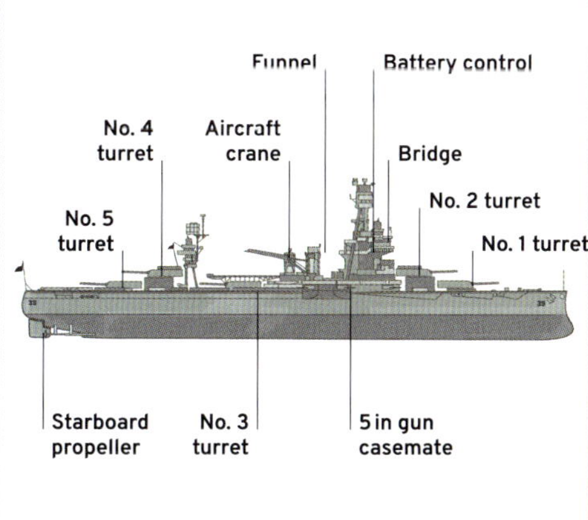

Nuclear-powered aircraft carrier

In 1961, the USS *Enterprise* became the first commissioned aircraft carrier to be powered by a nuclear reactor. The key advantage nuclear power brought to naval ships was that refueling could be avoided and, in consequence, a warship could travel significantly further and carry out deployments of much longer duration. At present, only the US and France deploy nuclear-powered carriers, but other countries, notably China, are looking to join this select band. Currently the US has 12 nuclear powered carriers in service; these carriers include the largest military machines ever built.

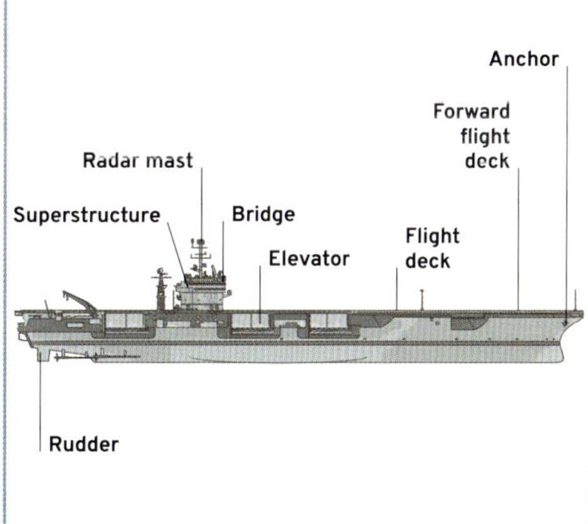

Modern destroyer

The destroyer started life at the end of the 19th century as a small, torpedo-carrying, light class of warship with limited range. However, as other warship types including battleships and cruisers became obsolete, the destroyer took on an increasing number of new roles. Today, the destroyer is the principal type of warship deployed by most modern navies. Equipped with stealth technologies, electronic warfare systems, helicopters, and missiles, destroyers now carry an enormous amount of weaponry compared to their predecessors, and they have grown in size to fulfil a range of roles.

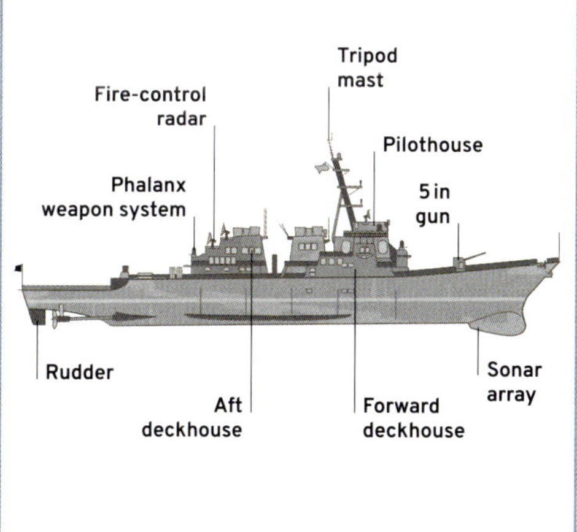

Protective Technology

The age of armor protection for vehicles began in earnest in the 19th century, when the hulls of wooden warships were reinforced with iron plates to defend against explosive and incendiary munitions. In World War I, protection extended to land vehicles, with steel plates fitted to armored cars and tanks to shield crews from enemy fire. Increasingly powerful guns and armor-piercing rounds drove military vehicle designers to develop ever-more resistant armor. Much modern armor is "composite," consisting of nonmetallic materials such as ceramics or plastics incorporated into steel layers. Supplementary armor is extra layers of material added to the exterior of an armored fighting vehicle.

THE DEVELOPMENT OF ARMOR

The "ironclad" warships of the 19th century had armor of wrought-iron plates. Iron armor was superseded by steel, which is stronger and weighs less. Plates of rolled steel were made by passing cast billets between rollers until the metal was the desired thickness. This repeated compression aligned the grain in the metal, eliminating weaknesses and creating tough "homogenous" steel. Another development, face-hardening, reheated steel plates with carbon to give the steel a hardened surface, or "face." Metals such as chromium, molybdenum, nickel, and tungsten were added to produce steel-alloy armor with differing characteristics. The development of anti-tank rounds that could burn through armor, rather than penetrating it by kinetic energy, led to ceramic blocks being fitted to vehicles; these blocks give modern tanks their angular appearance. Such armor, known as "Chobham" after the UK town where it was developed, greatly increases protection to anti-tank rounds. The armor of today's vehicles varies according to their use and theater of operation.

Yamato **battleship (1941)**

Warships
Early 20th-century warships relied on heavy armor—Japan's *Yamato* had up to 26½ in (650 mm) of armor. Modern warships are lightly armored, relying on stealth and electronic countermeasures.

Bell AH-1 Cobra (1965)

Aircraft
Armor on planes and helicopters concentrates on vital areas, such as the cockpit; trying to make the entire aircraft immune to damage would increase its weight and impair performance.

Merkava Mark 4 (2004)

Land vehicles
Modern combat vehicles, such as Israel's Merkava Mark 4 tank, are both fast and maneuverable, being protected by composite armor, which is typically lighter than all-metal armor alternatives.

Tiger I, German heavy tank (1942)
World War II saw a race to create the most effective plate-armored heavy tanks, and the Tiger I was among the most fearsome of these. Setting a tank's armor at an angle makes it likelier that rounds will deflect off the tank; it also increases the depth of armor to be penetrated. Surprisingly, the Tiger I had near-vertical armor, but the armor's thickness, rather than its geometry, made it impervious to many anti-tank weapons.

Thinnest armor on top

Front hull armor sloped at 13 degrees

Glacis armor was heavily sloped

Underbelly armor was relatively thin

Thin steel track guards

Interleaved wheels increased protection

25 mm | 60 mm | 80–100 mm | 100–120 mm

Smoke grenades

Smoke has been used to obscure battlefield targets since ancient times. From the 1940s, smoke has typically been delivered by grenades discharged from launchers mounted on the outside of vehicles. A salvo of grenades can quickly form a smoke screen to conceal a vehicle's movement. Smoke grenades today work in both the visual and infrared parts of the spectrum, so targets are also hidden from both optical and thermal imaging systems.

EXPLOSIVE REACTIVE ARMOR

A form of supplementary armor, explosive reactive armor (ERA) consists of relatively thin plates of armor with a backing of high explosive layers. When a plate is struck by a high-explosive anti-tank (HEAT) projectile, the jet of molten metal formed in the incoming round's warhead pierces the plate, but then detonates the high explosive layers beneath. The detonation blows the entire panel off the target vehicle before the HEAT round can penetrate the vehicle's main defensive armor below. ERA can, however, be defeated by "tandem charge" HEAT rounds. These use two charges, the second of which detonates just milliseconds after the first, by which time the vehicle's main armor has been exposed and is vulnerable.

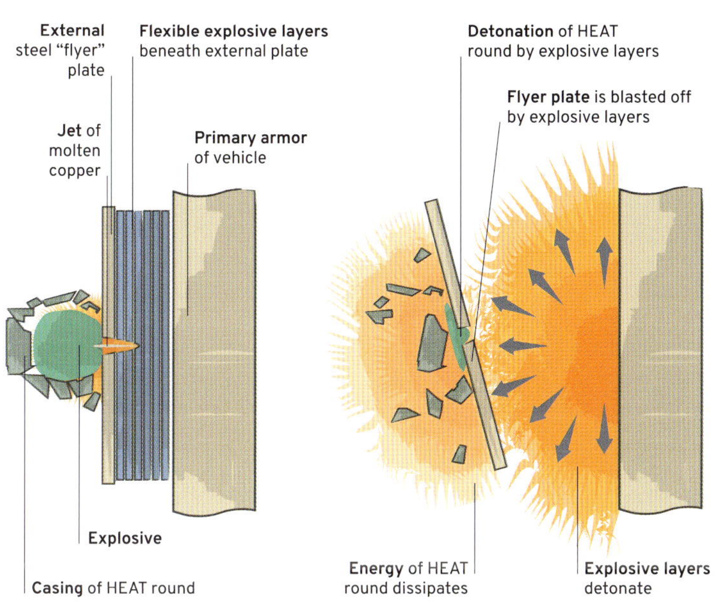

BAR ARMOR

The overall level of protection of light armored vehicles can be increased inexpensively by fitting bar armor. An alternative form of supplementary armor, bar armor involves mounting a framework of hardened steel bars (usually horizontally) over vulnerable parts of a vehicle. Bar armor is not effective against kinetic-energy rounds, but it can defeat lightweight HEAT rounds such as those delivered by grenade launchers. The bars can trap or detonate the rounds before they reach the body of the vehicle itself, minimizing impact and protecting the occupants inside.

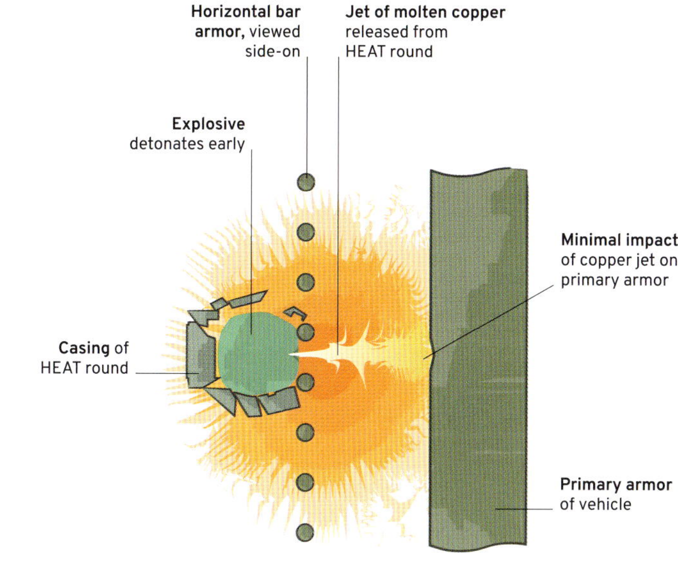

CAMOUFLAGE

Many modern military vehicles use camouflage patterns to disrupt their outlines and blend in with their surroundings, often mimicking natural habitats such as woodland, desert, or snowy terrain, or by using "dazzle" designs to obscure their direction of travel and distance from the enemy. Reducing a vehicle's heat footprint via thermal insulation and other means can help avoid detection, while radar-absorbent surfaces reduce long-range detectability.

Andrea Doria (1916)—dazzle camouflage

Pansarbil M40 (Lynx) (1939)—conventional camouflage

Lockheed F-117 Nighthawk (1981)—anti-radar surfaces and design, reduced thermal footprint

Challenger 2 (1998)—thermal insulation

Flight Technology

Winged craft stay aloft due to a difference in air pressure above and below their wings. This differential, which results from the wings' airfoil shape, produces lift—an upward force that acts together with weight, thrust, and drag (friction with the air) to produce flight. In level flight at constant speed, lift balances weight, and engine thrust balances drag. These basic principles are the same for modern jets as they were for the first heavier-than-air craft, while flight controls are also essentially the same as in the early days of aviation. The "stick-and-rudder" system, originally devised by French aviator Louis Blériot for his XI monoplane crossing of the English Channel in 1909, is still found in today's aircraft.

CHANGING WING SHAPES

To make aircraft wings as light as possible, early planes used very thin surfaces braced by wires. World War I biplane wings had thicker airfoil shapes that induced less drag. Until the advent of later aircraft such as the Spitfire, unbraced cantilever monoplane wings had to be thick for high-speed flight. Swept-back "laminar-flow" wings, which reduced turbulence, proved the best for transonic (near the speed of sound) flight. Improved materials enabled them to be made even thinner for supersonic speeds.

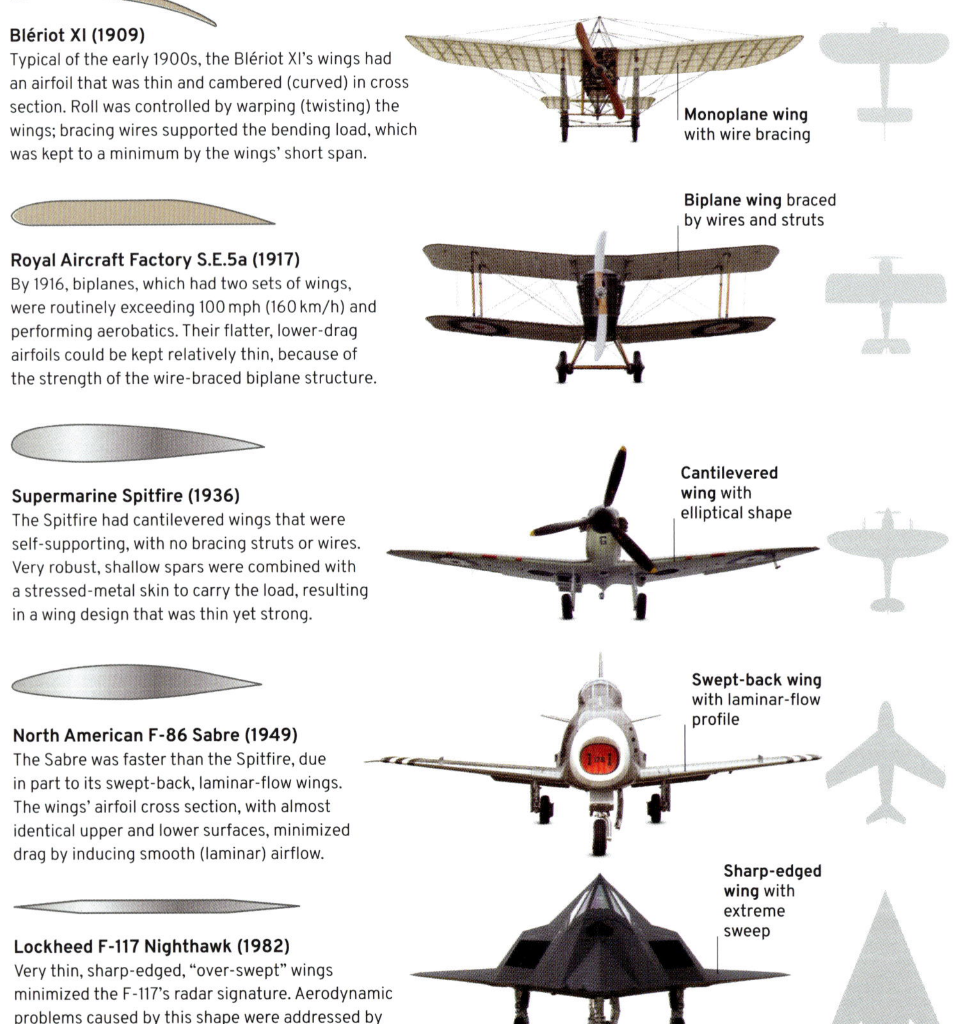

Blériot XI (1909)
Typical of the early 1900s, the Blériot XI's wings had an airfoil that was thin and cambered (curved) in cross section. Roll was controlled by warping (twisting) the wings; bracing wires supported the bending load, which was kept to a minimum by the wings' short span.

Royal Aircraft Factory S.E.5a (1917)
By 1916, biplanes, which had two sets of wings, were routinely exceeding 100 mph (160 km/h) and performing aerobatics. Their flatter, lower-drag airfoils could be kept relatively thin, because of the strength of the wire-braced biplane structure.

Supermarine Spitfire (1936)
The Spitfire had cantilevered wings that were self-supporting, with no bracing struts or wires. Very robust, shallow spars were combined with a stressed-metal skin to carry the load, resulting in a wing design that was thin yet strong.

North American F-86 Sabre (1949)
The Sabre was faster than the Spitfire, due in part to its swept-back, laminar-flow wings. The wings' airfoil cross section, with almost identical upper and lower surfaces, minimized drag by inducing smooth (laminar) airflow.

Lockheed F-117 Nighthawk (1982)
Very thin, sharp-edged, "over-swept" wings minimized the F-117's radar signature. Aerodynamic problems caused by this shape were addressed by computer-regulated fly-by-wire controls.

LIFT AND BALANCING FORCES

A moving wing's airfoil shape makes air flow faster over the top of it than underneath it, reducing the air pressure above the wing and generating lift. The angle at which the wing meets the oncoming air —the angle of attack—determines how much lift and drag are produced. If the critical angle is exceeded, the wing loses lift and stalling occurs.

FORCES

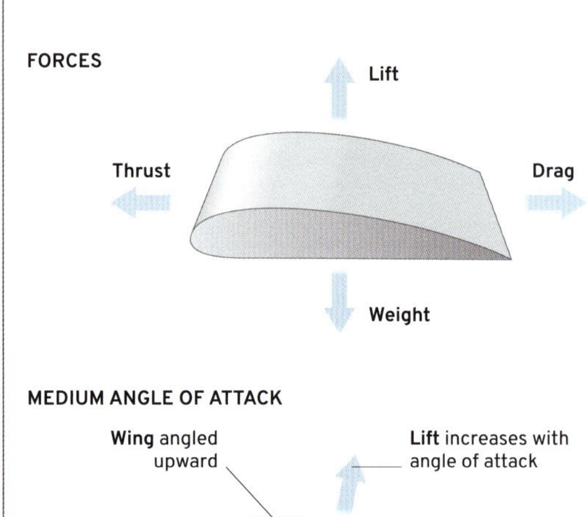

MEDIUM ANGLE OF ATTACK

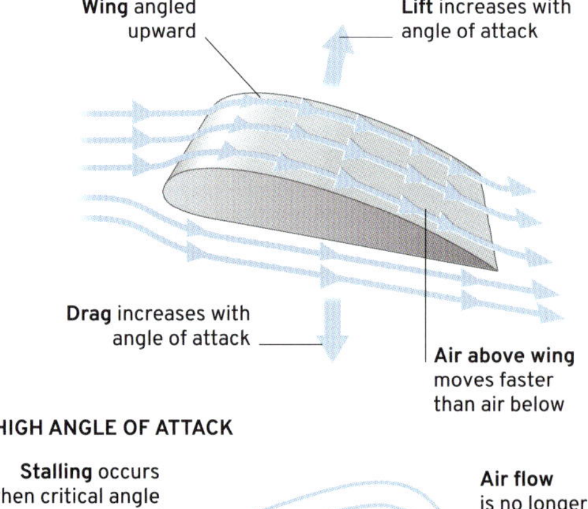

HIGH ANGLE OF ATTACK

Stalling occurs when critical angle is exceeded

Air flow is no longer smooth; air pressure above wing rises

Fall in air pressure differential reduces lift

STICK-AND-RUDDER CONTROL

An airplane's controls rotate it around three axes. The up or down movement of the nose, called pitch, is controlled by tail-mounted elevators. The pilot moves the control stick forward or back to operate the elevators and make the plane dive or climb. Roll—the up or down rolling motion of the wingtips—is controlled by ailerons on the trailing wing edges; the pilot operates them by moving the stick sideways, which turns the plane. The vertically mounted rudder, operated by the pilot's foot-pedals, controls yaw, the side-to-side movement of the nose. The pilot uses the rudder to point the airplane in the desired direction. Large aircraft and fast jets may have powered controls, but they are still maneuvered by the same basic stick-and-rudder input.

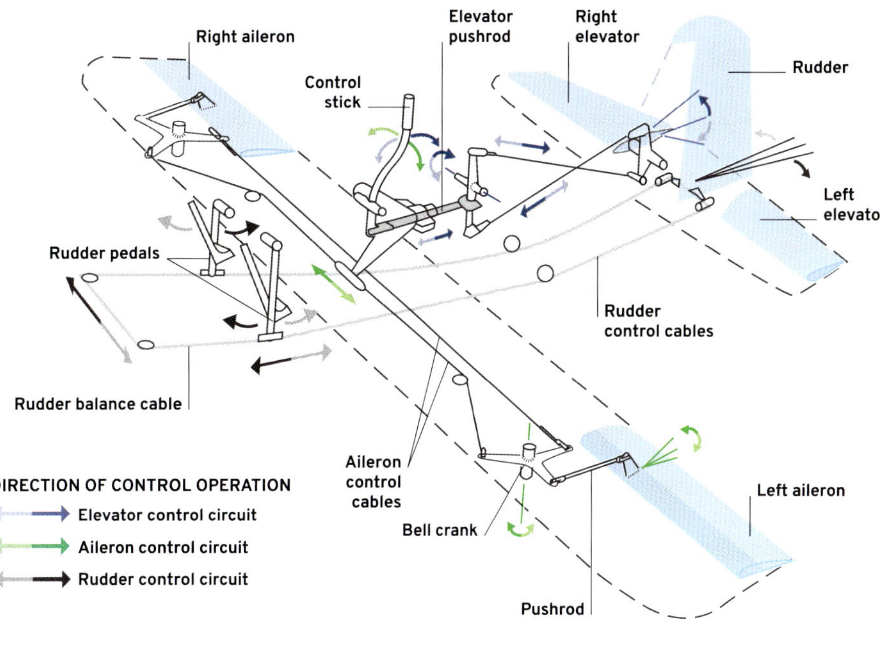

Nose comes up

Raised elevators push the plane's tail down

Steep angle of attack increases lift and drag

Pitching up
To pitch upward, the pilot pulls the control stick back, raising the elevators and causing the nose to rise. This increases the angle of attack, so the wing generates more lift and the aircraft begins to climb. The aircraft continues to pitch up until the pilot puts the stick to neutral, so that the elevators lie flat again.

Flat elevator keeps the plane level

Level flight
In level flight the tailplane, to which the elevators are attached, acts as a stabilizing surface that maintains the wings at a steady angle of attack. The elevators are kept flat, and during level flight the pilot will only move them up or down to compensate for the effects of air turbulence.

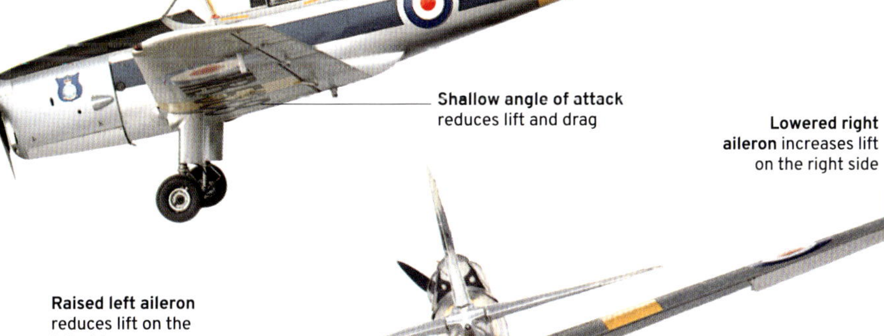

Lowered elevators push the tail up

Shallow angle of attack reduces lift and drag

Pitching down
To pitch downward, the pilot pushes the stick forward. This lowers the elevators, causing the nose to drop. As the angle of attack decreases, lift reduces, and the aircraft descends. With weight now acting in the same direction as thrust from the propeller, the descending aircraft rapidly gains speed.

Lowered right aileron increases lift on the right side

Raised left aileron reduces lift on the left side

Turning
When the pilot moves the stick to one side, the aileron on that side rises, reducing lift; at the same time, the opposing aileron lowers, increasing lift on the other side. Since overall wing lift is now acting to the side, the aircraft starts to turn. The pilot moves the rudder to balance the different amounts of drag generated by the up- and down-pointing ailerons.

Glossary

4×4
A four-wheeled vehicle in which the engine's power drives all four wheels; in a 4×2, only two wheels are driven.

active protection system (APS)
A method of defeating anti-tank weapons that does not rely on armor. Active systems use projectiles to shoot down missiles. Passive systems use jamming and smoke to defeat missile guidance systems.

add-on armor
Additional external armor that can be fitted to an AFV to increase protection. Also known as appliqué armor.

afterburner
A device that injects fuel into the hot exhaust gases produced by an engine and burns it to provide additional thrust.

aileron
A movable control surface on an aircraft wing's trailing edge, used to control roll, the up or down movement of the wingtips.

airfoil
A shaped surface, such as an airplane wing, tail, propeller, or helicopter rotor blade, that produces more lift than drag.

airframe
The basic structure of an aircraft, including the fuselage, wings, and tail assembly but excluding the engines and other fittings.

amphibious vehicle
A vehicle that can travel both on water and on land.

angle of attack
The angle at which a wing (or a propeller or helicopter blade) meets the oncoming air. Airplanes usually fly with the front of their wings higher than the back, so that air deflects downward, pushing the wings up.

armored car
A lightweight, wheeled AFV used for reconnaissance or armed escort duties.

armored fighting vehicle (AFV)
A vehicle combining armored protection, battlefield mobility, and offensive capability. AFVs include tanks, armored cars, troop carriers, air-defense vehicles, amphibious vehicles, and self-propelled artillery.

armored personnel carrier (APC)
A type of AFV, usually lightly armored, that transports troops to the battlefield, where they disembark to fight.

arrestor wire
A cable stretched across the landing area of an aircraft carrier that engages the tailhook of a plane to bring the aircraft to a halt.

autoloader
A device that inserts shells into the breech of a tank's main gun, replacing the need for a crew member dedicated to this task.

bar armor
Add-on armor in the form of a mesh of steel bars fitted to the hull of an AFV to protect against rocket-propelled grenades (RPGs). Also called cage or slat armor. *See also* add-on armor.

barbette
An armored cylinder supporting a gun turret on a warship.

battle management system
A computer-based system that gives near real-time information to aid the decision-making and effectiveness of commanders in the field and at headquarters.

battle cruiser
A class of heavily armed warship developed as a kind of fast battleship in the years leading up to World War I.

battleship
A large, heavily armored warship with a main battery of large guns.

biplane
A plane with two sets of wings, braced by wires and struts to form a light, rigid structure. The biplane design produces more drag than a cantilever monoplane. *See also* monoplane.

bogie
A pivoting group of wheels (typically two or three pairs) beneath a vehicle.

bore
The internal diameter of a gun's barrel. *See also* caliber.

bore evacuator
See fume extractor.

breech
The rear end of a gun barrel, opened to load ammunition and closed for firing.

bridge
The main control center of a ship, from where the captain and officers oversee the operations of the vessel.

bridge layer
A support vehicle that can deploy and retrieve a removable metal bridge to allow other military vehicles to cross obstacles such as rivers, craters, and trenches.

broadside
The simultaneous firing of all the guns on one side of a warship.

caliber
The internal diameter of a rifled gun barrel; since the 1950s, this has usually been expressed in millimeters (mm).

cantilever wing
A wing with no external support or bracing.

capital ship
A warship of the first rank in size and armament, such as a battleship.

caravel
A small, maneuverable ship with lateen sails developed in the 15th century.

carrack
A three- or four-masted sailing ship of the 15th and 16th centuries.

casemate
An armored enclosure or compartment for guns on a warship.

cemented armor
Steel-alloy armor that had a hardened outer face for protection but was fibrous and flexible beneath to resist spalling.

Chobham armor
Composite armor, developed at Britain's tank research center in Chobham, that includes ceramic tiles encased in metal mesh bonded to a backing plate with several elastic layers. Dorchester armor is a variant. *See also* composite armor.

Christie suspension
Tank suspension designed by J. Walter Christie in 1928. Each wheel had its own spring and could move freely vertically, allowing rapid travel over rough terrain.

coaxial machine gun
A machine gun mounted on the same axis as a vehicle's main gun and aimed using the same sights.

cog
A round-bottomed sailing ship developed in northern Europe in the Middle Ages.

combat engineer vehicle
An AFV, often fitted with mine-breaching devices, that is used to transport combat engineers around the battlefield. *See also* armored fighting vehicle (AFV).

combat weight
The mass of a tank when fully equipped for battlefield action.

command vehicle
A vehicle from which a commander leads a unit; it may carry equipment such as multiple radios and map boards, and include desk space for officers and aides.

composite armor
Vehicle armor made up of layers of different materials, such as metals, ceramics, and plastics.

conning tower
A raised structure on a submarine from which an officer conned (conducted or controlled) the boat. Today, this structure is called sail, because submarines are now controlled from below deck. *See also* sail.

corvette
Originally a small, three-masted sailing warship, a corvette is a fast, lightly armed naval vessel.

counterinsurgency (COIN)
Operations against an enemy that does not operate as a distinct military force. Counterinsurgency vehicles are often armored against mines or IEDs. *See also* improvised explosive device (IED).

cowl/cowling
The cover, often removable or partly removable, around a vehicle's engine. It is usually streamlined to reduce drag.

cruiser
In the 19th century, a steam warship, smaller than a battleship, able to operate in distant waters. Protected cruisers had armored decks; armored cruisers had a belt of armor around the hull. From 1930, cruisers were classed as light or heavy, according to their armament.

cupola
A mini turret on top of a tank's main turret, with ports that give the tank commander a (typically all-round) view of the battlefield.

destroyer
A type of warship conceived in the late 19th century to destroy torpedo boats, then adapted to fire torpedoes, and later used to escort warships and merchant convoys. Today, destroyers defend other ships from air, submarine, and surface attack.

diving plane
A control surface (also called a hydroplane) on a submarine that tilts the bow or stern up or down when submerging or surfacing, and helps control depth when submerged.

dogfight
A close-quarters battle between aircraft. It refers to individual duels, rather than to an attack by multiple planes in formation.

draft
The depth of a ship (to the lowest point of the hull) below the waterline.

drag
The force (air or water resistance) that impedes the motion of a vehicle.

dreadnought
A type of battleship, inaugurated by HMS *Dreadnought* in 1906, that surpassed previous ships for arms, armor, and speed.

drive sprocket
A toothed tank wheel that engages the track links to transfer torque from the engine and drive the track around.

drone
A more informal name for a UAV. *See also* unmanned aerial vehicle (UAV).

electronic countermeasures (ECM)
In modern warfare, any electronic devices designed to mislead the enemy's radar and other detection or targeting systems.

elevator
A control surface attached to the tailplane that affects the pitch of an aircraft (whether its nose points up or down, or is level).

explosive reactive armor (ERA)
See reactive armor.

fairing
A covering added to an aircraft, boat, or land vehicle to improve streamlining.

fire-control system
Technology that helps a weapons system to target, track, and hit targets with more speed and greater accuracy than a human operator could achieve. Fire-control systems today typically use sensors to detect the target, a computer to process data and calculate firing solutions, and stabilizing systems to ensure accuracy.

firing port
An opening on the side of an IFV through which infantry can fire without leaving the vehicle. *See* infantry fighting vehicle (IFV).

first-rate ship
A British designation for a ship of the line with more than 100 guns on three decks.

flame tank
A tank fitted with a flamethrower. Flame tanks are usually deployed for specialized operations, such as attacking fortifications.

flanking maneuver
An attempt to gain tactical advantage by moving an armed body around the side, or flank, of an enemy force.

flap
A control surface on the trailing edge of a wing that tilts downward and/or extends backward to increase the wing's lift.

fly-by-wire
A system that controls an aircraft's flight using electronics, rather than mechanical controls.

forecastle
On medieval ships, a raised structure at the front that served as a fighting platform for archers or marines; now a term applied to the front part of a ship's upper deck.

freeboard
The distance between the waterline and the deck of a ship.

frigate
Originally, a sail-powered warship that was faster than a ship of the line and had one gun deck. Modern frigates are used for escort and protection, especially against submarines and aircraft.

front-wheel drive (FWD)
The transmission of engine power only to a vehicle's front wheels. FWDs can be made lighter than 4×4 vehicles, since a drive shaft is not needed to send power to the rear wheels.

fume extractor
A vent in a tank gun barrel that stops toxic fumes released when a round is fired from entering the crew compartment. Pressure changes in the barrel expel fumes from the muzzle. Also called a bore evacuator.

fuselage
The main body of an airplane, excluding the wings and tail.

galleass
A large war galley developed in Venice in the 16th century to carry heavy guns.

galleon
The principal European warship of the 16th and 17th centuries, longer and narrower than the earlier carrack.

galley
A type of ship propelled primarily by oars, with a shallow draft, a long, narrow hull, and often a low freeboard. Used for more than 2,000 years, galleys had sails but relied heavily on the rowing of their oarsmen for maneuverability and speed.

gill armor
A type of spaced armor consisting of angled, external rubber panels, as used on some Soviet tanks. *See also* spaced armor.

glacis plate
An angled plate at the front of a tank's hull that helps to deflect projectiles. The plate's slope ensures that any projectile that does strike it horizontally must pass through a greater thickness of armor.

ground-attack aircraft
An aircraft specialized for low-level strikes on ground targets; its attacks are more precise than those of a conventional bomber. Today, many military jets combine ground-attack capability with other roles.

grousers
Treaded or studded extensions to a tank's tracks that are added to give more traction on loose materials such as soil or snow.

guided munition
Unlike a bullet, whose trajectory is wholly determined by its propellant charge and gravity, the path of a guided munition can be altered and directed toward a target.

gunsight
An optical device used by gunners to aim with greater accuracy. Telescopic sights for tanks were adopted prior to World War II.

half-track
A vehicle steered by wheels at the front and propelled by tracks at the rear, combining the handling of a road vehicle with a tank's cross-country capabilities.

head-up display (HUD)
A transparent screen in the pilot's line of sight that projects information, such as combat status or flight performance data.

heavy tank
A class of tank designed for infantry support; usually more heavily armed and armored than other tanks, but slower.

high-alpha performance
The ability of an aircraft to maintain controlled flight at high angles of attack, close to a stall, where the aircraft's nose is significantly higher than its flight path.

horsepower (hp)
A traditional unit of measurement of engine power; 1 hp is generally taken to be equal to 746 watts.

hydroplane
See diving plane.

hydropneumatic suspension
A type of suspension that uses oil and pneumatic pressure to keep a vehicle level and absorb shocks.

idler
An undriven end wheel on a tracked vehicle that serves to adjust the tension in the track.

improvised explosive device (IED)
A bomb made in an improvised manner, rather than being specifically designed and manufactured as an explosive device. Some IEDs use chemicals such as fertilizer as explosive materials, while others are adapted mines or artillery shells. Also called roadside bombs.

indirect fire
Fire aimed at a target the gunner cannot see. It usually requires a forward observer to correct the aim. Direct fire is firing at a visible target in the user's line of sight.

infantry fighting vehicle (IFV)
An AFV that carries troops to the battlefield and, being armed, can itself enter combat (unlike an APC). IFVs often have firing ports, and their armament may include anti-tank weapons. *See also* armored personnel carrier (APC).

infrared
A type of electromagnetic radiation given off by warm objects. Night vision and thermal imaging devices use infrared sensors that can detect the heat signals of troops, vehicles, and other objects.

interrupter gear
A mechanism that allowed a machine gun on an aircraft to fire through the arc of a spinning propeller. It paused the gun's fire when a blade was in line with its barrel.

ironclad
A type of mid-19th century warship, originally with armored iron plates over a wooden hull, later with an all-metal hull.

joystick
A lever in an airplane's cockpit that is used to control the ailerons and elevators.

kamikaze
The suicide attacks of Japanese pilots who intentionally crashed their airplanes into enemy ships at the end of World War II.

knot
A unit of speed; 1 knot = 1 nautical mile per hour (1³⁄₂₀ mph; 1.85 km/h).

landing gear
Wheels, skids, or floats on which an aircraft touches down when landing. Also called undercarriage.

laser range finder
A way of calculating a target's range, using the time taken for a laser pulse to reflect off the target and return to the range finder.

lateen sail
A triangular sail mounted at an angle on the mast. Lateen sails permitted ships to tack forward, even into light winds.

leaf spring
A basic form of suspension composed of overlaid arcs (or leaves) of steel that are fixed to the underside of a vehicle to form a shock-absorbing cushion onto which the axle presses. Also called a cart spring.

lift
The force exerted on a moving airfoil that causes a wing to rise.

light tank
A thinly armored tank designed for rapid movement rather than aggressive combat. Today, the light tank's role is largely confined to reconnaissance.

longship
A long, narrow, shallow-draft boat with a sail, oars, and a hull of overlapping planks, developed in Scandinavia.

Mach number
The ratio of an aircraft's speed to the speed of sound; an aircraft flying at Mach 3, for example, is traveling at three times the speed of sound.

machine gun
A gun that uses the gas or recoil from its fired projectile to cycle its action and so give continuous automatic fire.

magazine
A device that holds ammunition and feeds rounds to a gun; also, an area (such as on a ship) where ammunition or other explosive material is stored.

main battle tank (MBT)
The principle form of modern tank, MBTs combine composite armor, powerful firepower, and good mobility. They are designed for armor-protected direct fire.

mantlet
A plate of armor that protects the area where the main gun of a tank emerges from the turret. This area is exposed to the enemy when the gun is fired, so the mantlet tends to be the thickest part of the tank's armor.

materiel
All the hardware needed by a military force to complete a specific mission, from munitions, weapons, and equipment to vehicles such as tanks, fighter aircraft, and warships.

medium tank
A class of tank that is almost as mobile as a light tank and almost as well protected as a heavy tank.

military logistics
The science of planning and carrying out the movement and maintenance of military forces, from setting up and sustaining supply chains to directing personnel and materiel to battlefields.

mine
An explosive laid underground or left floating on or just below the water's surface. Mines can be detonated by a variety of means, depending on their design, including by pressure, sound, magnetism, and remote control.

Mine Resistant Ambush Protected (MRAP)
A class of vehicle designed in response to IEDs. A V-shaped hull limits the effects of IED blasts, while armor protects against direct-fire attack. *See also* improvised explosive device (IED).

monitor
A class of 19th-century ironclad warship that took its name from the USS *Monitor*. Often applied to shallow-draft vessels used for shore bombardment.

monobloc
An engine in which the cylinders are cast together as a single unit, rather than separately, which improves mechanical rigidity and the reliability of the sealing.

monocoque
A method of constructing an aircraft, land vehicle, or boat. The outer shell, rather than internal supports, provides the main strength and load-bearing ability.

monoplane
An airplane with a single pair of wings. *See also* biplane.

muzzle
The forward, open end of a gun's barrel, from which fired munitions emerge.

muzzle brake
A device at the end of the barrel of a tank's main gun, or artillery piece, that vents propellant gases and reduces recoil.

nacelle
A streamlined casing that supports and surrounds an engine or other structure.

NATO
An acronym for the North Atlantic Treaty Organization, an international alliance of countries from North America and Western Europe formed in 1949 in opposition to the Soviet Union.

nautical mile
One nautical mile is equivalent to 1³⁄₂₀ miles (1.85 km); 60 nautical miles = 1 degree of Earth's circumference.

NBC
Nuclear, biological, and chemical weaponry (often called weapons of mass destruction). Special protection systems are required if military personnel and equipment are to operate in areas where such weapons have been used.

optical range finder
An optical system that uses trigonometry to find a target's distance. Two prisms a known distance apart reflect images of the target into the operator's eyepiece. The operator adjusts the angle of the prisms until the two images appear as one; the distance is calculated from this angle.

ordnance
Weapons and ammunition, specifically relating to artillery.

outrigger
A structure that projects from the side of a boat. On an ancient Greek trireme, outriggers accommodated oarsmen.

pre-dreadnought
A battleship built or ordered in the period before HMS *Dreadnought* set new standards for armament, armor, and speed in 1906.

pylon
A structure that attaches engines, fuel tanks, or weapons to an aircraft.

radar
A system that detects and locates objects by sending pulses of radio waves that are reflected off the object back to the source.

rate of fire
The number of rounds that can be fired by a specific weapon in a given time, usually expressed in rounds per minute.

reactive armor
Add-on armor that reacts to incoming enemy projectiles to minimize damage. Explosive reactive armor (ERA) explodes if struck by armor-penetrating projectiles, damaging the projectile and dissipating its energy. *See also* add-on armor.

return rollers
Small wheels positioned above the road wheels of a tracked vehicle that ensure the top of the track runs straight between the drive sprocket and the idler. *See also* drive sprocket, idler, road wheels.

rifling
An arrangement of spiral grooves on the inside of a gun barrel. The rifling spins the fired projectile so that it travels through the air with greater accuracy.

road wheels
The main wheels that rotate within the tracks of a tank. They are unpowered and serve only to distribute the tank's weight.

rocket-propelled grenade (RPG)
An infantry anti-tank weapon that launches rocket-powered warheads. Most RPGs can be operated by a single soldier.

sail (submarine)
A towerlike structure on a submarine that houses the periscopes and antennas for radar and communications. It serves as an observation post when at the surface and provides stability when submerged.

self-propelled gun (SP)
A mobile artillery piece—for example, a howitzer—that is mounted on a motorized chassis with wheels or tracks.

ship of the line
A well-armed sailing warship between the 17th and 19th centuries, built to fight in the line of battle, exchanging broadsides with the enemy's line.

smart weapon
A precision-guided munition that is directed to its target by laser or a satellite-linked GPS (global positioning system).

smoothbore
An unrifled gun barrel designed to fire fin-stabilized projectiles. These projectiles do not spin when fired, so they travel faster and have greater armor penetration.

sonar
A system that detects and locates objects by sending pulses of sound waves that are reflected off the object back to the source.

spaced armor
Armor consisting of a thinner plate in front of, and separated by a space from, a thicker plate below.

spalling
Flakes that break off when armor plate is struck by a projectile. Some tanks are fitted with special linings that protect against high-velocity spalling.

sponson
A gun platform projecting from the side of a tank or battleship.

stealth bomber
A bomber plane that makes use of stealth technology; the name most commonly refers to the American Northrop B-2 Spirit.

stealth technology
Technology that aims to make an aircraft invisible to radar and other modes of detection using angular radar-deflecting surfaces and radar-absorbing materials.

strategic bombing
The planned destruction of specific targets by aerial bombing, with the intention of weakening the economy and war-making capabilities of an enemy state, and sapping the morale of its people.

stressed skin
A rigid construction in which the skin or covering takes a portion of the structural load; intermediate between monocoque, whereby the skin bears all or most of the load, and a rigid frame, which has a covering that is not load-bearing.

supersonic
Faster than the speed of sound.

suspension
A system that cushions the structure and occupants of a vehicle as the wheels move over uneven terrain.

swept wing
A wing angled backward toward the rear of an airplane to reduce drag. A swept wing also reduces lift, so it requires greater takeoff and landing speeds.

swing wing
A wing whose horizontal angle can be adjusted to give lower drag at high speeds and more lift at low speeds. The swing-wing mechanism itself adds to the aircraft's overall weight. Also called a variable geometry, or variable sweep, wing.

tail fin
The vertical part of an airplane's tail, to which the rudder attaches; the rudder controls yaw, the left or right movement of the aircraft's nose.

tailplane
The horizontal part of an airplane's tail, shaped like a small wing, that aids stability. The elevators attach to the tailplane. *See also* elevators.

tank
An AFV designed for frontline combat, featuring strong armor, heavy firepower, and tracks for battlefield maneuverability. *See also* armored fighting vehicle (AFV).

tank destroyer
An AFV armed with a direct-fire gun or missile launcher designed specifically to target enemy armored vehicles.

tankette
A tracked AFV resembling a small tank, used for light infantry-support duties and scouting. They were widely used after World War I and in World War II. *See also* tank.

thrust
The force that propels a powered aircraft through the air.

torpedo
A cylindrical, self-propelled missile that is launched from an aircraft, ship, or submarine. It follows an underwater path and explodes on contact with, or in the near vicinity of, its target.

torque
A measurement of the maximum twisting force generated by an engine. The higher the torque, the greater the capacity of the engine to perform work.

torsion bar suspension
Suspension that uses a twisting metal bar to cushion the vehicle's movement.

track
A continuous belt of linked steel plates (with or without rubber pads) that runs through or around the geared drive sprocket, idler, road wheels, and return rollers of a tank. *See also* drive sprocket, idler, return rollers, road wheels.

transmission
The electrical, hydraulic, or mechanical means by which a vehicle's engine power is converted into the rotary motion of the wheels or tracks.

transonic
Close to the speed of sound.

traverse
The ability of a gun or turret to rotate from the centerline of its mount. Traverse is described in degrees; a gun or turret that fully revolves has a traverse of 360 degrees.

trireme
An ancient Greek galley with three banks of oars. (A galley with two banks of oars was called a bireme.) *See also* galley.

turbofan
A jet engine developed from the turbojet. In a turbofan, the turbine powers both the compressor and a large fan at the front, which directs some of the incoming air past the combustion chamber and turbine. This cool, unburned air mixes with the exhaust at the rear, producing extra thrust and reducing noise.

turbojet
The original jet engine. Fuel is burned in a combustion chamber in a stream of air that has passed through a turbine-driven compressor. The hot, pressurized gases produced by combustion expand and emerge from the rear of the engine as an exhaust jet, creating thrust.

turboprop
An engine similar to a turbojet, except that the turbine extracts most of the energy from the hot gases and uses it to drive a propeller, so a turboprop does not actually use "jet power" for propulsion.

turboshaft
While very much like a turboprop in design, a turboshaft engine turns a shaft that powers other machinery, rather than driving a propeller. Turboshafts are used in helicopters, boats, and tanks.

turret
A rotating upper section of a tank, which accommodates the main gun and most of the crew, or a rotating structure housing one or more guns on a ship. Some aircraft of the past had machine-gun turrets.

unmanned aerial vehicle (UAV)
A pilotless aircraft controlled either remotely or by systems in the aircraft itself. UAVs are used for targeted ground attacks and reconnaissance. Also called drones or remotely piloted vehicles (RPVs).

V-twin engine
An engine with two banks of cylinders arranged in a V formation for compactness.

V4, V6, V8, V10, V12, V16
Designations for engines with cylinders arranged in a V formation, indicating how many cylinders each engine holds. In-line engines have cylinders arranged in a row.

Warsaw Pact
A defense treaty, signed in 1955, between the Soviet Union and its satellite states of Bulgaria, Czechoslovakia, East Germany, Hungary, Poland, Romania, and Albania. The Warsaw Pact was established as a counterweight to NATO. *See also* NATO.

"wet" ammunition storage
Surrounding shells with liquid containers to guard against ammunition fires.

Index

Page numbers in bold refer to main entries.

D

E

F

G

N

O

P

Q

R

U

V

W

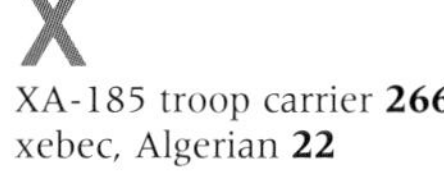

Y

Z

Acknowledgments

Dorling Kindersley would like to extend thanks to the following people for their help with making the book:

Senior Jackets Designer Suhita Dharamjit; Manish Upreti for DTP assistance; Vagisha Pushp for picture research assistance; Oliver Drake for proofreading; Helen Peters for indexing; Nic Dean for picture research; Nicholas Moran and Chris McNab for contents development; Steve Setford for additional text; Ciara Law for administrative assistance; Jane Ewart for additional design.

The publisher would like to thank the following for their kind permission to reproduce their photographs:

(Key: a-above; b-below/bottom; c-centre; f-far; l-left; r-right; t-top)

1 Dorling Kindersley: Dave King (c). **2-3 Dorling Kindersley:** Gary Ombler / Nationaal Luchtvaart Themapark Aviodome (c). **4 Dorling Kindersley:** Gary Ombler / Chris Till (bl); Gary Ombler / The Tank Museum, Bovington (br). **5 Dorling Kindersley:** Gary Ombler / Brooklands Museum (bl). **6 Dorling Kindersley:** James Mann / National Motor Museum, Beaulieu (bl); Gary Ombler / The Tank Museum, Bovington (br). **7 Alamy Stock Photo:** Inc (br). **Dorling Kindersley:** Gary Ombler / Shuttleworth Collection (bl). **8 Dorling Kindersley. 9 Shutterstock.com:** Frank L Junior (bl). **10-11 Alamy Stock Photo:** Newscom (c). **12 Alamy Stock Photo:** Album (cr); Niday Picture Library (clb). **13 Alamy Stock Photo:** Niday Picture Library (tc). **14 Alamy Stock Photo:** The Print Collector (cla, bl); Really Easy Star (cl); Zen Radovan (cra). **14-15 Alamy Stock Photo:** NMUIM (bc). **15 Alamy Stock Photo:** George Oze (tr); Zen Radovan (crb). **Bridgeman Images:** Dinodia (tl). **16-17 Getty Images:** De Agostini (c). **18 Alamy Stock Photo:** IanDagnall Computing (cl). **Getty Images:** DEA / G.Dagli Orti (br). **19 Alamy Stock Photo:** GL Archive (tc); GRANGER - Historical Picture Archive (br). **20 Paul Lipke:** (bl). **Shutterstock.com:** Konstantinos Livadas (tl). **21 Dorling Kindersley:** Hellenic Maritime Museum, (all). **22 akg-images:** Eric Vandeville (clb). **Alamy Stock Photo:** Ian G Dagnall (cla); Chris Hellier (cr); piemags / rmn (br). **Bridgeman Images:** Luisa Ricciarini (tc). **23 Alamy Stock Photo:** Newscom (c); Prisma Archivo (tr). **© The Trustees of the British Museum. All rights reserved:** (bc). **24 Alamy Stock Photo:** Imagedoc (tl). **Getty Images / iStock:** gorgios (bc). **25 Alamy Stock Photo:** Detail Heritage (cl); simon evans (tr); World History Archive (ca); mauritius images GmbH (cra); Douglas Lander (c); Manfred Gottschalk (crb); Nikreates (bl); Maurice Savage (br, bc). **26-27 Getty Images:** Culture Club (c). **28 Alamy Stock Photo:** Graham Hunt (cl); INTERFOTO (tl). **Premier Ship Models:** (tr). **Shutterstock.com:** Hans C. Schrodter (br). **29 Alamy Stock Photo:** US Navy Photo (br). **Dorling Kindersley:** Gary Ombler / Fleet Air Arm Museum (tc). **Wikipedia. 30-31 Dorling Kindersley:** Gary Ombler / Musée des blindés, Saumur, France (c). **32 Alamy Stock Photo:** INTERFOTO (clb); Ivy Close Images (cr). **33 Alamy Stock Photo:** Shawshots (tc). **34-35 Dorling Kindersley:** Gary Ombler / B&O Railroad Museum (c). **34 Alamy Stock Photo:** Mouseion Archives (cl); Stocktrek Images, Inc. (bc). **35 Alamy Stock Photo:** Chronicle (tl, cr); Hum Images (cra); KGPA Ltd (br); GRANGER - Historical Picture Archive (bl). **36 Alamy Stock Photo:** History and Art Collection (cl); U.S. Department of Defense Archive (bc). **Wikipedia. 37 Alamy Stock Photo:** Chronicle (clb); Niday Picture Library (tr). **Wikipedia. 38-39 Dorling Kindersley:** Chester Ong / Mikasa Preservation Society (bc). **38 Getty Images:** Photos.com (tl). **40-41 Dorling Kindersley:** Chester Ong / Mikasa Preservation Society (all). **42-43 Board of Trustees of the Science Museum:** Science Museum Group (cr, bc). **42 Alamy Stock Photo:** dpa picture alliance archive (clb). **Library of Congress, Washington, D.C.:** (cla). **Wikipedia. 43 Alamy Stock Photo:** Smudge Whisker (clb). **Wikipedia. 44-45 Alamy Stock Photo:** Stocktrek Images, Inc. (c). **46 Alamy Stock Photo:** Chronicle (tr); Pictorial Press Ltd (bc). **47 Alamy Stock Photo:** American Photo Archive (tr); Trinity Mirror / Mirrorpix (br). **48 Alamy Stock Photo:** piemags / NSC (tl). **SomeBlokeTakingPhotos:** (cl). **48-49 Alamy Stock Photo:** wyrdlight (bc). **Snapshooter46:** (tc). **49 Alamy Stock Photo:** Associated Press (br). **Dorling Kindersley:** Gary Ombler / Milestones Museum (crb). **Fondation de l'Automobile Marius Berliet, Lyon, France:** (tr). **50 Alamy Stock Photo:** EMU history (tl). **54-55 Brian Stephenson/RAS. 54 Alamy Stock Photo:** 2ebill (br); Inc (cl). **55 Dorling Kindersley:** Gary Ombler / Harzer Schmalspurbahnen (tl). **Brian Stephenson/RAS. Wikipedia. 56 Alamy Stock Photo:** Chronicle (cr). **Bovington Tank Museum. Dorling Kindersley:** Gary Ombler / Musée des blindés, Saumur, France (cl); Gary Ombler / The Tank Museum, Bovington (bl). **57 Alamy Stock Photo:** Argus (clb). **Dorling Kindersley:** The Tank Museum, Bovington (bc); Gary Ombler / Musée des blindés, Saumur, France (tc); Gary Ombler / The Tank Museum, Bovington (cr). **Bill Strouse:** (crb). **58-59 Dorling Kindersley:** Gary Ombler / The Tank Museum, Bovington (bc). **58 Alamy Stock Photo:** De Luan (tl). **59 Dorling Kindersley:** Gary Ombler / The Tank Museum, Bovington (tl, tr). **60-61 Dorling Kindersley:** Gary Ombler / The Tank Museum, Bovington. **62-63 Alamy Stock Photo:** De Luan (c). **64-65 Wikipedia. 64 Bovington Tank Museum. TopFoto:** Roger Viollet (cl). **65 akg-images:** ullstein bild (tr). **Alamy Stock Photo:** PJF Military Collection (bc). **Bovington Tank Museum. 66 Dorling Kindersley:** Gary Ombler / Richard Simms (tr). **Getty Images:** Hulton Deutsch (bl). **67 Getty Images:** Evening Standard / Stringer (tc); ullstein bild Dtl. (br). **68 Alamy Stock Photo:** Ivan Batinic (cl); planecollection (bc). **Wikipedia. 68-69 Alamy Stock Photo:** David Osborn (ca). **69 Alamy Stock Photo:** Chronicle (cra, br); PF-(sdasm3) (tl); Antony Nettle (c); History and Art Collection (clb). **70 Alamy Stock Photo:** Susan & Allan Parker (cl). **Dorling Kindersley:** Gary Ombler / Brooklands Museum (tc). **70-71 Dorling Kindersley:** Gary Ombler / Royal Airforce Museum, London (Hendon) (bc). **71 Dorling Kindersley:** Gary Ombler (tc); Gary Ombler / Royal Airforce Museum, London (Hendon) (cl). **72 Alamy Stock Photo:** Niall Ferguson (tl). **72-73 Dorling Kindersley:** Gary Ombler / Shuttleworth Collection (bc). **73 Dorling Kindersley:** Gary Ombler / Shuttleworth Collection (tl, tc). **74-75 Dorling Kindersley:** Gary Ombler / Shuttleworth Collection. **76-77 Getty Images:** Popperfoto (c). **78-79 Smithsonian National Air and Space Museum. 78 Alamy Stock Photo:** Antony Nettle (tr). **Canada Aviation and Space Museum:** (clb). **Phillip Capper:** (tl). **79 Dorling Kindersley:** Gary Ombler / Royal Airforce Museum, London (tc, c). **80 Getty Images:** Corbis Historical (cla); David Pollack / Corbis Historical (tr). **81 Getty Images:** Popperfoto (cra); Universal History Archive (bc). **82-83 Dorling Kindersley:** Gary Ombler / Fleet Air Arm Museum (cl). **82 Alamy Stock Photo:** PF-(bygone1) (br). **Wikipedia. 83 Alamy Stock Photo:** The History Collection (crb). **Getty Images:** Hulton Archive (cra). **SD Model Makers:** (tc). **84 Alamy Stock Photo:** Archive PL (tl). **88-89 SD Model Makers. 88 Alamy Stock Photo:** Chronicle (tr); The History Collection (cl). **Wikipedia. 89 Alamy Stock Photo:** Photo 12 (tl). **TopFoto:** World History Archive (crb). **Wikipedia. 90-91 Alamy Stock Photo:** GL Archive (c). **92 Alamy Stock Photo:** GL Archive (cla); INTERFOTO (clb). **Wikipedia. 92-93 SD Model Makers. 93 Alamy Stock Photo:** Hansrad Collection (br). **Wikipedia. 94-95 Dorling Kindersley:** James Mann / National Motor Museum, Beaulieu (cr). **96 Getty Images:** Pictures from History (tc). **97 Alamy Stock Photo:** Shawshots (tr). **Getty Images:** Universal History Archive (bl). **98 Paul Appleyard:** (tl). **Dorling Kindersley:** Gary Ombler / The Tank Museum, Bovington (cl). **Massimo Foti. Militaryfoto.sk:** (cr). **98-99 Dorling Kindersley:** The Tank Museum, Bovington (tc). **99 Alamy Stock Photo:** Martin Bennett (cl). **Arsenalen, The Swedish Tank Museum:** (br). **Dorling Kindersley:** Gary Ombler / The Tank Museum, Bovington (bl). **Shutterstock.com:** Sergey Ryzhov (tr). **100-101 Dorling Kindersley:** Gary Ombler / The Tank Museum, Bovington (tc). **100 Alamy Stock Photo:** Alexander Tolstykh (br); Universal Art Archive (bl). **Wikipedia:** JDankers (cl). **101 Cody Images:** (bl). **Dorling Kindersley:** Gary Ombler / The Tank Museum, Bovington (crb). **Library of Congress, Washington, D.C.:** Harris and Ewing Inc. (cra). **Chris Neel:** (tr). **Shutterstock.com:** Sergei Afanasev (clb). **102 Alamy Stock Photo:** piemags / ww2archive (tl). **Dorling Kindersley:** Gary Ombler / The Tank Museum, Bovington (clb, cb). **103 Alamy Stock Photo:** piemags / NBP (tr). **Dorling Kindersley:** Gary Ombler / The Tank Museum, Bovington (bc, tc). **104-105 Dorling Kindersley:** Gary Ombler / The Tank Museum, Bovington (all). **106-107 Getty Images:** Fox Photos (c). **108-109 Dorling Kindersley:** Gary Ombler / Yorkshire Air Museum (bc). **108 Dorling Kindersley:** Peter Cook / Planes of Fame Air Museum, Chino, California (cl); Gary Ombler / Sarl Salis Aviation (cr); Gary Ombler / Brooklands Museum (ca); Gary Ombler / Royal Airforce Museum, London (tl). **109 Dorling Kindersley:** Peter Cook / Planes of Fame Air Museum, Chino, California (cr); Gary Ombler / Royal Airforce Museum, London (Hendon) (tl); Gary Ombler / RAF Museum, Cosford (tr); Gary Ombler / Royal Airforce Museum, London (cl). **110-111 Getty Images:** Galerie Bilderwelt (tr). **110 Getty Images:** Hulton Archive / Stringer (ca); Keystone / Stringer (bl). **111 Getty Images:** George Rinhart (br). **112-113 Dorling Kindersley:** Gary Ombler / Eisenbahnfreunde Traditionsbahnbetriebswerk Stassfurt (bc). **112 colour-rail.com:** (tr). **Brian Stephenson/RAS:** (cl). **Wikipedia:** Rabensteiner (tl). **113 Alamy Stock Photo:** Islandstock (tl). **colour-rail.com. Dorling Kindersley:** Deepak Aggarwal / Rewari Steam Loco Shed (c). **Wikipedia:** (tr). **114 Dorling Kindersley:** James Mann / National Motor Museum, Beaulieu (br); Gary Ombler / National Motorcycle Museum (tc, ca). **115 Alamy Stock Photo:** CPC Collection (br). **Dorling Kindersley:** Dave King / National Motorcycle Museum, Birmingham (tl); Dave King / Motorcycle Heritage Museum, Westerville, Ohio (tr); Gary Ombler / Ian Stanley (cr); Dave King (cl); James Mann / National Motor Museum, Beaulieu (bl). **116 Nationaal Archief, Den Haag:** Collectie Spaarnestad / Wout van de Hoef. (tl). **116-117 Dorling Kindersley:** James Mann / National Motor Museum, Beaulieu (bc). **117 Dorling Kindersley:** James Mann / National Motor Museum, Beaulieu (tc, tr). **118-119 Dorling Kindersley:** James Mann / National Motor Museum, Beaulieu. **120 Dorling Kindersley:** Ted Bear, The War and Peace Show (cl); The Tank Museum, Bovington (tr); Matthew Ward / Peter Barber-Lomax (bc). **121 Alamy Stock Photo:** ZarkePix (cla). **Dorling Kindersley:** Gary Ombler / By kind permission of The Trustees of the Imperial War Museum, London (cr); George Paice / War and Peace Show (br). **122-123 Getty Images:** AFP (c). **124 Alamy Stock Photo:** Azoor Photo Collection (bl). **Dorling Kindersley. Massimo Foti:** (tr). **124-125 Dorling Kindersley.**

125 Dorling Kindersley: The Tank Museum, Bovington (tl, tr, cl).
126 Getty Images: ullstein bild Dtl. (tl).
127 Dorling Kindersley: Gary Ombler / The Tank Museum, Bovington (all).
128-129 Dorling Kindersley: Gary Ombler / The Tank Museum, Bovington (all). **130 Dorling Kindersley:** The Tank Museum, Bovington (cla, tr); Gary Ombler / The Tank Museum, Bovington (cb, bl). **130-131 Dorling Kindersley:** Gary Ombler / The Tank Museum, Bovington (bc). **131 Dorling Kindersley:** Gary Ombler / The Tank Museum, Bovington (tl, crb); Gary Ombler / I. Galliers / War and Peace Show (cra). **132 Dorling Kindersley:** Gary Ombler / Chris Till (bc, bl). **Getty Images:** Fred Ramage (tl). **133 Dorling Kindersley:** Gary Ombler / Chris Till (c). **134-135 Dorling Kindersley:** Gary Ombler / Chris Till (all).
136 Alamy Stock Photo: Zachary Frank (clb); Fraser Gray (br). **Bovington Tank Museum:** (ca). **Dorling Kindersley:** Gary Ombler / The Tank Museum, Bovington (tl, tr).
137 Bovington Tank Museum. Dorling Kindersley: The Tank Museum, Bovington (bl); Gary Ombler / The Tank Museum, Bovington (tc).
138-139 Dorling Kindersley: The Tank Museum, Bovington (tl).
138 Dorling Kindersley: The Tank Museum, Bovington (br); Gary Ombler / Gordon McKenna (c). **139 Dorling Kindersley:** The Tank Museum, Bovington (tr, cl, crb, br). **Dreamstime.com:** Victor Onyshchenko (cb). **140-141 Dorling Kindersley:** The Tank Museum, Bovington (tc). **140 Alamy Stock Photo:** Evgeny Haritonov (cl). **Dorling Kindersley:** Gary Ombler / Musée des blindés, Saumur, France (bc). **Shutterstock.com:** Karasev Viktor (cr).
141 Alamy Stock Photo: Alexander Blinov (tr). **Dorling Kindersley:** Gary Ombler / The Tank Museum, Bovington (cr). **Getty Images / iStock:** G0d4ather (bl). **Shutterstock.com:** Yakov Oskanov (br). **142 Getty Images:** Victor Temin (tl). **143 Dorling Kindersley:** Gary Ombler / The Tank Museum, Bovington (all). **144-45 Dorling Kindersley:** Gary Ombler / The Tank Museum, Bovington (all). **146 Dorling Kindersley:** The Tank Museum, Bovington (tc, c); Gary Ombler / The Tank Museum, Bovington (ca); The War and Peace Show (bl). **146-147 Dorling Kindersley:** Jez Marren, The War and Peace Show (bc). **147 Dorling Kindersley:** Gary Ombler / The Tank Museum, Bovington (tc, cr, br).
148 Getty Images: Mondadori Portfolio (bc). **149 Alamy Stock Photo:** CBW (tr); Hi-Story (br). **150 Dorling Kindersley:** Peter Cook / Planes of Fame Air Museum, Chino, California (cr); Gary Ombler / Flugausstellung (tl); Gary Ombler / Gatwick Aviation Museum (cb). **Shutterstock.com:** Ryan Fletcher (cl).
150-151 Dorling Kindersley: Gary Ombler / RAF Battle of Britain Memorial Flight (tc); Gary Ombler / Gatwick Aviation Museum (bc). **151 Dorling Kindersley:** Gary Ombler / Gatwick Aviation Museum (cl, br); Gary Ombler / Scale Model World, Steve Abbey (cr).
152 Getty Images: PhotoQuest (tl).
153 Dorling Kindersley: Gary Ombler / B17 Preservation (all).
154-155 Dorling Kindersley: Gary Ombler / B17 Preservation (picture nos: 2,4,6,9,12,13,14,15,16,17 & 18).
154 Alamy Stock Photo: Dave Block (clb); ZUMA Press, Inc (tr); Images-USA (crb); Albert Knapp (bc). **Shutterstock.com:** Frank L Junior (ca). **155 Alamy Stock Photo:** B. David Cathell (bl); ZUMA Press, Inc (bc). **156 Dorling Kindersley:** Peter Cook / Planes of Fame Air Museum, Chino, California (c); Gary Ombler / Royal Airforce Museum, London (clb); Gary Ombler / RAF Battle of Britain Memorial Flight (tr).
Rowhider: (tl). **156-157 Dorling Kindersley:** Gary Ombler / Musee de l'Air et de l'Espace / Le Bourget (bc).
157 Dorling Kindersley: Gary Ombler / Royal Airforce Museum, London (tr, c). **Shutterstock.com:** cpaulfell (tl). **158 Getty Images:** IWM (tl). **159 Dorling Kindersley:** Gary Ombler / RAF Battle of Britain Memorial Flight (all). **160-161 Dorling Kindersley:** Gary Ombler / RAF Battle of Britain Memorial Flight (all). **162-63 Getty Images:** Central Press (c). **164 Dorling Kindersley:** Gary Ombler / Royal Airforce Museum, London (Hendon) (tc); Gary Ombler / De Havilland Aircraft Heritage Centre (cla); Gary Ombler / RAF Museum, Cosford (cra). **Shutterstock.com:** Eugene Berman (bl). **164-165 Dorling Kindersley:** Peter Cook / March Field Air Museum, California (bc). **165 Dorling Kindersley:** Gary Ombler / Royal Airforce Museum, London (clb, tl). **Smithsonian National Air and Space Museum:** (c). **166 Alamy Stock Photo:** Trinity Mirror / Mirrorpix (cla). **Getty Images:** Bettmann (br).
167 Getty Images: Corbis Historical (bc); IWM (cra). **168-169 Dorling Kindersley:** Gary Ombler / Fleet Air Arm Museum (cb). **SD Model Makers. 168 Alamy Stock Photo:** Chronicle (tr). **Dorling Kindersley:** Gary Ombler / Model Exhibition, Telford (cra). **SD Model Makers. 169 Dorling Kindersley:** Gary Ombler / Model Exhibition, Telford (cra). **SD Model Makers. Courtesy of U.S. Navy:** Naval History & Heritage Command (br). **170 Alamy Stock Photo:** brystock (tl). **172 Alamy Stock Photo:** Craig Buchanan (tr); Greg Balfour Evans (cl, cb); Stelios Michael (cr, clb); Andrew Duke (bl); Selwyn (fcr); Zoonar GmbH (br).
Getty Images: Peter Dazeley (ca); Peter Dazeley (cra); NurPhoto (bc). **172-173 Alamy Stock Photo:** alias Ayub (tc).
173 Alamy Stock Photo: Philip Bird (cl); imageBROKER.com (tc); Steve Vidler (tr); Selwyn (c); Zoonar GmbH (cr, bl); Frank Nowikowski (ca). **174 Alamy Stock Photo:** allanbellimages (cla); VTR (tr). **Dorling Kindersley:** Gary Ombler / Model Exhibition, Telford (cra); Gary Ombler / Fleet Air Arm Museum (cb). **174-175 Dorling Kindersley:** Gary Ombler / Model Exhibition, Telford (bc). **175 SD Model Makers. Courtesy of U.S. Navy:** Naval History & Heritage Command (cr).
Wikipedia. 176-177 Dorling Kindersley: Gary Ombler / Model Exhibition, Telford (bc). **176 Dorling Kindersley:** Gary Ombler / Fleet Air Arm Museum (cb). **SD Model Makers. 177 Dorling Kindersley:** Gary Ombler / Scale Model World (ca); Gary Ombler / Scale Model World, Allan Toyne (cb). **SD Model Makers.**
178 Archive Deutscher Marinebund (German Naval Association), Laboe. 178-179 Alamy Stock Photo: Jürgen Wackenhut (bc).
180 Alamy Stock Photo: Penelope Barritt (crb); mauritius images GmbH (tc); mauritius images GmbH (cl, bl); Michael Piepgras (cr); Phillip Berg (c).
180-181 Alamy Stock Photo: mauritius images GmbH (tc); Zoonar GmbH (bc). **181 Alamy Stock Photo:** Penelope Barritt (clb); Paul Grove (tr); JB-2078 (cra, crb); Marek Slusarczyk (ca, cb). **Shutterstock.com:** rdp 15 (tc); rdp 15 (bc). **182 Dorling Kindersley:** Gary Ombler / Model Exhibition, Telford (ca). **SD Model Makers. 182-183 Dorling Kindersley:** Gary Ombler / Model Exhibition, Telford (clb). **183 SD Model Makers. 184-185 Ulrich Grueschow - MilitaryAircraft.de:** (bc). **184 Alamy Stock Photo:** Amy Lee (cr); chris mcloughlin (bl). **Dorling Kindersley:** Gary Ombler / RAF Museum, Cosford (tr); Gary Ombler / Old Flying Machine Company (clb).
Shutterstock.com: Pulpits (cla). **185 Alamy Stock Photo:** Rick Pisio\RWP Photography (tl). **Dorling Kindersley:** Gary Ombler / Fleet Air Arm Museum (c). **186-187 Getty Images:** Bettmann (c). **188-189 Dorling Kindersley:** Gary Ombler / Ukraine State Aviation Museum (c). **190 Getty Images:** Bettmann (cl). **191 Alamy Stock Photo:** dpa picture alliance (tc). **Getty Images:** Buyenlarge (cb). **192-93 Getty Images:** Rolls Press / Popperfoto (c). **194 Alamy Stock Photo:** Colin C. Hill (bl); Oleksiy Maksymenko (tr).
Dorling Kindersley: The Tank Museum, Bovington (br). **195 Dorling Kindersley:** Gary Ombler / The Tank Museum, Bovington (bl, cl).
Dreamstime.com: Yykkaa (crb).
Bron Pancema: (tl). **Shutterstock.com:** Karasev Viktor (tr). **196-197 Dorling Kindersley:** Gary Ombler / The Tank Museum, Bovington (c). **196 Dorling Kindersley:** Gary Ombler / The Tank Museum, Bovington (clb, bl).
Getty Images: Ahmad Al-Rubaye (tl).
198-199 Dorling Kindersley: Gary Ombler / The Tank Museum, Bovington (all). **200 Alamy Stock Photo:** Brent Beach (cl); Stocktrek Images, Inc. (bl).
Dorling Kindersley: The Tank Museum, Bovington (crb, bc).
Shutterstock.com: Kev Gregory (tc).
201 Alamy Stock Photo: Dorset Media Service (tl). **Dorling Kindersley:** The Tank Museum, Bovington (br). **Getty Images / iStock:** Getty Images Plus (c).
202-203 Getty Images: ullstein bild (c). **204-205 Dorling Kindersley:** Gary Ombler / The Tank Museum, Bovington (bc). **205 Dorling Kindersley:** Gary Ombler / The Tank Museum, Bovington (tr, tl). **206-207 Dorling Kindersley:** Gary Ombler / The Tank Museum, Bovington. **208 Alamy Stock Photo:** Panzermeister (clb). **Dorling Kindersley:** Gary Ombler / Musée des blindés, Saumur, France (tc); Gary Ombler / The Tank Museum, Bovington (cla). **Getty Images:** Leon Neal (br). **Shutterstock.com:** Art Konovalov (ca). **209 Dorling Kindersley:** Gary Ombler / Musée des blindés, Saumur, France (c). **Getty Images:** Michael Gottschalk (bl). **Jim Maurer:** (tl). **Shutterstock.com:** Leonard Zhukovsky (br). **210 Alamy Stock Photo:** Zoonar GmbH (cla).
Bri_J (Flickr): (tr). **Massimo Foti. Shutterstock.com:** DLeng (clb); M.J.J. de Vaan (br). **211 Alamy Stock Photo:** dpa picture alliance archive (tc); ZapperSiR (cr). **Shutterstock.com:** Free Wind 2014 (br). **212-213 Getty Images:** Eric Bouvet (c). **214-215 Dorling Kindersley:** Gary Ombler / Musée des blindés, Saumur, France (bc).
214 Shutterstock.com: Om_Joshi (cr); viper-zero (bl). **Wikipedia:** Johan Elisson (tr); PD-Self / Loss688 / Japan Ground Self-Defence Force (cl).
215 Dorling Kindersley: Gary Ombler / Norfolk Tank Museum (c).
Shutterstock.com: Dmitriy Feldman svarshik (tr). **216 Alamy Stock Photo:** Grzegorz Czapski (tr). **Stuart Mitchell:** (cr). **Shutterstock.com:** Art Konovalov (bl). **Wikipedia:** Steve F-E-Cameron (Merlin-UK) (cl). **217 Alamy Stock Photo:** Radharc Images (bc). **Bonhams:** (tl). **Wikipedia:** Darkone (tr). **218-219 Alamy Stock Photo:** De Luan (tc).
218 Getty Images: Corbis Historical (cr). **219 Alamy Stock Photo:** Pictorial Press Ltd (br); U.S. Department of Defense Archive (bl). **220-221 Dorling Kindersley:** Peter Cook / The American Airpower Museum, Farmingdale, New York (c); Gary Ombler / City of Norwich Aviation Museum (tc). **220 Dorling Kindersley:** Gary Ombler / Flugausstellung (tl, br); Gary Ombler / Midlands Air Museum (cla). **221 Alamy Stock Photo:** Dean West (br). **Dorling Kindersley:** Peter Cook / Intrepid Sea, Air and Space Museum, New York (tr); Gary Ombler / Yorkshire Air Museum (cla). **222-223 Getty Images:** Anadolu (c). **224 Getty Images:** Interim Archives (tl). **225 Dorling Kindersley:** Gary Ombler / Golden Apple Operations Ltd (all). **226-227 Dorling Kindersley:** Gary Ombler / Golden Apple Operations Ltd (all). **228 Alamy Stock Photo:** Allstar Picture Library Ltd (cl); horsemen (ca). **Dorling Kindersley:** Gary Ombler / Yorkshire Air Museum (tr); Gary Ombler / Ukraine State Aviation Museum (bl). **228-229 Alamy Stock Photo:** Nir Ben-Yosef (bc). **229 Alamy Stock Photo:** Bob Graham (cr); Tami Ruble (tc). **Dorling Kindersley:** Peter Cook / Pima Air and Space Museum, Tuscon, Arizona (cla). **230 Dorling Kindersley:** Gary Ombler / Flugausstellung (cr); Gary Ombler / Royal International Air Tattoo 2011 (clb). **Getty Images:** Athanasios Gioumpasis (tl). **230-231 Alamy Stock Photo:** Konstantinos Koronakis (br).
Dorling Kindersley: Gary Ombler / Fleet Air Arm Museum (tc). **231 Alamy Stock Photo:** Stocktrek Images, Inc. (ca). **Dorling Kindersley:** Gary Ombler / Royal International Air Tattoo 2011 (cb).
Getty Images / iStock: ILya Oslyakov (tc). **232-33 Getty Images:** Patrick Aventurier (c). **234 Alamy Stock Photo:** Avpics (bc); Lloyd Horgan (tl).
235 Dorling Kindersley: Gary Ombler / RAF Wittering, Cambridgeshire (all).
236 Dorling Kindersley: Gary Ombler / Flugausstellung (tl); Gary Ombler / Nationaal Luchtvaart Themapark Aviodome (cla); Gary Ombler / Imperial

War Museum, Duxford (c). **236-237 Dorling Kindersley:** Peter Cook / Pima Air and Space Museum, Tuscon, Arizona (bc). **237 Dorling Kindersley:** Gary Ombler / Royal International Air Tattoo 2011 (tl, cb); Gary Ombler / Flugausstellung (cla). **238 Shutterstock.com:** VanderWolf Images (tl). **239 Dorling Kindersley:** Gary Ombler / Ukraine State Aviation Museum (all). **240-241 Dorling Kindersley:** Gary Ombler / Ukraine State Aviation Museum (all). **242-243 Alamy Stock Photo:** Stocktrek Images, Inc. (c). **244 Alamy Stock Photo:** Dino Fracchia (tr); JJ (br). **245 Alamy Stock Photo:** CHM (bc); Classic Picture Library (tr). **246-247 SD Model Makers. 246 Alamy Stock Photo:** NB / ROD (bl). **Dorling Kindersley:** Gary Ombler / Fleet Air Arm Museum, Eric Dyke (cla). **SD Model Makers. The US National Archives and Records Administration. 247 SD Model Makers. Wikipedia:** Javier Bueno Iturbe (cl); Nathalmad (cra). **248-249 SD Model Makers. 248 Getty Images:** Science & Society Picture Library (br). **SD Model Makers. 249 Model by Ingemar Caisander:** (clb). **Dorling Kindersley:** Gary Ombler / Fleet Air Arm Museum (crb). **SD Model Makers. 250 Alamy Stock Photo:** Ewing Galloway (tl). **The US National Archives and Records Administration:** (bc). **251 Dorling Kindersley:** Gary Ombler / Historic ship Nautilus and Submarine Force Museum, Connecticut (all). **252-253 Getty Images:** U.S. Navy (c). **254-255 Alamy Stock Photo:** Grobler du Preez (c). **256 Alamy Stock Photo:** World History Archive (tc). **257 Alamy Stock Photo:** American Photo Archive (cr). **Getty Images:** Anadolu (bl). **258 Alamy Stock Photo:** Grobler du Preez (tr). **Shutterstock.com:** Grobler de Preez (tl). **Witham Specialist Vehicles Ltd:** Ministry of Defence, UK (cl). **259 Alamy Stock Photo:** Aviation Visuals (tr); Hot Shots (cr). **Ministry Of Defence UK © Crown copyright 2021:** Sgt Wes Calder RLC (tl). **260 Wikipedia:** Chamal Pathirana (tl). **264-265 Getty Images:** Global Images Ukraine (c). **266 Alamy Stock Photo:** Esa Hiltula (cla). **Shutterstock.com:** Stefan Holm (tr). **Wikipedia:** Outisnn (bc). **267 Alamy Stock Photo:** Sergei Butorin (cb); Imago (cr); Mike Needham @ digitally_challenging (br). **Getty Images:** Ludovic Marin (ca); Leon Neal (tr). **268 Alamy Stock Photo:** Sergii Popsuievych (br). **Shutterstock.com:** Karolis Kavolelis (tc); StockPhotoLV (cb); OlegDoroshin (cl). **269 Alamy Stock Photo:** Associated Press (bc); Oleg Zaslavsky (cl). **Combat Camera Europe:** (tc). **Getty Images / iStock:** vicnt (cr). **270-271 Image courtesy of General Dynamics Ordnance and Tactical Systems:** (bc). **270 Alamy Stock Photo:** 501 collection (tl). **271 USAASC:** (tl); photo by SGT Richard Wiley, 2nd Armoured Brigade Combat Team, 3rd Infantry Division, Public Affairs (tr). **272-273 U.S. Army photo:** (all). **274-275 Getty Images:** Fred Marie / Art in All of Us (c). **276 Courtesy Leidos, Inc.:** © Salty Dingo 2023 (bc). **Courtesy of U.S. Navy:** (cla). **277 Getty Images:** Park Ji-Hwan (br). **Courtesy of U.S. Navy:** US Navy Sixth Fleet (tc). **278 Alamy Stock Photo:** Stocktrek Images, Inc. (cr); Martin Witte (clb). **Getty Images:** michaelbwatkins (tr). **Shutterstock.com:** Joris van Boven (cla). **278-279 Alamy Stock Photo:** U.S. Department of Defense Archive (bc). **279 Alamy Stock Photo:** Rob Arnold (cla); Stocktrek Images, Inc. (tc). **Getty Images:** Hindustan Times (bc). **280-281 NAVY.mil:** Photographer's Mate 3rd Class Summer M. Anderson (c). **280 Alamy Stock Photo:** ZUMA Press, Inc (tl). **282-283 Dorling Kindersley:** Gary Ombler / USS George Washington and the US Navy (all). **284-285 Dorling Kindersley:** Gary Ombler / Fleet Air Arm Museum (tc). **284 Alamy Stock Photo:** one-image photography (c); Focke Strangmann (br). **Getty Images:** Mark Wilson (tl). **285 Alamy Stock Photo:** Associated Press (bc); PJF Military Collection (cl); dpa picture alliance (cr). **286-287 Dorling Kindersley:** Gary Ombler / Fleet Air Arm Museum (c, bc). **286 Dorling Kindersley:** Gary Ombler / Fleet Air Arm Museum (clb, bl). **287 Dorling Kindersley:** Gary Ombler / Fleet Air Arm Museum (cb). **SD Model Makers. 288 Alamy Stock Photo:** Andrew Harker (bl); NASA Photo (tr). **289 Alamy Stock Photo:** CNP Collection (tc); PA Images (br). **290 Alamy Stock Photo:** Marco McGinty (cla). **Dorling Kindersley:** Gary Ombler / Royal International Air Tattoo 2011 (tr); Gary Ombler / RAF Museum, Cosford (bl). **290-291 Alamy Stock Photo:** Malcolm Haines (c); James Hancock (bc). **291 Alamy Stock Photo:** Kris Christiaens (br); Gary Stedman (tc). **Getty Images:** Dibyangshu Sarkar (cl). **292 Alamy Stock Photo:** Avpics (tl). **293 Dorling Kindersley:** Gary Ombler / RAF Coningsby (all). **294-295 Dorling Kindersley:** Gary Ombler / RAF Coningsby (all). **296-297 Alamy Stock Photo:** Ukrinform (c). **298 U.S. Air Force:** Lt. Col. Leslie Pratt (c). **298-299 Getty Images:** Anadolu (c). **299 Getty Images:** Global Images Ukraine (br). **Wikipedia:** Mike 1979 Russia (tr). **300 Alamy Stock Photo:** US Air Force Photo (tl). **Getty Images:** Isaac Brekken (bc). **301 Alamy Stock Photo:** American Photo Archive (br); Contraband Collection (tl); ZUMA Press, Inc (tr); Wildfire Image (cra); Michael Fitzsimmons (crb); Operation 2024 (bc). **New York National Guard:** (cb). **302 Alamy Stock Photo:** piemags (bl). **304 Dr. Zachi Evenor:** (bl). **Getty Images:** Shaul Schwarz (br). **SD Model Makers. 305 Arsenalen, The Swedish Tank Museum:** (crb). **SD Model Makers. 306 Dorling Kindersley:** Gary Ombler / Shuttleworth Collection (tc, ca); Gary Ombler / RAF Battle of Britain Memorial Flight (c); Gary Ombler / Golden Apple Operations Ltd (cb)

Endpapers: Shutterstock / 19srb81

DK LONDON

Senior Art Editors Katie Cavanagh, Helen Spencer
Senior Editors Hugo Wilkinson, Victoria Heyworth-Dunne
Editors John Andrews, Steve Setford
US Editor Sharon Lucas
US Executive Editor Lori Cates Hand
Senior Production Editor Andy Hilliard
Senior Production Controller Laura Andrews
Managing Editor Gareth Jones
Managing Art Editor Luke Griffin
Art Director Maxine Pedliham
Design Director Phil Ormerod
Publishing Director Georgina Dee

DK DELHI

Senior Editor Janashree Singha
Senior Art Editor Nidhi Mehra
Project Art Editor Shipra Jain
Art Editor Arshti Narang
Managing Editor Soma B. Chowdhury
Senior Managing Art Editor Arunesh Talapatra
Senior Pre-Production Designer Harish Aggarwal
Pre-Production Designer Raman Panwar
Pre-Production Image Editors Vikram Singh, Ashok Kumar
Pre-Production Manager Balwant Singh
Pre-Production Image Manager Pankaj Sharma
Project Jacket Designer Juhi Sheth
Senior Jacket Coordinator Priyanka Sharma Saddi
Creative Head Malavika Talukder

Consultant David Willey
Contributors Chris McNab, David Willey

First American Edition, 2026
Published in the United States by DK Publishing,
a Division of Penguin Random House LLC
1745 Broadway, 20th Floor, New York, NY 10019

25 26 27 28 29 10 9 8 7 6 5 4 3 2 1
001–350185–Feb/2026

Published in Great Britain by Dorling Kindersley Limited

ISBN: 979-8-2171-2831-0

Printed and bound in UAE

www.dk.com